SISTER STATES, ENEMY STATES

SISTER STATES ENEMY STATES

The Civil War in Kentucky and Tennessee

Edited by Kent T. Dollar, Larry H. Whiteaker,
and W. Calvin Dickinson

THE UNIVERSITY PRESS OF KENTUCKY

Scholarly publisher for the Commonwealth,
serving Bellarmine University, Berea College, Centre
College of Kentucky, Eastern Kentucky University,
The Filson Historical Society, Georgetown College,
Kentucky Historical Society, Kentucky State University,
Morehead State University, Murray State University,
Northern Kentucky University, Transylvania University,
University of Kentucky, University of Louisville,
and Western Kentucky University.
All rights reserved.

Editorial and Sales Offices: The University Press of Kentucky
663 South Limestone Street, Lexington, Kentucky 40508-4008
www.kentuckypress.com

Library of Congress Cataloging-in-Publication Data

Sister states, enemy states : the Civil War in Kentucky and Tennessee /
edited by Kent Dollar, Larry Whiteaker, and W. Calvin Dickinson.
     p.   cm.
  Includes bibliographical references and index.
  ISBN 978-0-8131-2541-1 (hardcover : alk. paper)
  1. Kentucky—History—Civil War, 1861–1865. 2. Tennessee—
History—Civil War, 1861–1865. 3. Kentucky—History—Civil
War, 1861–1865—Social aspects. 4. Tennessee—History—Civil War,
1861–1865—Social aspects. 5. Kentucky—History—Civil War,
1861–1865—Influence. 6. Tennessee—History—Civil War,
1861–1865—Influence. I. Dollar, Kent T. II. Whiteaker, Larry H.
(Larry Howard), 1946– III. Dickinson, W. Calvin.
  E509.S576 2009
  973.7—dc22
                      2009004604
ISBN 978-0-8131-3382-9 (pbk.: alk. paper)

This book is printed on acid-free paper meeting
the requirements of the American National Standard
for Permanence in Paper for Printed Library Materials.

Manufactured in the United States of America.

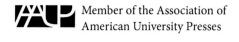 Member of the Association of
American University Presses

Contents

Preface

The idea for this book was born in the faculty lounge of the History Department at Tennessee Tech University in the spring of 2006. My fellow historians Larry Whiteaker and Calvin Dickinson and I were sitting around discussing the fact that, despite the historical ties between Kentucky and Tennessee, little has been written focusing exclusively on these two states during the Civil War period. We agreed that a collection of essays on the subject was warranted and would constitute an important contribution to Civil War scholarship. After brainstorming among ourselves on the names of historians who had written on the war in either of these states, we soon found ourselves with an impressive list of potential contributors—long-established historians as well as up-and-comers. We promptly contacted the names on our list, and the response to our query was overwhelmingly positive. Most of those we contacted agreed to contribute essays; a handful declined but submitted the names of other scholars who might be interested. All, however, thought the project was a good idea. Our next step was to contact Joyce Harrison, then editor-in-chief at the University Press of Kentucky, who immediately and enthusiastically expressed interest in the project. We all agreed to move forward. The rest is, as they say, history.

There is to be found in this volume a wealth of material not previously published. Those looking for an account of the military campaigns in these states will not find it here. The essays in this volume focus instead on the political, economic, and social conditions in Kentucky and Tennessee before, during, and immediately after the Civil War. But, as they demonstrate, there is much of value to be learned about the Civil War other than military matters.

Taking a book from the point of inspiration to the publication stage requires the involvement of many individuals. First of all, we would like to thank the scholars who contributed essays. Their enthusiasm for this project and eagerness to contribute to it made the endeavor much less burdensome than it might have been. We would also like to acknowledge our debt to the University Press of Kentucky, in particular, Stephen Wrinn, Laura Sutton, Mack McCormick, Ila McEntire, Pat Gonzales, Ann Malcolm, and Joseph Brown. Without their expertise and nurture, this book would not have been possible. We are very grateful to Charles P. Roland, Nat Hughes, and John V. Cimprich for reading the manuscript and offering their support for the project.

We would also like to thank our colleagues in the History Department at Tennessee Tech, who continually expressed interest in and support for this project through all its stages.

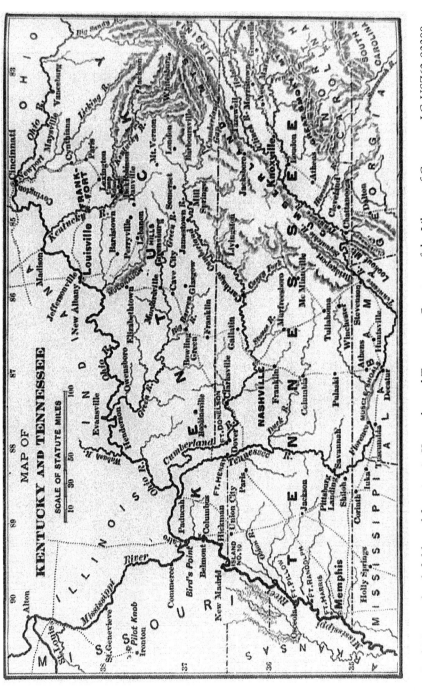

Civil War–era battlefields and fort sites in Kentucky and Tennessee. Courtesy of the Library of Congress, LC-USZ62-93300.

Introduction

Larry H. Whiteaker

Kentucky and Tennessee. Tennessee and Kentucky. Sister states. Enemy states. From the 1770s, when settlers from Virginia and North Carolina began to move into the lush valleys of East Tennessee and central Kentucky, these two states would be linked—whether the residents wished this or not—in the national consciousness. Even with many similarities—terrain, climate, settlers' background, and religion, to name a few—there would always be major differences. By the 1820s, for example, a huge political rift would develop, pitting the followers of Kentucky's Henry Clay against the followers of Tennessee's Andrew Jackson. The ultimate difference would come in 1861—a difference that constitutes a major theme of this essay collection—when Tennessee joined the Confederate States of America and, after a failed attempt to remain neutral in the Civil War, Kentucky remained in the Union.

Kentucky and Tennessee. Even the names had something in common. Anthropologists and historians believe that they came from Native American terms, but no agreement has been reached on what the terms meant. That the two areas were named by Indians does reveal, of course, that the first people to live in Kentucky and Tennessee were Native Americans, who probably moved into the region thousands of years before Europeans began to arrive in the sixteenth century. By the eighteenth century, powerful tribes such as the Cherokee and the Chickasaw had claimed the area all the way north to the Ohio River as their hunting lands and had chased out competing tribes such as the Shawnee.

In the 1740s and 1750s, Thomas Walker and other surveyors from east of the Appalachian Mountains began to explore part of the region, and their activities were followed in the 1760s and 1770s by efforts to buy the land from the Cherokees and other tribes. Further interest in the region arose when "long hunters" such as Thomas "Big Foot" Spencer and Daniel Boone ventured into the area in pursuit of deer hides and other animal pelts. Their descriptions of the region helped spark land fever back in Virginia and North Carolina. By the early 1770s, settlers had begun to move into both Kentucky and Tennessee, causing conflict with British officials trying to keep settlers from moving west of the mountains and with anti-settlement factions of the Cherokees.

What a region to struggle for! Bounded on the north by the Ohio River, on the east by the Appalachian Mountains, on the west by the Mississippi River, and, more vaguely, on the south by an informal line close to the thirty-fifth parallel, this area of some eighty-three thousand square miles had already been a prize in the war between the French and the British in the 1750s and was another prize in the American Revolution. After the Revolution canceled British claims to the region, a new challenge to American possession came from the Spanish in Louisiana when during the 1780s they tried to lure Kentucky and Tennessee residents into withdrawing allegiance from the United States and giving it to Spain.

Frontier loyalties to the nation held firm through the shaky Articles of Confederation period, but this time produced both political tumult and progress toward statehood. In 1776, for example, Kentucky, long considered a part of Virginia, saw Virginia create Kentucky County from the whole region. To the south, North Carolina soon made what would become Tennessee the county of Washington. More counties were created in the years that followed, but Kentuckians and Tennesseans alike complained loudly about the poor government that Virginia and North Carolina provided and the difficulties that frontier people had in traveling to the state capitals east of the mountains. Subsequently, in 1792, Kentucky, with Virginia's acquiescence, became the fifteenth state. In 1796, after a brief existence as a territory, Tennessee entered the Union as the sixteenth state.

Including their similar paths toward statehood, early Kentuckians and Tennesseans had much in common. Most of the settlers in both states had migrated from Virginia and North Carolina and were largely English, Scots-Irish, or German in background. In religion, most were Presbyterians, Baptists, or Methodists, but the region also contained Catholics, Episcopalians, Lutherans, and members of smaller denominations. English was certainly the dominant language, even if spoken with a frontier twang. As late as 1860, schools were scarce in the two states, but each had them and had several private colleges within their borders by the 1820s and 1830s.

Economically, the two states shared a largely agricultural way of life. After the initial lure of abundant game had brought the long hunters, the permanent settlers came because of the rich soils, temperate climate, and excellent water sources. In Kentucky, farmers raised the usual food crops such as corn but also planted large amounts of hemp, flax, and tobacco. Tennessee farmers subsisted on corn and other vegetables and raised tobacco and—in the middle and western sections of the state—cotton commercially. Both states produced enough cattle and hogs not only to satisfy their own needs but also to export some to adjacent states. By 1860, some development of coal mining had occurred in the region as well as the development of small industries, but neither mining nor industry played significant roles in the states' economies.

Raising tobacco, hemp, or cotton involved intensive labor and, to be profitable, large acreage. To meet these needs, Kentucky and Tennessee farmers—at least the large landowners—brought into the region African slaves. The first, of course, arrived with the original settlers. Virginia and North Carolina had long before established a slavery-based agricultural system, and, thus, as the western migration began, the slaves went with their owners. As the wilderness gave way to farms and plantations, commercial crops demanded more slaves. In 1800, Kentucky, more agriculturally developed than its sister state, had 40,343 slaves, while Tennessee had only 13,584. After the purchase of western Tennessee territory from the Chickasaws in the late 1810s, cotton cultivation greatly expanded and, with it, Tennessee's slave population. By 1840, Kentucky had 182,258 slaves and Tennessee 183,059. Tennessee's slave population continued to increase at a faster rate than that of its neighbor to the north, as is revealed by the 1860 census: Tennessee slaves, 275,719; Kentucky slaves, 225,483. By this time, approximately one in five Kentuckians was a slave, while in Tennessee the ratio was closer to one in four. Although there were many other reasons why Tennesseans joined the Confederacy in 1861, their commitment to slavery and to cotton cultivation certainly tied them to the lower Southern states—the Cotton Belt—in ways that many Kentuckians did not share.

Political developments in the two states both bound them and separated them. Initially, the vast majority of the region's voters were die-hard Jeffersonians, with the rival Federalists being virtually nonexistent. Further, both states enthusiastically supported the War of 1812, with War Hawks such as Henry Clay of Kentucky and Felix Grundy of Tennessee leading the way. By the 1820s, however, the growing rivalry between Clay and Andrew Jackson would split the two states' political allegiances. Calling Clay the "Judas of the West" in 1825 when he supported Jackson's rival, John Quincy Adams, in the presidential election, Jackson and his supporters became even more furious with Clay when he accepted the secretary of state position in Adams's administration. This rivalry played a huge role in just a few years in the emergence of two new political parties: the Democrats and the Whigs. (Personal animosity between Clay and Jackson led Clay to remark about Jackson that killing two thousand British soldiers at New Orleans certainly did not qualify him to be president and caused Jackson allegedly to claim that one of his major regrets as a politician was that he had not been able to "shoot Henry Clay.")

The differences between Clay's political program and Jackson's went far beyond personality. Both men were staunch nationalists, but Clay's American System put much more emphasis on the development of industry and government-sponsored internal improvements than did Jackson's program of limited, frugal government. With the founding of the Whig Party in 1834—a party that incorporated most of Clay's goals—the Whigs would have a vigorous and popular presence in Kentucky and, somewhat surprisingly, Tennessee. In 1836, the first Whig presidential contest, the Whig William Henry Harrison carried Kentucky and the Whig Hugh Lawson White outpolled Martin Van Buren in Tennessee. Until 1856—even when Tennessee's own James Knox Polk ran in 1844—Kentucky and Tennessee gave their electoral votes to the Whig candidates. At the state and local levels as well, the states' Whigs maintained active and successful opposition to the Democrats. Not until 1856 did the states' voting majority choose the Democratic candidate—James Buchanan—and, by then, the Whig Party had collapsed, and the Democrats were beginning to have great difficulty in maintaining national unity.

Beginning with the Wilmot Proviso in 1846, the sectional crises that wracked the nation during the next fifteen years ripped apart the political parties, created new ones, and eventually resulted in civil war. Kentuckians and Tennesseans alike participated in the turmoil that the crises caused and saw their own political allegiances twisted and, in some instances, redefined. A major blow for the Whigs in both states was the collapse of the national Whig Party after the 1852 election, a collapse that sent Whigs everywhere searching for a new party. Some dabbled with the upstart and nativist American ("Know Nothing") Party, but its anti-immigrant stance and lukewarm attitude toward slavery failed to gain much support from Kentucky and Tennessee voters. After the 1856 election, its national existence ended as well. By the end of the decade, former Whigs would find a more attractive party in the short-lived Constitutional Union Party.

The states' Democrats and Whigs did agree on one thing during the 1850s, however: they hated the newly emergent Republican Party. Joining with their fellow Southerners, they condemned the Republicans not only for opposing slavery's expansion but also for being closet abolitionists (at least in the minds of many Republican opponents). The prospect of a Republican victory in the 1856 presidential election played a large role in Kentucky and Tennessee voters opting for James Buchanan. Though thwarted in that election for the presidency, the Republicans made significant gains in Congress and at state and local levels, engendering fear and anger throughout the South, and opening the door once again for a South-wide debate over secession.

Thus, these two states, Kentucky and Tennessee, entering the Union as part of the New West, serving as the home of national political figures such as Henry Clay and Andrew Jackson, boasting of folk heroes such as Daniel Boone and David Crockett, waited to see what the remainder of the 1850s would accomplish in dealing with the sectional crises. Would the Republicans win in 1860? Would a new party arise to replace the Whigs? If the Republicans ever came to national power, would slavery be safe? Would the South secede? And, if secession came, which way would Kentucky and Tennessee go? Today we know the answers to these questions, but, as this book's essays reveal, we are still—nearly 150 years later—assessing the consequences of the decisions the states' residents made.

Part 1

★ ★ ★

Secession in Kentucky and Tennessee

Beleaguered Loyalties

Kentucky Unionism

Gary R. Matthews

On the eve of the Civil War, as the Southern states began to organize under the banner of a nascent confederacy, Jefferson Davis looked toward Kentucky with no less covetous eyes than did Abraham Lincoln and the federal government. Both presidents, Kentuckians by birth, measured the worth of the Bluegrass State to their respective nations in relative terms. Lincoln, always the gifted and pragmatic politician, viewed Kentucky much like a politician would the votes of a needed swing state in a presidential election and remained determined to deny the state's resources to the South. Davis, a West Point graduate, instinctively assessed Kentucky's value in military terms and recognized the defensive advantage of an unbroken Confederate line along the Ohio River. In the end, a pragmatic respect for Northern economic dominance and a love for the historic national identity bolstered by a trust in the democratic process inspired a majority of Kentuckians to seek preservation of property and self by resisting the temptations of secession. This decision, however, did not stop thousands of Kentuckians from heading south to fight for the Confederacy. Nor did it deter the ex-Confederates from assuming a high degree of political and social ascendancy in post-Appomattox Kentucky, an ascendancy that in many ways made Kentucky seem more Confederate after the guns stopped firing than it had a historic right to claim.

The postwar ascendancy of the Kentucky Confederates has created an unavoidable temptation to assess why Kentucky did not hitch its horse to the secession wagon as opposed to why it chose to remain in the Union. Such an assessment has a tendency to misinterpret Kentucky's character in 1860 by overestimating the state's enthusiasm for a confederacy controlled by the cotton states. For, although Kentucky was Southern, it was not, as Thomas Clark so aptly concluded, "a Southern state, comparable to Mississippi, Alabama, and South Carolina." William Freehling has further pointed out that Kentucky was not even as Southern as its mother state, Virginia; it was more Western, a point that should be well taken. Conversely, pointing to its geographic proximity to the North, and identifying certain border state characteristics as determinative in Kentucky's decision to remain in the Union, ignores the more subtle reasons for that decision. That being the case, it becomes incumbent to analyze the historic cultural, economic, and political components of Kentucky's antebellum character in order to understand the determining factors in Kentucky's stand.[1]

The Kentuckian of 1861 could generally trace his or her roots to the English and Scots-Irish settlers and their African American slaves who migrated over the Wilderness Trail from Virginia, North Carolina, and, to lesser degree, Pennsylvania and Maryland in the last quarter of the eighteenth century. In the settlement years preceding statehood, Kentucky was a political subdivision of Virginia. Finding itself deeply involved in the American Revolution, Virginia was unable to govern or protect Kentucky effectively. Thus, Kentuckians learned quickly that they would have to fend for themselves against the frequent Native American incursions, often inspired by the British. Richmond was also particularly inept at regulating land distribution after the American Revolution. This ineptness resulted in a land system that was mired in a swamp of confusion. It was during these years that many of the large estates of central Kentucky were put together through the purchase, more often than not by absentee Virginians, of many small squatter claims. Unlike the typical pioneer, who cleared and settled his own land, many of these absentee owners sent their overseers and slaves ahead to perform this function. Thus, by 1800, almost all the early squatters in central Kentucky were supplanted by large estate owners, who introduced slavery as a protected property right.[2]

With Virginia's preoccupation with the American Revolution, Kentucky's early settlers were thoroughly isolated and continued to be for many years, creating a society that, but for slavery, was more similar to that developing in the old Northwest territories of Indiana and Illinois than in the Southern states. Southern influences, however, were pervasive and over the years, particularly among the Bluegrass gentry of central Kentucky, developed into mainstays of society. Within a generation of Fort Boonesborough, these gentlemen farmers began to fashion their society and behavior after the plantation life of the Southern seaboard and Tidewater areas of Virginia and the Carolinas. By 1820, they had achieved a level of prosperity and permanence that matched that of the grand Southern estates on the eastern side of the Appalachians. The society and culture of the Bluegrass elite were, however, the exception and not the rule. The yeoman farmers in other parts of the state lived in a much less pretentious style and, like their brethren to the north, personally worked the soil. Slavery and its attendant culture, however, influenced Kentucky society more than any other institution, and the Bluegrass elite essentially controlled slavery. It was slavery and the gentry society, as perpetuated in the Bluegrass, that identified Kentucky with the South.[3]

The first half of the nineteenth century also witnessed thousands of second- and third-generation Kentuckians settling in Ohio, Indiana, and Illinois. In part, much of this northern migration was prompted by slavery. Although many of the migrating Kentuckians had a moral distaste for the institution, most objected to it as a deterrent to the economic prosperity of nonslaveholders. They had discovered that it was difficult to compete with the slaveholders unless they themselves became slaveholders. The majority of these migrants were either unwilling or unable to make this compromise. Thus, an impressive number of Kentucky's yeomen farmers of egalitarian stock sought what they believed to be more fertile fields in the free states of the Midwest. By 1860, some sixty-five thousand native-born Kentuckians were living in Indiana and another sixty thousand in Illinois. Likewise, a number of free-state natives, although a considerably smaller population than the northward-migrating Kentuckians, migrated southward to Kentucky. These migrations and comminglings of peoples created strong ties that bound together families and friends on both sides of the Ohio River, ties that would have a significant impact on Kentucky's decisionmaking process in 1861.[4]

Despite the lack of guidance from Virginia, Kentucky emerged from the pioneer wilderness with a mind-set characterized by an egalitarian-based nationalism. In 1792, it became the first Southern state, and only the second in the nation, not to require a property qualification for either voting or holding public office. In time, its budding political philosophy would be nurtured and irrevocably molded into a strong desire for national unity through the immeasurable influence of Henry Clay, who for more than forty years dominated Kentucky politics. Although a slave owner, Clay understood the limitations of the slaveholding system, particularly its economic deterrence to industrialization. Despite a reputation for being a self-seeking, ambitious politician, he was also an adept businessman with a vision for America and Kentucky. Like most visionaries, he was an idealist. From 1820 until his death, his ideology was centrist and focused on compromise among competing interests—those of the North and the South—in order to advance economic progress. His continuous efforts to mediate those differences in sectional perspective resulted in the concept of compromise becoming deeply rooted in the Kentucky psyche as an ideal of progress.[5]

Clay's vision for the future of America and Kentucky was based on what was called the *American System*. The American System demanded progress through industrialization. Clay adroitly politicized the need for a larger federal monetary presence in developing the national infrastructure while respecting the property rights of the slave owner. His call to the future would require Southerners, including Kentuckians, to diversify and adopt economic innovations. It was not surprising that both Northerners and Southerners determined that such a program would eventually abrogate slavery. Although many Southerners, particularly Kentuckians, understood and fully appreciated Clay's program, few were willing to infringe on the slavocracy.[6]

Clay's opinions on slavery were well known. Although he perceived slavery as a protected state right not to be infringed on by the federal government, Clay strongly believed in and publicly advocated gradual emancipation. (He was also noted for his work with colonization societies to find homes in Africa for freedmen.) This position bolstered the fledgling antislavery movement in Kentucky, and, by 1849, the movement had gathered sufficient steam to push—although unsuccessfully—for a state constitutional amendment abolishing slavery.

Clay's belief in the Constitution and love for the Union was legendary among his constituents. Over the years, his fundamental belief that the preservation of the Union was in the best interest of all Kentuckians was more than once demonstrated by the employment of his political skills to effectuate his ideology of compromise during the heat of a sectional crisis. Kentuckians admired Clay for his successes and began to see their state as being in a unique geographic position to mediate grievances between North and South. With an ability to appreciate both sides of the ongoing arguments, Kentuckians were less likely to advocate any form of political extremism. Such was the case when Kentucky resisted sending a delegate to the 1850 Nashville Convention of slave states called to discuss what recourse, including secession, should be taken in the event the Compromise of 1850 became law. Likewise, in 1861, Kentucky never called a convention to determine the question of secession. Both instances suggest that political leadership in Kentucky was in the hands of conservatives who, when pressed, would disdain secession. The Kentuckians who followed Clay in Congress, particularly John J. Crittenden, also viewed compromise as a viable alternative to disunion.[7]

That Kentuckians were comfortable with the principles expounded by Clay was not an impediment to their supporting the rights of the slave states. They still believed in the inviolability of states' rights. This view would come to forefront with the formation of the Republican Party, which most Kentuckians despised with the same vehemence as those in the Deep South. Generally, Kentucky congressmen sided with the slave states on roll call votes that addressed issues regarding the institution of slavery. A review of the voting patterns during the presidential elections held between 1840 and 1856 reveals that Kentuckians overwhelmingly supported candidates who were protective of states' rights and did not threaten the slavocracy. Kentucky politicians, however, were more conservative on votes relating to the expansion of slavery, an issue that generally differentiated Kentucky from the Deep South.[8]

During the 1850s, Kentucky, like the rest of the nation, experienced the reshaping of political parties and the realignment of voters. For twenty years, Kentucky had been a state whose vote could be counted on to fall in the Whig Party column. Although the Whig Party suffered a shattering defeat in the 1852 presidential election, it still had a tenuous control over the Kentucky statehouse. For almost two years after the 1852 presidential election, a cadre of politically powerful Kentuckians still held to the hope of a resurgent Whig Party, a hope that dissipated with the passage of the Kansas-Nebraska Act in 1854. This piece of legislation also destroyed the relative sectional calm following the Compromise of 1850. In January 1854, Senator Archibald Dixon, a Kentuckian, introduced a bill that would have effectively repealed the Compromise of 1850. Dixon had based his political career on supporting the proslavery demands of his power base. His bill was nothing more than an attempt to influence the proslavery faction–controlled Kentucky legislature to reelect him to the Senate. Southern Democrats viewed Dixon's bill as a Whig power play. Not to be outdone by the Whigs, they forced Stephen Douglas to introduce a similar bill to reestablish their "proslavery credentials." John J. Crittenden and other politically astute Kentuckians immediately saw that the passage of either bill would generate a new and potentially more explosive round of sectional strife. The Dixon bill fell to the wayside as Douglas orchestrated his bill through the Senate. Crittenden, soon to take over Dixon's Senate seat, pleaded with all the Kentucky congressmen, including Dixon, not to vote for the Douglas bill. His efforts reaped little success as the Kentucky congressional delegation backed the bill to a man.[9]

The implications of the passage of the Kansas-Nebraska Act were not as revolutionary in the border states as they were in the North and South. Northerners were appalled and took great exception to the passage of the act. Most Northerners viewed the machinations employed by Douglas to ensure passage of the act as morally corrupt. What followed was the destruction of the Northern Democratic and Whig parties and a search for a new sectional political entity to fight the slavocracy. By the mid-1850s, only one party, the Democratic, survived in the South. Although somewhat in need of repair, Kentucky, however, still maintained a basis for a viable two-party system.

With the demise of the Whig Party, many stalwart ex-Whigs joined the Know Nothings—a fast-growing nativist organization that formed under the nebulous banner of the American Party. The American Party was something of an anomaly in Kentucky and the rest of the South, opposed as it was to immigrants and Catholics, who posed no direct threat to the homogeneity of the political power base. What apparently attracted Kentucky voters was not so much the political philosophy of the Americans, which many found shameful at best, as their in-place organization. Astute ex-Whigs viewed this political infrastructure as an opportunistic mechanism to keep the Democrats from control of the state until a more agreeable opposition party could be formed. This goal was realized in

1855 when the Know Nothings carried the state election. By that time, the American Party was already in its death throes as a nationally viable political entity. Most Northern members of the party were joining the newly formed Republican Party, resulting in a shift of the party's power base to the border states. This became apparent in 1857 when die-hard party members staged their last national political convention in Louisville.[10]

It was evident by the late 1850s that the American Party had served its purpose in Kentucky and elsewhere. The growing strength of the Republican Party in the North and the rhetoric spouting from "Fire-Eaters" in the South caused old Whigs like John J. Crittenden to feel that there was a need and, perhaps, an opportunity for the formation of a national conservative opposition party. In February 1859, the path to realizing this need was initiated in Kentucky when two thousand delegates from eighty-four counties met in Louisville. Robert Letcher, an old Whig and ex-governor, presided over an assembly that included most of the men who would constitute the Union leadership in Kentucky during the next decade. The convention passed a rather weak platform that pronounced no specific program other than some platitudes about preserving the Union and the peace of the nation. This lack of direction, most likely, contributed to the overwhelming victory of the Democratic Party in the August elections that summer. Beriah Magoffin, a man with strong pro-Southern sentiments, was elected governor. All the other incoming state officials were Democrats, as were six of ten congressmen and the overwhelming majority of the state legislature. Almost two-thirds of the incoming legislators were slave owners, and a little over a third were lawyers. It would be hard to argue that the legal interests of the Kentucky slave owners were not well represented as the state was about to enter the secession crisis.[11]

The short-lived truce following the Compromise of 1850 was replaced by an ever-increasing sectional animosity, the strength of which destroyed the South's faith in the two-party system. Kentuckians, unlike the Southern oligarchy, were not overcome with the fear that the political results of a Republican victory could not be controlled. They, in large part, still believed that the competition generated by a healthy two-party system was the most appropriate means to contain the sectional crisis. With the advent of the Kansas-Nebraska Act and the formation of the Republican Party, this belief was no longer shared by Kentucky's sister states in the Deep South. The Deep South believed that it was no longer a question of which party but one of which *section* controlled the White House. Editorials in Republican-backed newspapers in the North stressing the need for an exclusive Northern party "to resist slave power aggressions" tended to support this belief. Consequently, by 1856, there was only one party in the Deep South—the Democratic Party. The lack of two-party competition in the Deep South permitted sectional extremism to flourish to the extent that normal political processes would, ultimately, be rejected when secession appeared to be the only means to achieve the region's political goals. Kentuckians, on the other hand, "not only continued to believe that they could achieve those goals at the national level through the normal political process, but . . . also thought that they were being attained already within their state so that there was no need to create a new government." This fundamental difference would play itself out during the presidential election of 1860.[12]

It is hard to imagine that the sectional animosity reached in the 1850s would have been so extreme in the absence of slavery. Naturally, being a slave state that was bordered by three free states, Kentucky was a frontline recipient of this animosity. Slavery became a pervasive part of Kentucky history the minute the first African American bondsman set foot on the Wilderness Trail. In the first years of settlement, slaves were used to clear fields, build houses, and do whatever else was needed to help close the frontier. It soon became evident, however, that, but for the extreme southwest section of the state, where cotton was raised, Kentucky's climate and crops were not as conducive to the profitable use of slave labor as were those of the plantations of the Deep South. Ironically, the farmers in the Bluegrass area, where the great majority of slaves were located, found their land to be far more valuable for raising livestock than any labor-intensive crop. Hemp was the only exception, owing in most part to the abundant use of its by-products, twine and rope, by Southern planters to bind their cotton bales and the U.S. Navy for the rigging on its ships. It was axiomatic that the demand for hemp production rose proportionately with the demand for cotton. Owing in large part to large slave populations, Lexington and the surrounding Bluegrass counties became the center for the production and manufacturing of hemp and its by-products. In time, strong commercial and social ties developed between the Bluegrass hemp producers and the Southern planters.[13]

Although slave labor was used extensively in hemp production and manufacturing, the industry was not a panacea for the growing number of relatively underutilized slaves in the Bluegrass. From 1800 to 1833, when Kentucky passed a law forbidding the importation of slaves, the state's slave population witnessed its greatest rate of growth. Although this rate slowed after 1833 and the proportion of black to white Kentuckians began to decrease marginally until it reached 19.5 percent in 1860, the existence of an underutilized slave population was alarming to the slave owner. In the legal terms of the nineteenth century, slaves were property and treated as a capital investment. However, when a capital investment is producing little or no income, it quickly becomes a liability. To resolve this economically unattractive dilemma, the slave owner had either to maximize the use of his property or liquidate it. Some Kentuckians moved with their slaves to take advantage of the opening of more cotton-producing lands in Mississippi and Alabama. Others purchased cotton fields in these states but retained their Bluegrass farms, moving slaves between the two locations as needed. These movements and the ever-expanding need for slaves in the Deep South created a market for Kentucky's abundant slave population. With the repeal in 1849 of Kentucky's Slave Importation Act of 1833, the state became an even more active commercial center for domestic slave traffic. In his seminal work on the history of blacks in Kentucky, Marion Lucas has calculated that approximately seventy-seven thousand slaves were sent to the Deep South from the state from 1830 to 1860. With the cotton market booming, the demand for Kentucky slaves in the Deep South became so substantial after 1849 that their commercial value reached its highest level in the decade before the Civil War.[14]

The Kentucky slave owner's comprehension of his property rights and their inherent value unquestionably tethered him to the Southern slavocracy. Yet, unlike in the Deep South, a slaveholding planter class, and its attendant caste system, was not created in Kentucky, owing to its lack of labor-intensive crops. Instead, the state's settlement and development patterns produced a wealthy middle class supported by artisans, mechanics, and small farm owners. Thus, slave ownership in Kentucky was more widespread than it was in the Cotton Belt states, with a majority of slave owners owning fewer than five slaves. The 1850 census shows that only fifty-three Kentuckians owned more than fifty slaves. Nevertheless, Kentucky slaveholders were just as adamant about their property rights as were the slave owners of the Deep South and generally would not entertain thoughts of emancipation, at least emancipation without compensation. There were, however, numerous Kentuckians, including some slave owners, who felt strongly that the state would, ultimately, benefit from some form of emancipation. The more conservative antislavery proponents viewed slavery as a means of race control and recommended emancipation only if it was used in tandem with the removal of the freed slaves from the state. Most nonslaveholding Kentuckians, however, believed that slavery was evil but were intent on being "patient until some safe and practical solution to the problem could be found."[15]

Although the average midcentury Kentuckian may have been ambivalent about slavery, he was not ambivalent about blacks. Swayed by racially motivated concerns about an uncontrolled African American population, Kentuckians never considered championing political and social equality for the emancipated slaves. Such concerns also likely contributed to their continued susceptibility to the rhetoric proffered by the state's proslavery element.[16]

Antislavery attitudes in Kentucky can be traced almost to the importation of the first slaves. By and large, the first settlers were not wealthy men but common farmers and artisans with strong egalitarian and republican beliefs. For various reasons, most had a disdain for slavery. Yet, by the time statehood was achieved in 1792, the institution had become strongly entrenched and attempts to ban it in the first state constitution failed. There were recurrent attempts to introduce some form of gradual emancipation, but these efforts were defeated. Emancipators' most favorable opportunity appeared in 1849 under the color of constitutional reform. When the dust settled, not only was the reformers' call for gradual emancipation soundly defeated, but it was also obvious that slavery had become even more entrenched in Kentucky. The Third Constitutional Convention held in 1855 tended to confirm this conclusion. The 1849 convention was the last serious effort to move for emancipation in Kentucky before the Civil War. Kentuckians never did agree to emancipation of their own volition. It would, ultimately, take a civil war and a national constitutional amendment before Kentuckians begrudgingly accepted it.[17]

The existence of an active core of Kentuckians willing to support some form of emancipation is indicative of a democratic society unafraid to air its own laundry. Aside from the moral issues attendant to the evil necessity, many Kentuckians never were able philosophically to reconcile slavery with a republican form of government. Perhaps this dichotomy, more than any other factor, continued to breathe life into Kentucky's antislavery movement.[18]

Kentuckians' tolerance of antislavery activity within their state far exceeded that of residents of the Lower South. Indicative of this toleration was the existence of an antislavery press within the state. The most famous was the *True American,* published in Lexington for several months during the spring and summer of 1845 by Henry Clay's eccentric cousin Cassius Marcellus Clay. Cassius Clay believed that slavery retarded economic progress, particularly when it came to the industrialization of the South. Although he preached emancipation, he did not advocate equality of rights. His editorials in the *True American* added nothing more than what he had advocated publicly for years, but they were now printed and circulated throughout Kentucky. This agitation stretched beyond the proslavery forces' limit of toleration when the *True American* carried an article advocating equality for free blacks. When a committee was appointed to dismantle the newspaper's presses and transport them to Cincinnati, Thomas Marshall delivered a speech advising Clay that he should have known Kentuckians better. If the suppression of Clay's press failed to concern most Kentuckians, neither did the further establishment of newspapers of like kind, such as the *Louisville Examiner,* which tended to deliver a milder message of emancipation.[19]

A small core of abolitionists also patronized the antislavery movement in Kentucky. Abolitionists could be differentiated from other antislavery advocates by their strong belief in the "immediate emancipation of slaves and equal rights for blacks in the United States." Of course, antebellum Kentuckians considered those favoring even the most limited form of emancipation extremists. Extreme or not, Northern abolitionists targeted Kentucky all through the 1840s and 1850s as their beachhead in the South. Just across the river from an active abolition stronghold in Cincinnati, Kentucky was too tempting a target for these crusaders to pass up. Abolitionists also believed that, owing to the state's history of antislavery politics, Kentuckians would be more receptive to their dogma than the residents of the Deep South. Such freedom of thought, the Lower South strongly believed, would lead states like Kentucky to side with Illinoisans rather than with South Carolinians and hasten the death of slavery on its northern flank.[20]

The story of John Fee and his abolitionist colony in Berea, Kentucky, has been told many times. It is a remarkable story in the sense that Kentucky slave owners tolerated the colony's presence for several years before forcing its inhabitants out of the state in early 1860. Situated in the slave-intense Madison County, Fee and the Berea colony preached a biblically based abolitionism. This was not in itself unique, for, at one time or another, all the major Protestant denominations, with the Presbyterian ministry being the most vocal, preached some form of antislavery in Kentucky. What was unique was that Fee intended to colonize Kentucky with Northerners and make it a free state. Although experiencing very little success, Fee found that his presence, in tandem with proslavery's deep-rooted fear of an imminent slave uprising, was more than enough of a catalyst for the residents of Madison County to remove the Bereans. It was this "constantly increased ascension of northern men" that was cited by Kentuckians as one of the primary reasons why they deemed it necessary to force Fee and his followers to leave the state.[21]

It has been written many times that slavery in Kentucky, and the Upper South in general, was of a milder form than what African Americans experienced in the Lower South. Despite the incongruity of this statement, there is ample evidence to support such an argument, but there are also sufficient examples to be found highlighting the harsh reality of slavery. Kentuckians then were, and still to some extent today are, quick to point out what they considered to be the benevolent aspects of slavery as one way of ameliorating their complicity in perpetuating the peculiar institution. For example, there were no legal restrictions in Kentucky forbidding teaching slaves to read or write, as there were in the states of the Deep South. In fact, it has been estimated that at least 20 percent of Kentucky's runaways could read. Kentucky slaves also had far more freedom of movement than was previously thought. This liberality is particularly interesting in a state where a slave's proximity to freedom was the width of the Ohio River. One would think that it could be far easier for a mobile slave to bolt than for one who was sedentary. Yet the 1860 census for Kentucky reported only 119 fugitives out of a slave population of 225,483.[22]

Perhaps no slave state, other than Virginia, openly debated emancipation as did Kentucky. Although this debate sometimes had violent consequences, the fact that it was carried on at all indicated the willingness of Kentuckians to address the issue. This permissive attitude was not present in the other slave states. Indeed, the slave states in general took great pains to suppress such attitudes. By 1860, every Southern state but Kentucky had passed laws restricting free speech and freedom of the press in order to curtail antislavery influences. The willingness to debate these issues openly, in tandem with apparently more liberal laws toward slaves in general, would tend to suggest that, in 1860, Kentuckians had less fear of the racial consequences resulting from a Northern-dominated Congress than did the white citizens of the Lower South.[23]

Written history is so focused on the sectional crisis during the decade before the Civil War that it would lead one to believe that Kentucky, along with the entire borderland, was constantly in turmoil. To some degree, Kentuckians were assaulted from the north by abolitionist and other free-state propaganda, from the south by challenges questioning the state's loyalty to slavery and the region, and from within by attempts to reconcile these contrasts, but the reality was that life went on as usual, with very few people recognizing the historical significance of their time. Most Kentuckians recognized that slavery was economically harmful to the state, but they were willing to accept the institution as a necessary evil. Such a conception of slavery was far different from that of the other slave states like Virginia, which viewed slavery as a "social, political and moral blessing." Kentuckians, however, much like the rest of the South, easily convinced themselves that, without slavery, a large free black population within the state would disrupt social harmony and, ultimately, lead to some sort of violent racial confrontation. This thought process helped them explain away the incongruity of slavery within the democratic society they so strongly cherished.[24]

Kentucky's geographic position historically permitted it to reap the benefits of trade with both the North and the South. However, with the advent of the railroad and, particularly, the unprecedented miles of track built by the Northern railroads in the 1850s, the state's political-economic outlook was significantly altered. By 1860, except for the Louisville and Nashville Railroad's brand-new southern main line, Kentucky's rail connections were oriented north. These Northern connections benefited Louisville perhaps more than any other city in the state. The city had experienced both an economic and a population boom between 1840 and 1860. Louisville in 1860, with a population of almost seventy thousand people, was the twelfth largest city in the country. Its vibrant commerce and trade created a wealthy and politically conservative business class. These politically active and powerful businessmen viewed their lucrative economic ties with a jealousy that would suppress the exigencies relating to any thoughts of secession. They clearly understood that "a southern confederacy, conceived and controlled by the cotton states, had serious economic disadvantages for the Upper South," particularly if its primary goals were "cheap slaves, free trade, and expansion." Consequently, they became highly motivated in protecting their "growing manufacturing and commercial commitments." The only rational way to ensure deliverance in that direction was to back, even in a titular manner, the North in the upcoming war for national political and economic dominance.[25]

Thus, as the two sections of the country marched toward war, it is really not so difficult to understand the position that a majority of Kentucky leaders chose to take regarding secession. They were Southern men with a national perspective very different from that of the oligarchic Deep South. Most important, they were men who strongly believed in the two-party system and the potential for the political resolution of controversial issues. Although many were slave owners, they were neither afraid to debate the issue of emancipation nor willing to support the institution's expansion in a manner that would threaten national unity. Slavery was never the determinative factor in Kentucky's decision to take the high road. Nor does it seem to have been the determining factor for the vast majority of the state's nearly thirty-five thousand sons who fought for the Confederacy.

Through family and commercial ties, many Kentuckians, particularly the state's business and political leaders, had been inculcated with Northern economic power and Yankee determination. Unlike their brethren farther south, they were convinced that the North would fight and, most likely, win. Furthermore, politically astute Kentuckians as early as 1850 recognized that "as to the boys up the hollows, and in the bush who form a considerable part of our country they are not to be relied on in any contest against the Union." Perhaps these understandings alone were enough of an incentive for most Kentuckians to avoid a war that would certainly turn Kentucky into a battlefield and threaten their way of life.[26]

Notes

1. Thomas D. Clark, *Kentucky: Land of Contrast* (New York: Harper & Row,

1968), 122; William W. Freehling, *The Road to Disunion: Secessionists at Bay, 1776-1854* (New York: Oxford University Press, 1990), 464.

2. Thomas D. Clark, *A History of Kentucky* (Lexington, Ky.: John Bradford, 1950), 62–64; Stephan Aron, *How the West Was Lost: The Transformation of Kentucky from Daniel Boone to Henry Clay* (Baltimore: Johns Hopkins University Press, 1996), 79–81.

3. Aron, *How the West Was Lost*, 126.

4. Nicole Etcheson, *The Emerging Midwest: Upland Southerners and the Political Culture of the Old Northwest, 1787-1861* (Bloomington: Indiana University Press, 1996), 67; U.S. Bureau of the Census, *Population of the United States in 1860* (Washington, D.C.: Bureau of the Census, 1864), 168–87.

5. Ralph A. Wooster, *Politicians, Planters and Plain Folk: Courthouse and Statehouse in the Upper South, 1850-1860* (Knoxville: University of Tennessee Press, 1975), 13.

6. Daniel Walker Howe, *The Political Culture of the American Whigs* (Chicago: University of Chicago Press, 1979), 132–39.

7. Arthur C. Cole, *The Whig Party in the South* (Gloucester, Mass.: Peter Smith, 1962), 161; Albert D. Kirwan, *John J. Crittenden: The Struggle for the Union* (Lexington: University of Kentucky Press, 1962), 432–33.

8. Ruth McQuown and Jasper B. Shannon, *Presidential Politics in Kentucky, 1824-1948: A Compilation of Election Statistics and an Analysis of Political Behavior* (Lexington: University of Kentucky, College of Arts and Sciences, Bureau of Government Research, 1950), 10–40.

9. Michael F. Holt, *The Rise and Fall of the American Whig Party: Jacksonian Politics and the Onset of the Civil War* (New York: Oxford University Press, 1999), 808–10.

10. Ibid., 956; Tyler Anbinder, *Nativism and Slavery: Northern Know Nothings and the Politics of the 1850s* (New York: Oxford University Press, 1992), 247.

11. *Louisville Journal*, February 23–25, 1859; Wooster, *Politicians, Planters and Plain Folk*, 33, 38.

12. Michael F. Holt, *The Political Crisis of the 1850s* (New York: Wiley, 1978), 255.

13. J. Winston Coleman, *Slavery Times in Kentucky* (Chapel Hill: University of North Carolina Press, 1940), 42–44.

14. Marion B. Lucas, *Blacks in Kentucky*, vol. 1, *From Slavery to Segregation, 1760-1891* (Frankfort: Kentucky Historical Society, 1992), 99; Coleman, *Slavery Times in Kentucky*, 122.

15. Harold D. Tallant, *Evil Necessity: Slavery and Political Culture in Antebellum Kentucky* (Lexington: University Press of Kentucky, 2003), 3.

16. Ibid., 17; *Louisville Democrat,* January 8, 1857.

17. Lowell H. Harrison, *The Antislavery Movement in Kentucky* (Lexington: University Press of Kentucky, 1978), 59–60; Tallant, *Evil Necessity,* 158.

18. Asa E. Martin, *Anti-Slavery Movement in Kentucky Prior to 1850* (1918; reprint, New York: Negro Universities Press, 1970), 67–68.

19. David L. Smiley, *Lion of White Hall: The Life of Cassius M. Clay* (1962; reprint, Gloucester, Mass.: Peter Smith, 1969), 111; W. L. Barre, ed., *Speeches and Writings of Hon. Thomas F. Marshall* (Cincinnati: Applegate, 1858), 209; Clement Eaton, *The Freedom-of-Thought Struggle in the Old South,* rev. and enlarged ed. (New York: Harper Torchbooks, 1964), 190.

20. Stanley Harold, *Abolitionists and the South, 1831–1861* (Lexington: University Press of Kentucky, 1995), 106, 120; Freehling, *The Road to Disunion,* 24.

21. William E. Ellis, H. E. Everman, and Richard D. Sears, *Madison County: 200 Years in Retrospect* (Richmond, Ky.: Madison County Historical Society, 1985), 145–51; Harold, *Abolitionists and the South,* 124.

22. Eaton, *Freedom-of-Thought Struggle,* 212; U.S. Bureau of the Census, *Population of the United States in 1860,* 168–87.

23. Sean Wilentz, *The Rise of American Democracy: Jefferson to Lincoln* (New York: Norton, 2005), 734; Martin, *Anti-Slavery Movement in Kentucky,* 138.

24. *Richmond Enquirer,* April 20, 1857; Tallant, *Evil Necessity,* 13–14.

25. Maury Klein, *History of the Louisville and Nashville Railroad* (Lexington: University Press of Kentucky, 2003), 1–3; William L. Barney, *The Road to Secession: A New Perspective on the Old South* (New York: Praeger, 1972), 180.

26. Barney, *The Road to Secession,* 113; Richard F. Bensel, *Yankee Leviathan: The Origins of Central State Authority in America, 1859–1877* (New York: Cambridge University Press, 1990), 39.

Not a Pariah, but a Keystone

Kentucky and Secession

Thomas C. Mackey

In 1926, E. Merton Coulter, Kentucky's Lost Cause historian, published *The Civil War and Readjustment in Kentucky,* his still widely cited interpretation of the Bluegrass commonwealth in the era of the U.S. Civil War.[1] Included in it is a December 7, 1864, report by Asst. Insp. Gen. E. H. Ludington to Secretary of War Edwin M. Stanton. In that report, Ludington noted the pro-Confederate guerrilla bands that had appeared in the commonwealth and the hostility of the "loyal" state citizens toward the recruitment of black soldiers for the Union army. He blamed Governor Thomas E. Bramlette for encouraging these signs of disorder and disloyalty. "He knows his people are disloyal," Ludington wrote, "so he qualifies his Unionism." Worse, for Ludington, but perhaps capturing the mood of many Kentuckians in late 1864: "The Governor's policy is simply self first, State second, Union last."[2]

With this interpretation in mind, Coulter added in a footnote: "The feeling was unquestionably rather general throughout the North that Kentucky was a pariah among the elect." It is that word and image, *pariah,* that pro-Kentucky modern historians have built on to describe the state in the Union and its relationship with the federal government during secession and the Civil War.[3] But the image does not fit well over the course of the Civil War, and it especially does not fit well in the crucial time of 1860–1861—the era of the secession winter through the ending of Kentucky's illusion of neutrality. Rather, far from being a pariah, Kentucky played a key role in the secession drama of those months, and the actions of the state's political leadership and of President Abraham Lincoln's administration demonstrate the importance of Kentucky to the Union cause. Securing Kentucky to the Union constituted one of the major goals and turning points in the eventual success of the Union in the western theater even if some Kentuckians were frustrated in their desire both to remain in the Union and to retain their property in persons, a frustration that extended to both the commonwealth and the federal government.[4]

Secession was a political process that started as early as the Democratic and Republican nominating conventions in the summer of 1860 and was not completed until the last of the border states, Kentucky, fell willingly into Union hands in September 1861. And, while the major newspapers of the era focused on the East and what would become the eastern theater of military operations, it was the West (what today is the Middle West of the Ohio River valley from the western counties of Virginia to Kentucky to Missouri) where the key actions actually occurred. And, without disparaging or downplaying the importance of Delaware, the need to cross Union troops over Maryland to secure the capital city of Washington, D.C., or the shifting tides of loyalties and politics in Missouri, Kentucky formed the keystone of the border states.

Setting aside for a moment the natural resources of the commonwealth—from horses, to crops, to human-power—geography demonstrates the significance of Kentucky. Its waterways—the long, winding northern border of the Ohio River (one of the major natural water highways of the nineteenth century) and the western border on the Mississippi—formed a natural southern border with the loyal states of Ohio, Indiana, and Illinois. To lose Kentucky to the Confederacy meant placing the front lines of the war at Cincinnati, Ohio, New Albany, Indiana, and Cairo, Illinois, not the Cumberland Gap and Bowling Green, Kentucky, and Knoxville, Nashville, and Memphis, Tennessee. Furthermore, two of the four major rivers into the Upper South drain into the Ohio River at or near Paducah, Kentucky—the Tennessee and the Cumberland. Therefore, just considering Kentucky's western rivers in terms of defending the Union homeland and pressing the military front south, the state's significance as the keystone of the West is hard to overstate.

While geography explains why the Lincoln administration pursued different policies toward Kentucky than it did other border states like

Maryland or Missouri, geography alone does not explain the significance of Kentucky in terms of secession. Ties of blood and livelihood must also be factored in. It is often overlooked that three of the four primary residents of the two White Houses of the Civil War years were Kentucky born— Abraham Lincoln, Mary Todd Lincoln, and Jefferson Davis. Furthermore, Kentucky's ties to the rest of the nation ran east and west. From the East had come Daniel Boone and other settlers through the Cumberland Gap, and, by 1860, the largest number of non-Kentucky-born residents of the state came from Virginia, not surprising as Kentucky constituted the farthest western county of Virginia until its separation and statehood in 1792. As a result of this heritage, Kentuckians looked to Virginia (and, to a lesser but notable extent, North Carolina) for political leadership even if that leadership was a love/hate relationship. The historian Russell Weigley describes Kentucky as a "self-conscious daughter of Virginia," as indeed it was.[5]

In addition, Kentuckians had been a restless people, populating at least the southern parts of the western states of Indiana, Illinois, and Missouri. The distinguished historian James A. Rawley went so far as to call Missouri "the child of Kentucky" because of the 100,000 residents of that state who claimed Kentucky birth.[6] Thus, kinship and family ties stretched from the Old Dominion to the muddy banks of the Ohio to the Missouri River and beyond.

With these attachments came Kentucky's ambiguous political responses to the secession crisis and its attachment to the "peculiar institution" of the South, slavery. No person better symbolizes Kentucky's importance in the Union prior to the Civil War than the Virginia-born Henry Clay.[7] Clay loomed over Whig politics and Kentucky like no other figure, and, although he was frustrated four times in his bid for the presidency, his personality, his vision of the American System, and his sheer political weight cannot be overlooked or discounted. Although he died in 1852, his shadow hung over the commonwealth through the 1850s because of both his nationalism and his slaveholding. Not only did Kentuckians search for the next Henry Clay among their political leadership to maintain their national significance (in vain, it turns out);[8] they also resisted the drift of the Northern and Midwestern parts of the country into antislavery (opposing slavery, not because they were sympathetic to the plight of African Americans, but because of the economic threat posed by slavery to free, white labor), as opposed to abolitionism, as they thought Clay might have done. Kentuckians read Clay's heritage as one of both prosperity in the Union because of the state's natural resources, rivers, and geographic position and maintaining their mixed labor force of free and slave laborers. As a result, many in the Bluegrass found themselves Unionist in their wallets and Southern in their sentiments.

What made many Kentuckians culturally Southern was not just their predominant roots in Virginia but their attachment to a labor system based on master and slave. Slavery, unevenly present across the state, constituted a political and social issue in the commonwealth from colonial times into the late 1850s. The mountain areas of the eastern part of Kentucky had few to no slaves, yet the far western part of the state, with its strong economic ties to Tennessee, had some slaves and embraced the institution, while the central part of the state, the classic Bluegrass area, held the bulk of Kentucky's slave population. Urban slavery existed as well, especially in the river cities of Covington and Paducah, and also in the most important city in the state then and currently, Louisville. By 1860, Kentucky ranked ninth among the states supporting slavery, and it held more slaves than three of the states that joined the Confederacy. While few farms held large numbers of slaves, Kentucky ranked third in the nation in slaveholders, suggesting that, in those areas that employed slave labor, the practice was widespread among the white population. While the slave percentage of the overall population had been dropping in Kentucky, slaves constituted 19.5 percent of the state's 1860 population.

Thus, by 1860, combining the Union heritage of Henry Clay with the Southern heritage of slavery resulted in a mixed message being sent to the rest of the nation. As the Kentucky historian Lowell Harrison put it: "Many Kentuckians who cherished the Union saw nothing wrong with slavery."[9] This duality and Kentuckians' failure to grasp that the current was shifting against slaveholding in the Midwest and the North placed the state out of step with both the nation and certainly the policies of the Lincoln administration. Kentuckians' efforts through the secession crisis and the war both to stay within the Union and to maintain their property in persons looked back to the world before the war and resulted in disenchantment and resentment on the part of both the Union and Kentuckians.

And so, with these geographic, cultural, and economic values, Kentuckians confronted the election of 1860. They heard the secessionist rhetoric of the Fire-Eaters of the Deep South and the Republican Party's position on the nonextension of slavery into the federal territories and reacted ambiguously. Again, Rawley nicely captures the dilemma with which Kentuckians were confronted: "[They were] Southern in their hearts, but they thought as national citizens. They were conservatives, who disapproved unilateral exercise of the right of secession—as well as the use of force against seceded states."[10] Not surprisingly, Kentucky's political leaders searched for a middle path that, if it ever existed, quickly disappeared during the secession crisis of 1860–1861.

With the collapse of the national Whig Party by 1854–1855, Kentucky's Whigs found themselves wandering in a political desert. They flirted with the Know Nothings in 1855 when that party won the governorship of the state. Then, in 1859, they opposed the Democratic Party candidate, Beriah Magoffin, a lawyer and rising pro-South politician from Harrodsburg, Kentucky, to whom they lost the election.[11] As a result, when the political crisis came, the political leadership of the commonwealth fell to the Democrat Magoffin and to what turned out to be a fickle and Unionist state legislature made up of old Whigs, Unionist Democrats, and a few Republicans.

A four-way race for the presidency developed in 1860 featuring two native Kentuckians—Abraham Lincoln for the Republicans and Senator John C. Breckinridge for the Southern wing of the Democratic Party. The other candidates were Stephen Douglas of Illinois, representing the Northern portion of the Democratic Party, and John Bell of Tennessee of the Constitutional Union Party, which sought to buy time and craft a middle political ground that avoided further sectional battles. In November 1860, a plurality of Kentuckians eschewed their favorite son candidate, Breckinridge, and split their votes, giving 45 percent to Bell, 36 percent to Breckinridge, 18 percent to Douglas, and less than 1 percent to the national winner, Lincoln. Moderation appeared to be the message of the Kentucky voters at a time when the middle ground held less and less weight in other slaveholding states.

During the secession crisis from November 1860 to March 4, 1861, it was Kentucky's other senator, John J. Crittenden, who sought to play Henry Clay's role of compromiser and Governor Magoffin who sought to gather support for a regional proposal to counter both the threat of secession by Southern states and the use of coercion by Northern states to preserve the Union. On December 9, 1860, Magoffin acted first by sending a circular letter to slave-state governors restating their terms for a compromise of the political crisis. Magoffin's letter called for the federal government to beef up its enforcement of the 1850 Fugitive Slave Act, the division of the remaining federal territories along the thirty-seventh parallel so that slavery could move into the southern half of that area, the continued guarantee of the use of the Mississippi River for commerce, and a Southern veto in the Senate for federal legislation touching on slavery. Magoffin proposed a two-part process for adopting these demands: first a conference of the Southern states to adopt his proposals and then a second conference of all the states to approve them. Nine days later, on December 18, Crittenden introduced into the Senate his more famous compromise proposals, which included the extension of slavery into the federal territories—thereby dooming its chance of passing because it violated the fundamental value of the Republican Party, the nonextension of slavery into the federal territories.

In any case, the advanced wing of the Southern secessionists was not listening to proposals of compromise as the heart of secession, South Carolina, declared itself seceded from the Union on December 20. Six other Deep South states rushed to assert their exit from the Union and, along with South Carolina, set up their Gulf Coast–centered Confederacy before the new federal administration took over on March 4, 1861. Opening shop in Montgomery, Alabama, the Provisional Confederate Congress set about the work of nation building, which included the calling for and gathering of military forces. On February 18, 1861, the Confederacy's only president, the Kentucky-born Mississippian Jefferson Davis, took the oath of office. These events, all before the Lincoln administration took office, established the context of the crisis that came to be focused on the harbor fortification in Charleston, South Carolina—Fort Sumter.

Both sides understood that, while that last federal installation constituted an important symbol of federal authority in the Confederacy, the deeper question was what the states of the Upper South and the border states would do if the Lincoln administration used force to maintain its officers, men, and property. Thus, parallel to the better-known events unfolding in Montgomery and Charleston, the story of the border states is crucial to understanding the larger context of secession. And that shifts the focus back to Governor Magoffin and Kentucky's struggle with where its loyalties lay.

Events moved at a faster pace than Magoffin's (and Crittenden's) calls for more talk and more meetings; therefore, by late December, after South Carolina had declared its secession, Magoffin believed that he had to seize the leadership of the pro-South, prosecession movement in Kentucky from Breckinridge, and he did so by calling a special session of the state legislature. Magoffin admitted that events had passed by his suggestion of a Southern convention, so he urged the legislators to authorize a separate Kentucky convention to chart a path for the commonwealth through the dangerous political waters. "We, the people, of the United States are no longer one people, united and friendly," Magoffin told the legislature in his message. He pointed to Virginia and North Carolina, both of which had called for a special convention within their states to discuss the situation, and he urged the Kentucky legislators to take the same action to determine "the future Federal and interstate relations of Kentucky." Of the Gulf Coast Confederacy, Magoffin stated: "Their cause is right and they have our sympathies." He also called on the legislature to provide funding for arms and equipment for the state guard. He also urged the legislators to participate in a scheduled February border states conference, but his efforts to appear noncommittal fooled no one. As a Frankfort, Kentucky, newspaper explained: "The Governor of Kentucky is a secessionist."[12]

Not surprisingly, Magoffin's December actions and statements motivated Kentuckians of Unionist sentiment to secure Kentucky for the Union. Men such as Robert J. Breckinridge, Garret Davis, James and Joshua Speed, and the Louisville newspaper editor George Prentice opened communications with each other and other Unionists as well as the Lincoln administration. And, in the legislature, the John C. Breckinridge faction failed to manage a majority to call for a state convention or to raise funds for arming the state guard.[13] Both houses, however, revealed the state's difficult position: they issued a resolution that warned the federal government against using coercion against the South and condemned Southern secession. Kentuckians, it was clear, saw themselves between the rock of coercion and the hard place of secession.

A sort of political ballet between a governor who wanted to move Kentucky south and a legislature with some Southern sympathies but enough

Union sentiments to frustrate any definitive movement one way or the other occurred during the months of the secession winter. The legislature adjourned from February 11 until March 20, 1861, but not before supporting a call for a border convention in Frankfort on May 27, a meeting that went nowhere toward resolving the crisis in Kentucky, much less in the nation.

On April 12, as the South fired on Fort Sumter, Kentucky's situation remained foggy. When the legislature met again after the military beginning of the Civil War, the legislators, not Magoffin, took the lead in setting the state's course and public policies. Magoffin rejected a call for troops from both Jefferson Davis and, in much more emphatic and emotional language, from Abraham Lincoln, yet he was hardly neutral. In an April 16, 1861, letter to Secretary of War Simon Cameron, he stated his position in one sentence: "In answer, I say emphatically that Kentucky will furnish no troops for the wicked purpose of subduing her sister Southern States."[14] Plus, Magoffin supported the state guard (headed by Simon B. Buckner) and allowed Confederate recruiting agents to enter the state. In response, the legislature stripped Magoffin of control of the state guard and placed it in a Unionist-dominated military board. At the same time, Lincoln followed a generally hands-off policy toward the commonwealth; nevertheless, with the arming of the state guard, and after speaking with William Nelson, a former naval officer, in Louisville, Lincoln agreed to supply covert aid in the form of the shipment and distribution of "Lincoln guns" to supporters of the Union. As a result, two armed forces began to form in Kentucky, the pro-South state guard and the pro-Union home guard.

On the political front, leadership fell on the members of the Kentucky House. On May 16, 1861, by a vote of 69–29, the House, without the support of the state Senate or Governor Magoffin, voted in favor of a resolution of neutrality. It read:

Considering the deplorable condition of the country and for which the State of Kentucky is in no way responsible, and looking to the best means of preserving the internal peace and securing the lives, liberty, and property of the citizens of the State; therefore,

Resolved, by the House of Representatives, that this State and the citizens thereof should take no part in the civil war now being waged, except as mediators and friends to the belligerent parties; and that Kentucky should, during the contest, occupy the position of strict neutrality.

Resolved, that the act of the governor in refusing to furnish troops or military force upon the call of the executive authority of the United States under existing circumstances is approved.[15]

Four days later, this House resolution became the template for Magoffin's May 20 statement supporting neutrality. In that statement, he urged that the troops of all states, Union and Confederate, not enter or pass through Kentucky, and he told Kentuckians not to make "any warlike or hostile demonstration." He urged his fellow state citizens "to refrain from all words and acts likely to engender hot blood and provoke collision," telling them that the only reason to arm themselves was self-defense.[16] Kentucky's Senate adopted a similar resolution on May 24, 1861.

Neutrality reflected the divided state government, but it also reflected the divided opinion of the population. While wholehearted Unionists such as James and Joshua Speed and wholehearted supporters of the South such as Simon B. Buckner could be found, the evidence suggests that, in April and May 1861, Kentucky's general population was as befuddled by what was happening to the Union as were the legislators and the governor. A negative public policy such as neutrality—the argument that the state of Kentucky had a right *not* to participate—while far from perfect for all parties at least constituted enough of an ad hoc policy that all parties could agree on it. With Kentucky neutral, the historian Lowell Harrison has speculated, an outside observer might conclude that the United States had "become three countries: the Union, the Confederacy, and Kentucky."[17]

Modern historians agree that neutrality formed a viable, though clumsy, public policy option. For example, Russell Weigley concludes that "no policy could have accorded more closely with the mixed feelings engendered by Kentucky's Southern heritage and the legacy of Henry Clay,"[18] and the noted Civil War historian James M. McPherson believes with Lincoln and "other pragmatic unionists" that "neutrality was the best they could expect for the time being. The alternative was actual secession."[19] Rawley provides the fullest assessment of the policy, saying: "Neutrality was the expression of Kentucky's uniqueness; it was not the outgrowth of timidity." Concluding that "neutrality was a wise response to the state's dilemma and a logical result of her history," he explains that this policy "meant an interim victory for the anti-secessionist forces, and was perhaps the only course that could keep the state from seceding. Neutrality also served the short-range political ends of both extremes during a period of agonizing incertitude." Perhaps most important, and often overlooked and underemphasized in historical accounts, "neutrality provided a cooling-off period for the sorely divided commonwealth until sentiment could crystallize." Neutrality, then, was, according to Rawley, "the happiest expedient that could be devised in that hour's quandary."[20] Because the state was genuinely divided and most of the political leadership and the population preferred fence-sitting to taking a definitive position and defending it, buying time to both watch and participate in unfolding events constituted an acceptable option. At that point in their history (to use a modern metaphor), Kentuckians punted—they played it safe, played for more time, pursued their own self-interest, and waited.

While waiting, Kentuckians set about profiting from the fluid economic and political situation in the state and the West. Trade across Kentucky via wagons and the Louisville and Nashville Railroad increased as the state's natural resources (including manpower) went south. Weigley nicely describes the situation as "Kentuckians gladly proceed[ing] to act as though their state was Switzerland, maintaining their commercial ties across both their northern and southern borders."[21] Trade boomed from late spring through early fall 1861, engendering concern among the pro-Union home guard and Kentucky Unionists, but the Lincoln administration tolerated the situation. Hoping that, in time, Kentuckians' ties to their economic well-being and Unionist heritage would trump their Southern sentiments, the president pursued a policy of toleration and covert aid. Even after Congress prohibited trade with the Confederacy and especially the trade across Kentucky, Lincoln deftly administered the policy by issuing permits that, while cutting the trade, did not end it. He believed that, through careful cultivation, the apple of Kentucky would fall from the tree of secession and land in the Union basket.

Kentucky, it was clear, could not remain a domestic Switzerland forever. Kentuckians took sides regardless of official state policy; moreover, over the course of the summer of 1861, Lincoln's gamble that a majority of Kentuckians would support the Union proved correct. Led by Simon Buckner, and tacitly supported by Governor Magoffin, the state guard championed the Southern cause; and, led by William "Bull" Nelson, who was openly supported by the legislature, the home guard backed the Union cause. Both sides wanted recruits, both sides sought arms, and both sides desired recognition from either Washington, D.C., or Richmond. By June 1861, Buckner had worked out a gentleman's agreement with the Union general George B. McClellan and Tennessee governor Isham Harris for both sides to uphold Kentucky's neutrality. While friction existed between these armed factions of the state, no open conflict occurred—an interesting lack of military and political action if ever one existed.

Nor did Lincoln overlook Kentucky's decisions. After all, Kentucky was a part of the Union, and its failure to comply with his request for troops and its insistence that federal troops not be allowed to trespass on Kentucky soil challenged his, and the nation's, authority. In this situation, Lincoln's forbearance (what Rawley has called "pragmatic circumvention of the issue")[22] proved a virtue. Four days after Magoffin's announcement of neutrality on May 28, Lincoln established the Military Department of Kentucky, which covered an area within one hundred miles of the state nearest the Ohio River (and, thus, those areas of the state with the most Union loyalties), and placed in command of that department a native son, the Union hero of Fort Sumter, Maj. Robert Anderson. Prudently, Anderson set up his command in Cincinnati, just across the river from Kentucky, but, by setting up this military department, Lincoln sent a message about his wishes for his native state. With the bureaucratic structure in place and Nelson on the ground recruiting troops and seeing that the covert arms reached the right people, long-term Union goals could not be clearer.

Lincoln himself made it clear in his July 4, 1861, message to Congress that, because of his oath to "preserve, protect, and defend" the Constitution, he could not recognize neutrality. As the president pointed out about the states that followed a policy of "armed neutrality":

An arming of those States to prevent the Union forces passing one way, or the disunion, of the other, over their soil . . . would be disunion completed . . . for, under the guise of neutrality, it would tie the hands of Union men, and freely pass supplies from among them, to the insurrectionists which it could not do as an open enemy. . . . It recognizes no fidelity to the Constitution, no obligation to maintain the Union; and while very many who have favored it are, doubtless, loyal citizens, it is, nevertheless, treason in effect.[23]

Thus, in public, Lincoln repudiated the idea of a state acting as a Switzerland-like neutral body while privately tolerating the delicate situation in the Bluegrass so as not to lose the key border state.

At the same time, Buckner's Southern faction interacted and opened correspondence with Confederate military and political leaders.[24] Some Kentuckians traveled across the state's southern border to join Kentucky and Tennessee Confederate units forming in northern Tennessee. Manpower, horses, and food all traveled south over the course of the summer of 1861, and, though no open hostilities broke out in the commonwealth, both sides recognized opportunity in Kentucky's neutrality.

Two elections in Kentucky track the state's political drift and political choices over the course of the summer of 1861. On June 20, the state held congressional elections, and, in nine of the state's ten election districts, voters sent Unionists to Congress—conservative Unionists perhaps, but Unionists nonetheless. The only congressional district not to support the Union lay in the far western part of the state where the four rivers of the Mississippi, Ohio, Cumberland, and Tennessee flowed; that district returned Henry C. Burnett to office.[25] Coulter and later Harrison claimed that Southern supporters deliberately did not vote in these elections and that, if they had, Southern support would have manifested itself. As a gauge to measure who did *not* vote has not yet been devised, the argument that Southern support was stronger in the state than the June elections suggest amounts to a verdict of not proved.

Less than two months later, on August 5, Kentuckians went to the polls to select state legislators, and, once again, Union men won. Once the tally came in, Unionists controlled the Kentucky House 76–24 and held a 27–11 margin in the Kentucky Senate. These results may reflect the actions of Southern supporters who stayed away from the polls; but, if they did stay away, they in fact conceded what almost everyone suspected—a majority of the Kentucky population did not favor the Confederacy or secession as the state's future path. But the vote may not have signaled support for the Lincoln administration either; rather, it may have signified only that the population voting desired peaceful relations and a continuation of the status quo.

Regardless, Unionists took these election results to heart and acted on them. On August 6, 1861, now General Nelson moved his headquarters into Kentucky to about thirty miles south of Lexington in Garrard County, where he established Camp Dick Robinson. Nelson concentrated his home guard in this camp and continued his recruiting and training efforts.

While Magoffin protested the establishment of Camp Robinson to President Lincoln, he also wrote to Jefferson Davis to protest a buildup of Confederate forces along the Tennessee border, including the establishment of Camp Boone for the organizing and training of Kentuckians who wished to support the Confederacy.[26] On August 28, Davis wrote Magoffin and tried to reassure him about the good intentions of the Confederacy toward Kentucky's neutrality, but Davis was clearly troubled by the establishment of Camp Robinson and Magoffin's reaction to it. Davis warned Magoffin: "Neutrality to be entitled to respect, must be strictly maintained between both parties."[27] Davis's shot across Magoffin's bow reminded Magoffin about the dangers of neutrality and the high stakes at play.

Lincoln's August 24 response to Magoffin's protest letter of August 19 reminded the governor of the president's position on secession and Union.[28] Lincoln acknowledged the presence of Camp Robinson and admitted that it was established by the authority of the United States, but he added that the force was "not very large, and is not now being augmented." He clarified that "this force consists exclusively of Kentuckians, having their camp in the immediate vicinity of their homes, and not assailing, or menacing, any of the good people of Kentucky." Warming to his topic, Lincoln argued that everything he had done came at the "urgent solicitation of many Kentuckians" and was in line with "what I believed, and still believe, to be the wish of the majority of all the Union-loving people of Kentucky." Like a lawyer layering on his evidence, he stated that no one other than Magoffin, the individual bearers of the letter Magoffin sent to Lincoln, and "one other very worthy citizen of Kentucky" had urged him to remove the camp and that, in fact, a large number of people urged him to maintain it. "I do not believe," Lincoln warned Magoffin, "it is the popular wish of Kentucky that this force shall be removed beyond her limits; and, with this impression, I must respectfully decline to do so."

This exchange might have ended here, but Lincoln could not resist taking a poke at Kentucky's pro-South, prosecession governor. Claiming that he sympathized with Magoffin "in the wish to preserve the peace of my own native State, Kentucky," Lincoln noted his great regret that, in Magoffin's "not very short letter," there was no "declaration, or intimation, that you entertain any desire for the preservation of the Federal Union."[29] Thus, Camp Robinson remained.

Occasional incursions occurred, both Confederates testing the Kentucky waters and Federals crossing into Kentucky to break up informal pro-South camps of men. When the break came, it was not in the political centers of Frankfort, or Washington, or Richmond, but in the far western part of the state. The Confederate generals Gideon Pillow and Leonidas Polk (the "fighting bishop" of the Confederacy and West Point friend of Jefferson Davis) had long considered the heights overlooking the Mississippi River at Columbus, Kentucky, as a key strategic location.[30] Whoever controlled those heights, they thought, would have a choke point on the river; control Columbus, and control the upper Mississippi. More enticing still, the residents of the area possessed Southern sympathies and had, as early as April 22, 1861, invited the Confederates into the town as a starting point to seizing the Mississippi River town of Cairo, Illinois. Not surprisingly, the day after the residents of Columbus asked for Confederate intervention, Illinois troops countered by occupying Cairo.[31]

Confederate desires for Columbus could be postponed only so long, and, on September 1, 1861, Polk wrote Magoffin and warned him that he, Polk, believed that he ought to be "ahead of the enemy in occupying Columbus and Paducah."[32] On September 2, the commander of Illinois's volunteer forces in the area, Brig. Gen. Ulysses S. Grant, ordered his forces into Belmont, Missouri, across the river from Columbus. In response, Polk ordered his forces to violate Kentucky's neutrality and enter the state. They did so the next day. Moving north, the Confederates entered and took Columbus on September 3, 1861.[33]

While Polk hailed this movement as a great achievement, neither Grant, the Kentucky legislature, nor the Confederate authorities in Richmond were so convinced. Grant fought war on a map better than Polk and most other generals, North or South. Having received confirmation of the Confederate capture of Columbus, on September 6, 1861, on his own initiative, he ordered his men to move, not against Columbus, but against a town nicknamed "Little Charleston" because of its Southern sympathies: Paducah, Kentucky, on the Ohio River. He ordered them to seize the mouth of the Tennessee River and then move up the Ohio around the large bend to seize the mouth of the Cumberland River at Smithland, Kentucky. By using those waterways, Union forces could travel upriver and flank and then get behind Columbus and the Confederates, thus making the town an indefensible position on the Mississippi. Militarily, Grant checked and checkmated Polk's move into Columbus.

On the political front, the Confederate move also backfired. While Polk found some of the people of Columbus happy to see him and his forces, his actions enraged the Kentucky legislature and embarrassed Governor Magoffin. On September 7, the legislature ordered the flag of the United States flown over the state capitol in Frankfort, and four days later, on September 11, the legislature passed a resolution demanding that Magoffin order the Confederate forces to leave Kentucky. Magoffin had called for both sides to withdraw from Kentucky and had said that he held both sides responsible for "equally palpable and open violations of the neutral rights of Kentucky." But the legislature rejected Magoffin's language and called for only a Confederate withdrawal. After Magoffin vetoed its resolution, the legislature overrode him by overwhelming margins: 68–26 in the House and 25–9 in the Senate. On September 18, the pro-Union legislature effectively took over the running of the commonwealth and implemented its policies: it placed the Union general Robert Anderson in charge of loyal forces to expel the Confederates, instructed the governor to call out the militia, and petitioned the federal government for aid and assistance.[34] With this series of resolutions, Kentucky cast its lot with the Union and Abraham Lincoln. While Magoffin vetoed all these actions, the legislature overrode his vetoes and refused to ask Union forces to leave the state. Magoffin had become superfluous; the pro-Union legislature controlled the state and its future involvement in the conflict.[35]

Not only did Kentuckians doubt the political and military wisdom of Polk's actions; some of the Confederacy's highest political leaders doubted his actions as well. The Confederate secretary of war, Leroy P. Walker of Alabama, opposed the move into Columbus as unnecessary and unwise. Polk appealed to his old West Point colleague and friend Jefferson Davis, claiming that federal actions in Belmont, Missouri, necessitated his move into Columbus. Some controversy exists as to what and when Polk told Davis. The evidence suggests that Polk modified the story he told Davis, changed the language and dates of dispatches between himself and Davis, and manipulated Davis into supporting him.[36] Regardless, Davis did back Polk and defended the move into Kentucky to the Confederate Congress on November 18, 1861.

Sharing Davis's position, Kentuckians with Confederate sympathies called a convention in Russellville, Kentucky, along the Tennessee border, on hearing of the actions of the state legislature. That convention drew up a declaration of independence and put together a provisional Confederate government of Kentucky with its capital at Bowling Green, Kentucky. On December 10, 1861, the Confederate Congress "admitted" Kentucky into the Confederacy and added a star on its flag for the state. But this "Confederate Kentucky" reflected a thin minority of the overall population of the state; as Rawley describes this provisional government, it "never amounted to more than a rump of the people."[37]

Lincoln understood just how close a call Kentucky had been and how delicately the state had to be handled because, at the same time that these military movements and political events unfolded within the commonwealth, he had problems with his general in Missouri, John C. Frémont, who threatened that state's loyalty. On August 30, Frémont had issued a proclamation to deal with disloyalty and the low-intensity conflict that had developed in Missouri. In it, he designated a line across Missouri and stated that any person who took up arms against the United States north of that line would be court-martialed and, if convicted, shot. His proclamation was so broad that it included properly enlisted Confederate soldiers and, thus, all but asked for reprisals by the Confederates in Missouri against Union soldiers. Worse for Lincoln and the Kentucky situation, it stated that any and all personal and real property of persons who took up arms against the United States would be confiscated, including slaves, whom Frémont declared to be free.[38] While abolitionists cheered Frémont's proclamation, border states men cringed. Raising the issue of uncompensated military emancipation at just the moment when Kentucky looked to be dropping into the Union fold worried Lincoln.

On September 2, Lincoln sent Frémont a letter by special messenger urging the general to reconsider both parts of his proclamation. The president pointed out the problem of retaliation and called attention to the First Confiscation Act of 1861, which provided for the forfeiture of slaves only when they were actively engaged in support of the rebellion. Frémont remained obstinate in defense of his proclamation despite Lincoln's letter and despite visits by prominent Union commanders and politicians attempting to change his mind. Because Frémont would not take the hint, he forced Lincoln into ordering him to bring his proclamation in line with the First Confiscation Act. Nevertheless, the damage had been done; emancipation arose to worry Kentuckians.

That Kentucky's situation and Frémont's action became linked in Lincoln's thinking can be seen in the president's September 22, 1861, letter to his friend O. H. Browning. Browning had written Lincoln on September 17 defending Frémont's actions regarding emancipation and criticizing Lincoln's actions in reversing Frémont's policy. Most of this letter deals with Lincoln's conception of the limits of confiscation under the law and the Constitution, but Kentucky's situation loomed. "The Kentucky Legislature would not budge till [sic] that proclamation was modified," Lincoln lectured Browning. He then stated that he had heard of "a whole company of our Volunteers" throwing down their weapons and disbanding rather than support emancipation. Lincoln was aghast that "the very arms we had furnished Kentucky would be turned against us." Then he touched the heart of the matter, stating: "I think to lose Kentucky is nearly the same as to lose the whole game. Kentucky gone, we can not hold Missouri, nor, as I think, Maryland. These all against us, and the job on our hands is too large for us. We would as well consent to separation at once, including the surrender of this capitol."[39] Frémont overstepped his authority in his August 30 proclamation, he embarrassed his political leader without providing him prior knowledge of his actions, he raised emancipation as a potential war goal far too early, and he potentially derailed the Kentucky situation. As a result, he was forced to rescind parts of his proclamation and, in time, was sacked. By chastising Frémont and repudiating emancipation at that point in the conflict, Lincoln had reassured Kentuckians about the stability of their property in persons while the Union maintained the loyalty of the keystone state of the West, Kentucky.

Emancipation and the enlistment and use of black troops in the state went a long way toward souring the relationship between the Union and Kentuckians, but that difficult relationship lay in the future.[40] In 1860–1861, just as Magoffin's and Buckner's efforts to effect Kentucky's secession failed, so too did the halfway house of neutrality. Ironically, while Kentucky's population drifted toward the Union—a drift tracked in the summer 1861 election results—it was not the drift but a bad choice by Confederate General Polk that triggered Kentucky to abandon neutrality and declare for the Union on September 18, 1861. No doubt Kentuckians were a divided people, but a political majority of them initially believed that their best interests lay in crafting a middle-ground policy between secession and support for the Union. Only later did they realize that no such middle ground exists in civil war. Thus, by the late summer of 1861, Kentucky shifted toward supporting the Union, even if only in a begrudgingly and conservative Unionist fashion. Lincoln's light touch with the land of his birth and his fending off the hydra of emancipation raised by General Frémont's August 30 proclamation helped keep Kentucky in the Union. On the other side of the battle lines, the Confederate government acted rashly. While Lincoln tolerated the trade across Kentucky, the Confederacy moved to cut off all trade with the Union. The Confederate Congress required that the South's goods had to be moved through the Confederacy's own seaports or across the Mexican border, thereby strangling the Kentucky trade lines. As Coulter summed up the situation: "The South, too impatient to be tolerant and too impetuous to be tactful [on the trade issue], lost the greatest prize of the West—Kentucky."[41] Polk's impatience, ineptitude, and political deafness in "invading" Kentucky pushed the state's pro-Union lawmakers to go where they had wanted to go for a while—not onto the Stars and Bars of the Confederacy, but to stay a star in the blue field of the Stars and Stripes of the United States. Thus, contrary to E. Merton Coulter's 1926 claim that "the feeling was unquestionably rather general throughout the North that Kentucky was a pariah among the elect," Kentucky was no pariah. Instead, the Bluegrass state is better understood as the keystone—geographically, logistically, militarily, and politically—of the Union cause in the western theater even if it took a few extra months for the people of the commonwealth and its political leaders to reverse their governor's emphasis on "self first, State second, Union last."

Notes

1. E. Merton Coulter, *The Civil War and Readjustment in Kentucky* (Chapel Hill: University of North Carolina Press, 1926; reprint, Gloucester, Mass.: Peter Smith, 1966).

2. U.S. War Department, *The War of the Rebellion: A Compilation of the Official Records of the Union and Confederate Armies, 1861–1865* (hereafter cited as *OR*), 70 vols. in 128 pts. (Washington, D.C.: U.S. Government Printing Office, 1880–1901), ser. 1, vol. 45, pt. 2, pp. 93–94.

3. Coulter, *Civil War and Readjustment,* 210 n. 118.

4. Kentucky's history in this era is in much need of updating and rethinking. In addition to Coulter's *Civil War and Readjustment,* the standard secondary sources are Robert M. McElroy, *Kentucky in the Nation's History* (New York: Moffat, Yard, 1909); James R. Robertson, "Sectionalism in Kentucky from 1855 to 1865," *Mississippi Valley Historical Review* 4 (June 1917): 49–63; Wilson P. Shortridge, "Kentucky Neutrality in 1861," *Mississippi Valley Historical Review* 9 (March 1923): 283–301; Edward C. Smith, *The Borderland in the Civil War* (New York: Macmillan, 1927); and Thomas Speed, *Union Cause in Kentucky, 1860–1865* (New York: Putnam's, 1907).

5. Russell F. Weigley, *A Great Civil War: A Military and Political History, 1861–1865* (Bloomington: Indiana University Press, 2000), 46.

6. James A. Rawley, *Turning Points of the Civil War* (1966; reprint, Lincoln: University of Nebraska Press, 1989), 16.

7. While a large historiography exists on Henry Clay, the best modern biography and historical assessment is Robert V. Remini, *Henry Clay: Statesman for the Union* (New York: Norton, 1991). Clay as a constitutionalist is nicely analyzed in Peter B. Knupfer, *The Union as It Is: Unionism and Sectional Compromise, 1787–1861* (Chapel Hill: University of North Carolina Press, 1991).

8. Not until the likes of Albert B. "Happy" Chandler (1898–1991) and Addison Mitchell "Mitch" McConnell Jr. (1942–) would a Kentucky politician possess a reputation and influence on the national political stage anywhere close to Henry Clay's.

9. Lowell Harrison, *The Civil War in Kentucky* (Lexington: University Press of Kentucky, 1975), 1.

10. Rawley, *Turning Points of the Civil War,* 16.

11. Lowell H. Harrison, "Beriah Magoffin," in *The Kentucky Encyclopedia,* ed. John E. Kleber (Lexington: University Press of Kentucky, 1992), 603–4.

12. Harrison, *The Civil War in Kentucky,* 7.

13. In time, Breckinridge cast his lot with the Confederacy (see William C.

Davis, *Breckinridge: Statesman, Soldier, Symbol* [Baton Rouge: Louisiana State University Press, 1974]; and Frank H. Heck, "John C. Breckinridge in the Crisis of 1860–1861," *Journal of Southern History* 21 [August 1955]: 316–46).

14. Beriah Magoffin to Simon Cameron, April 16, 1861, quoted in J. Stoddard Johnston, *Kentucky*, vol. 9 of *Confederate Military History: A Library of Confederate States History*, ed. Clement A. Evans, 12 vols. (New York: Thomas Yoseloff, 1899), 19.

15. Quoted in ibid., 22–23.

16. Robert W. Goebel, "'Casualty of war': The Governorship of Beriah Magoffin, 1859–1862" (master's thesis, University of Louisville, 2005), 88; Coulter, *Civil War and Readjustment*, 55.

17. Harrison, *The Civil War in Kentucky*, 9.

18. Weigley, *A Great Civil War*, 46.

19. James M. McPherson, *Battle Cry of Freedom: The Civil War Era* (New York: Oxford University Press, 1988), 294 (see also 293–97).

20. Rawley, *Turning Points of the Civil War*, 32.

21. Weigley, *A Great Civil War*, 46.

22. Rawley, *Turning Points of the Civil War*, 33.

23. Ibid., 34; Don E. Fehrenbacher, ed., *Abraham Lincoln: Speeches and Writings, 1859–1865* (New York: Library of America, 1989), 251–52.

24. In time, Buckner too cast his lot with the Confederacy (see Arndt M. Stickles, *Simon Bolivar Buckner: Borderland Knight* [Chapel Hill: University of North Carolina Press, 1940]). On the dilemmas faced by Southern Unionists, see Daniel W. Crofts, *Reluctant Confederates: Upper South Unionists in the Secession Crisis* (Chapel Hill: University of North Carolina Press, 1989).

25. Berry F. Craig, "Henry Cornelius Burnett: Champion of Southern Rights," *Register of the Kentucky Historical Society* 77 (Autumn 1977): 266–74.

26. Coulter, *Civil War and Readjustment*, 104–5.

27. Beriah Magoffin to Jefferson Davis, August 1861, in *OR*, ser. 1, vol. 4, p. 378. The letter was hand delivered to Davis. For the response, see Jefferson Davis to Beriah Magoffin, August 28, 1861, *OR*, ser. 1, vol. 4, pp. 396–97.

28. Beriah Magoffin to Abraham Lincoln, August 19, 1861, Abraham Lincoln Papers, Library of Congress, ser. 1, General Correspondence, 1833–1916.

29. Abraham Lincoln to Beriah Magoffin, August 24, 1861, in Fehrenbacher, ed., *Abraham Lincoln*, 265–66.

30. For more on Pillow, see Nathaniel Cheairs Hughes Jr. and Roy P. Stonesifer Jr., *The Life and Wars of Gideon J. Pillow* (Chapel Hill: University of North Carolina Press, 1993). For more on Polk, see Glenn Robins, *The Bishop of the Old South: The Ministry and Civil War Legacy of Leonidas Polk* (Macon, Ga.: Mercer

University Press, 2006); Joseph H. Parks, *General Leonidas Polk, C.S.A.: The Fighting Bishop* (Baton Rouge: Louisiana State University Press, 1962); and Bryan Bush, "'My whole life must speak for me': Southern Honor and Confederate General Leonidas Polk" (master's thesis, University of Louisville, 2005).

31. Coulter, *Civil War and Readjustment,* 106. On Cairo, see Matthew E. Stanley, "'City of soldiers': The Military Occupation of Cairo, Illinois, 1861–1862" (master's thesis, University of Louisville, 2007), 1–19.

32. *OR,* ser. 1, vol. 4, p. 179.

33. Coulter, *Civil War and Readjustment,* 108–9; Rawley, *Turning Points of the Civil War,* 38–39; Weigley, *A Great Civil War,* 48; Harrison, *The Civil War in Kentucky,* 12.

34. Rawley, *Turning Points of the Civil War,* 39; Harrison, *The Civil War in Kentucky,* 13.

35. Magoffin lasted in office until August 18, 1862, when he finally resigned and was replaced by James F. Robinson, a conservative Unionist (Weigley, *A Great Civil War,* 48).

36. Bush, "'My whole life must speak for me,'" 84–88.

37. Rawley, *Turning Points of the Civil War,* 40.

38. Weigley, *A Great Civil War,* 88–89.

39. Fehrenbacher, ed., *Abraham Lincoln,* 269 (see also 268–70).

40. See Jacob F. Lee, "'The Union as it was and the Constitution as it is': Unionism and Emancipation in Civil War Kentucky" (master's thesis, University of Louisville, 2007).

41. Coulter, *Civil War and Readjustment,* 80.

The Vortex of Secession

West Tennesseans and the Rush to War

Derek W. Frisby

Meredith P. Gentry, like many Tennesseans of the antebellum era, "had always loved the Union" and never believed in secession as "a remedy for any evil, real or imagined." Indeed, prior to 1860, the state had been instrumental in quashing the idea of secession and its intellectual cousin, nullification. Andrew Jackson's victory at New Orleans with his Tennessee Volunteers had stifled the resolutions of the Hartford Convention in 1815 and ushered in a wave of nationalism. Jackson's resolve, bolstered by Tennesseans' enthusiastic support, had also cowed the nullifiers of South Carolina in 1831–1832. In 1850, when Fire-Eaters from the Lower South infected Tennessee and advocated secession during the Nashville Convention of 1850, Tennessee moderates took control of the convention and diffused the crisis.

Yet, within the course of a few months in 1860–1861, secessionists overturned Tennesseans' strong Unionist traditions and carried the state into the Confederacy and civil war. The secessionist tide was so swift, according to Gentry, that resistance was futile. Although secession was "contrary to his feelings," Gentry's "friends, neighbors, and kinsmen, all rushed pell-mell aboard" the secessionists' "d——d old worm-eaten, rickety, stem-wheel boat" against his warnings. Suddenly, he looked around and found himself "alone on the bank of the stream, and they were pulling the gang plank. I shouted to the captain: 'Hold on! Hold on!' I'll get aboard too and we'll all go to hell together."[1]

Peer pressure alone, however, has failed to explain the secessionist triumph in Tennessee. The secessionist minority radicalized Tennessee's political climate and utilized fraud, intimidation, and coercion to engineer a coup d'état. Tennessee's historical example during the secession crisis provides a chilling reminder that those with superior numbers do not always win contests and that a determined minority can often achieve political ascendancy. As the English philosopher Edmund Burke observed, the majority, feeling secure in its power to overcome the minority's influence, often becomes apathetic, advocating patience and the peaceful resolution of conflicts. Thus, they are often caught off guard and ill prepared to meet the minority's challenge in a crisis. The minority that is "more expedite, awakened, active, vigorous and courageous" will campaign incessantly for its cause with a "superabundance of velocity." "When men are furiously and fanatically fond of an object," Burke predicted, "they will prefer it to their own peace, to its own property, and to their own lives."[2]

As the country prepared to elect a new president in 1860 amid concerns over the future of slavery in the territories, Tennesseans were ready to stand firm and "rebuke fanaticism." Unable to agree on a party candidate at their Charleston convention, Tennessee Democrats later reconvened with their colleagues in Baltimore, determined to encourage moderation and promote compromise on the slavery issues. To many Tennesseans, breaking up the Union seemed inconceivable. "If you divide the Union how would you divide it? I would not like to part with Pennsylvania, the keystone state, it contains the hall of our independence, it was there American liberty was born," declared one Memphis citizen. "I cannot give up Massachusetts—even such a devil as she has grown up—Disunion would be a stain of infamy upon all our brows." The possible secession of the Lower South states in response to a Republican victory in the 1860 presidential election would spell commercial disaster as well as disrupt Tennessee's thriving border state economy, especially that of the western section of the state. In the event of war to restore the Union, Tennessee and the Upper South might well become a major battleground and incur great losses measured, not only in dollars, but also in lives. Tennesseans therefore searched frantically for a national compromise that could preserve the Union. Their efforts failed, and the last remaining national party, the Democrats, split into sectional factions: the Northern faction, led by Stephen Douglas, appealing for compromise and party unity and the Southern faction, headed by John Breckinridge, strongly advocating states' rights.[3]

Meanwhile, remnants of Tennessee's Whig/American Party, reconstituting themselves statewide as the Opposition Party, endorsed the native son John Bell and his new Constitutional Union Party as a moderate alternative to the extremism they believed now pervaded both the Democratic and Republican parties. The once-dominant anti-Democratic forces had not carried a statewide election in nearly a decade, though the Opposition Party had stiffly challenged the Democrats each time and appeared to be regaining strength amid the growing talk of disunion. Tennessee Opposition leader Gustavaus A. Henry advised his fellow citizens to support Bell because he stood for "a union for the sake of the Union" to avoid the "untold horrors" of secession. Other state Opposition Party leaders seemed less certain of Bell's chances to stem the tide of secession given the number of candidates currently in the race. The West Tennessee Opposition congressman Emerson Etheridge predicted as early as June 1860 that, with Douglas, Bell, and Breckinridge splitting the slave-state vote, the Republicans stood poised to sweep the fifteen free states, making Lincoln's election, and, thus, the secession of the Lower South, a "foregone conclusion."[4]

In the 1860 presidential contest, moderates carried the day in Tennessee with a plurality voting for Bell. Surprisingly, the Constitutional Union Party made its strongest statement in West Tennessee, the state's predominant slaveholding region. Although Breckinridge captured 45 percent of the statewide vote, he polled only 31 percent in West Tennessee and a paltry 11 percent in Memphis. Either Douglas or Bell carried many of the planter counties with significant slave populations. Meanwhile, Bell and his Constitutional Union Party polled almost as many votes in West Tennessee as the Democrats Douglas and Breckinridge combined. Thus, despite the sectional agitation over slavery, West Tennessee's Democrats and a high percentage of West Tennessee slaveholders favored the moderate positions of Douglas or Bell over Breckinridge's more militant Southern rights stance. Despite Tennesseans' pleas for moderation expressed at the Democratic convention and at the ballot box, the nascent Republican Party prevailed, and its antislavery candidate, Abraham Lincoln, became the sixteenth president of the United States on the strength of the electoral vote of the free states alone.[5]

Although somewhat dismayed over the Republicans' victory in the national presidential contest, most Tennesseans adopted a wait-and-see attitude toward the new Lincoln administration. After all, the Congress remained in Democratic hands, and the Supreme Court, a conservative group that had been appointed mostly by Democrats, would surely prove a barrier to any presidential assault on slavery. The editor of the *Memphis Bulletin* urged his readers to recognize the constitutionally elected administration "however much we may deplore the result." According to the *Nashville Banner,* Tennesseans had expressed their opinion in the presidential election that "disunion is no remedy for existing evils," perceived or real. The *Memphis Enquirer* agreed, saying: "Let every man put his foot on secession, it is no remedy for Southern wrong, or it is only a madman's remedy."[6]

Chief among those expressing dismay at the November 1860 results was Governor Isham G. Harris. Having cooperated with the Fire-Eaters throughout the presidential campaign, Harris had remained in constant communication with secessionist leaders in other states. Some political observers even suspected him of having already made secret promises to officials in the Lower South that he would carry the state out of the Union if Lincoln was elected. Unwilling to accept Lincoln as the newly elected president, Harris called a special session of the state legislature to meet in Nashville on January 7, 1861, to consider the present condition of the country.[7]

Harris must have known that secession faced an uphill struggle in the state, and he likely pinned his hopes on the ability of secessionist agitators to stir up a popular revolution that would eventually carry the state out of the Union. He would begin this revolution in his home region of West Tennessee, an area that was dependent on slave labor and whose broad, flat geography made it easy to control with a relatively small contingent. By late October 1860, a group of South Carolinians had arrived in Memphis to establish a prosecession organization known as the Minute Men to "fire the Southern heart—instruct the Southern mind—give courage to each other, and at the proper moment, by one organized and concerted action, we can precipitate the Cotton States into a revolution." The Minute Men were to act as a revolutionary vanguard to incubate secessionist sentiment in Tennessee. Despite what one paper described as their predisposition to violence and attraction to the "gullible and curious," the Minute Men's ranks in and around Memphis began to grow throughout the fall of 1860, and they began to create a climate of fear through intimidation and violence directed against their political opponents. These radicals seized every opportunity to sport their blue cockades and promote their cause. Those who dared resist became targets of physical and economic bullying. The secessionists' favorite targets were immigrants and nonnative Southerners, whom they blamed for having prevented Breckinridge from carrying Tennessee.[8]

In the wake of Lincoln's election, the atmosphere grew steadily more intolerant. The secessionists' editorial mouthpiece, the *Memphis Daily Avalanche,* deemed the Minute Men's efforts "noble work" and begged them to purge the city of those who would falter in the defense of slavery or oppose secession. "Hunt up the cowardly ingrates," the *Avalanche*'s editor implored, "and if necessary nail their vile carcasses to their own doors or hang them upon the public lamppost. . . . When you find a traitor consign him to a dishonored grave, with no monument to mark the accursed spot save a rough stake driven through the body of the miserable ingrate." Other newspapers decried such vitriolic rhetoric because it supposedly encouraged a "spirit of mobocracy" antithetical to "the better impulses of a peaceful and orderly community."[9]

When the South Carolina convention adopted an ordinance of secession on December 20, 1860, the Memphis Minute Men and their supporters poured into the streets, playing loud music, and firing sporadic cannon salvos. The following evening, secessionists held a torchlight procession, and, intoxicated by emotion as well as the abundant champagne and whiskey, the crowd burned an effigy of Tennessee's U.S. senator Andrew Johnson, who just days before had made a passionate pro-Union speech on the Senate floor. They later sent the scorched rope used to hang Johnson's blazing effigy to the Minute Men's national headquarters. The crowd wildly cheered a subsequent motion to hang the real Johnson should he ever visit Memphis again.[10]

Memphis Unionists charged that secessionist claims of several thousand people attending the December 22 rally were wildly exaggerated, declaring that the event had drawn no more than 250 persons and only "a contemptuable monority [*sic*] of the citizens" supported secession. Former governor Neill S. Brown reported to Johnson: "All this was the work of a few, and has the sympathy of no respectable class anywhere. It amounts to nothing." Across West Tennessee, other Unionists gathered to discuss remedies for the crisis sparked by South Carolina's "demented folly." Within a week of the Memphis Minute Men's demonstration, a group of Memphis Unionists, many of whom were reportedly among the city's most respected and wealthy citizens, met to form a Unionist society to counteract the fiery secessionist agitators. Bolstered by this show of strength, Tennessee Unionists hoped that their organizations, as well as similar groups in Virginia, could form "a great breakwater to Northern Abolitionism and Southern secession."[11]

On January 7, 1861, the Tennessee legislature met in special session, and Governor Harris's opening message attempted to set a prosecession tone. He lectured the members on the "systematic, wanton, and long continued agitation of the slavery question" by Northern states. These "actual and threatened aggressions" of the North on Southern citizens' constitutional rights should not be allowed to stand, Harris said. He then proposed five amendments to the Constitution in order to safeguard Southerners' rights, yet he clearly held out little hope that constitutional adjustment could be worked out, saying: "The only practical question for the State to determine will be whether she will unite her fortunes with a Northern or Southern Confederacy." The governor concluded with a wildly optimistic hope: "I am certain there can be little division in sentiment [in Tennessee], identified as we are in every respect with the South."[12]

Mississippi's decision to secede just two days into this special legislative session, combined with the speeches of secessionist agents from Alabama and Mississippi, whipped prosecession Tennessee legislators into a frenzy. They quickly introduced resolutions to sever political and economic ties with the North and to create a state army under Governor Harris's command. Unionists managed to defeat these measures, so secessionists proposed calling a special convention.

Unionists publicly blasted this secessionist plan as an attempt to "rush the people of the state into the vortex of secession." The West Tennessee congressman and Unionist Emerson Etheridge noted that similar tactics had induced the Lower South to act on the matter of secession "with less deliberation than is usually displayed at a coroner's inquest." The Unionists charged that holding a convention to adopt a secession ordinance and create a standing army within the state not only violated democratic principles and bypassed the will of the people but also threatened to establish a military despotism. Unionists, however, faced a difficult political quandary. Their constituents might perceive outright opposition to a convention as a sign of political weakness, yet secessionists would never risk losing a direct referendum on the matter, at least not at this time. Therefore, the two sides agreed on a compromise measure whereby Tennesseans would decide by popular referendum whether a convention should be held and, if so, whether they preferred sending Unionist or secessionist delegates to the convention. The "disastrous rout" of Harris and the secessionist movement during this special legislative session led many Unionists to conclude that their opponents were finished.[13]

The General Assembly set February 9, 1861, as the date for the convention referendum. To preempt their adversaries, the Unionists added a provision requiring that a majority of the number of the votes cast at the previous gubernatorial election were necessary to approve the convention, not just a simple majority of votes cast on that particular election day, as the secessionists had proposed. Furthermore, the call for a statewide vote on secession could not take place until twenty days after any such convention had adjourned. By raising the political bar on secession and delaying the vote, Unionists hoped to blunt the secessionists' call for quick, decisive action. Many Unionists actually began favoring a convention themselves because they believed that they could use it to quash secession once and for all. Because a significant number of Unionists and almost all secessionists favored a convention, the crucial issue in the February election became, not whether to hold a convention, but whether to select Unionist or secessionist delegates to attend it.[14]

The anticipation and excitement grew as the February 9 vote neared. Both sides used every possible means of persuasion available, including newspaper editorials, stump speeches, and handbills. "States' Rights Anti-Coercion" supporters derisively labeled their opponents "submissionists." They denied that immediate secession was their goal and, instead, predicted that calling a convention would pressure the Northern people and the new administration into respecting Southern rights. For their part, Unionists accused secessionists of attempting to capitalize on the heat of the moment and stampede the state into secession. One newspaper

called on Tennesseans "to accomplish the salvation of our beloved Union
. . . [and] stand at the great breakwater to Northern Abolitionism and
Southern secession." The pro-Union *Nashville Banner* pleaded for calm
deliberation, warning: "If the PEOPLE do not rise in their strength and put
back meddling politicians, the latter will *chloroform* them with 'sectional
prejudice,' and then ride over them rough-shod before they can recover.
. . . The political tricksters who see their *power* slipping from their grasp
are playing a desperate game and will not 'lose a trick' if they can help it."
Emerson Etheridge reported that the people "or the noisy portion of them
seem mad." "A panic prevails," he continued, "which is made to feed itself
[off terror]." Confident Unionists held only a modest torchlight parade
through Memphis on election eve, with marchers strutting around the
city's statue of Andrew Jackson carrying banners declaring "Secession is
Treason" and "Don't give up the Ship."[15]

On election day, people arrived early at the polls and remained to
mill about much of the day, anxiously awaiting the outcome. Brass bands
entertained the crowds with alternating refrains of "The Star-Spangled
Banner," "Dixie," and other patriotic tunes. One observer described the
atmosphere at polling places across the state as one of "perfect political
saturnalia." Spectators jammed the polls, and, as each voter cast his ballot,
the crowds filled the air with chanting and cheers, and each voter had "his
hand shaken 'till his very arm aches and tears of pain attest his heartfelt
repentance at having voted at all." The secessionists' well-oiled publicity
campaign led Unionist candidate Robertson Topp to leave Memphis when
the polls closed, certain his side would be defeated. He was wrong.[16]

Tennesseans narrowly rejected the calling of a convention and voted
almost four to one for Unionist delegates. Comparing both the convention
and the delegate results of the February 1861 vote illustrates the complex-
ity of deciphering the voters' message. East Tennesseans perceived a convention as a step toward their state's secession instigated by slaveholders
in Middle and West Tennessee, and they opposed a convention while
largely supporting Unionist delegates with a ratio of six Union delegates
for every secessionist delegate. Middle Tennessee was more divided on the
convention question but still chose Unionist delegates four to one. West
Tennesseans believed that they could use the convention to outmaneuver
the secessionists and place Tennessee in a position to broker a compromise
between the already-seceded states and the national government. At least

two-thirds of the West Tennesseans preferred a convention with double the number of pro-Unionist delegates as secessionist ones.

Regardless of party affiliations or connections to slavery, Tennesseans were obviously not yet ready in February 1861 to embrace secession. The real significance of the February 1861 vote, however, lies not so much in statistical correlations to party, slaveholding, or to future loyalties as in how the results shaped future political strategy. Unionist leaders emerged from the election with a sense of confidence that lulled them into believing that keeping Tennessee in the Union would be relatively easy. On the other side, the February 1861 vote initially stunned secessionists and caused considerable consternation among their leaders but, in the end, only made them more determined to carry Tennessee out of the Union.[17]

Unionists' overconfidence also encouraged political apathy. On hearing the results of the February vote, the director of the Tennessee State Historical Society, A. Waldo Putnam, proclaimed: "Thank God a thousand times! Tennessee has not been moved from her propriety; neither terrified, hoodwinked, corrupted or ensnared [by fanatics from the North or South]." The secessionists, he continued, "are few indeed,—and *we trust and believe,* (that, like dogs,) 'they have had their day.'" On hearing of the "most glorious victory" of the Union ticket, the Carroll County attorney Alvin Hawkins noted that the secessionists were angry and had promised to inflict their "wrath" on him for their defeat but that he expected "the storm will soon pass away."[18]

Of course, not all Unionists became complacent, and some warned their leaders of overconfidence. Some worried that the secessionists' defeat would make them "more desperate." During a tour of several states that had already seceded, the Memphis physician Jeptha Fowlkes found secessionists "up &c doing" and feared that Unionists might be inclined to bend before their "active and intolerant" opponents unless they devised some "*avowed, direct* and *fixed* measures" to conciliate the Southern states. Another Memphian, Benjamin D. Nabers, concurred that "the Seceders here altho writhing under a Waterloo defeat are calling their Scattered forces together for another effort" to remove the "foul blot" cast on the state by the February vote.[19]

The Union party had "swept like an avalanche over the State," the West Tennessean Charles Faxon declared, adding that, for the time being, Governor Harris is "Check-Mated." The Unionist and former governor

Neill S. Brown also rejoiced that the "mad waves of secession had found an iron embankment around this commonwealth which defied all their fury." Yet he and the other Unionists continued to worry about the future. "The secession party per se, is small," Brown warned, "but there is a large body of Union men who are such under the assurances of a fair settlement—many of whom would be carried off in a storm—Thus would be produced in our midst a formidable division animated by bitterness and violence." The gradual atrophy of the traditional political party system over the last few years meant that the fragmenting electorate was severely weakened. Tennesseans were desperately searching for the sort of political stability that had existed in the previous decades and ready to embrace any political movement that offered some sense of vigor. Any emotionally charged incident during this delicate stage would dramatically alter the political dynamic. Had any firmness, like that of Jackson in the nullification crisis, been displayed against the seceded states, lamented the Unionist Waldo Putnam, "the spread of this contagion might have been stayed," but now if Lincoln were "to fire a single gun into these infatuated states—whilest the people of the other Slave States not seceded, are in such a sensitive, nervous, emotional condition—will not war kindle instantly and rage furiously?"[20]

In the early months of 1861, the prospect of armed confrontation or "collision" at Fort Sumter or Fort Pickens loomed as a Unionist nightmare. Tennessee Unionists admitted that their political position rested on "fragile defenses, ill-suited to withstand the tremors of crisis and war hysteria." The *Louisville Journal* encouraged Unionists in Tennessee and other border states to organize, "rouse up," and express their position else the "timid, conservative majority is overawed by violence and clamor into passive acquiescence." Unionists therefore urged Andrew Johnson to find a "fair solution" to the crisis before "a collision at some of our southern points" would "create no small excitement & give us much trouble." Charles Faxon and other Unionists feared that much Unionist support was "conditional" and that any further "excitement" of the national crisis might tip the scales in favor of those "infected with the secession epidemic." Jeptha Fowlkes suggested that "if no act of violence and no new cause of irritation be furnished the Secession feeling will rapidly lessen," but he also feared that the uncertainty and hesitancy of the Unionist leadership was stifling the growth of Unionist sentiment.[21]

Unionists from across the state implored the state's Unionist leader, Andrew Johnson, to show "Stronger backbone" during the crisis. They detested the "apologetic *ifs, peradventures* and *contingencies*" implicit in his Unionist appeals that prevented more Tennesseans from rallying to their side. In other states, such as Georgia and Alabama, secessionism had been allowed to grow into "a most savage raving lunacy" by Unionist inaction, making the Unionist cause appear "over awed by the reign of intolerance and terror." According to one Unionist: "Once I thought it strange that the first Napoleon should have become so universally popular in France by the successful use of strong and prompt coercive measures upon a raging mob. Now I think I can appreciate it." The Unionist William Lellyett feared that "whenever the piratical forces of the conspirators shall attempt the capture of Fort Sumter or Fort Pickens, many of our so-called Union men will be found to be wolves in sheep's clothing. . . . They will cry 'Murder!' and throw down the stripes and stars. Others of them are so slenderly fortified in their position, that should they prove true, all their work must be done over." Tennessee Unionists, it was proposed, must "meet the domineering career of this raging fanaticism in Tennessee by presenting a bolder, more threatening and determined front. . . . No half way measures will do." Another fearful Unionist admitted that his side's arguments were "weak, impotent weapons" and that, unless their "blank cartridges" were replaced with real ammunition, they faced certain defeat.[22]

The haphazard, convoluted Unionist arguments stood in stark contrast to the well-orchestrated, straightforward secessionist campaign. For the last decade, Americans had debated the future of slavery. West Tennesseans depended on slavery, and the uncertainty of the peculiar institution's expansion into the new territories caused many to question their place within the Union. The diversity of the possibilities proffered by the Northern free states regarding slavery's future made this uncertainty more pronounced. Gradually, many Southerners formulated the opinion that the only way to ensure slavery, their livelihoods, and their culture was through secession. Jeptha Fowlkes claimed that Unionists in West Tennessee were converting daily to the secessionists' side because the Southern position was "fixed" and "definite" while "doubt, hesitation and uncertainty" characterized their "Northern friends'" position. Furthermore, Unionists' arguments seemed mired in the past, while secessionists spoke of the future, couching their appeals in the rhetoric of progress, and

infusing them with religious themes. Revolution, as one Memphis secessionist newspaper declared, was a means to advance "society towards a
higher freedom and more perfect civilization . . . upward towards that
ideal perfection, that millennial glory, pictured in the golden dreams of
poets and prophets."[23]

For their part, secessionists carefully crafted their language to avoid
alienating "conditional" Unionists, those who supported the Union but
would protest the use of force to bring the seceded states back into the fold.
As early as January 1861, it had become apparent to the secessionists that
terms such as *coercion* and *revolution* carried enough intellectual weight to
expose chinks in the armor of Unionist solidarity that they could exploit.
Conditional Unionists were more likely to support *independence* but abhorred the term *secession*. This might appear to be a distinction without
a difference, but to conditional Unionists, especially in the western areas
steeped in frontier republicanism, it meant everything. Should the secessionists make a first strike, many Unionists believed, "the act of [federal]
resistance will not be *coercion* but the constitutional defense and mainte-
nance of the Union." If the federal government resorted to the use of force
first, then secessionists could invoke the right of revolution and carry with
them the conditional Unionists, who would have to defend their homes
against Northern aggression regardless of their opinions on secession or
slavery. The *West Tennessee Whig*, a Constitutional Union and antiseces-
sionist newspaper, warned: "While Tennessee disapproves [of secession]
. . . she utterly repudiates and will, in all proper ways, resist any attempt to
coerce [seceded states] back into a Union." However, it remained clear that,
unless the federal government resorted to force or could be coaxed into doing so, secessionists would remain on the defensive in West Tennessee.[24]

Fearing that Unionists, whatever their doubts about the Lincoln
administration, might still seek some sort of Union-saving compromise,
secessionists urged their supporters to "strike now for independence."
Just four days before the February 1861 vote, delegates from the seceded
states gathered in Montgomery, Alabama, while border-state representatives met in Washington at a so-called peace conference. Governor Harris
and the secessionist members of the General Assembly tried to convince
the legislators to send a delegation to Montgomery rather than Washington but failed, and eventually Tennessee delegates made their way to
the nation's capital. The *Memphis Appeal*, a recent convert to secession,

chastised Tennesseans for defeating secessionist measures and ridiculed the Unionists' faith in the federal government's ability to protect Southern rights. Those who hesitated about leaving the Union now were submissionists who maintained a "devotion to the *dead glories* of an *expired nationality.*" February's "shameful verdict," the editor continued, had revealed the "ignorance of the masses as to the true state of the country." The *Appeal* urged "every true Southron" to attend an upcoming meeting of secession supporters: "The fires of the great revolution have but commenced to burn upon our prairies. They will continue to spread until all opposition to southern freedom shall be consumed amid its annihilating flames." With increasingly militaristic rhetoric, secessionists instructed their supporters to "buckle on the armor, draw their swords, throw away the scabbards, and enter upon the contest with redoubled ardor." Another speaker commanded them "to keep their flints in order and their powder dry for another contest, which must sooner or later come."[25]

The collision that Unionists had long feared came in the early hours of April 12, 1861, in Charleston, South Carolina. After enduring a siege for several months, the Union garrison at Fort Sumter came under attack from Confederate shore batteries. Almost immediately on hearing the news, crowds began to congregate around the Memphis telegraph office, eagerly awaiting further word from Washington and Charleston. Three days later, President Abraham Lincoln requested troops from the states, including Tennessee, to put down this insurrection. The secessionists had provoked the federal government into action, yet the wily secessionist propaganda machine made it appear that Lincoln was the aggressor. Lincoln's call for volunteers sparked great furor throughout the Volunteer State. Militia meetings, drill parades, cannon salutes, and nighttime fireworks commenced almost immediately. Not surprisingly, Governor Harris defiantly responded to Lincoln's call: "Tennessee will not furnish a Single Man for the purposes of Coercion but 50,000 if necessary for the defense of our rights and those of our Southern brothers."[26]

Many Unionists did, indeed, perceive Lincoln's call for troops as an act of coercion, and it transformed these conditional Unionists into reluctant Confederates. The events sparked by Fort Sumter produced a dramatic change in the state's mood. One Tennessee Unionist remarked: "Our most influential and strongest Union men of yesterday are today carried by the vortex of circumstance into the powerful stream of public opinion." The pressure placed on Unionists to defend their homes and oppose Lincoln's actions was intense.

Perhaps nowhere was the change of sentiment more evident than in West Tennessee. The *Memphis Appeal* declared that Lincoln's war proclamation had "made a unit of our people" and created a "perfect unanimity beyond our wildest expectations." Prominent Unionist politicians, including the Constitutional Union presidential candidate John Bell and former governor Neill S. Brown, briefly pondered their situation and then reluctantly switched to the secessionist side. At a Memphis rally, one Unionist after another took to the podium, where they "repented" and "converted" to the secessionist cause. The one-time Unionist delegate Robertson Topp was among these and offered to transport all Confederate troops on his Memphis and Ohio Railroad free of charge.[27]

It appeared obvious from the outset that Tennessee would be a key Confederate defensive position, and preparations for war began almost immediately. West Tennessee, with its proximity to key rivers and railroads, became a priority. Within a week, Memphis's civic leaders had appropriated $50,000 for construction of new defensive works and other military preparations. Men quickly filled the ranks of numerous militia units. Women too offered to do their "patriotic duty" by collecting materials and making clothing and flags. "War with the inexperienced is very popular," a McNairy County citizen perceptively noted, declaring: "Every man and Boy becomes a Genl. [Andrew] Jackson."[28]

Presenting a united front became such a priority that secessionists turned to intimidation and violence to suppress dissent. Warnings appeared all over the state or in the press stating: "You are either with us or against us. Let every citizen remember that 'Eternal vigilance is the price of Liberty.'" Throughout Tennessee, secessionists were determined to move against anyone with "Black Republican proclivities." They organized "Committees of Safety" within communities "for the purpose of hanging or getting rid of all abolitionists . . . [and] Northern unsound men." Secessionists warned any potential "agitators" in their midst "to be cautious as to how they conduct themselves in the South. This latitude, just at this time, is not healthful for such individuals."[29]

The secessionists' first targets were the "sixteen or eighteen hundred foreign suffragans" in Memphis believed to have voted in "a solid phalanx for the Union ticket" in February. The later determination that at least 15 percent of these immigrants had voted in favor of secessionist delegates forced secessionists to rationalize their previous prejudices and shift the blame onto Unionist operatives who had spread rumors that a vote for secession would violate citizenship oaths and pose a risk of deportation. Unionists had also reportedly warned immigrants that the newly formed Confederate government would impose heavy taxes and might even disfranchise the propertyless.[30]

The Minute Men units and the "Committees of Safety," sometimes referred to as the "Vigilance Committees," carefully searched for signs of dissent. Tennesseans were asked to watch their neighbors and inform officials immediately if anyone left the area for an extended time and then returned. One Memphian of Northern origins felt obliged to publish a letter declaring his Southern loyalties. He wrote: "Let all who are not actually with us in this struggle, from whatever country or clime, quietly and as speedily as convenient, take their departure; and those unwilling to do so be compelled by a prudent and proper manifestation of public sentiment." Businesses were urged to report anyone who "could not be trusted as friends of the South. . . . It is important that this be done—the security of our property and the safety of our families demand it." Secessionists portrayed the act of informing on "disloyal" persons as a patriotic duty. Those volunteering for service in the field could take comfort in knowing "that they have not left behind them the lurking enemy, who, while lingering around their homes and firesides, would incite our negroes to insurrection, and bring the worst calamities upon our wives, our mothers, and our daughters."[31]

Reports of "mob action" or isolated acts of violence against those brave enough to voice their contrary opinions or those thought to be acting suspiciously soon filled the local papers. One German man announced his support for Lincoln while raising a barn just outside Memphis. Others repeatedly warned him to keep quiet, but he ignored their advice until he was struck with an axe and seriously wounded by a secessionist coworker. In another incident, a Northerner traveling through Memphis was supposedly overheard telling someone how he would fight against the Confederacy on his return home. He was quickly placed under citizens' arrest and had his head shaved before being allowed to continue his trek upriver, thus serving as a powerful warning to others with similar inclinations.[32]

Many Unionist residents witnessed the growing secessionist intolerance since the February election and the war hysteria in the wake of Fort Sumter and concluded that it would be impossible to remain neutral and left Tennessee. An estimated two to five thousand Northern or foreign-born persons left Memphis in the week following the attack on Fort Sumter alone. Many residents fled in such haste that they left behind unpaid bills and houses full of furniture. Even in the interior of West Tennessee, mobs descended on Unionist citizens and demanded they take an oath of loyalty to the Confederacy, enlist, or leave. Posted notices in Brownsville, Tennessee, gave Unionist residents, particularly those born in the North, just ten days to put their affairs in order and depart. After this grace period had expired, anyone still in the area was expected "to stand by and aid us in defending ourselves against invasion, and to all such we pledge the protection of this community." One Northern-born Unionist who waited until the deadline discovered that many secessionists had already commenced searching trains and pulling off suspect passengers. Most West Tennessee Unionist refugees managed to get north to the area around Cairo, Illinois, soon dubbed by Unionist refugees as "Little Egypt," before secessionists closed the last transportation routes. Unionists who stayed behind found themselves "obliged to become secessionists whether they liked it or not," claimed one Memphis Unionist refugee who reached St. Louis.[33]

Governor Harris capitalized on this war hysteria by pushing for quick and decisive action to take Tennessee out of the Union. On May 6, the General Assembly emerged from a secretly called two-week-long session and declared the state independent. Carefully choosing his words, Harris declined to call this action *secession,* preferring to justify it as Tennessee's exercise of the "right of revolution" against a government that was antithetical to its interests. But the legislators believed that they lacked the authority "to put Tennessee out of the Union, or to place it among the Confederate States." Instead, the people would decide the issue in a referendum to be held June 8, 1861. This method would avoid "the delays, embarrassments, and expense of a convention" and supposedly refute the Unionists' charges that "trickery or political management" was being used to undermine the will of the people. Despite his nuanced language and apparent victory in the legislature, Harris must have remained uneasy about the referendum's outcome given the stinging defeats of prosecession forces in February 1861. Therefore, he tried to create a fait accompli by signing a military alliance with the Confederacy on May 7. He also declared a state of emergency and seized the state's financial and military assets to construct defenses and protect Tennessee against an imminent invasion.[34]

Secessionists ensured that the June 8 vote would not lead to another embarrassment. Again violence and intimidation were their primary tools. With most of the Northern- and foreign-born citizens having departed, the focus of the secessionists' efforts became the native Southern Unionists who had stood firm in their beliefs and chose to remain. As the *Troy Press* of Obion County stated, certain "stumbling blocks" in the vicinity "must be crushed *out*." Memphis secessionists made certain that they could tell friend from foe during the upcoming June referendum. Subsidized by the *Memphis Appeal*, they printed red paper ballots indicating a preference for separation in the upcoming election and ballots of a different color for Unionist voters. Some locations printed no Unionist ballots at all. Voting against separation was, of course, a constitutional right, the prosecession *Appeal* said, but these "traitors" should also have "no objection to their position as Union men being known to the community."[35]

The Unionist Emerson Etheridge, or, as the secessionist press dubbed him, "Emerson Blatheridge," vowed to fight secessionists "with a torch in one hand and a sword in the other; and so help me God, so long as the Stars and Stripes wave over my state, or any part of it, I will never bow to the storm of disunion." He attempted to speak in his congressional district, but threats and mobs frequently deterred him. The *Memphis Daily Avalanche* suggested that the people "nail him to the public pillory and cut his black tongue from his sooty mouth." An editorial in Tipton County warned that, should Etheridge appear there, "if he is not shot or hung, he will be treated to a new coat of tar and feathers, free gratis, and rode on a rail out of town to the tune of the rogues' march." "Let him come if he like, and his men too," the editorial continued, "we will greet them just as kindly as powder and ball will receive them." The threats of violence grew during the campaign when Etheridge attempted to debate the secessionist Robert G. Payne in Trenton prior to the election. Payne later canceled his appearance but issued a statement saying: "If Etheridge speaks for the South, we have no reply. If against it *our only answer to him and his backers must be cold steel and bullets.*" Indeed, that was the response during an April 22 pro-Union rally in Paris when a group of secessionists attacked Etheridge and his supporters, leaving one dead and several others wounded.[36]

The "Vigilance Committees" and local secessionist officials in Tennessee banned Northern newspapers, shut down Union presses, and rummaged through mail searching for expressions of disloyal sentiments. Secessionists shut down Unionist newspapers prior to the June 8 election. The pro-Unionist publishers of the *Carroll Patriot,* Isaac Hawkins and his cousins Alvin and Ashton, soon found themselves the target of new secessionist threats. Such intimidation efforts, along with the censorship of the press, hamstrung the Unionists' organizing efforts.

In striking contrast, the secessionists campaigned freely throughout the state with dramatic calls for public unity. As the secessionist Alfred Robb pointed out to the Unionist Isaac Hawkins: "If the vote on the 8th of June next shall show a *division* that fact will do more for Mr Lincolns army than 50,000 men and millions of money." "The only hope they have of making a successful foray on the South," Robb continued, "was in the divisions of her own People." He begged Hawkins "not to cause a division among our *people* but let us all go forth together and establish our *independence.*" Once Tennessee established its independence, there would be plenty of time to debate reconstruction with the federal government or permanent connection with the Confederacy. "We have got to fight now," Robb argued, "and after the fight is over we may adjust our political states." Hawkins ignored his friend's advice and remained a steadfast Unionist.[37]

As the June 8 vote neared, it became obvious that the election was to be merely a hollow ritual designed to ratify Harris's push for Tennessee's secession. Recording the names of voters who cast ballots and implementing "open ticket" voting were tactics meant to intimidate and discourage Unionists from expressing their true sentiments. According to the *Memphis Appeal:* "Every man should now show his hand, should let his neighbors know where he stands on the great question to be decided." "Anyone failing to vote," according to the *Appeal,* should be the "object of suspicion within the community." Secessionists deemed a Unionist voter as "an enemy of his state and as the enemy of liberty. . . . We sincerely trust that the election of the 8th of June will not discover a single man of that stripe. We hope that no son of Tennessee will have the insufferable mortification to see a brother untrue." The *West Tennessee Whig* even accepted a challenge from a Rutherford County newspaper to see which county could cast the largest percentage of votes for separation.[38]

Secessionists used intimidation and fraud very effectively on election day. Gibson County resident William T. Dickens sympathized with the

Union and believed it "the best govt under the sun," so he voted against secession in February. Yet he voted for secession in June, explaining his change of sentiment by referring to death threats issued by secession supporters in his community. Dickens said that secessionists told him that "any man who voted at my precinct for the Union would be hung and that every man who did not vote at all was as bad and would be held as guilty as if he voted for the Union." Secessionists patrolled West Tennessee prior to the June election and threatened to punish those who voted against secession. With his wife ill, and caring for eight children, Dickens believed that he had no choice but to yield to the political pressure. "I would have fled to the country if I could, but could not," he exclaimed. "I feared I would be arrested and dragged about the country by the soldiers if I did not vote and I voted for the state to go out."[39]

Gray B. Medlin of Haywood County had also voted "no convention" in February but "for separation" in June because he "was afraid to do otherwise, as the rebels were 'spotting' those who voted against it and who did not vote at all." Others in Obion County claimed that "Union men were deterred from the polls by rebel bayonets." According to William P. Orne, an election clerk in Shelby County and Memphis, "all the clerks were ordered to turn over the tickets, to number every one of them with the same number as the poll books and opposite put the man's name who voted it, so that upon examination of the votes any person was found voting against secession he should be *spotted*. I mean by 'spotted' that he would be handed over to the Vigilance Committee and separated from his family, property, and influence."[40]

The secessionists won an overwhelming victory on June 8. Overall, the state voted nearly two to one for separation. East Tennessee, where the valleys, ridges, and a paucity of slave owners, made it difficult for the secessionists to coordinate a successful campaign, remained the only section of the state to oppose disunion. But the Middle and West Tennessee results showed a four to one margin in favor of separation. Only five West Tennessee counties (Carroll, Decatur, Henderson, Weakley, and Hardin) voted to remain in the Union. Several counties recorded unanimous secession votes or seemingly preposterous margins. Shelby County recorded but five Union votes and Lauderdale County only seven. But even this result was a source of great disappointment for the *Memphis Appeal,* which had promised to "outdo Richmond [Virginia]" with its four pro-Union votes cast in the referendum. Obion County had nearly double the number of voters participate in the June election as in February, and, of course, these new voters overwhelmingly, if not unanimously, seemed to favor separation.

In counties where the usual number of voters went to the polls, significant numbers of Unionists cast ballots, while, in counties where turnout lagged significantly or increased more than 5 percent from the previous November, Unionist votes were almost nonexistent. Fraud, intimidation, and coercion likely played a role in these areas where turnout was suppressed or exaggerated, and few men could have been expected to vote their conscience under such circumstances.

The dramatic swing in the public mood bewildered Unionists, who believed that they had won a decisive and lasting victory in February. In the words of the Middle Tennessee Unionist Alvan C. Gillem, it seemed unfathomable "that in the short interval from February to May 104,500 intelligent American citizens could have changed their minds on so important an issue as the dismemberment of a nation" over the seemingly minor confrontation pitting "a major and a few half-starved officers and men at Fort Sumter against 'Davis and Beauregard.'"[41]

The secessionists' turn toward more coercive measures to achieve their goals should hardly have been surprising. The Minute Men had proved in the November presidential contest and in the weeks leading up to Tennessee's convention vote that the secessionist minority was willing to utilize all possible means, including violence and intimidation, to achieve their goals. They had seen their cause soundly defeated in February 1861, and, being "furiously and fanatically fond" of establishing a Southern nation, they preferred war to peace, disregarding their property and their own lives.

West Tennessee secessionists initiated a coordinated campaign of fear and repression that brought Tennessee ever closer to the precipice of secession by April 1861. All the hesitant electorate needed was a push. Events in Charleston provided the strong shove necessary to send Tennessee over the edge. The secessionists' organizational strength and brutal tactics of intimidation allowed them to take advantage of the political upheaval generated by the attack on Fort Sumter and Lincoln's subsequent call for troops. Unionists were caught off guard and were ill prepared to meet these challenges from the more expedite and vigorous secessionist forces. Many chose to leave their homes temporarily and move north until the chaos subsided or the Union army advanced south to occupy that area and restore a sense of stability and order. Other Unionists, unable to leave their families and property but too scared to resist, had little choice but to weather the crisis and acquiesce to Confederate authority, at least temporarily. A small core group of unconditional Unionists, now finding themselves as the minority and being "furiously and fanatically" fond of the Union, resolved to stay and fight the Confederates to regain control of their communities, regardless of the risk to their property, their families, or themselves.

As war approached, Confederates instituted a reign of terror in the Unionist areas in Tennessee as they constructed a thin defensive perimeter along the presumed Yankee invasion routes, the rivers and railroads. Outnumbered and outgunned, Tennessee Unionists held out hope that Federal soldiers would soon deliver them from their oppressors and pined for the opportunity to aid in restoring the Union and their cherished sense of stability and order.

Notes

1. Oliver P. Temple, *Notable Men of Tennessee* (New York: Cosmopolitan, 1912), 244.

2. Edmund Burke, *The Writings and Speeches of Edmund Burke,* 12 vols. (Boston: Little, Brown, 1901), 7:88.

3. Marguerite Bartlett Hamer, "The Presidential Campaign of 1860 in Tennessee," *East Tennessee Historical Society Publications* 3 (January 1931): 6–14 (quote, 9).

4. Ibid., 8–9 (Henry quote); Emerson Etheridge to Isaac Hawkins, June 25, 1860, Hawkins Letters, private collection. Because state officials in many Southern states (including Tennessee) had barred the Republicans from appearing on the ballot, the presidential contest in those states narrowed to a field of three: Bell, Douglas, and Breckinridge.

5. Election results have been tabulated from Mary Campbell, *The Attitude of Tennesseans towards the Union, 1847–61* (New York: Vantage, 1961), 284–87; *Nashville Union and American,* December 2, 1860; and University of Virginia, Geospatial and Statistical Data Center, Historical Census Browser, http://fisher.lib.virginia.edu/census/ (accessed November 28, 2002). West Tennessee's voting patterns appeared largely undisturbed by sectional turmoil. The Democrats' combined totals were just under half a percentage point lower than the Demo-

cratic returns from the 1859 gubernatorial contest and only 2 percentage points above their decade-long average. Furthermore, an estimated 96 percent of Bell's supporters came from the old Whig/American/Opposition Party strongholds throughout West Tennessee. West Tennessee's newspapers played a key role in the presidential campaign, with both Bell and Douglas enjoying the support of well-established partisan newspapers in Memphis and West Tennessee. This organizational advantage that the moderate forces enjoyed may account for their strength on election day over the smaller, but vocal, prosecession Breckinridge elements. Douglas's emphasis on the economic repercussions of secession may also have swayed many West Tennesseans to his camp, especially in Memphis, the commercial hub of West Tennessee.

6. *Memphis Bulletin,* November 12, 1860; *Nashville Banner,* November 13, 1860; *Memphis Enquirer,* November 13, 1860; Paul Bergeron, *Antebellum Politics in Tennessee* (Lexington: University Press of Kentucky, 1982), 163–66. Bergeron notes that the election of 1860 "conveyed the theme of politics as usual" (ibid., 164) owing to the continuity of party strength from the antebellum period. This voter continuity is even more striking when considering the volatile issues of the campaign and the first-ever three-man race for president in Tennessee's history. Bergeron further indicates that the 1860 results should not be interpreted as a referendum on secession (ibid., 166), a statement that needs some qualification. Of course, no candidate proposed immediate secession, and, until December 20, 1860, secession from the Union remained only a theoretical option. Nonetheless, early proponents of secession would have supported the Breckinridge Southern rights platform to protect slavery rather than the more moderate positions offered by Douglas or Bell. So, while it can be said that the 1860 vote was not a true test of support for secession, it does offer an early snapshot of support for moderation vs. extremism, at least within Tennessee's Democratic Party.

7. Stanley F. Horn, "Isham G. Harris in the Pre-War Years," *Tennessee Historical Quarterly* 19 (1960): 195–207. In a decidedly sympathetic biographical sketch of Harris's prewar years, Horn downplays the governor's secessionist sentiments, saying that he "counseled moderation and restraint until the fatal hour of decision in April, 1861" (196). Contemporaries contradict this assertion and believed that Harris played an early and integral role in taking Tennessee out of the Union. For example, Lincoln's secretaries, John Nicolay and John Hay, noted his suspicions of Harris's secret negotiations in their *Abraham Lincoln: A History,* 10 vols. (New York: Century, 1914), 4:249–50.

8. Bruce Catton, *The Coming Fury* (New York: Doubleday, 1961), 111; William L. Yancey to James Slaughter, June 15, 1858, quoted in Allen Nevins, *Emergence of Lincoln,* 2 vols. (New York: Scribner's, 1950), 1:406 ("fire the Southern heart");

Memphis Appeal, October 30, 1860 ("gullible and curious"), December 18, 1860; William H. Carroll to Andrew Johnson, January 2, 1861, in LeRoy Graf and Ralph Haskins, eds., *The Papers of Andrew Johnson* (hereafter *Johnson Papers*), 16 vols. (Knoxville: University of Tennessee Press, 1967–2003), 4:117; Charles Lufkin, "Secession and West Tennessee Unionism, 1860–61" (Ph.D. diss., Memphis State University, 1988), 55–61. The Minute Men was one of several paramilitary groups formed following Lincoln's election to persuade Southerners to join the secessionist cause. The first of these groups was organized in 1858 when William L. Yancey of Alabama had suggested southern "Committees of Safety" to perpetuate secessionism. These groups adopted the blue cockade to show support for this cause or designate oneself as a member of the group. The cockade, an ornamental knot of ribbon usually worn on a hat, was a historical symbol of revolution or resistance and had been used previously during the Nullification Crisis of 1832 to show support for South Carolina.

9. *Evansville Daily Journal,* December 22, 1860, quoting the *Memphis Daily Avalanche* (no date given).

10. Nancy D. Beard, "A Kentucky Physician Examines Memphis," *Tennessee Historical Quarterly* 36 (1978): 199.

11. Reuben F. Alexander to Andrew Johnson, December 25, 1860, Henry G. Smith to Andrew Johnson, December 23, 1860, and Neill S. Brown to Andrew Johnson, February 17, 1861, in *Johnson Papers,* 4:79–80, 88, and 301. On December 18–19, 1860, and February 5–6, 1861, Andrew Johnson rose on the Senate floor, delivering speeches against secession, and outlining his reasons for supporting the Union. As a result, Johnson, a Democrat, was widely seen by secessionists as a traitor to the South, his state, and his party. For the text of these speeches, see *Johnson Papers,* 4:3–51, 204–55.

12. Robert H. White and Stephen V. Ash, eds., *Messages of the Governors of Tennessee,* 11 vols. to date (Nashville: Tennessee Historical Commission, 1952–), 5:261–65; Jonathan M. Atkins, *Parties, Politics, and the Sectional Conflict in Tennessee, 1832–1861* (Knoxville: University of Tennessee Press, 1997), 235–38. Governor Harris's call for a convention to "consider relations" between Tennessee and the Union certainly lacked clarity. Some have speculated that Harris was intentionally vague in order to win support for a convention from both sides, realizing that, once that convention was convened, secessionist delegates could take the state out of the Union. Unionists presumably viewed the convention as a way to promote compromise measures. Those straddling the fence on the issue would see it as nothing more than a political meeting with little authority to take drastic action.

13. Jordan Stokes to William B. Campbell, January 7, 1861, David Campbell

Papers, Perkins Library, Duke University, Durham, N.C.; Emerson Etheridge to Isaac Hawkins, January 20, 1861, Hawkins Letters; Return J. Meigs to Andrew Johnson, in *Johnson Papers*, 4:263–64; Campbell, *Attitude of Tennesseans*, 171–72; Atkins, *Parties, Politics*, 235–40.

14. Meigs to Johnson, February 7, 1861, in *Johnson Papers*, 4:263–64; Atkins, *Parties, Politics*, 235–38.

15. *Trenton, Tenn., Southern Standard,* February 16, 1861; *Nashville Banner* quoted in *Memphis Appeal,* February 7, 1861; Emerson Etheridge to Isaac Hawkins, January 20, 1861, Hawkins Letters; Atkins, *Parties, Politics*, 239–41.

16. *Memphis Argus,* February 11, 1861; *Nashville Patriot,* February 12, 1861; Sam Vance to W. L. Vance, February 13, 1861, Robertson Topp Papers, Memphis Public Library, Memphis; *Memphis Appeal,* February 10, 1861.

17. Daniel Crofts, *Reluctant Confederates: Upper South Unionists in the Secession Crisis* (Chapel Hill: University of North Carolina Press, 1989), 164–97. See also Mary Campbell, "The Significance of the Union Victory in the Election of February 9, 1861 in Tennessee," *East Tennessee Historical Society Publications* 14 (1942): 11–30.

18. A. Waldo Putnam to Andrew Johnson, February 13, 1861, William Lellyett to Andrew Johnson, February 12, 1861, Neill S. Brown to Andrew Johnson, February 17, 1861, and Benjamin D. Nabers to Andrew Johnson, February 13, 1861, in *Johnson Papers*, 4:278, 281–82, 289–90, and 300; Alvin Hawkins to Isaac R. Hawkins, February 10, 1861, Hawkins Letters.

19. Jeptha Fowlkes to Andrew Johnson, March 21, 23, 1861, and Benjamin D. Nabers to Andrew Johnson, February 13, 1861, in *Johnson Papers*, 4:274, 422–23, and 425–26.

20. Neill S. Brown to Andrew Johnson, February 17, 1861, Charles O. Faxon to Andrew Johnson, February 11, 1861, and A. Waldo Putnam to Andrew Johnson, February 18, 1861, in *Johnson Papers*, 4:289–90, 300–301, 310–11. See also Charles Lufkin, "Secession and Coercion in Tennessee: The Spring of 1861," *Tennessee Historical Quarterly* 50 (1991): 98–109; and LeRoy Graf, "Andrew Johnson and the Coming of the War," *Tennessee Historical Quarterly* 19 (1960): 208–21.

21. Jeptha Fowlkes to Andrew Johnson, March 21, 23, 1861, and Charles O. Faxon to Andrew Johnson, February 11, 1861, in *Johnson Papers*, 4:422–23, 425–26, and 289–90; *Louisville Journal,* February 26, 1861; Lufkin, "Secession and West Tennessee Unionism," 55–61.

22. William Lellyett to Andrew Johnson, February 12, 1861, and John Lellyett to Andrew Johnson, January 23, 1861, in *Johnson Papers*, 4:184–85, 281–82.

23. Jeptha Fowlkes to Andrew Johnson, March 21, 23, 1861, in *Johnson Papers*, 4:425; *Memphis Daily Avalanche,* June 8, 1861.

24. *West Tennessee Whig* (Jackson), January 18, 1861; Lufkin, "Secession and West Tennessee Unionism," 55–61.

25. *Memphis Appeal,* February 12, 13, 1861. The Washington peace conference, derogatorily termed the "Old Gentleman's Convention" in reference to many delegates' old age, was the last attempt at reconciliation before the firing on Fort Sumter. After three weeks of intense debate held in secret sessions, delegates managed to agree on resolutions extending the Missouri Compromise line to the Pacific by constitutional amendment, strengthening the Fugitive Slave Law, and compensating slaveowners for fugitive slaves not returned by Northerners under "personal liberty laws." Extremists on both sides criticized the conference's proposals, which were very similar to those of the Crittenden Compromise rejected in January, and defeated them when they were presented in Congress. The conference, called at the request of Virginia, met from February 4 to February 27, 1861, concurrent with the first meeting of the Confederate States of America in Montgomery, Alabama. The conference revealed the persistence of border-state Unionism but proved to be an exercise in futility. Consequently, the gathering never offered any viable options to solve the crisis of the Union.

26. White and Ash, eds., *Messages,* 5:273; J. Milton Henry, "The Revolution in Tennessee, February 1861, to June 1861," *Tennessee Historical Quarterly* 18 (1959): 113–19.

27. *Memphis Appeal,* April 14–17, 1861.

28. *Memphis Appeal,* April 14–17, May 5, 1861; Pitser Miller to Andrew Johnson, February 27, 1861, in *Johnson Papers,* 4:341–42.

29. Frank Moore, ed., *The Rebellion Record,* 12 vols. (New York: Arno, 1977), 2:58; *Memphis Appeal,* December 12, 1860, April 14–17, 1861.

30. *Memphis Appeal,* February 13, 1861; Charles Lufkin, "The Northern Exodus from Memphis," *West Tennessee Historical Society Papers* 42 (1988): 6–29. An estimated 56 percent of people living in Memphis had been born either in the North or in a foreign county. In the preceding decades, an influx of Northern-born citizens and immigrants had arrived in Memphis to seek new opportunities. Many had come during the economic depression of 1857, when mechanics and laborers flocked south to assist the growing cotton trade and its attendant industries in the strategic river port. Others sought employment in Tennessee's railroad construction boom of the 1850s. Immigrants, especially the large Irish population, tended to stay, choosing to side with Confederacy rather than fight for equal rights with blacks, whom they saw as potential competitors for jobs. Germans remained more subdued in their support for secession but did form several companies composed of European war veterans.

31. *Memphis Daily Avalanche,* April 26, May 1, 1861; Moore, ed., *Rebellion Record,* 2:58.

32. *Memphis Daily Avalanche,* April 28, 1861; *Chicago Tribune,* April 27, 1861; Lufkin, "The Northern Exodus from Memphis."

33. *Cleveland Plain Dealer,* April 30, 1861; *Louisville Journal,* May 31, June 1, 7, 1861; *Daily Missouri Democrat* (St. Louis), April 24, 1861; Lufkin, "The Northern Exodus from Memphis." By the first week in May, the Union army had fortified Cairo, Illinois, and stopped almost all river and railroad traffic south. This area provided sanctuary for Unionist refugees.

34. White and Ash, eds., *Messages,* 5:279–87, 298; *Memphis Appeal,* May 8, 1861; *Nashville Daily Press,* January 11, 1861.

35. William B. Gibbs to Isaac Hawkins, May 5, 1861, Hawkins Letters; *Memphis Appeal,* May 12, 1861.

36. Speech of Emerson Etheridge, January 23, 1861, *Congressional Globe,* 36th Cong., 2nd sess., 1861, app., 113; Emerson Etheridge to Isaac Hawkins, January 20, 1861, Hawkins Letters; *Paris Sentinel,* March 6, 1861; *Memphis Daily Avalanche,* April 20, 1861; *Weekly Spy* (Covington, Tenn.), May 18, 1861; James W. Patton, *Unionism and Reconstruction in Tennessee, 1860–1869* (1934; reprint, Gloucester, Mass.: Peter Smith, 1966), 14.

37. Alfred A. Robb to Isaac Hawkins, May 15, 1861, Hawkins Letters.

38. *Memphis Appeal,* May 21, June 8, 1861; *Nashville Patriot,* May 8, 1861; *West Tennessee Whig* (Jackson), June 7, 1861.

39. Disallowed Claim No. 10378, William T. Dickens, Gibson County, in *Barred and Disallowed Case Files of the Southern Claims Commission, 1871–1880,* microfilm publication M1407, National Archives and Records Administration, Washington, D.C.

40. Disallowed Claim No. 7517, Minerva J. McGough, Obion County, Disallowed Claim No. 10137, Catherine Pursley, Obion County, Disallowed Claim No. 8660, Gray B. Medlin, Haywood County, and Disallowed Claim, No. 21986, William P. Orne, Shelby County, in ibid.

41. Alvan C. Gillem to Andrew Johnson, August 16, 1861, in *Johnson Papers,* 4:679.

"An unconditional, straight-out Union man"

Parson Brownlow and the Secession Crisis in East Tennessee

Robert Tracy McKenzie

Most in the auditorium on that May evening in 1862 were surely disappointed by the guest of honor's appearance. From his reputation, they had expected the "celebrated exile" from the Confederacy to look more imposing, to embody physically the undaunted courage and unflinching resolve that all knew to be his defining traits. Instead, the "martyr" from East Tennessee looked thin and frail, his shoulders stooped, his face haggard and—to be candid—homely. (What else could you say about a man whom a sympathetic reporter characterized as "not quite as handsome as Mr. Lincoln"?) Yet, when the speaker was led on the stage by the president of the Young Men's Republican Union, the packed assembly at New York City's Academy of Music sprang to their feet as one. As a member of the audience described the scene: "The clapping of hands seemed almost to shake the very walls; gentlemen waved their hats and ladies their handkerchiefs; and all this was followed by cheer upon cheer, indicating the 'irrepressible' enthusiasm of the crowd." The speaker did nothing to dampen their enthusiasm, for he proceeded to enrage and inspire his admirers with a graphic account of the "reign of terror" that gripped his native land and a moving tribute to its persecuted patriots "whose only offense was love of country." Relating how his business had been shut down and his life threatened because of his faithfulness to the Constitution and the Union, he hastened to add that East Tennessee was teeming with suffering heroes just like him. The Union men of East Tennessee, he assured his listeners, were "uncompromising" in their loyalty. Indeed, they would readily imperil both life and property in defense of the Stars and Stripes. "We have thought that we loved our country," the *New York Times* confessed, "[but] our patriotism, with its many flags and applause of men, 'pales its ineffectual fires' before the noontide glory of theirs." In sum, if readers were searching for examples of truly selfless devotion to the Union in the most trying of circumstances, the *Times* advised them to look south to the loyalists of East Tennessee or, better yet, to their triumphant leader now in New York City, that "sturdy and much-suffering lover of the Union," William G. Brownlow.[1]

It was good advice—up to a point. The *Times* was correct in two crucial particulars: whoever would understand Unionism within the Confederacy must surely pay attention to East Tennessee, and whoever would understand Unionism in East Tennessee must come to know that region's most outspoken Unionist, the minister turned journalist whom both friends and enemies called "the Parson." The name William Brownlow is rarely recognized today, but in 1862 its bearer was a celebrity across the war-weary North. As the editor of the *Knoxville Whig,* the pugnacious parson had waged war against the cause of secession until Tennessee seceded in June 1861, at which point he aimed his acid pen at the "Satanic Confederacy" and its hellish agenda. After tolerating his defiance for nearly half a year, Confederate authorities in Knoxville finally arrested Brownlow for treason in November and, after holding him through the winter, ordered him beyond the lines of the Confederacy in March 1862. He headed for Cincinnati and soon began a triumphal speaking tour that took him to Chicago, Detroit, Indianapolis, Pittsburgh, Philadelphia, Washington, New York, Boston, and countless smaller venues along the way. At each stop, enraptured crowds hailed the "unflinching hero," paid tribute to the patriot "unwavering and bold." They snapped up more than 100,000 copies of his hastily written autobiography, purchased his likeness on "cartes de visite" and stationery, read dime novels about his exploits, danced to "The Parson Brownlow Quick Step," and in numerous other ways so lionized the Tennessee journalist that at least one religious newspaper had to caution its readers about "idol worship." The Parson, it would seem, had become the very personification of Southern Unionism.[2]

Yet, if our goal is to gain insight into East Tennesseans' original response to the collapse of the Union, it is imperative to disregard much of what Parson Brownlow actually told Northern audiences after his banishment from the Confederacy. Although they could not have been aware of it at the time, the audience in the New York Academy of Music who came to learn about Southern Unionism heard, not an accurate characterization, but a caricature.[3] The Brownlow who addressed *Northern audiences during the war* presented Southern Unionism as the product of a pure and "unconditional" patriotism that valued fidelity to the Union above all other attachments. The Brownlow who addressed *other Tennesseans during the secession crisis* took a decidedly different tack. A close reading of the Parson's public pronouncements in 1860 and 1861 reveals that, although this quintessential Unionist categorically denounced secession, he never actually espoused a literally unconditional commitment to the Union.[4] Furthermore, when he exhorted his readers to stand by the Union, he most often did so by appealing to a variety of more parochial commitments—to party, region, and class—which combined to make not so much a positive case *for Union* as a compelling negative case *against disunion.*

"East Tennessee is my horror," Union general William T. Sherman once complained to Ulysses S. Grant. "That any military man should send a force into East Tennessee puzzles me."[5] On the whole, latter-day historians of the Civil War have seemed to share Sherman's aversion to the region; most broad histories of the Confederacy are written as if it did not exist. To cite but a few examples, a recent work focused on "anti-Confederate Southerners" devotes all of two paragraphs to East Tennessee, a survey of Confederate politics allocates two sentences, and a major study of "the failure of Confederate nationalism" allots three sentences.[6] Perhaps the region is just too much of an anomaly for works geared toward broad generalization. Certainly, East Tennessee was a world far removed from the land of cotton fields and white-columned mansions that has for so long fascinated both scholars and buffs interested in "the South." Proud of the region's uniqueness, East Tennesseans were prone to exaggerate it; they accepted the label *mountaineers* and referred to their homeland as the "Switzerland of America." In reality, proportionally few East Tennesseans actually lived in the mountains per se—whether the Smokies to the east or the Cumberland Plateau to the west—most opting instead for the more fertile and accessible lands of the Great Valley of East Tennessee. A census official once dubbed the area *the poor man's rich land,* a phrase that nicely captures the combination of opportunity and limitation that the land afforded. The soil and climate were well suited for the production of foodstuffs and livestock, and the plain folk who lived there could reasonably expect the land to yield a comfortable existence. They knew better than to expect handsome profits, however. The short growing season rendered cotton cultivation impractical (fewer than one in one hundred farmers tried to plant it), and most farmers would never be able to purchase slaves, a luxury restricted to less than one-tenth of households.[7]

In sum, East Tennessee was a mixed-farming region of small farms worked primarily by white labor, almost the antithesis of the Black Belt regions that led in the creation of the Confederacy. When the secession crisis erupted, this economically distinct area asserted its political distinctiveness as well. As Mark Neely has observed: "The mountains may have isolated East Tennesseans physically, but they did not do so politically." The region was "in the vanguard" of the Jacksonian party system, "the scene of strenuous political campaigns, the home of enthusiastic voters, and the nursery of able politicians."[8] As was true in the Upper South generally, in East Tennessee the two-party system survived the national collapse of the Whig Party. The Whigs survived locally, albeit under a succession of different names. Lifelong Whigs like Parson Brownlow typically became Know Nothings in the mid-1850s, members of the "Opposition" Party toward the end of the decade, and finally backers of the Constitutional Union Party during the 1860 presidential election. Such name changes aside, the Democratic and Whig factions were impressively stable well into the secession crisis, and voter turnout regularly exceeded 80 percent.[9]

East Tennessee voters formally considered separation from the Union not once but twice. In mid-January 1861, as several Lower South states were in the process of seceding, Tennessee's prosecession governor, Isham G. Harris, urged the General Assembly to call for a statewide referendum a mere three weeks later. As prescribed by the legislature, voters would cast two ballots, the first indicating whether they favored holding a special convention to consider the desirability of secession, the second choosing delegates to represent them in such a convention should it be held. When voters went to the polls on February 9, Middle Tennesseans were closely divided, and West Tennesseans strongly favored holding a convention, but fully 81 percent of East Tennessee voters were opposed, and the resulting twenty-five-thousand-vote margin against the convention was more than enough to offset the eighteen-thousand-vote margin in favor in the rest of the state.[10] Four months later, Tennesseans returned to the polls, this time to approve or reject a "declaration of independence" passed by the General Assembly in the aftermath of the battle at Fort Sumter and President Lincoln's call for troops to put down the rebellion. By then, nearly seven-eights of Middle and West Tennesseans favored disunion, yet East Tennesseans still opposed separation by more than two to one, making the region an island of Unionism within the Confederacy.[11]

Although East Tennessee has long been marginalized in the grand narrative histories of the South during the Civil War, historians of Southern Appalachia such as Charles F. Bryan Jr., Noel Fisher, John D. Fowler, W. Todd Groce, and John C. Inscoe have begun to pay close attention to the region, and in recent years they have done much to underscore its importance and to highlight the complex and engaging story that unfolded there. In particular, they have significantly complicated our understanding of the area's predominant "Unionism" by showing the sheer number of variables—class, kinship, geography, religious ties, partisan affiliation, and regional self-image, among others—that helped shape patterns of loyalty in the region.[12] Curiously, however, they have not given focused attention to Parson Brownlow, the man who by the time of Tennessee's secession was indisputably the preeminent voice of East Tennessee Unionism.

They are not alone. To be sure, works that deal significantly with dissent within the Confederacy normally mention the Parson, and occasionally broader studies of the Civil War include cursory references as well. Only a handful of scholars, however, have written about him in any detail. You have to go back three-quarters of a century to find the only book-length scholarly biography of him. In the mid-1930s, E. Merton Coulter turned his attention toward Brownlow, holding his nose as he did so. Brownlow was a "deluded crusader," Coulter averred, who whipped "up patriotism through singing his hymn of hate." Writing unabashedly as a Southern partisan, Coulter condemned Brownlow for "treason" against the Confederacy, questioned his mental stability, assaulted his character, and attributed his large following among East Tennesseans to their "ignorance and prejudice." So great was Coulter's contempt for the Parson that, at times, his biography reads like a nineteenth-century melodrama. Regarding Brownlow's decision in the 1830s to retire as a Methodist circuit rider and "locate" in the small village of Jonesborough (where he would live for about a decade before moving to Knoxville), Coulter observed sadly: "It was an evil day for this little mountain town when Brownlow came here to live."[13]

Although somewhat more balanced, most subsequent scholarly assessments since Coulter's evince the same basic dislike for the Parson. Probably, at least into the 1980s, much of this scholarly disdain reflected distaste for his postwar career. As the war was coming to a close, Brownlow embraced the Republican Party (which he had earlier denounced), won the governorship (thanks to the disfranchisement of white Confederates), claimed a second term (thanks to the enfranchisement of blacks, whom he had long proclaimed inferior), and then contrived to have himself elected to the U.S. Senate just before the state legislature was "redeemed" from Republican rule by a Democratic resurgence. At any rate, a 1981 survey of Tennessee historians ranked Brownlow dead last among the state's governors to that point in terms of "ability, accomplishments, and statesmanship"—one slot below Ray Blanton, a convicted felon, and some thirty-two places behind Isham G. Harris, the prosecession governor who maneuvered to ally the state with the Confederacy even before a popular referendum could be held on secession.[14]

Even scholars with no obvious dislike for Brownlow have typically found it hard to take him seriously, and this, I am convinced, has more to do with his shocking prose than with any other single factor. And it *is* shocking to our modern ears, accustomed as we are to journalists who, most of the time anyway, make at least a pretense of professional objectivity. In the pages of the *Whig,* an antislavery opponent became "an unwashed, unmitigated, unregenerate, and God-forsaken Abolitionist." Local secessionists were "imps of hell," a rival newspaper editor a "low-down, ill-bred, lying, debauched, drunken scoundrel." My favorite "Brownlowism" involves the Parson's response to an invitation, shortly after Tennessee seceded, from the Confederate general Gideon Pillow to serve as a chaplain for a Tennessee brigade. Brownlow replied in print. Thanking Pillow for his invitation, he nevertheless declined. "Should I ever decide to go to Hell," he explained, "I will simply cut my throat and go direct, and not by way of the Southern Confederacy."[15] Brownlow made no apology for such language. He gloried in it, bragging early in his career about his gift for "piling up epithets," and boasting that, in its "wholesale abuse of individuals," his newspaper was "without a parallel in the history of the American Press." No wonder that one of Brownlow's biographers dismissed the *Whig* as an "advertisement against the First Amendment."[16]

Yet Brownlow's world was not our own. Antebellum readers typically expected their newspaper of choice to be overtly, aggressively, even viciously partisan.[17] Granted, the Parson elevated the ad hominem attack to an art form, but he hardly monopolized the tactic. (Indeed, he was often on the receiving end of it. To cite one example, a Democratic editor once blasted him in print as "monstrously corrupt, desperately wicked, a pest to society, a common tattler, a shameless blackguard, an unblushing hypocrite, a deliberate calumniator, and a convicted libeler.")[18] It would be a mistake, in other words, merely because of his salty vocabulary, to ignore the editor whose newspaper reached more readers than all other newspapers in East Tennessee combined, who indeed may have had the largest readership of any journalist in the Confederacy at the outbreak of the war.[19] What is more, Brownlow's political positions were identical with those of the majority of East Tennesseans throughout the secession crisis, and both his friends and his enemies testified that this was no coincidence. The Parson's political allies pointed to his "phenomenal" personal magnetism and persuasiveness as well as his unerring grasp of the views of the common folk who constituted the bulk of his subscribers.[20] Critics also acknowledged his influence, bitterly denouncing the *Whig* as "the great and deadly engine in deluding and poisoning the public mind" against secession. "The rabble," one enemy condescendingly complained, "have it as their guide and textbook."[21] No, the editor of the *Whig* was not a sophisticated political theorist. He was, however, a masterful polemicist and political catechist, and a close reading of his columns can do much to further our understanding of the complicated phenomenon of Appalachian Unionism.

"I am an unconditional, straight-out Union man," Parson Brownlow told cheering Northern audiences after his banishment from the Confederacy. He had left behind a legion of like-minded patriots in his beloved East Tennessee, common folk characterized by an "uncompromising devotion" to the Union and an "unmitigated hostility" to those who would rend it asunder.[22] Other Unionist refugees from the region quickly picked up the refrain. "The Union is with the Union men of East Tennessee the paramount question," Hermann Bokum proclaimed in a book published in Philadelphia during the war. "Every other is secondary." A group of prominent East Tennesseans appealing to Congress for financial relief in the fall of 1863 expanded on the theme. As the secession crisis unfolded, they explained, East Tennesseans "did not stop to consider their local or pecuniary interests. Their innate love of country rose above the narrow and selfish considerations that controlled the people and dictated the policy of other states." In sum, East Tennesseans' "deep and strong love for their *whole country*" was a near mystical attachment. It trumped all other loyalties, all other bonds, all other interests.[23]

We need to take such post-1861 pronouncements with more than a grain of salt. Ulterior motives lurk everywhere. In Brownlow's case, there was his undeniable love of public acclaim, the desire to place East Tennessee in the most favorable light, the hope of drumming up support for a military campaign that would redeem his homeland from Rebel rule. Of all the different forms of expression, behavior is the one that most rarely lies, however, and the course that the Parson actually pursued during the secession crisis indicates that he doubted that a simple appeal to patriotism could succeed. For some East Tennesseans, such a straightforward approach might have been sufficient, but it is telling that by far the most influential Unionist newspaper in the region adopted a much more complicated editorial strategy.

It is not that Brownlow eschewed appeals to patriotism. In fact, they were fairly common in the pages of the *Whig*. As early as the spring of 1860, the editor began to warn his readers that the perpetuity of the Union could be at stake in the forthcoming presidential campaign. Once the Democratic Party had split into Southern and Northern wings, with Southern Democrats nominating the current vice president, John C. Breckinridge, Brownlow announced that the "controlling spirits" behind the Breckinridge candidacy "are for disunion." To underscore the connection, he took to labeling the Southern Democratic Party "the Disunion Party," their ticket the "disunion ticket." The Breckinridge Democrats were engaged in a "conspiracy to break up the Union," he insisted, and "deserve the scorn, contempt, and hatred of every patriot in the land."[24] As summer gave way to autumn and the election of the Republican Abraham Lincoln seemed more and more likely, the Parson boldly declared that the mere election of a Republican as president would not constitute grounds for secession. The editor professed no love for the Illinois rail splitter. Should Lincoln gain the White House, it would be "the greatest calamity that ever befell our country." Yet Lincoln's election alone, "under the forms of law and the Constitution, will by no means be a sufficient reason to dissolve this Union." The "Disunionists" would have no cause to act, Brownlow maintained, and, what is more, they would have no right to act. "I even deny the right of secession," the Parson proclaimed.[25]

These are strong words, but not as unequivocal as they might at first appear. As Brownlow defined the matter, the "calamity" of a Republican victory in November would present white Southerners with *three* options, not two. They could "stand by the Union," they could secede, or they could *revolt.* Although the latter two alternatives would both sever the Union, technically they were far from equivalent. Secession was the expression of an alleged constitutional right of states, revolution the expression of a natural right of citizens. The legitimacy of the former was hotly contested, that of the latter not only accepted but venerated in both North and South as a sacred principle enshrined in the American founding. Indeed, the Tennessee constitution opened with the avowal that the people possess, "at all times, an inalienable and indefeasible right to alter, reform, or abolish the government in such manner as they may think proper."[26]

If any public figure in East Tennessee dared to question this right, I have not discovered it. Certainly, Parson Brownlow did not. "The right of *Revolution* I admit," he acknowledged early in 1861, "but I deny that such remedy is called for in the present crisis of our affairs." The qualification was crucial. Although revolution was a *natural right,* it was not a *moral act* unless undertaken as a last resort against a government that had forfeited its legitimate authority by ceasing to protect the constitutional rights of its citizens.[27] This was exactly the situation that existed after the election of Abraham Lincoln, early advocates of disunion insisted. Although in East Tennessee proponents of separation rarely spoke in terms of revolution per se, they nevertheless argued that, with the election of a Republican president, all the necessary criteria for a legitimate revolution were in place. They maintained that, by endorsing a "higher law" than the law of the land, ridiculing the Dred Scott decision, supporting the Underground Railroad, and lionizing the abolitionist murderer John Brown, the Northern Republican majority had repeatedly shown its contempt for the Constitution and its willingness to pervert the federal compact in pursuit of its sectional agenda. If justice was the true end of government, as Madison had argued in the *Federalist* essays, then a Republican-dominated federal government was, by definition, illegitimate. "Can we hope for justice from Abolitionism and its rulers?" a prominent East Tennessee secessionist asked. The answer, this speaker avowed, was obvious. "There is no hope but under the banner and shield of our own State, co-operating with the South."[28]

Not so, Brownlow countered. "What the people of the Southern States should do," the editor recommended shortly after the votes were in, "may be summed up in a single word: PAUSE!" No Southern right had yet been violated. No Southern interest had yet been thwarted. Lincoln had been elected constitutionally, and the men of the South had no right to judge him except by his actions, "and these can only be appreciated *after* his inauguration." As repugnant as Lincoln's election might be, the South should "stand by the Union and the Constitution with him, as long as he stands by them himself." If the future president should dare to initiate "unfriendly legislation" against the South (e.g., attempting to abolish the interstate slave trade), Brownlow would wait to see whether Congress sustained him. Should it fail to do so, he would look to the Supreme Court, and, if that body also ignored its constitutional obligations, then—and only then—the time for revolution would be at hand. With right on their side, the Southern states would rise up in revolt. "AND I WILL GO WITH THEM," the Parson proclaimed, "AND FIGHT THE ENEMY TO THE DEATH!"[29] In context, Brownlow was rebuking those who demanded immediate secession in response to a Lincoln victory, but he was hardly proclaiming the "unconditional" Unionism that he so often boasted of after his exile to the North.[30]

In sum, disunion per se was morally indeterminate. If "Fire Eating" secessionists dissolved the Union *without cause,* their course would be "treasonable" and "diabolical." If, on the other hand, "Black Republicans" co-opted the government and waged war on Southern rights, revolution would be both justified and honorable. Both scenarios were real possibilities, furthermore, because border-state moderates were plagued by threats from both extremes of the political continuum, from the "hell-deserving Abolitionists of the North, and the God-forsaken Disunionists of the South." Because Parson Brownlow perpetually attacked both groups, he found it necessary both to condemn disunion as currently unwarranted and to threaten disunion should circumstances change. Given his unabashedly polemical temperament, he made both kinds of declarations as dogmatically as possible.[31]

As framed in the pages of the *Whig,* then, the real issue before East Tennessee voters was the question of whether circumstances currently warranted that they exercise their indisputable natural right of revolution. This was a question much less of constitutional philosophy than of political judgment, and, sooner or later, questions of political judgment always came down to perceptions of competence and character. Which side of the debate did voters find more trustworthy? To win such a contest in the court of public opinion, Brownlow pursued a twofold strategy. First, he set out to prove that East Tennessee Unionists were utterly loyal to the institution of slavery and the pattern of white supremacy it undergirded. Second, he relentlessly impugned the motives of the secessionists, in the process reminding his readers of all they had to fear from a Southern Confederacy.

If the Unionist position was to stand a chance with the electorate, it was imperative, Brownlow understood, to rebut the secessionist claim that opposition to disunion was equivalent to support of abolition. Even before the presidential election, Breckinridge supporters had libeled the Constitutional Union Party as engaged in an insidious coalition with "Abolitionists" and "Douglasites" to ensure the defeat of the only candidate truly committed to preserving slavery. Before election day, they even damned the Parson himself for "going over to the Abolitionists." After Lincoln's victory, they relentlessly hammered on the purported connection, calling all opponents of disunion "Lincolnites" and "submissionists" who would spinelessly acquiesce in the "Black Republican agenda." Representative of this view was the public advertisement posted by six Knoxville voters who later cast their ballots in favor of secession in the February 1861 referendum. "By our votes for the 'Secession Ticket,'" they explained, "we intended to express . . . our abhorrence of Abolition aggression."[32]

There had been a time, more than a generation earlier, when white East Tennesseans could publicly disagree about slavery. During the 1820s, there were perhaps as many as sixteen chapters of the Tennessee Manumission Society in the eastern part of the state. When a convention was held in 1834 to revise the state constitution, eleven East Tennessee counties sent in petitions, signed by perhaps 5 percent of their adult white male populations, advocating some form of gradual abolition. Some of these denounced human bondage as "morally wrong" and "contrary to the law of God." Others shifted the focus away from the slaves themselves and lamented slavery's effects on the region's economy and society. Significantly, even William Brownlow—at the time still riding the Methodist circuit—endorsed a petition that condemned slavery for saddling Southern whites "with some of the most odious features of aristocracy." The constitutional convention tabled the petitions, however, and it was not long before such public condemnations of slavery had totally vanished, silenced by the "omnipotent despotism of public opinion," as one East Tennessean remembered. With the emergence of radical abolitionism in the North during the early 1830s, any expression of doubt about the South's defining institution became "unsouthern" and unsafe.[33]

Nearly thirty years later, the Unionist cause would be doomed in East Tennessee if secessionists succeeded in portraying themselves as the only true champions of slavery. Parson Brownlow contested the secessionist strategy early and often. During the course of the presidential campaign, the editor published an ongoing exchange with Abram Pryne, a Pennsylvania abolitionist whom he had debated in 1858 concerning the question, "Ought American slavery to be perpetuated?" The Parson denounced his fellow clergyman as "a heartless, unfeeling, unprincipled *knave*" who proposed to "turn the brutal negro upon unsuspecting white men and the defenseless white woman, and see them gloat on murder and rapine." As a defender of John Brown—that "murderous old Imp of Hell"—Pryne deserved the gallows every bit as much as Brown. He was pathetically typical "of that class of God forsaken fanatics, who lie, and rant, against slavery, and the cruelties of slavery in the South, without knowing anything about the institution." In fact, Brownlow lectured, Southern slaves were healthy and happy in the position that God had ordained for them. Abuses might occur elsewhere, the editor conceded, but, "so far as America is concerned, slavery is a blessing to the slave."[34]

Thus, the "Republican North" was deluded, the Parson proclaimed early in 1861, if it thought for a moment that white Southerners were less than unified in their commitment to slavery. Unionists and secessionists "differed" only "as to the *time* and *mode* of resistance" to the threat of Republican aggression. Should convincing evidence emerge that the new administration "contemplated the *subjugation* of the South or the *abolishing* of slavery," the editor assured a New York correspondent later in the spring, "there would not be a Union man among us in twenty-four hours." Turning his sights on Southern secessionists, Brownlow argued that—for the present, at least—slavery was perfectly safe within the Union. Taking the offensive, he contended that secession would actually jeopardize slavery. By precipitating civil war and presenting the North with a rationale for invading the slave states, the fanatic Fire-Eaters would "actually bring about the overthrow of Slavery, one hundred years sooner than the Republican Party could have done it." Far from being "soft" on slavery, Southern Unionists were its only reliable defenders, Brownlow insisted. Rightly understood, the secessionist scheme was "a more consummate Abolition contrivance than ever was devised at the North, by the most ultra anti-slavery men."[35]

While proving to his satisfaction that slavery was safe within the Union and that secession would actually endanger it, the Parson simultaneously asked his readers why so many Southerners were clamoring for secession when it was such an obviously unwise course. The rank and file of secessionists might be dismissed as simply "deluded," he acknowledged, but their leaders were clever and cunning men who must be "seeking their own and not their country's good."[36] What motivated them? In answering his own query, the editor repeatedly stressed partisan, geographic, and class loyalties designed to render the secessionist leadership suspect in the eyes of his audience.

Brownlow began by reminding his readers that the secessionist movement was spearheaded by Democrats. Although both secessionists and Unionists frequently claimed that old party ties had been rendered moot by the sectional crisis, it is impossible to exaggerate the importance of partisan themes in the Parson's case against disunion. The editor had been warring against the devil and the Democratic Party for decades, and, even as the Union was collapsing, there was an eerie continuity to his rhetoric. Part of his role was simply to remind his readers of the moral bankruptcy of the Democratic leadership. At the national level, there were Northern opportunists such as that "wicked liar" James Buchanan, who had spawned an administration remarkable for its "thieving, lying, all-pervading corruption, and wasteful extravagance." Farther South were Fire-Eaters such as the Alabama senator William L. Yancey, a convicted murderer who perfectly embodied the "political charlatanism, truculence, imprudence, unsoundness, and unfaithfulness of the Southern extremists." Democratic leaders closer to home also received their fair share of scorn. The former Tennessee congressman John H. Crozier, the Parson announced, was "one of the most unmitigated scoundrels, cold-blooded hypocrites, insincere and selfish villains" to walk the streets of Knoxville. The local Democratic editor Jacob Sperry was "a contemptible puke" and "the tool of scoundrels," an "unscrupulous liar," "revolting drunkard," and "contemptible coward."[37]

More generically, the editor assaulted the Democratic Party as "a bundle of corrupt factions" led by "corrupt, designing, and unprincipled demagogues." The Breckinridge faction was especially "hypocritical" and "insincere," given that for years they had cynically agitated the slavery question in search of political advantage. Through their hysterical ranting, they had persistently provided the Republican Party with priceless political ammunition, so much so that it was but small exaggeration to say that Southern Democrats were primarily to blame for Republican popularity. Even before Lincoln's election, the Parson had proclaimed: "If the Union is dissolved, and the institutions of the country are overthrown, this vile, designing, corrupt and abominable Democracy are responsible for it." When Lincoln subsequently won the White House, Southern Democratic leaders realized that they would lose out on the patronage and plunder to which they had grown accustomed under the corrupt Buchanan. They then discovered their "principles" and conspired to create a Southern Confederacy, a new vehicle for patronage that promised to be nothing more than "a revival of corrupt Southern Democracy."[38]

This was not entirely bombast. In point of fact, almost every prominent Democrat in East Tennessee did ultimately support secession, with Andrew Johnson being the one glaring exception. Conversely, although not all prominent former Whigs remained Unionists, in East Tennessee almost every prominent Unionist had been a former Whig. It is no surprise, then, that a large part of Parson Brownlow's case for loyalty to the Union was, in fact, a plea for continued loyalty to the old Whig Party. After the Whig Party formally collapsed in the mid-1850s, most East Tennessee Whigs had followed Brownlow into its subsequent incarnations, including the nativist Know-Nothing (or American) Party and the border-state Constitutional Union Party. Echoes of both abounded in the pages of the *Whig*. In early 1861, for example, the editor exhorted his readers in a column titled "Put None on Guard but Union Men!"—a phrase all would have recognized as but one word removed from the old masthead slogan of the *Whig* during its Know-Nothing days: "Put None on Guard but Americans." The editorial went on to exhort readers to support no politician who could not give the countersign "the Union, the Constitution, and the enforcement of the Laws"—the motto of the Constitutional Union Party during the recent presidential campaign. Brownlow assured his readers that four years of Republican rule under Lincoln could be no worse than another four years of Democratic corruption under Buchanan or Breckinridge. The only time that he wavered in that view was when word reached him that the new Republican president planned to take his cues on patronage appointments in East Tennessee from the Democrat Johnson. The Parson's disgust was unreserved. "Whilst I am a Union man, in every sense of the word," he observed bitterly, "I am not to be used in the name of UNION to help re-construct the Democratic Party, whose corruptions, insincerity, demagoguism, and general policy, have brought the country to the verge of ruin."[39]

Complementing the Parson's partisan rhetoric was his castigation of disunion as a plot of the Lower South to serve its own interests. From the moment of South Carolina's secession in December, East Tennessee secessionists maintained that all other issues were superseded by the imperative that the South remain united. Anticipating the argument that Tennessee must stand shoulder to shoulder with its "Sister Southern States," even before Lincoln's election the editor was warning East Tennesseans that, if disunionists should succeed in forming a Southern Confederacy, the wealth and power of the cotton states would inevitably control it, to the detriment of the border states. "We have no interest in common with these Cotton States," he lectured his readers the following January. "We are a grain-growing and stock-raising people, and we can conduct a cheap Government, and live independent, inhabiting the Switzerland of America." As the secession of the Lower South became a reality, and, even more troubling, as support for separation in Middle and West Tennessee became strong, Brownlow even proclaimed that East Tennessee should be prepared to secede from the rest of the state. "We can never live in a Southern Confederacy," he declared, "and be made hewers of wood and drawers of water for a set of aristocrats."[40]

This was not the first time that Brownlow had recommended independent statehood for East Tennessee. Two decades earlier, angry and impatient with the state legislature for ignoring East Tennessee's dire need for transportation improvements, the region's politicians had introduced multiple resolutions calling for an independent mountain state, and the Parson had endorsed them with almost identical language. "We have long enough been 'hewers of wood and drawers of water,' in the hands of Middle Tennesseans," Brownlow had written in 1841. Denouncing Nashville as the *"seat of Dictation,"* he applauded independent statehood as the only way for East Tennesseans to end their subservience to the "lordly inhabitants" of the "Nashville Temple." The proposal actually came close to fruition early in 1842, when both houses of the Tennessee General Assembly passed differing versions of an enabling bill but could not agree on how to reconcile the particulars.[41]

The internal improvements controversy was only the most pronounced episode in a pattern of intrastate rivalry that had long characterized Tennessee politics. In truth, by 1861 East Tennesseans had been suffering from a regional inferiority complex for decades. Knoxville had been the first capital of Tennessee, and the East Tennessee Valley had been the first center of population and wealth in the state. The area had soon been eclipsed by Middle and West Tennessee, however, as migrants from North Carolina and Virginia began bypassing East Tennessee for the more fertile and accessible lands west of the Cumberland Plateau. For the rest of the antebellum period, East Tennessee would remain decidedly the poorest section of the state; on the eve of the Civil War, the average wealth per free family was 60 percent lower there than in the rest of Tennessee. Acknowledging this economic reality, in 1812 the state legislature had voted to move the capital to Nashville. Thereafter, East Tennessee politicians were wont to portray their section of the state as an outlying "province," a political backwater now "passed over and left behind." In warning his readers during the secession crisis that it might be unwise to follow Nashville's lead, the Parson was merely renewing a hoary theme in East Tennessee politics.[42]

Significantly, running throughout Brownlow's condemnation of the Lower South or of Middle and West Tennessee was a thread of populist, class-based rhetoric. Subservience to the Southern Confederacy would be subservience to a "set of aristocrats," the editor stressed. This, too, was but a variation on a tried and true theme. Over the years, the Parson had frequently condemned demagogic politicians who attempted to "array the poor against the rich," but the context of such denunciation was usually an editorial in which he was arraying the poor against the rich. Brownlow regularly stressed that he was a poor man, alluded to his background as a carpenter prior to becoming a Methodist preacher, and identified himself as in sympathy with the "Mechanics, Farmers, and laboring classes." As long as Brownlow was part of a national political party that sought to appeal to all sections of the country—the Whigs or Know Nothings, for example—he confined his assault on "aristocrats" to the members of the "scrub aristocracy" that allegedly dominated his hometown. The Constitutional Union Party garnered almost no support south of Tennessee, however, and, by the presidential campaign of 1860, Brownlow felt little compunction about populist attacks on the Lower South; after the beginning of the secession crisis, he felt none at all.[43]

A new Southern Confederacy would be ruled by a "Slave Oligarchy," Brownlow announced toward the end of the presidential campaign. Only slaveholders would be accorded the franchise, which would eliminate not only the Irish and German vote but also "the native poor of our own country." When the Alabama senator William Yancey stopped off in Knoxville to speak on behalf of John Breckinridge, he played right into the Parson's hands. Seeking to underscore the importance of slavery to nonslaveholding whites, the Fire-Eater reminded his audience that slavery preserved for them a privileged position by sparing them from "menial service." Yancey contrasted this with the degradation of white workers in the North, where "white women stand over the tub and cook" and white men "black boots and drive carriages." Brownlow seized on the comment, and the next several issues of the *Whig* featured a crude drawing of a white woman standing at a washtub, accompanied by the editor's explanation that she was "degrading" herself by "menial service." "That sort of slur upon honest labor may do in South Alabama, among purse-proud aristocratic Democrats," Brownlow observed caustically, but not in East Tennessee, where only a tenth of white men actually owned slaves and their wives and daughters often "wash, cook, and milk cows, without ever suspecting that they were performing menial services!"[44]

In truth, Brownlow's audience was likely quite sensitive to a perceived "slur upon honest labor." As the editor suggested, most East Tennesseans were no strangers to hard work. What is more, many were undoubtedly dependent on others for their daily bread. In the Parson's hometown, for example, nearly three-quarters of adult white males in 1860 held "blue-collar" jobs, and nearly half of these were unskilled or semiskilled workers, laboring as gardeners, cooks, waiters, woodcutters, teamsters, or generic "day laborers." In the countryside, a similar pattern could be found. Perhaps as many as one-fourth of agricultural households were headed by men who hired out as farm laborers, while almost as large a proportion rented the farms that they worked. In four counties of upper East Tennessee that have been systematically studied, fully 43 percent of farm families owned no land of their own. By comparison, studies of landholding patterns in the Lower South place the proportion of free agricultural households without land at 19 percent in southern Alabama, 25 percent in the Mississippi Delta, 24 percent in southern Georgia, and 26 percent in east Texas. Clearly, landlessness was much greater in East Tennessee than in the Black Belt of the Lower South, which also suggests that whites were much more likely to engage in the kind of "menial labor" that Yancey derided.[45]

As the states of the Lower South began to secede, then, it is small wonder that Parson Brownlow increased his populist assault against disunion. The Southern Confederacy would make the ownership of land and slaves a qualification for voting, he again insisted. "The border States can never live in peace with such men." Their goal was to establish a "Slavery Aristocracy" which would "overshadow and dishonor poor white men." Although they decried the "Black Republican" quest for racial equality, they were secretly just as opposed to equality among whites. "We never thought it a disgrace to labor, or to eat bread and meat 'by the sweat of the brow,'" the editor boasted. In contrast, the "nabobs of Cottonocracy" had nothing but contempt for laboring men; indeed, they welcomed the collapse of the Union as an opportunity to roll back the democratic advances of the past two generations. In the war that was bound to ensue, however, they would force the "honest yeomanry" of the border states to leave their wives and children and "fight for the purse-proud aristocrats of the Cotton States, whose pecuniary abilities [would] enable them to hire substitutes!" In sum, secession would be devastating for the common folk, who had little to gain and much to lose in the slaveholders' irresponsible and reckless "revolution."[46]

That revolution proceeded, of course, and, notwithstanding all the Parson's efforts, Tennessee formally joined in it during those furious and frenzied first weeks after the attack on Fort Sumter. Once the majority had spoken, however, most East Tennessee Unionists remained opposed to the Confederacy and supported it begrudgingly. They actually petitioned the state legislature (yet again) for permission to form a separate state, and, when their request was predictably denied, most opted for what amounted to a course of neutrality, staying home, keeping their mouths shut, and hoping to be left alone. Although the vast majority rejected outright resistance to the Confederacy as suicidal, from the beginning there were those who believed otherwise. Small bands participated in sensational acts of sabotage in the fall of 1861, while hundreds more made the dangerous trek through the mountains into Kentucky in order to enlist in the Union Army. When the Confederate Congress passed its first Conscription Act in April 1862, furthermore, the trickle of refugees to Kentucky became a flood, as East Tennesseans concluded that Parson Brownlow had been right in his prediction: the Confederate government was going to force the "honest yeomanry" to finish a war that wealthy slaveholders had begun. The Confederate commander in East Tennessee estimated that as many as seven thousand East Tennesseans crossed the border into Kentucky during the first ten days after the measure was passed. Before all was said and done, the region would send more than thirty thousand men into the Union army, a total greater than from such officially loyal states as Rhode Island, Delaware, and Minnesota. Consequently, when Brownlow addressed the New York Academy of Music in May 1862, it was not difficult to convince his admiring audience of the "uncompromising" and "unconditional" Unionism of his homeland.[47]

The evidence presented here has pointed to a different understanding, however. During the secession crisis, William Brownlow never encouraged voters simply to choose between their commitment to the Union and all other loyalties. Rather, he understood that for East Tennesseans—as for Americans generally—allegiance to the Union coexisted with numerous other forms of group loyalty, which either weakened or reinforced it. When Fire-Eaters began to clamor for secession, he countered their arguments, not primarily by appealing to patriotism, but by stressing a combination of other, more parochial attachments—to slavery, to the Whig Party, to East Tennessee, and to the working class. While the *New York Times* might marvel at how East Tennesseans' patriotism overwhelmed every other commitment, it seems more likely that their opposition to secession was so persistent because they could view Unionism as entirely compatible with a number of other forms of allegiance they held dear.

Notes

1. *New York Daily Tribune,* May 14, 1862; *New York Times,* April 1, May 22, 1862; *National Anti-Slavery Standard* (New York), May 24, 1862; W. G. Brownlow, *Sketches of the Rise, Progress, and Decline of Secession* (Philadelphia: George W. Childs, 1862), 7.

2. I discuss Brownlow's Northern tour in some detail in *Lincolnites and Rebels: A Divided Town in the American Civil War* (New York: Oxford University Press, 2006), 111–15.

3. Richard B. Drake correctly notes that Brownlow was a primary architect of one of the first popular stereotypes of the Southern mountaineer: the image of the "hard-pressed lover of freedom who held strongly to the Union" (Drake quoted in Steve Humphrey, *"That D——d Brownlow"* [Boone, N.C.: Appalachian Consortium Press, 1978], viii). Brownlow fleshed out the stereotype in a series of public lectures across the North in the spring and summer of 1862. For coverage of those speeches, see *Chicago Tribune,* April 11, 1862; *New York Times,* April 1, 3, May 14, 22, 1862; *New York Daily Tribune,* May 16, 20, 1862; *National Anti-Slavery Standard,* May 24, 1862; *Public Ledger* (Philadelphia), April 19, June 14, 1862; *Boston Daily Evening Transcript,* May 24, 1862; *Christian Recorder,* May 31, June 21, 1862; *Saturday Evening Post,* April 26, 1862; and *Ladies Repository* 22, no. 7 (July 1862): 388. After the war, other East Tennessee writers enthusiastically perpetuated the stereotype. See Thomas W. Humes, *The Loyal Mountaineers of Tennessee* (Knoxville: Ogden Bros., 1888); Will A. McTeer, *Among Loyal Mountaineers* (Maryville, Tenn.: n.p., n.d.); William Rule, *The Loyalists of Tennessee in the Late War* (Cincinnati: H. C. Sherick, 1887); Oliver P. Temple, *East Tennessee and the Civil War* (Cincinnati: Robert Clarke, 1899); and William R. Carter, *History of the First Regiment of Tennessee Volunteer Cavalry in the Great War of the Rebellion* (Knoxville: Gaut-Ogden, 1902).

4. Because opposition to separation could reflect a variety of motives other than an ideological commitment to the Union per se, there is an argument for dispensing altogether with the label *Unionist.* In his recent study of the Civil War in the north Georgia mountains, e.g., Jonathan Sarris labels opponents of secession *anti-Confederates,* rightly noting that, while *Unionism* could mean many things in North Georgia, "rarely did it mean a philosophical commitment to the ideals of national unity." The label *anti-Confederate* is technically more applicable in East Tennessee as well, but I prefer the traditional term *Unionist* as less cumbersome and truer to the terminology employed at the time. See Jonathan Dean Sarris, *A Separate Civil War: Communities in Conflict in the Mountain South* (Charlottesville: University of Virginia Press, 2006), 79.

5. William T. Sherman to Ulysses S. Grant, December 1, 1863, in U.S. War Department, *The War of the Rebellion: A Compilation of the Official Records of the Union and Confederate Armies, 1861–1865* (hereafter cited as *OR*), 70 vols. in 128 pts. (Washington, D.C.: U.S. Government Printing Office, 1880–1901), ser. 1, vol. 31, pt. 3, p. 297.

6. William W. Freehling, *The South vs. the South: How Anti-Confederate Southerners Shaped the Course of the Civil War* (New York: Oxford University Press, 2001); George C. Rable, *The Confederate Republic: A Revolution against Politics* (Chapel Hill: University of North Carolina Press, 1994); Paul Escott, *After Secession: Jefferson Davis and the Failure of Confederate Nationalism* (Baton Rouge: Louisiana State University Press, 1978).

7. Hermann Bokum, *The Tennessee Handbook and Immigrants' Guide* (Philadelphia: J. B. Lippincott, 1868), 8; Humes, *Loyal Mountaineers of Tennessee*, 19–35; J. B. Killebrew, *Introduction to the Resources of Tennessee* (Nashville: Tavel, Eastman & Howell, 1874), 423–47; Eugene W. Hilgard, *Report on Cotton Production in the United States* (Washington, D.C.: U.S. Government Printing Office, 1884), 409–11; Robert Tracy McKenzie, "Wealth and Income: The Preindustrial Structure of East Tennessee in 1860," *Appalachian Journal* 21 (1994): 260–79.

8. Mark E. Neely Jr., *Southern Rights: Political Prisoners and the Myth of Confederate Constitutionalism* (Charlottesville: University Press of Virginia, 1999), 104.

9. For overviews of the second-party system in Tennessee, see Paul H. Bergeron, *Antebellum Politics in Tennessee* (Lexington: University Press of Kentucky, 1982); and Jonathan M. Atkins, *Parties, Politics, and the Sectional Conflict in Tennessee, 1832–1861* (Knoxville: University of Tennessee Press, 1997).

10. The statewide tally was 69,387 against secession and 57,798 in favor. See Paul H. Bergeron, Stephen V. Ash, and Jeanette Keith, *Tennesseans and Their History* (Knoxville: University of Tennessee Press, 1999), 134–35; and Mary E. R. Campbell, *The Attitudes of Tennesseans toward the Union, 1847–1861* (New York: Vantage, 1961), and "The Significance of the Unionist Victory in the Election of February 9, 1861 in Tennessee," *East Tennessee Historical Society's Papers* 14 (1942): 25–27.

11. Statewide, the vote was 108,418–46,996 in favor of the declaration. In East Tennessee, the count was 32,753–14,617 against it. Campbell, *Attitudes of Tennesseans*, 291–94.

12. Charles Faulkner Bryan, "The Civil War in East Tennessee: A Social, Political, and Economic Study" (Ph.D. diss., University of Tennessee, 1978); Noel C. Fisher, *War at Every Door: Partisan Politics and Guerilla Violence in East Tennessee, 1860–1869* (Chapel Hill: University of North Carolina Press, 1997); John

Derrick Fowler, *Mountaineers in Gray: The Story of the Nineteenth Tennessee Volunteer Infantry Regiment, C.S.A.* (Knoxville: University of Tennessee Press, 2004); W. Todd Groce, *Mountain Rebels: East Tennessee Confederates and the Civil War, 1860–1870* (Knoxville: University of Tennessee Press, 1999); John C. Inscoe, "Mountain Unionism, Secession, and Regional Self-Image: The Contrasting Cases of Western North Carolina and East Tennessee," in *Looking South: Chapters in the Story of an American Region,* ed. Winfred B. Moore Jr. and Joseph F. Tripp (New York: Greenwood, 1989), 115–29.

13. E. Merton Coulter, *William G. Brownlow: Fighting Parson of the Southern Highlands* (Chapel Hill: University of North Carolina Press, 1937), 36, 61, 225. For a brief discussion of Coulter's aggressive defense of the South, see Thomas J. Pressly, *Americans Interpret Their Civil War* (New York: Free Press, 1955), 286–87. There have been two other extended treatments of Brownlow, but both are narrowly focused. See Royal Forrest Conklin, "The Public Speaking Career of William Gannaway (Parson) Brownlow" (Ph.D. diss., Ohio University, 1967); and Humphrey, "*That D——d Brownlow.*" Conklin's work was a School of Communications dissertation that focused on the effectiveness of Brownlow's public speaking. Humphrey was a retired newspaper reporter who concentrated primarily on Brownlow's success at generating a wide readership.

14. William Gillespie McBride, "Blacks and the Race Issue in Tennessee Politics, 1865–1876" (Ph.D. diss., Vanderbilt University, 1989); *Tennessee Historical Quarterly* 41 (1982): 100. For assessments of Brownlow since Coulter's, see esp. Thomas B. Alexander, "Strange Bedfellows: The Interlocking Careers of T. A. R. Nelson, Andrew Johnson, and W. G. (Parson) Brownlow," *East Tennessee Historical Society's Publications* 24 (1952): 68–91; Ralph W. Haskins, "Internecine Strife in Tennessee: Andrew Johnson versus Parson Brownlow," *Tennessee Historical Quarterly* 24 (1965): 321–40; Conklin, "Public Speaking Career of Brownlow"; Humphrey, "*That D——d Brownlow*"; and James C. Kelly, "William Gannaway Brownlow," *Tennessee Historical Quarterly* 43 (1984): 25–43, 155–72.

15. *Knoxville Whig,* May 12, 1860, April 27, May 25, October 12, 1861; *Brownlow's Knoxville Whig and Rebel Ventilator,* January 9, 1864.

16. *Jonesborough Whig,* May 14, 1840; Kelly, "William Gannaway Brownlow," 169.

17. On this point, see esp. Kelly, "William Gannaway Brownlow," 31.

18. *Tennessee Sentinel* (Jonesborough), quoted in Humphrey, "*That D——d Brownlow,*" 63.

19. Kelly, "William Gannaway Brownlow," 31; R. N. Price, "William G. Brownlow and His Times," in *Holston Methodism: From Its Origin to the Present Time,* 5 vols. (Nashville: Methodist Episcopal Church, 1906–1913), 3:320.

20. See, e.g., Oliver P. Temple, *Notable Men of Tennessee from 1833 to 1875: Their Times and Their Contemporaries* (New York: Cosmopolitan, 1912), 29; and Samuel Mayes Arnell, "The Southern Unionist," 57, unpublished manuscript, Special Collections Division, University of Tennessee Libraries.

21. *Knoxville Daily Register,* October 23, 1861; Bird G. Manard to Thomas A. R. Nelson, June 28, 1865, in Thomas A. R. Nelson Papers, McClung Historical Collection, Knox County Public Library. See also *Knoxville Daily Register,* February 9, 1862.

22. *Portrait and Biography of Parson Brownlow, the Tennessee Patriot* (Indianapolis: Asher, 1862), 30; Brownlow, *Sketches of Secession,* 5; *Chicago Tribune,* April 11, 1862. See also *Public Ledger,* April 19, 1862; *New York Daily Tribune,* May 14, 1862.

23. Hermann Bokum, *Wanderings North and South* (Philadelphia: King & Baird, 1864), 13, 18; "Message of the President of the United States Transmitting an Address of the 'East Tennessee Relief Association,'" 38th Cong., 1st Sess., Senate Executive Document 40 (Washington, D.C.: U.S. Government Printing Office, 1864), 2; Humes, *Loyal Mountaineers of Tennessee,* 11.

24. *Knoxville Whig,* April 28, July 21, 28, August 25, September 8, 1860.

25. *Knoxville Whig,* October 13, 1860. See also *Knoxville Whig,* February 9, 1861.

26. *The Official and Political Manual of the State of Tennessee* (Nashville: Marshall & Bruce, 1890), 81.

27. *Knoxville Whig,* February 9, 1861.

28. William H. Sneed, "To the Voters of Knox County," *Knoxville Whig,* February 2, 1861. Significantly, even the Tennessee General Assembly eventually defined the question of disunion in terms of revolution. Alone among the states that joined the Confederacy, Tennessee never formally seceded. When the state legislature voted in May 1861 to sunder its tie with the Union, it explicitly "waiv[ed] any expression of opinion as to the abstract doctrine of secession," passing instead a "declaration of independence." See *Official and Political Manual of the State of Tennessee,* 84.

29. *Knoxville Whig,* October 6, 20, November 24, 1860.

30. See, e.g., *Portrait and Biography of Parson Brownlow,* 30.

31. *Knoxville Whig,* March 30, April 27, 1861.

32. *Knoxville Register,* September 27, 1860; *Knoxville Whig,* October 27, 1860, February 23, 1861.

33. Temple, *East Tennessee and the Civil War,* 85–105, 111–20; Richard B. Drake, "Slavery and Antislavery in Appalachia," *Appalachian Heritage* 14 (1986): 29–30; Durwood Dunn, *An Abolitionist in the Appalachian South: Ezekiel Birds-*

eye on Slavery, Capitalism, and Separate Statehood in East Tennessee, 1841–1846 (Knoxville: University of Tennessee Press, 1997); Petitions 25-1834, 40-1834, Legislative Petitions, Tennessee State Library and Archives.

34. *Knoxville Whig*, February 25, May 12, June 23, November 10, 1860. On Brownlow's earlier debate with Pryne, see *Ought American Slavery to Be Perpetuated? A Debate between Rev. W. G. Brownlow and Rev. A. Pryne* (Philadelphia: Lippincott, 1858).

35. *Knoxville Whig*, December 15, 1860, January 19, May 18, 1861. For similar arguments from other East Tennessee Unionists, see Temple, *East Tennessee and the Civil War*, 119–20; Horace Maynard, "How, by Whom, and for What Was the War Begun? Speech of Hon. Horace Maynard Delivered in the City of Nashville, March 20, 1862" (n.p., n.d.), Special Collections, University of Tennessee Libraries.

36. *Knoxville Whig*, May 4, 1861.

37. *Knoxville Whig*, April 28, June 16, October 27, 1860, May 25, June 1, 1861.

38. *Knoxville Whig*, March 10, May 5, 1860, March 23, May 4, 1861.

39. *Knoxville Whig*, February 23, March 9, April 6, 1861.

40. *Knoxville Whig*, September 29, 1860, January 26, 1861.

41. Eric Russell Lacy, *Vanquished Volunteers: East Tennessee Sectionalism from Statehood to Secession* (Johnson City: East Tennessee State University Press, 1965), 111–27; Stanley J. Folmsbee, "Sectionalism and Internal Improvements in Tennessee, 1796–1845" (Ph.D. diss., University of Pennsylvania, 1939), 177–215; *Jonesborough Whig and Independent Journal*, December 8, 15, 1841. Even had the General Assembly been able to agree on an enabling measure, it is far from certain that the U.S. Congress would have given its consent as well. Northern congressmen, in particular, may have been loath to approve the creation of a new slave state from within an existing one.

42. Inscoe, "Mountain Unionism," 125; Lacy, *Vanquished Volunteers*, 47–50.

43. *Knoxville Whig*, June 2, July 29, 1849, January 12, 1850.

44. *Knoxville Whig*, September 22, 29, October 13, 1860.

45. For occupational data and landownership patterns in Knoxville and East Tennessee, see McKenzie, *Lincolnites and Rebels*, 40–41, and "Wealth and Income," 265–69. For statistics on the Lower South, see Frederick A. Bode and Donald L. Ginter, *Farm Tenancy and the Census in Antebellum Georgia* (Athens: University of Georgia Press, 1986), app. D; and Randolph B. Campbell and Richard G. Lowe, *Wealth and Power in Antebellum Texas* (College Station: Texas A&M University Press, 1977), 108–11.

46. *Knoxville Whig,* January 26, March 2, 30, 1861, December 22, 1860.

47. *OR,* ser. 1, vol. 10, pt. 2, pp. 453–54, 521; Richard Nelson Current, *Lincoln's Loyalists: Union Soldiers from the Confederacy* (Boston: Northeastern University Press, 1992), 215. There are no precise figures relating to Federal enlistments specifically from East Tennessee, but Current conservatively estimates the number of white Union volunteers from the state as a whole at about forty-two thousand. Because nearly three-quarters of the ballots against secession in the state referendum were cast in East Tennessee, it seems reasonable that at least three-quarters of Union enlistments originated from there as well.

"We can never live in a southern confederacy"

The Civil War in East Tennessee

John D. Fowler

"We can never live in a southern confederacy and be made hewers of wood and drawers of water for a set of aristocrats and overbearing tyrants," asserted William G. "Parson" Brownlow, the publisher of the *Knoxville Whig*, as the debate over secession echoed through the hollows, coves, and mountains of East Tennessee. The itinerant Methodist minister and newspaper editor's words reached a receptive audience. While Middle and West Tennessee embraced secession following Lincoln's call for troops to quell the rebellion in the Deep South, the majority of East Tennesseans refused to abandon their allegiance to the old Union. This precipitated an internecine struggle within the unfolding national conflict. East Tennessee's stance involved more than just state sectionalism; it also involved a rejection of the Confederate South and its values. Historians have long studied the story of how and why these "loyal mountaineers" resisted the Confederacy but have until recently ignored their secessionist neighbors. Fortunately, modern scholars are now examining all aspects of the Civil War in Appalachia.[1]

What follows is an analysis of East Tennessee's struggle. Why was East Tennessee so different from the rest of the South? Why did some East Tennesseans support the Confederacy while most did not? How did the war and Reconstruction affect the people of this region—Rebels, loyalists, and slaves? The answers to these questions reveal a personal war waged not only by the Federal and Confederate armies but also by secessionist and Unionist guerrillas and brigands. Each of these groups had different agendas, and, as a result, East Tennessee fought a complex war on the economic, social, and intellectual levels as well as the traditional political and military ones.[2]

East Tennessee rejected the rest of the state and the South for three interrelated reasons: economics, politics, and, most important, geography. The state's terrain provides a natural boundary between Tennessee's three Grand Divisions. West Tennessee is generally flat, and Middle Tennessee is characterized by rolling hills. East Tennessee, however, is predominantly a land of steep and rugged mountains and narrow coves. Only the Great Valley running through East Tennessee contains large farm acreage. Consequently, East Tennessee's geography has isolated it from the rest of the state and nation since early white settlement.[3]

This geographic isolation influenced the economic development of the region. East Tennessee, with its small subsistence farms and limited number of slaves, shared little in common with the slave-based plantation economy that dominated most of the South. Not until the construction in the 1850s of the East Tennessee and Virginia and the East Tennessee and Georgia railroads did the region have a cheap and reliable means to deliver agricultural products to market and, thus, join the national economy. Even with this new mode of transportation, only those farmers closest to the few shipping routes really profited from access to the market economy.[4]

The railroads also spawned new urban commercial classes in the towns now connected to the larger world. Almost at once, a growing economic disparity developed between the minority living near the rail lines of the Great Valley and the majority inhabiting the more isolated areas of the region. As the Civil War drew near, the townspeople and commercial farmers linked to the rest of the Southern and national economy enjoyed greater wealth and a higher standard of living than the subsistence farmers. This disparity cultivated resentment. Indeed, early accounts of the conflict between the region's secessionists and loyalists pointed to economics as the key factor separating the two sides and creating, in essence, a class war. A comparison of the wealth of an East Tennessee Confederate regiment and an East Tennessee Union regiment supports this notion. The households of a sample of the Nineteenth Tennessee Volunteer Infantry, CSA, held 122 percent greater real and personal property than their Unionist counterparts in the Third Tennessee Volunteer Infantry, USA. Astonishingly, the Nineteenth held a combined wealth of more than $3 million, which was more than fifteen of East Tennessee's thirty-one counties combined.[5]

The economic discord ties in with a final divisive factor: political affiliation. The isolated mountaineers of the region traditionally had supported the Whig Party and its remnant, the "Opposition" Party. This party supported economic expansion and development. At first glance, therefore, it may appear odd that the large-scale farmers and urban elite who constituted the region's secessionists were more often Democrats than Whigs. Traditionally, such professions, residence patterns, and market orientation were associated with Whig ideology. However, antebellum party affiliation cannot always be explained in tidy generalizations. It had as much to do with intangibles such as community and family heritage, the persuasiveness and charisma of political leaders, the party preference of rivals, and the influence of elite families as it did with the ideological and political issues. Moreover, those linked to the new towns and Deep South trade joined the other regions of Tennessee and the greater South in supporting the Democratic Party, which had dominated Southern politics at least since the 1850s. Resentful of Middle Tennessee's power, most East Tennesseans preferred to remain Whigs.[6]

Closely tied to political affiliation was the belief in republicanism prevalent during the antebellum period, a belief that, in part, warned the electorate to be ever vigilant for those who would attempt to destroy the Republic and establish a tyranny. The majority of East Tennesseans then rejected the Confederacy out of the belief that such a government, dominated by large slaveholding aristocrats, threatened republican liberty—the very soul of the great American democratic experiment. For the loyalists of East Tennessee, the protection of republicanism required a rebellion against the tyranny of Governor Isham Harris and Jefferson Davis. Conversely, the region's secessionists, like most of their Southern brethren, came to view Abraham Lincoln's administration as the threat to republican government.[7]

While geography, economics, and politics can explain much of the division between secessionists and loyalists in East Tennessee, they cannot explain support in every case. For example, only one-third of the men in the sample of the Nineteenth Tennessee were wealthy; the other two-thirds owned little or no property. Factors such as the influence of local elites, community pressure, kinship, and patriotism cannot be overlooked

as motiving factors for them, other Confederates, or their Unionist neighbors. Indeed, myriad factors spurred the people of the eastern counties to
choose sides in the coming conflict. In essence, the region's white inhabitants fought to determine the fate not only of two nations but also of their
own homes, farms, families, and futures since the losers in this struggle
could hardly expect to remain in the region they called home.[8]

Following Abraham Lincoln's election in November 1860, the Lower
South left the Union. The secession crisis presented Tennesseans with a
dilemma. While most whites abhorred abolitionism, they perceived disunion as a threat to the future of the republican experiment. A cautious
wait-and-see attitude struck most East Tennesseans as the prudent course.
Governor Harris, however, viewed the situation much differently. He saw
little hope in a compromise to save the old Union and wanted to place Tennessee in the new Confederacy. The General Assembly, however, chose to
let the people decide. It authorized a February 1861 referendum to decide
whether to hold a state convention on secession and, if so, which delegates
to send. When the votes were counted, Unionists across the state had won
an overwhelming victory. The convention itself was narrowly defeated,
but Union delegates accounted for more than four-fifths of the total. East
Tennessee gave the strongest support to the loyalists, with 80 percent of
the voters rejecting the convention and about 85 percent voting for Unionist delegates. The outcome proved that most citizens of the Volunteer State,
especially East Tennesseans, wished to remain in the Union.[9]

The assault on Fort Sumter and Lincoln's subsequent call for volunteers changed everything. Amid cheers at the state capitol on the evening
of April 17, 1861, Governor Harris declared that, before he would fulfill
the secretary of war's request for two regiments to help conquer the South,
he would sever his right arm. The telegram the governor sent in response
to Lincoln's call for troops defiantly asserted: "Tennessee will not furnish
a Single Man for the purposes of Coercion but 50,000 if necessary for the
defense of our rights and those of our Southern brothers."[10]

Harris and the legislature hastily prepared to excise Tennessee from
the Union and ally it with the Confederacy. In early May, Tennessee declared its independence from the United States. Cognizant of the need
for popular support for such actions, the legislature authorized a second
referendum on June 8 on the issue of independence. East Tennesseans
responded immediately. In mid-May, a group of prominent Knoxvillians,

including Brownlow and Oliver P. Temple, called for a Unionist convention. On May 30, four hundred delegates convened in Knoxville for two days, issuing proclamations condemning secession, and preparing to canvass the region to drum up support for the Unionist cause. Despite their efforts, the results of the referendum stunned East Tennessee Unionists. While 69 percent of East Tennessee rejected secession, 70 percent of the state's voters approved of it. The Volunteer State had joined the Confederacy.[11]

Undeterred, nine days after the June vote, 285 loyalist delegates convened in Greeneville to plan a course of action. After much debate between moderates, who advocated negotiation with Nashville, and radicals, who demanded immediate action, the convention decided to petition the state legislature for separate statehood. The General Assembly listened politely and then quashed the request. East Tennessee would remain part of a state and of a nation that it had rejected. Confederate authorities at the state and national level now hoped that the loyalists of the eastern counties would align with the state in secession, but this was not to be the case. The region's Unionists would never willingly submit to Confederate rule, and East Tennessee would soon be plunged into a state of violence and bloodshed that would not end until long after the final shots of the Civil War.[12]

The Confederacy needed East Tennessee's railroads, which linked the resources of the Deep South to the battlefields in Virginia. As Confederate soldiers began patrolling the rail lines, Unionists began organizing and drilling militia companies. The proximity of these two opposing groups made armed conflict a real threat. Nonetheless, Governor Harris was confident that the region's loyalists could be won over, and he initiated what would be the Confederacy's first policy toward East Tennessee's Unionists—that of conciliation. Anxious to calm the fears of military despotism, Harris advised President Jefferson Davis to limit the number of Confederate troops in the region and to employ only Tennessee troops. He also successfully urged Davis to appoint Brig. Gen. Felix K. Zollicoffer, a Tennessee native, as the head of the newly created Department of East Tennessee. Harris argued that Zollicoffer's ties to the old Whig Party would allow him to influence the Unionists.[13]

Through the summer of 1861, Zollicoffer attempted to mollify loyalists by doing little to quell Unionist activities. This was partially because of the appeasement policy and partially because of his lack of manpower. With limited numbers of troops, all lacking proper equipment and training, the general could only garrison the major towns and mountain passes, guard the railroads, and conduct sporadic patrols into the hinterland. He certainly could not prevent determined Unionist meetings and drills.[14]

The state's congressional and gubernatorial elections in early August revealed that, despite the best efforts of Harris and Zollicoffer, East Tennessee's loyalists had not acquiesced to Confederate rule. The Unionists demonstrated their determination and disaffection by voting for Harris's rival for the governor's seat, William H. Polk, by a large margin. Moreover, they rejected the ratification of the Confederate Constitution and, worse still, elected four representatives to the U.S. Congress rather than the Confederate Congress. The election results embarrassed and angered both Harris and Zollicoffer. The defiance of the region's loyalists in the face of leniency exacted a swift change in Confederate policy. Throughout East Tennessee, Confederate troops began to disperse loyalist groups and arrest their leaders.[15]

Harris's change in attitude mirrored Richmond's harsher policy against Unionist sympathizers. In August 1861, the Confederate Congress passed key legislation that profoundly affected East Tennessee. The first piece, an alien enemies act, stated that citizens of a hostile nation over fourteen years of age living within the Confederacy were liable for arrest and expulsion. President Davis applied the law to East Tennessee and demanded that all residents of the region swear an oath of allegiance by October. The Confederate Congress also passed the "sequestration law," which provided for the seizure of real and personal property belonging to alien enemies. East Tennessee Unionists faced the loss not only of their livelihood but also of their liberty if they did not comply with the laws. Civil authorities in East Tennessee strictly enforced the new legislation, generating animosity that would haunt the region for years.[16]

East Tennessee was a powder keg of disaffected loyalists and frustrated secessionists. In the summer of 1861, the keg exploded. While Zollicoffer moved most of the region's Confederate troops into eastern Kentucky as part of Gen. Albert Sidney Johnston's defensive line protecting the western Confederacy, Confederate fears of insurrection in East Tennessee mounted, and rightly so. The ardent Unionist and Presbyterian minister William B. Carter journeyed to Washington, D.C., where he presented a daring plan to Federal officials, including Abraham Lincoln, Maj. Gen.

George B. McClellan, the general-in-chief, and Senator Andrew Johnson. Carter proposed that he organize a group of saboteurs that would destroy nine key railroad bridges stretching across East Tennessee from Alabama to Virginia while a Federal force under Maj. Gen. George Thomas invaded the region from Kentucky. A mass uprising of Unionists would then surface amid the chaos. Unable to receive reinforcements because of the destroyed bridges, and facing invasion and a revolt, Confederate resistance would disintegrate.[17]

The plan appeared sound, and Carter left for home believing that he had secured the requisite support. He had not. On November 8, 1861, the saboteurs struck, burning only five bridges but disrupting Confederate communications and generating panic. Maj. Gen. William T. Sherman failed, however, to issue Thomas the order to move into East Tennessee, preferring instead to hold his forces for a strike into Middle Tennessee. Uninformed of any change in plan, bands of Unionists gathered for an uprising that did not occur.[18]

News of the bridge burnings and armed Unionists traveled quickly, and Confederate authorities moved to secure the railroads and crush the "revolt." Zollicoffer, then in Kentucky, declared martial law, ordered the arrest of Unionist leaders, and directed the disarming of all Unionists. Ultimately, Confederate authorities in East Tennessee hanged five of the bridge burners and sent four to prison in a massive roundup of loyalists. All across the region, jails overflowed with those accused of complicity or disloyalty to the Confederacy. Frustrated with the situation, the Davis administration replaced Zollicoffer as commander of the Department of East Tennessee with Maj. Gen. George Crittenden. The subsequent rout of Confederate forces at Mill Springs in January 1862, however, coupled with an agonizing retreat into Middle Tennessee, left Zollicoffer dead and revealed Crittenden's inadequacies as a general.[19]

The bridge burnings and the Confederate disaster at Mill Springs threw East Tennessee Confederates into a panic, and this panic ignited retaliation. Mass arrests and confiscations replaced conciliation as Rebel authorities initiated a new phase in their rule of East Tennessee, a phase that sought to terrorize the region's loyalists into submission. Under this new onslaught, Unionists could submit, passively resist, or flee to Kentucky to join the Union army. Many chose the latter. Those crossing the mountains into Kentucky faced increased Confederate patrols. Guides called *pilots* led thousands into the Bluegrass State. Once there, most joined the Federal Army. Indeed, nearly all the thirty thousand or so white Tennesseans who joined up came from East Tennessee.[20]

Guerrillas who wished to fight augmented this massive number of volunteers. Unionist partisans began raiding into the region by the winter of 1861–1862. Because of their knowledge of the terrain and the local support they received, they proved impossible to eradicate. The partisans sought revenge for the harshness of Confederate rule by ambushing isolated Rebel troops or raiding secessionists' homesteads. As this guerrilla war continued into 1862, Confederate soldiers grew increasingly frustrated and more brutal in their attempts to destroy the insurgents. Atrocities on both sides mounted.[21]

In March 1862, the Confederate War Department ordered Maj. Gen. Edmund Kirby Smith to the region to restore order and defuse the tense situation. His arrival initiated a third phase in the Confederate occupation of the region. During this phase, Smith and the Confederate authorities in Richmond vacillated between conciliation and coercion. From his arrival, Smith viewed the region as an "enemy's country" and endeavored to convince the Davis administration to assume the same stance. He held local East Tennessee Confederate troops in contempt and petitioned Richmond to send them south, where they could be made loyal. He also wanted to arrest Unionist leaders in order to curb their influence on the population and eagerly enforced the new congressional act requiring loyalty oaths for all civil servants, under threat of arrest for noncompliance. Responding to Smith's pleas for martial law, in April Davis suspended the writ of habeas corpus in East Tennessee and rewarded Smith with control of the courts. The families of prominent Unionists such as William G. Brownlow, Horace Maynard, and Andrew Johnson were expelled from the region, and Smith threatened to expel the families and seize the property of all Unionists fighting in the Union army as well. Worse still, on April 16, the Confederate Congress passed the first of three conscription laws making every white male between the ages of eighteen and thirty-five eligible for the draft. Most citizens across the South resented conscription, even in areas of strong Confederate support. In East Tennessee, the act generated a virtual exodus of Unionists heading for Kentucky. Not since the bridge burnings had there been a more polarizing event.[22]

Having wielded his authority and power, Smith hoped that he could

now win over loyalists with benevolence. On April 18, he issued a proclamation offering amnesty to any East Tennessean taking an oath to the
Confederacy, including those in the Union army, provided they returned
within thirty days. He also suspended service in the state militia. On August 13, he sweetened the deal by offering to buy any arms brought in by
East Tennesseans leaving Federal service. Smith even suspended Confederate conscription in the hope of mollifying the Unionists and stopping
the flood of recruits into the Federal army. Despite this carrot-and-stick
approach, the hearts and minds of the region's loyalist population did not
waver.[23]

When Smith left East Tennessee in the ill-fated invasion of Kentucky
in the summer of 1862, the Confederate War Department insisted that
his temporary successors—John P. McCown, a native East Tennessean,
and Maj. Gen. Samuel Jones—enforce conscription. Endeavoring to win
Unionist support, Jones persuaded Unionist leader T. A. R. Nelson to issue
a public statement condemning the preliminary Emancipation Proclamation, encouraging the acceptance of Confederate rule, and urging Richmond to suspend again the draft in East Tennessee. Nelson's statement fell
on deaf ears, as did Jones's call to suspend conscription.[24]

Smith's return in October 1862 did nothing to change Confederate
policy in the region, and the general left East Tennessee for good in early
1863, to be replaced by Maj. Gen. Daniel Donelson, who subsequently
would be replaced by Maj. Gen. Simon B. Buckner in May 1863. The administration of these two generals marked the last phase of Confederate
occupation, in which Richmond accepted that East Tennessee was, indeed, an "enemy's country." Neither Donelson nor Buckner could woo the
Unionist population. Confederate policies of conscription, sequestration,
and taxation, as well as the increasingly antagonistic attitude of Confederate occupation forces, prevented any hope of a peaceful coexistence.[25]

Unionist guerrillas, with the open support of the local population,
continued to raid the region, and, by late August 1863, as Buckner moved
his forces out of upper East Tennessee to link up with Gen. Braxton Bragg's
army contesting Gen. William S. Rosecrans's advance on Chattanooga,
Confederate control began to dwindle. It collapsed outright when Maj.
Gen. Ambrose Burnside's twelve-thousand-man army advanced from
Kentucky and occupied Knoxville on September 1, 1863. East Tennessee's
Unionists greeted Burnside's men as liberators, showering them with food

and cheers. A little more than a week later, Rosecrans's occupation of lower East Tennessee effectively ended the Confederate occupation of the region.[26]

The years of Confederate rule had taken a heavy toll on the Unionists of the region, both male and female. While many men fled East Tennessee to join the Union army or avoid conscription, the women, children, and elderly men stayed to fend for themselves. Subsistence farming was never as precarious for the region's Unionist sympathizers as during the Civil War. With the men gone, Unionist women and their children labored in the fields and worked to keep self-supporting farms operating in the face of harassment from secessionist neighbors, confiscations by Confederate soldiers, and raids by Rebel guerrillas. Undoubtedly, self-preservation was difficult enough, yet many Unionist women also served as couriers, safe-house operators, and spies for Unionist guerrillas and Federal soldiers. As early as the start of the war, women supported the Underground Railroad for Unionists escaping into Kentucky. By providing food, shelter, and information to Unionists and escaped Federal soldiers, these abettors forced thousands of Confederate soldiers, needed elsewhere, to guard the mountain passes, patrol isolated trails, and search homesteads. Largely at the mercy of Confederates, East Tennessee women risked much to help the cause of the Union.[27]

Like Unionist women, the region's slaves were also at the mercy of others during the years of Confederate occupation. While the loyalist-secessionist conflict in East Tennessee was unique to most of the South, the wartime experiences of the region's black population were similar to those of their brethren elsewhere in the Confederacy. Due to its geography, East Tennessee had few slaves and masters, yet the region's whites, whether loyalist or secessionist, united in their racism. Slaveholders were found on both sides, and many Unionist masters believed that the institution would be better protected in the Union than in what they viewed as a doomed Confederacy. Blacks had in East Tennessee, as they did elsewhere in the South, few, if any, white allies. Seeking a better life for themselves and their families, many followed white Unionists over the Cumberland Mountains into Kentucky in a search for freedom. This exodus increased after Lincoln issued the Emancipation Proclamation. Although the proclamation did not apply to Tennessee, blacks still fled to Federal lines in hopes of securing their freedom.[28]

In retrospect, given the continued resistance of white Unionists of both sexes and slaves, it is clear that the Confederate government never had full control of East Tennessee. It simply lacked the resources to garrison the region adequately, and it always faced an active and armed resistance from loyalist guerrillas. Moreover, Richmond's inconsistent policies of conciliation and suppression only alienated and emboldened a population determined to resist the Confederacy. In effect, the Confederacy could have done nothing politically or militarily to secure the acceptance or loyalty of the region's inhabitants.[29]

In the fall of 1863, large-scale conventional warfare ushered in new horrors to the area. The first and last major battles fought in East Tennessee occurred at this time as the Confederates strove to retain control of this strategic region. Following his pyrrhic victory at Chickamauga in September, Bragg followed the retreating Federals back to their defenses at Chattanooga. Unable and unwilling to mount an attack or maneuver past the city, Bragg chose instead to besiege Rosecrans's army in the hope of capturing the town and the Federals without a fight. Lincoln responded swiftly by dispatching Gen. Ulysses S. Grant to take command of the situation. Grant immediately broke the tentative siege and brought in supplies and reinforcements. At the very moment he needed every man, Bragg sent a large force under the command of Gen. James Longstreet to defeat Burnside, capture Knoxville, and theoretically siphon forces away from Grant as he attempted to protect upper East Tennessee. In reality, all Bragg did was weaken his army prior to Grant's advance. Union forces would eventually rout Bragg's Army of Tennessee at the Battle of Missionary Ridge, sending them into headlong retreat into Georgia. Meanwhile, Longstreet failed to storm the defenses of Knoxville and, subsequently, retreated into upper East Tennessee. With the defeat and retreat of Bragg and Longstreet, all but the extreme northwest corner of the region fell permanently under Union occupation, and a new chapter in the region's war began.[30]

With the capture of Chattanooga, the Federal War Department planned massive offensives for Georgia and Virginia in 1864. East Tennessee became a secondary theater, and its northeast counties were abandoned to Longstreet's forces around Bull's Gap. The Rebels would remain there until the spring of 1864, foraging liberally off the land and generating widespread shortages of food and fodder. Even after Longstreet left to rejoin the Army of Northern Virginia, Union forces failed to oust Confederate cavalry under Brig. Gen. John Hunt Morgan, and loyalist farmers could only watch while Rebel raiders plundered their farms.[31]

As Union forces endeavored to evict the last remaining Rebel troops, secessionist guerrillas operating out of western North Carolina and north Georgia entered the region during the winter of 1863. Sweeping through areas of East Tennessee, the guerrillas looted and burned Unionists' homes and barns and ambushed Federal garrisons. Militia, loyalist guerrillas, and Federal troops responded against both the insurgents and the local secessionists, which intensified the guerrilla war. Moreover, an increasing number of deserters from both armies and brigands with no real allegiance to either side prowled the region in search of the unwary and undefended. Federal attempts at counterinsurgency failed, as had earlier Confederate efforts. The violence simply could not be contained with the current resources.[32]

The new Federal district commander, Ambrose Burnside, faced a daunting challenge. Not only did he have to continue to wage war against Rebel forces both regular and irregular, but he also had to formulate and implement reconstruction policies for the devastated region. Burnside, however, had a well of experience from which to draw—both his own as commander of the Department of the Ohio, which had included a sizable majority sympathetic to the Confederacy, and that of other Union commanders across the South. Burnside believed that he first had to crush immediately any and all opposition to Federal authority. He chose Brig. Gen. Samuel P. Carter, a cousin of Rev. William B. Carter's, as provost marshal general for the District of East Tennessee and empowered him to execute martial law throughout the region. Carter, lacking adequate troop strength, employed the members of the local loyalist population as deputy provost marshals for each county. Burnside also established a "secret police" force of loyalists under Robert A. Crawford to be his eyes and ears, and he organized home guard units called the "National Guard of Tennessee" to suppress guerrillas.

Although determined to establish Federal control, Burnside's occupation policy followed Lincoln's Proclamation of Amnesty of December 1863, which, among other things, offered a pardon to all Rebels except high-ranking officials provided that they took an oath of loyalty and agreed to accept the abolition of slavery. While hopeful of conciliation, Burnside was, nevertheless, prepared to imprison or banish secessionists who continued to resist Federal authority. By early 1864, Burnside ordered Confederate prisoners in East Tennessee north to Federal camps, and he deported to the Deep South numerous outspoken civilian secessionists, including some women and ministers. Both groups had advocated secession and continued to resist Federal authority. This was something neither Burnside nor the region's loyalists would tolerate.[33]

Burnside's policies won over the region's moderate Unionists such as T. A. R. Nelson, who hoped to see an end to the bloodshed and suffering. They did not, however, appease the most influential Unionist in East Tennessee—William Brownlow. Arriving on the heels of the Union army, Brownlow returned from exile to Knoxville with both official and unofficial powers. Officially, he served as a special treasury agent for East Tennessee, a post that gave him the authority to issue or withhold licenses to trade, seize goods traded without a license, and confiscate and dispose of property abandoned by traitors. Brownlow energetically used his office to reward his friends, punish his enemies, and increase his influence. Unofficially, Brownlow became a demagogue for the Unionists of the region. Through his newspaper, now christened the *Knoxville Whig and Rebel Ventilator,* he spewed forth a torrent of anti-Confederate propaganda and near obscene calls for retribution against the Rebel population of East Tennessee. Referring to secessionists as "Imps from Hell," he declared that Union men who had suffered at their hands would be "justified in shooting them down on sight." He challenged the manhood of Unionists who did not do so, declaring: "We shall regard hundreds of them [Unionists] as wanting in courage and in resentment if they do not dispatch them [secessionists] whenever they meet their rotten carcasses."[34]

Brownlow's rhetoric fell on receptive ears, and many of his followers joined him in demanding retribution for real and perceived wrongs committed during the Confederate occupation. Burnside was in the awkward position of trying to control the violence against former secessionists who accepted Federal rule without alienating the loyalists on whom he greatly depended. Tensions between the region's Unionists and their liberators were exacerbated further by the behavior of Federal troops that foraged indiscriminately from loyalists and secessionists alike.[35]

As the war dragged on into 1864, East Tennessee faced economic disaster. Guerrillas and brigands continued to destroy homes and barns, steal food and livestock, and murder the farmers. Worse still, the region had not recovered from Confederate confiscations before Federal authorities arrived to continue the practice. Many poor East Tennesseans now moved north in search of opportunity to cities such as Cairo, Louisville, and Cincinnati, where they received mixed receptions by Northern citizens.[36]

Not all East Tennesseans wanted to leave, nor could they. Those who remained faced starvation and homelessness. Thousands moved to Federal garrison cities such as Nashville, Knoxville, and Chattanooga, where Union commanders provided temporary shelters and provisions. As Federal offensives in Georgia and Virginia demanded more provisions, however, this aid evaporated. One newspaper correspondent with the *Louisville Journal* recalled the pitiful refugees of Chattanooga arriving daily to beg for food that the military would no longer supply. The situation for blacks was even worse. Crowded into contraband camps in Knoxville and Chattanooga, black families subsisted solely off military aid in the form of tents, foodstuffs, and other supplies. The lack of sanitary camp conditions led to outbreaks of smallpox that ravaged the refugees. Although black men in the camps often performed manual labor for the government, in many cases they were not paid and, thus, could not afford better conditions for themselves or their families. Moreover, while some blacks voluntarily joined the U.S. Colored Troops for money and freedom, others were coerced by white Federal officers eager to fill the ranks by any means available.[37]

So grave were the economic conditions in East Tennessee that leading citizens of Knoxville formed the East Tennessee Relief Association. Unable to receive substantive Federal aid, agents traveled to the Midwest and Northeast to secure funds. Ultimately, the association would purchase, transport, and distribute $250,000 in aid to East Tennesseans. Preference was given to Unionist families, especially those that had suffered for their loyalty. Ironically, poor Rebel families could secure aid, but none would be given to black families, even those with members in the Union army. Despite its best efforts, the poverty of the region was so widespread that the association did not disband until 1868, well after the war was over.[38]

In fact, poverty was not the only carryover after the war. While the spring of 1865 brought the surrender of all major Confederate armies and an end to violence in most places, the "official peace" did not extend to East Tennessee. The Unionist-secessionist conflict continued unabated in the coves, mountains, and villages of eastern Tennessee. The great issues of the war concerning secession and slavery had been decided, but the local issue of who would now control the region had not. Moreover, as Unionist guerrillas and those who had joined the Union army returned to the region for good, they were determined to shape the peace. Revenge was on the minds of many Unionists who wanted satisfaction for the wrongs they and their families had suffered at the hands of the secessionists. These veterans, like their loyalist neighbors who had remained, were determined to control the politics and economics of postwar East Tennessee, and they initiated a systematic campaign of terror to drive the Rebels from the region. All across East Tennessee, ex-Confederates endured intimidation, beatings, arson, and murder as they struggled to rebuild their lives in the aftermath of the Civil War.[39]

Less dramatic but no less serious were the legal actions brought against the Confederates. Unionists used the courts to obtain compensation for losses or level treason charges against the Rebels. President Johnson's executive pardons, coupled with the actions of moderate Unionist jurors and judges throughout East Tennessee, meant that, while many ex-Confederates were temporarily jailed or fined, treason cases generally ended in acquittal.[40]

The violence and legal actions leveled against the region's secessionists convinced many to flee East Tennessee. Indeed, most of East Tennessee's secessionist leaders, as well as a great number of their followers, left the area for good. Although some of the exiled Confederates returned after 1870 when conditions improved, most never did. The magnitude of this forced exodus is astonishing. An examination of veterans from the Nineteenth Tennessee regiment reveals that few of the men were present for the 1870 census and that those who were lived in counties that had strongly supported secession in 1861. Sullivan County, in particular, became something of a haven for ex-Confederates during the violence of the immediate postwar period. It appears that those who fled East Tennessee permanently migrated mainly to the pro-Confederate areas of the Volunteer State or to other parts of the former Confederacy, especially the Deep South.[41]

In March 1865, William Brownlow came into office as the governor of Tennessee with the vindictive intention of driving ex-secessionists from the state—or at the very least stripping them of political influence. Through a series of legislative acts, the governor and his radical followers barred ex-Confederates from voting or holding political office. Nonetheless, when Brownlow left Nashville to become one of the state's senators in Washington, the radical regime he built began to crumble, and some Rebels not only regained the franchise but also quickly assumed power in the state. Reconstruction in Tennessee was over by 1870.[42]

The end of radical politics meant that some secessionists eventually did return to East Tennessee. Yet this small number of ex-Rebels, surrounded by Unionists, lived quietly among their old enemies. They made only feeble attempts to join the South's celebration of the "Lost Cause," and few United Confederate Veterans camps or United Daughters of the Confederacy chapters existed in East Tennessee. In a sense, Brownlow had achieved his dream of driving the region's Rebels into obscurity, as future generations and historians remembered only the region's Unionist majority.[43]

While white East Tennesseans fought to determine the region's future, blacks struggled to find their own way. With the passage after the war of the Thirteenth Amendment, the fate of the region's African American population became another concern of the Unionists who sought to control the region they had fought so hard to win. As long as the freedmen remained in rural areas and functioned as sharecroppers, the white population was content. However, the blacks in the towns who received aid from the Freedmen's Bureau and Northern benevolent societies became objects of resentment. Moreover, when Governor Brownlow and the radical government in Nashville granted blacks the franchise and civil rights, a wedge between former Unionists developed. White East Tennesseans increasingly spurned black attempts at improvement, including attending schools, voting, and holding political office. Once the radicals fell from power, many former Unionists and ex-Confederates could unite to limit the political and economic aspirations of blacks. For most East Tennessee Unionists, emancipation was a necessary by-product of the struggle to defeat the rebellion and was always more about destroying the wealth and power of the planter elite than about caring for the plight of blacks. The century of virtual apartheid that existed across the South, including East Tennessee, following Reconstruction demonstrates this point.[44]

In looking back over East Tennessee's experience during the Civil War and Reconstruction, it is clear that the war devastated victor and vanquished alike. The region's secessionist population had been permanently reduced as hundreds, if not thousands, fled to other parts of Tennessee or the South. Never again would they challenge their Unionist neighbors.

Indeed, the region's Confederates faded into obscurity, partly because of their limited numbers, and partly because of their desire to reacclimate themselves—a defeated people living in a hostile land.

For East Tennessee's blacks, the war and its immediate aftermath brought the cherished dream of emancipation but also the reality of economic dependence through sharecropping and debt peonage. Unionists were no more likely than secessionists to accept African Americans as political or economic equals. Like blacks throughout the South, those and their descendants in the towns and on the farms of East Tennessee would have to endure discrimination and poverty until a century later when the civil rights movement sparked a second Reconstruction.

Finally, although the region's Unionists had triumphed over their secessionist enemies and managed to maintain their racial hierarchy over blacks, they could boast of little else. Radical Unionists controlled the state only for a brief time before a coalition of moderate Unionists and ex-Confederates regained power and reestablished Democratic rule. Indeed, as East Tennessee's Unionism transformed into Republicanism, the region remained out of step with the rest of the Volunteer State and the South. Additionally, the ravages of the war had destroyed the economy. Subsistence farmers had always lived on the edge of ruin, and no greater disaster ever swept the region than the Civil War. A population increase exacerbated endemic postwar poverty and put even more pressure on overworked and shrinking farmlands. In fact, not until the New Deal would the region begin to emerge from the poverty of the post–Civil War period. Sadly, the region's Unionists had won their war only to be forgotten by the rest of the Union. In this they had company. No two groups, East Tennessee secessionists or Unionists, sacrificed so much for their respective causes only to be abandoned by a rapidly modernizing world. They, like others in Appalachia, became "yesterday's people."[45]

Notes

1. *Knoxville Whig,* January 12, 1861. The most important works covering the Civil War in southern Appalachia include Durwood Dunn, *Cades Cove: The Life and Death of a Southern Appalachian Community, 1818–1937* (Knoxville: University of Tennessee Press, 1988); Kenneth W. Noe, *Southwest Virginia's Railroad: Modernization and the Sectional Crisis* (Urbana: University of Illinois Press, 1994); Noel C. Fisher, *War at Every Door: Partisan Politics and Guerilla Violence in East*

Tennessee, 1860–1869 (Chapel Hill: University of North Carolina Press, 1997); Kenneth W. Noe and Shannon H. Wilson, eds., *The Civil War in Appalachia: Collected Essays* (Knoxville: University of Tennessee Press, 1997); David Williams, *Rich Man's War: Class, Caste, and Confederate Defeat in the Lower Chattahoochie Valley* (Athens: University of Georgia Press, 1998); W. Todd Groce, *Mountain Rebels: East Tennessee Confederates and the Civil War, 1860–1870* (Knoxville: University of Tennessee Press, 1999); John C. Inscoe and Gordon B. McKinney, *The Heart of Confederate Appalachia: Western North Carolina in the Civil War* (Chapel Hill: University of North Carolina Press, 2000); Martin Crawford, *Ashe County's Civil War: Community and Society in the Appalachian South* (Charlottesville: University Press of Virginia, 2001); John W. Shaffer, *Clash of Loyalties: A Border County in the Civil War* (Morgantown: West Virginia University Press, 2003); John Fowler, *Mountaineers in Gray: The Story of the Nineteenth Tennessee Volunteer Infantry Regiment, C.S.A.* (Knoxville: University of Tennessee Press, 2004); and Robert Tracy McKenzie, *Lincolnites and Rebels: A Divided Town in the American Civil War* (New York: Oxford University Press, 2006).

2. Fisher, *War at Every Door*, 62–63.

3. Fowler, *Mountaineers in Gray*, 1–2; Stanley John Folmsbee, Robert E. Corlew, and Enoch L. Mitchell, *Tennessee: A Short History* (Knoxville: University of Tennessee Press, 1976), 5–11; Paul H. Bergeron, Stephen V. Ash, and Jeanette Keith, *Tennesseans and Their History* (Knoxville: University of Tennessee Press, 1999), 1–2; Harry L. Law, *Tennessee Geography* (Norman, Okla.: Harlow, 1964), 15–18; Charles Faulkner Bryan Jr., "The Civil War in East Tennessee: A Social, Political, and Economic Study" (Ph.D. diss., University of Tennessee, 1978), 8; Donald L. Winters, *Tennessee Farming, Tennessee Farmers: Antebellum Agriculture in the Upper South* (Knoxville: University of Tennessee Press, 1994), 1–2, 4.

4. Groce, *Mountain Rebels*, 9–20; Donald W. Buckwalter, "Effects of Early Nineteenth Century Transportation Disadvantage on the Agriculture of Eastern Tennessee," *Southeastern Geographer* 27 (1987): 21–23, 33; Winters, *Tennessee Farming*, 31–36, 48, 84–87, 191; J. B. Killebrew, *Introduction to the Resources of Tennessee* (Nashville: Tavel, Eastman & Howell, 1874; reprint, Spartanburg, S.C.: Reprint Co., 1974), 6–25, 277–78, 432–33; Folmsbee, Corlew, and Mitchell, *Tennessee*, 244, 249; Bergeron, Ash, and Keith, *Tennesseans and Their History*, 113, 115–17; James W. Holland, "The East Tennessee and Georgia Railroad, 1836–1860," *East Tennessee Historical Society's Publications* 3 (1931): 89–107, and "The Building of the East Tennessee and Virginia Railroad," *East Tennessee Historical Society's Publications* 4 (1932): 83–101; Philip M. Hamer, ed., *Tennessee: A History, 1673–1932*, 4 vols. (New York: American Historical Society, 1933), 1:262–63, 399–420, 448–54; Fowler, *Mountaineers in Gray*, 2–5.

5. Robert Tracy McKenzie, "Wealth and Income: The Preindustrial Structure of East Tennessee in 1860," *Appalachian Journal* 21 (1994): 271–74, and *One South or Many? Plantation Belt and Upcountry in Civil War–Era Tennessee* (New York: Cambridge University Press, 1994), 53–54; David C. Hsiung, *Two Worlds in the Tennessee Mountains: Exploring the Origins of Appalachian Stereotypes* (Lexington: University Press of Kentucky, 1997), 128, 162–63; Walter Lynn Bates, "Southern Unionists: A Socio-Economic Examination of the Third East Tennessee Volunteer Infantry Regiment, U.S.A., 1862–1865," *Tennessee Historical Quarterly* 50 (1991): 226–39; Fowler, *Mountaineers in Gray,* 4–5, 20–29.

6. Jonathan Atkins, *Parties, Politics, and the Sectional Conflict in Tennessee, 1832–1861* (Knoxville: University of Tennessee Press, 1997), 15, 87–88; Paul H. Bergeron, *Antebellum Politics in Tennessee* (Lexington: University Press of Kentucky, 1982), 9–34, 64–102, 152, 156; Fisher, *War at Every Door,* 15; Bryan, "Civil War in East Tennessee," 12; Folmsbee, Corlew, and Mitchell, *Tennessee,* 178–94; Hamer, ed., *Tennessee,* 1:277–94; Daniel W. Crofts, *Reluctant Confederates: Upper South Unionists in the Secession Crisis* (Chapel Hill: University of North Carolina Press, 1989), 47.

7. Hamer, ed., *Tennessee,* 1:265; Atkins, *Parties, Politics,* 2–3; Crofts, *Reluctant Confederates,* 47, 49.

8. Fowler, *Mountaineers in Gray,* 29–38.

9. Ibid., 7–9; Folmsbee, Corlew, and Mitchell, *Tennessee,* 317; Mary Emily Robertson Campbell, *The Attitude of Tennesseans toward the Union, 1847–1861* (New York: Vantage, 1961), 159, 175–76, 288–90; Robert H. White and Stephen V. Ash, eds., *Messages of the Governors of Tennessee,* 11 vols. to date (Nashville: Tennessee Historical Commission, 1952–), 5:265; Hamer, ed., *Tennessee,* 1:522–33; Atkins, *Parties, Politics,* 241.

10. Crofts, *Reluctant Confederates,* 289–352, 358; Hamer, ed., *Tennessee,* 2:537–39; James Welch Patton, *Unionism and Reconstruction in Tennessee, 1860–1869* (Chapel Hill: University of North Carolina Press, 1934; reprint, Gloucester, Mass.: Peter Smith, 1966), 14; Fowler, *Mountaineers in Gray,* 10–11.

11. For the situation in East Tennessee following the attack on Fort Sumter, see Fowler, *Mountaineers in Gray,* 11–14; Atkins, *Parties, Politics,* 247, 252; Hamer, ed., *Tennessee,* 2:542, 545–46, 549–51; Fisher, *War at Every Door,* 29–30, 33–35; Bryan, "Civil War in East Tennessee," 37–51, 53–55; Oliver P. Temple, *East Tennessee and the Civil War* (Cincinnati: Robert Clarke, 1899), 184–86, 192–94, 340–43, 588; *Knoxville Whig,* April 2, 1861; Thomas William Humes, *The Loyal Mountaineers of Tennessee* (Knoxville: Ogden Bros., 1888), 100, 105–15, 120–21, 347; Patton, *Unionism and Reconstruction,* 14; and Campbell, *Attitude of Tennesseans,* 291–94.

12. Fisher, *War at Every Door*, 37–40; Temple, *East Tennessee*, 343–65, 565–73; Patton, *Unionism and Reconstruction*, 24–25; Humes, *Loyal Mountaineers*, 115–19; Bryan, "Civil War in East Tennessee," 55–63.

13. Fowler, *Mountaineers in Gray*, 43–44; Fisher, *War at Every Door*, 41–45, 102; U.S. War Department, *The War of the Rebellion: A Compilation of the Official Records of the Union and Confederate Armies, 1861–1865* (hereafter cited as *OR*), 70 vols. in 128 pts. (Washington, D.C.: U.S. Government Printing Office, 1880–1901), ser. 1, vol. 4, p. 374; James C. Stamper, "Felix K. Zollicoffer: Tennessee Editor, Politician, and Soldier" (M.A. thesis, University of Tennessee, Knoxville, 1967), 1–68; Isham Harris to Jefferson Davis, July 13, 1861, Harris Papers, Tennessee State Library and Archives.

14. *OR*, ser. 1, vol. 4, pp. 201, 374, 377; Circulars, Letters, Orders Issued by Various Commands, Brigadier General Felix K. Zollicoffer, East Tennessee Brigade, 1861, and General Order No. 5, August 23, 1861, Orders and Letters Sent, Brigadier General Felix K. Zollicoffer, August 1861–January 1862, Record Group 109, National Archives, Washington, D.C.; Fisher, *War at Every Door*, 44–48.

15. Fowler, *Mountaineers in Gray*, 45–46; Fisher, *War at Every Door*, 47–50; Folmsbee, Corlew, and Mitchell, *Tennessee*, 325–26; Atkins, *Parties, Politics*, 253–58; Temple, *East Tennessee*, 224–44; *OR*, ser. 1, vol. 4, pp. 379, 389, 393.

16. *OR*, ser. 4, vol. 1, pp. 586–93; *Knoxville Register*, October 17, 1861; *OR*, ser. 2, vol. 2, pp. 1368–70; Bryan, "Civil War in East Tennessee," 75–76.

17. Fowler, *Mountaineers in Gray*, 49; Fisher, *War at Every Door*, 51–54; Temple, *East Tennessee*, 370–72, 375–77; David Madden, "Unionist Resistance to Confederate Occupation: The Bridge Burners of East Tennessee," *East Tennessee Historical Society's Publications* 52–53 (1980–1981): 22–39; Bryan, "Civil War in East Tennessee," 85–86.

18. Humes, *Loyal Mountaineers*, 133–35; Temple, *East Tennessee*, 381–83; Madden, "Bridge Burners," 30–34; Bryan, "Civil War in East Tennessee," 87–88.

19. Fisher, *War at Every Door*, 59–61; Madden, "Bridge Burners," 35–37; Bryan, "Civil War in East Tennessee," 88–89; Fowler, *Mountaineers in Gray*, 51–59.

20. *Tennesseans in the Civil War: A Military History of Confederate and Union Units with Available Rosters of Personnel*, 2 vols. (Nashville: Civil War Centennial Commission, 1964–1965), 1:1; Bryan, "Civil War in East Tennessee," 90–95; Fisher, *War at Every Door*, 65–68, 102.

21. Fisher, *War at Every Door*, 68–78.

22. *OR*, ser. 1, vol. 10, pt. 1, pp. 20–21, and pt. 2, pp. 14, 369, 385–86, 397–402, 429–30; Albert B. Moore, *Conscription and Conflict in the Confederacy* (New York: Macmillan, 1924), 148–49; Georgia Lee Tatum, *Disloyalty in the Confederacy* (Chapel Hill: University of North Carolina Press), 13–17, 150–51; Bryan,

"Civil War in East Tennessee," 99–103; Groce, *Mountain Rebels,* 83–85; Fisher, *War at Every Door,* 103–8.

23. *OR,* ser. 1, vol. 16, pt. 2, p. 756; Bryan, "Civil War in East Tennessee," 103–6; Groce, *Mountain Rebels,* 85–87; Fisher, *War at Every Door,* 108–10.

24. *OR,* ser. 1, vol. 16, pt. 2, pp. 790, 797–98, 841, 851, 866, 884–85, 890; Bryan, "Civil War in East Tennessee," 107–11; Fisher, *War at Every Door,* 110–18.

25. *OR,* ser. 1, vol. 23, pt. 2, pp. 621, 631, 651–52; Fisher, *War at Every Door,* 102, 118–21; Bryan, "Civil War in East Tennessee," 111–12.

26. Fisher, *War at Every Door,* 126; Temple, *East Tennessee,* 480; Bryan, "Civil War in East Tennessee," 113–14; Humes, *Loyal Mountaineers,* 211–12.

27. William A. Strasser, "'A terrible calamity has befallen us': Unionist Women in Civil War East Tennessee," *Journal of East Tennessee History* 71 (1999): 73–75; W. B. Hesseltine, "The Underground Railroad from Confederate Prisons to East Tennessee," *East Tennessee Historical Society's Publications* 2 (1930): 63.

28. Bryan, "Civil War in East Tennessee," 300–304, 307–13, 318–19.

29. Ibid., 115–17; Fisher, *War at Every Door,* 119–21.

30. Among the best sources for the struggle for East Tennessee in 1863 are Thomas Lawrence Connelly, *Autumn of Glory: The Army of Tennessee, 1862–1865* (Baton Rouge: Louisiana State University Press, 1995), chaps. 7–10; Steven E. Woodworth, *Six Armies in Tennessee: The Chickamauga and Chattanooga Campaigns* (Lincoln: University of Nebraska Press, 1998); Peter Cozzens, *This Terrible Sound: The Battle of Chickamauga* (Urbana: University of Illinois Press, 1992), and *The Shipwreck of Their Hope: The Battles for Chattanooga* (Urbana: University of Illinois Press, 1994); and Harold S. Fink, "The East Tennessee Campaign and the Battle of Knoxville in 1863," *East Tennessee Historical Society's Publications* 29 (1957): 79–117.

31. Fisher, *War at Every Door,* 129–30.

32. Ibid., 79–95; Bryan, "Civil War in East Tennessee," 147–58.

33. Fisher, *War at Every Door,* 130–37; Bryan, "Civil War in East Tennessee," 123–25.

34. James B. Campbell, "East Tennessee during the Federal Occupation, 1863–1865," *East Tennessee Historical Society's Publications* 19 (1947): 66–67; Bryan, "Civil War in East Tennessee," 121–23; Fisher, *War at Every Door,* 135, 144; *Knoxville Whig and Rebel Ventilator,* January 9, 1864.

35. Fisher, *War at Every Door,* 143–47.

36. William C. Harris, "The East Tennessee Relief Movement of 1864–1865," *Tennessee Historical Quarterly* 48, no. 2 (1989): 88, and "East Tennessee's Civil War Refugees and the Impact of the War on Civilians," *Journal of East Tennessee History* 64 (1992): 3–19.

37. Harris, "Relief Movement," 88; Bryan, "Civil War in East Tennessee," 138–40, 325–27.

38. Strasser, "Unionist Women," 82; Campbell, "Federal Occupation," 71–75; Harris, "Relief Movement," 89–95; Bryan, "Civil War in East Tennessee," 140–44.

39. Fowler, *Mountaineers in Gray,* 188–89. For a general overview of conditions in postwar East Tennessee, see Groce, *Mountain Rebels,* 127–51; Fisher, *War at Every Door,* 154–77; Bryan, "Civil War in East Tennessee," 160–86; and Thomas B. Alexander, "Neither Peace nor War: Conditions in Tennessee in 1865," *East Tennessee Historical Society's Publications* 21 (1949): 41–42, and *Political Reconstruction in Tennessee* (Nashville: Vanderbilt University Press, 1950), 58–68.

40. Fowler, *Mountaineers in Gray,* 193–94; Fisher, *War at Every Door,* 159–63; Groce, *Mountain Rebels,* 135–40; Bryan, "Civil War in East Tennessee," 166–73.

41. Fowler, *Mountaineers in Gray,* 194–95; Groce, *Mountain Rebels,* 145–49; Fisher, *War at Every Door,* 163–64; Bryan, "Civil War in East Tennessee," 182–84.

42. Fisher, *War at Every Door,* 167–71.

43. Fowler, *Mountaineers in Gray,* 198–99; *Confederate Veteran* (Nashville) 1 (1893): 343; "Confederates in East Tennessee," *Confederate Veteran* 1 (1895): 277; J. W. Lillard, "Confederates in East Tennessee," *Confederate Veteran* 5 (1897): 593–94; George Moorman, "Reorganization of Georgia Division," *Confederate Veteran* 8 (1900): 17–18; J. C. Hodges, "Model Camp at Morristown, Tenn.," *Confederate Veteran* 15 (1907): 28–29; James L. Douthat, *Roster of Upper East Tennessee Confederate Veterans* (Signal Mountain, Tenn.: Mountain, n.d.); Groce, *Mountain Rebels,* 156–57; Anne Cody, *History of the Tennessee Division of the United Daughters of the Confederacy* (Nashville: n.p., n.d.), 259–336; *Minutes of the One Hundred and Ninth Annual General Convention of the United Daughters of the Confederacy Incorporated Held at Richmond, Virginia, October 31–November 5, 2002, United Daughters of the Confederacy* (Nashville: n.p., n.d.), 27–28; Web page of the Sons of Confederate Veterans, http://www.scv.org. (accessed December 14, 2007); "Distinguished Surviving Confederates," *Confederate Veteran* 19 (1911): 420–21. For a discussion of how the South attempted to come to grips with the Confederacy's defeat, see Gaines M. Foster, *Ghosts of the Confederacy: Defeat, the Lost Cause, and the Emergence of the New South, 1865 to 1913* (New York: Oxford University Press, 1987); and Charles Regan Wilson, *Baptized in Blood: The Religion of the Lost Cause, 1865–1920* (Athens: University of Georgia Press, 1980).

44. Bryan, "Civil War in East Tennessee," 331–42.

45. For a detailed examination of East Tennessee's economic problems fol-

lowing the Civil War, see Robert Tracy McKenzie, "'Oh! ours is a deplorable condition': The Economic Impact of the Civil War in Upper East Tennessee," in Noe and Wilson, eds., *Civil War in Appalachia*, 199–226. "Yesterday's people" is a reference to Jack E. Weller, *Yesterday's People: Life in Contemporary Appalachia* (Lexington: University of Kentucky Press, 1966). For a broad overview of Appalachia's economic problems and its struggle with modernization, see Richard B. Drake, *A History of Appalachia* (Lexington: University Press of Kentucky, 2003); John Alexander Williams, *Appalachia: A History* (Chapel Hill: University of North Carolina Press, 2002); and John D. Fowler, "Appalachia's Agony: An Historiographical Essay on Modernization and Development in the Southern Appalachians," *Filson Club Quarterly* 72, no. 3 (July 1998): 305–28.

Part 2
★ ★ ★

Traitors, Blacks, and Guerrillas in Wartime Kentucky and Tennessee

"Battle against the traitors"

Unionist Middle Tennesseans in the Ninth Kentucky Infantry and What They Fought For

Kenneth W. Noe

According to Richard Nelson Current, as many as 100,000 white Southerners from the seceded states fought in Union blue during the Civil War, fully a tenth of all white soldiers the Confederacy furnished. Nearly half of them, 42,000 men, came from East Tennessee. That region's loyalty to the Union is familiar to students of the war, of course, while the Unionism of other mountain residents is routinely discussed, if often overstated. In contrast, despite welcome recent attention from scholars, the experiences of the South's non-Appalachian Unionists remain greatly overshadowed by both the war fought by their highland comrades and especially the overwhelming popular memory of their Confederate neighbors.[1] Among those neglected Southern Unionists are the Middle Tennesseans who served in the Ninth Regiment, Kentucky Volunteer Infantry. From its creation in November 1861 until its end three years later, roughly 1,070 men served in the Ninth Kentucky. Of the 425 soldiers whose home counties have been established, at least 184, 43 percent, were Middle Tennesseans.[2] An examination of those Tennesseans in the Kentucky regiment and their motivations for going to war thus promises to illuminate the motives and experiences of non-Appalachian Southern Unionists in uniform further.

Moreover, consideration of these men promises to enrich a broader general debate about Civil War soldiers. Why did men join the armies? Why did they stay in the ranks? Why did they fight and not run from the battle line? Over the last two decades, several lively and important books have appeared regarding the motives that drove the men on both sides to take up arms. Bell Irvin Wiley's pioneering work emphasized social and cultural factors as motivators while largely dismissing ideology. Most men did not, in his estimation, fight for ideas such as liberty or republican government; rather, they rallied to the colors because of peer and family pressure, community expectations and pride, a taste for excitement and adventure, hatred of the enemy, a desire to prove courage and manhood, and the need of a regular paycheck. A vague patriotism, narrowly defined as emotional and nonideological, further spurred Federals. Loyalty to their comrades and solid yeoman values rather than ideological causes kept soldiers in the armies once they mustered into service.[3]

Wiley's conclusions proved powerful and durable. Only in the 1980s did a new generation of historians influenced by the Vietnam War, the domestic struggle for civil rights, and the so-called new social history again take up the topic. Many, however, continued to deemphasize ideology as Wiley had done. Michael Barton stressed sectional conceptions of what characteristics made good men and identified patriotism as a "psychosocial" value rather than an expression of ideology. Gerald Linderman primarily depicted soldiers as the products of the Age of Romanticism, aching to prove their manhood in the crucible of war until the brutal realities of the battlefield left them disillusioned with the Victorian values they brought to field and camp. Paul Christopher Anderson and Stephen Berry placed masculinity center stage for understanding why men fought, while Kenneth Greenberg emphasized the masculine demands of honor.[4]

In contrast, Reid Mitchell gave more credit to the power of patriotism and especially the nation's revolutionary heritage while still emphasizing how family, community, and personal concerns involving masculinity persuaded men to join the army. Scholars such as Earl Hess, Randall Jimerson, Chandra Manning, and especially James McPherson increasingly turned even further away from Wiley's shadow and pointed to a more broadly defined political ideology that included patriotism as the keystone of soldier motivation. While not dismissing social factors, these scholars stressed that men ultimately entered the ranks and lines of battle to defend liberty, whether that liberty meant republican government in a preserved Union or in an independent, slaveholding Confederacy. Drawing from the work of the military historian John Lynn, McPherson additionally provided a useful framework for all historians of the war grappling with soldier motivations. Factors that spurred enlistment constituted *initial motivation*. Once soldiers were in the army, he posited, the same ideology as well as loyalty to comrades enabled them to stay and fight. Morale generally remained high, at least among veterans. McPherson terms the factors that kept commitment and morale high *sustaining motivation*. *Combat motivation,* finally, enabled men to take part in battle. Here again, Hess and McPherson emphasized the importance of ideology while refuting the charges of demoralization and dehumanization argued by others. Ultimately, as the title of McPherson's work suggests, Civil War soldiers fought "for cause and comrades."[5]

In retrospect, much of the historical debate over soldier motivations has been semantic, especially involving whether one considers patriotism to be an expression of ideology. Yet the question of how important ideas were in encouraging Civil War soldiers to fight remains a crucial one. And what of the pro-Union Tennesseans of the Ninth Kentucky? Did they indeed enlist initially to fight for an ideological cause? A single regimental memoir exists to help answer the question. William Marcus Woodcock of Company B, a nineteen-year-old from Macon County, Tennessee, joined the Union army in September 1861. He served in the Ninth Kentucky until the end of 1864, rising to the rank of lieutenant before mustering out. He returned home on Christmas Day only to seek and gain election to the Tennessee state legislature. As he waited for the term to begin, he worked on a never-completed memoir of his "soldier experiences." That memoir, coupled with other sources, offers vital clues about the mind-set of uniformed Southern Unionism.[6]

In his memoir, Woodcock dealt directly with his decision to enlist. He attributed it to patriotism. He described the American government before the war as "the Star of the world." Americans had enjoyed peace and "all the blessings of a Republican Government, the right of suffrage being extended to all honest men, the advancement of education becoming more popular everywhere, the people becoming every day more able to prove to the world the greatness, glory, and justice of self-government." The secessionists had threatened to destroy that government and replace peace with desolation. "Incarnate fiends, political demagogues of the South," he wrote, "why were ye not content to fill your pockets with Northern Gold without using every exertion to bring about this most disastrous war?" At such an hour, it had been the duty of every citizen to rise up in defense of

William Marcus Woodcock,
ca. 1864. Courtesy of Ed Arn-
ing and the Woodcock family.

the nation. "I felt that I had done what every loyal citizen of the United States should do," he maintained. "Ever since the fall of Fort Sumpter [*sic*] I had resolved that if ever I had an opportunity, I would enlist in the U.S. Armies."[7]

Woodcock further stressed the nation's republican heritage. Secession, he maintained, was not just treason but a betrayal of "the noble heroes of '76. . . . I have always, from my earliest infancy, cherished an ardent feeling of love and admiration for my country," he wrote. "Have read books that only tended to increase the intensity of that feeling. . . . And now I felt that I was but doing justice to my self, to my country, to my forefathers, and to future generations." Later, he exclaimed in the same vein: "What sacrifices did [George Washington] make for our happiness! How long and earnestly did our forefathers toil for our liberty while suffering from all that a suffering people can be brought to endure! And now how are we repaying them for all their anxieties? We have grown too proud—have come to the conclusion that we are wiser, better, and more patriotic than our illustrious ancestors."[8]

While Woodcock stressed his patriotism, a closer examination of the memoir suggests that more was involved in his initial decision to join the Union army than simply an individual commitment to republicanism and the survival of the Union. Social and personal factors were at work as well. The most obvious is that his enlistment came in the context of a wider community response. Using incomplete records involving less than half the regiment's companies, the historian Geoff Michael identified at least 126 natives of Macon County, Tennessee, in the regiment. At least 58 other soldiers came from just to the east in Jackson County, the "Switzerland of the Cumberlands." Both counties lay northeast of Nashville along the border with Kentucky. Crucially, both were also divided in two geographically. Tennessee's Highland Rim delineated the northern neighborhoods of the counties as well as eastern Jackson County, while the more accessible southern topography of the Nashville Basin, drained by the Cumberland River, characterized the rest. In the latter, a degree of commercial farming, slavery, and prosecession sentiments thrived among the "river people." Those areas would produce several Confederate companies.

In contrast, according to Stephen Ash, the rugged northern neighborhoods had more in common politically, socially, and culturally with East Tennessee. Farms were smaller, slaves were fewer, and trade flowed, not south, but north along two roads that led to Tompkinsville, Kentucky, and the surrounding county of Monroe. Indeed, county seat and state politics aside, the northern Jackson-Macon area joined with Monroe County to form a single rural world along tributaries of the Barren River. The Tennesseans routinely traded in Monroe and educated their children there. They also traditionally supported the Union. Families like the Woodcocks had received their initial land grants from the federal government for War of 1812 service under Andrew Jackson, but the somewhat more moderate sectional ideology of the Whig Party and Henry Clay dominated the area politically by the early 1850s.[9]

As the secession crisis reached its crescendo in the spring of 1861, divergent state politics and the border cleaved the region. Unionism dominated Tennessee politics until Fort Sumter, but, after that, the state government quickly aligned itself with the newborn Confederacy. Kentucky's divided government, in contrast, declared its neutrality in the coming contest, threatening if invaded to join the other side. Along the border, the result was chaos. In Jackson and Macon counties, as elsewhere in Middle Tennessee's Upper Cumberland region, local secessionists and state officials moved with dispatch against suspect Unionist "Tories" in the Highland Rim, driving many into Kentucky. Meanwhile, across the border in strongly Unionist Monroe County, the local home guard sprang to life. Created by the commonwealth's legislature after Fort Sumter to counter the prosecession Kentucky State Guard, and sometimes armed surreptitiously by the Abraham Lincoln administration, the home guard quickly became a main avenue for militant Unionists. Pro-Union Tennesseans as well as Kentuckians significantly took part in it. Woodcock was one. While attending school in Gamaliel, Monroe County, he joined the home guard company in that village. The commander in Tompkinsville was another Tennessean, Jackson County's William J. Henson.[10]

In September 1861, Kentucky's neutrality ended when Confederate troops under the command of Leonidas Polk occupied the Mississippi River city of Columbus. While Federal troops poured into the state from the Midwest, Confederate forces moved north from Tennessee into Kentucky, establishing positions at Bowling Green and in eastern Kentucky's Cumberland Plateau. In Monroe County, the home guard sprang to action. Members secured weapons and began to drill in anticipation of a fight. After a local invasion scare passed, Henson announced that he was forming a company for Federal service. Woodcock was among the first to step forward.[11]

Woodcock's reminisces of those heady days in the autumn of 1861 are filled with neighbors' expressions of support. When rumors of a Confederate incursion into Monroe County surfaced, a meeting occurred at Woodcock's schoolhouse. "A large collection of people" gathered, "attaching more importance to the matter than even *we* had. . . . The old men had assembled, to devise means of defense and the younger ones were present to act on the dictation of the older." The next morning "a large crowd assembled and ready to furnish the required number of men" to march to Cave City for weapons. Arriving in Tompkinsville, the marchers found the town "strung to the highest pitch of excitement." All along the march, community members expressed their support.[12]

Yet Woodcock's enlistment involved more than following friends and neighbors. Despite widespread expressions of community Unionism, most of his classmates in fact did not join the army, and he admitted that, once in the ranks, he knew personally only one other member of his company.

Of the 167 men ultimately to serve in Company B, 62 were Tennesseans, but only 3 other Macon County men joined Woodcock in it. The rest hailed from Henson's home county of Jackson. Still other motivators thus must be considered. In Woodcock's case, not just neighbors but especially kin crucially supported the Union cause. The Woodcocks were among the best-known Unionists in Macon County, a fact that would soon make them targets of the Confederate authorities. Before his enlistment, Woodcock returned home to Tennessee. His father, the farmer and physician Wiley Woodcock, expressed pride in his son for his home guard activities, telling him: "You did right."[13]

Coming in tandem with Kentucky's sudden and frenzied entrance into the war, Woodcock's enlistment was clearly in part also an emotional response to events. Marching and countermarching with the home guard left him exhausted, yet he could neither sleep nor eat during those heady days of *rage militaire.* "I was in a continued whirl of excitement during the whole evening," he wrote, describing his last trip home before his enlistment, "continually walking back and forth over the floor around the yard and through the fields." He had what hindsight would reveal to be unrealistic expectations for the war. Told that his enlistment would run three years instead of two, he did not worry, for he "felt very confident that the war would terminate ere in six months." Finally, there was ambition. Woodcock openly coveted an officer's rank but was defeated in the balloting for lieutenant and begrudgingly had to settle for an appointment as corporal. "I *did* to some extent cherish a desire to obtain with my own arms a right to distinction while I should be defending my Country's rights," he admitted. "These hopes had been in a measure, seemingly rendered hopeless by my defeat, yet I still hoped, for I knew I would at least *do my duty* and this I had resolved to do at all hazards." Patriotic ideology propelled Woodcock into Federal service, in short, but so did personal ambition, emotion, expectations of a brief war, his family's Unionism, the widespread support of his Unionist neighbors, and a lifetime of reading patriotic schoolboy histories. Conspicuously missing from the list, one should note, is slavery. There is no evidence that Woodcock opposed the institution in 1861. Indeed, the Woodcocks had owned slaves in the past, although they did not hold any in 1861.[14]

With regard to the second of the three Lynn-McPherson categories, sustaining motivation, Woodcock's memoir suggests similar complications. McPherson stressed the continuing importance of ideology and comradeship in keeping men in the field and the armies in existence. In many ways, Woodcock's memoir bears out this interpretation. Indeed, it is noteworthy how Woodcock's politics radicalized as the war progressed. In 1861, he, like his father, was a Democrat who wanted the Union preserved but said little about slavery. But, as the war passed, like many Union soldiers of similar political background, he moved step by step toward supporting Abraham Lincoln and the Republicans. On February 22, 1863, anticipating Lincoln's Gettysburg Address by nine months, he eulogized George Washington in his diary and linked his cause to that of the "patriots" of the revolutionary generation. A year later, the Democrat Woodcock sat down to write an address supporting George B. McClellan's presidential candidacy. Intending to criticize Lincoln, Woodcock wrote several pages before realizing: "I could make no point. . . . I mentally asked myself what McLellan [*sic*] might do were he to be elected. The result was that in a short time I tore up the message . . . and I soon discovered a complete change in my principles."[15]

Perhaps more surprising is how Woodcock's army experiences drove him to attack slavery, "the most abominable institution that ever stained the bright escutcheon of our country," and racism. Union soldiers often abused African Americans for amusement, and such "fun" sometimes turned brutal. For Woodcock, the son of a sometimes slaveholder, one incident of taunting became a turning point. One evening in February 1863, some of his comrades acquired whiskey and then began to throw stones at a slave who was passing through the camp. The victim responded in kind, striking a Kentuckian with near deadly force. Only the imposition of the slave owner prevented the slave's lynching. Woodcock found it all contemptible:

I have seen so many *little meannesses* practiced toward the negro race that I cannot help expressing my *true feelings* on the subject. . . . Many a time has my blood fairly boiled with rage when I have seen some of these poor fellow[s], whose only fault is a *black skin,* and the fact that they have always been *slaves,* stunned by a stone thrown by some specimen of the *noble* and *magnanimous* Anglo Saxon race. And as a general thing the persons who were continually despising and insulting the negro . . . were generally men superiors to whom in point of bravery, patriotism, morality, education, and natural intelligence could be found among the free Africans and even among the *slaves* by the hundred.[16]

The next step in the evolution of his racial views was his support of arming African American soldiers. At first he opposed it "violently," admitting: "I had not yet got rid of all the prejudices to the negro race that had been instilled into my mind as a consequence of living in a Southern State." Yet "the opposition in our regiment was so universal" that he worried that question would destroy the army. He began to argue for the measure, at first "only to allay the excitement among the members of our company," but then: "Almost to my horror I found myself partially convinced of the truth of the arguments that I had been advancing . . . and then by degrees I came sincerely to advocate this, one of the wisest and most prudent acts of the United States Government during the war." The war was about the Confederacy's desire to preserve slavery, he concluded, "and if our country's history is stained with the black spot of one civil war, it will be the brighter by the removal of the blacker one of *slavery*."[17]

Woodcock's attitudes would continue to evolve after the war. As a Tennessee legislator, he aligned himself with Radical Republicans, supported the Fourteenth Amendment, and voted to extend civil rights, including the vote, to the state's freedpeople. The voters of Macon County agreed enough with him to reelect him in 1867. One must be careful, however, not to assume that all the Tennesseans in the regiment followed Woodcock's political arc. Few, in fact, did; Woodcock far outdistanced most of his peers in supporting equality as well as Lincoln and emancipation. Several members of the regiment, including Col. Benjamin C. Grider, were slave owners who even brought body servants with them to camp. Many other men in the Ninth Kentucky ached to leave the army and endlessly debated exactly when their enlistments expired. Others simply deserted, angry that they had been forced to serve away from their homes. Emancipation led to more dissension and desertion. Woodcock admitted: "There was always a class of persons in our army who were continually croaking about the measures of the administration, and their strongest point they could ever bring up to excuse their *disloyalty* or opposition to every great and wise action of the lamented president . . . the subject upon which they lived principally to discant was the subject of *Negro Equality,* and these same *croakers* were always first to attempt to bring themselves into this hated (by them) sphere of social equality with the negro." Having decided to support Lincoln in 1864, Woodcock tellingly admitted: "I did not have the courage to mention it for a considerable time." When the fall elections came, Woodcock indeed voted for Lincoln, but a majority of his regimental comrades did not. "We cannot get the vote of our Tennesseans," he wrote, "but the Kentuckians vote 45 for Lincoln and 90 for McLellan [*sic*]."[18]

Despite such ideological differences of opinion, camaraderie nonetheless did help sustain Woodcock. His general affection for many of his fellow soldiers is obvious throughout the memoir. "I *know*," he wrote, "that I possessed as warm feelings of admiration, love or respect for the Regiment as any one, and I also acknowledge that I had cause for this feeling."[19] Specifically, he praised fellow soldiers who nursed him during bouts of illness, expressed his devastation when they marched toward the front without him early in 1862 as he recovered from measles, and enjoyed a pleasant reunion after returning from furlough early in 1864. His pride in their battlefield performance was immense, his pain at their loss was real, and he protested when outsiders appeared to assume regimental offices his comrades deserved. His affections seem to have been returned to an extent, especially when the men of his company twice petitioned that he be promoted to fill vacancies. Yet, in the end, Woodcock surprisingly does not seem to have closely bonded with many men in Company B. Throughout much of 1862, he notably messed with seven men, but only one from the Ninth Kentucky, the others representing Indiana and Ohio regiments. His closest friend from home died at Stones River, and he later described a subsequent mess as almost accidental in its origins.[20]

In addition to ideology and camaraderie, other factors must be considered. Hatred of the enemy looms as one crucial element. Scholars from Bell Wiley to Jason Phillips have emphasized the role that it played in soldier motivation and maintained that blue-gray soldier solidarity has been overstated. McPherson, moreover, specifically discussed the ache to wreak vengeance on the part of Southern Unionists. While occasionally admitting that the Confederates in the field believed that they too fought for a just cause, Woodcock not surprisingly was generally dismissive of his foes. Local and family concerns especially combined to push him toward an increasing hatred of the enemy. Confederate troops harassed and arrested Unionists in Macon County, including his brother and father, notably forcing the latter to ride twelve miles to jail despite a painful illness. There the Confederate commander "had the audacity to insult my father by speaking lightly of his sufferings, and also by making some *slang* remarks concerning myself and of the fact of my being a soldier in what he termed the Lincoln army, saying that I had 'gone to Abraham's bosom.'" They also threatened Woodcock himself, asserting that, if he became a prisoner, he would be treated as a Confederate deserter for not answering his call to service through conscription. "Those were the days when the rebels ruled with a heavy hand in our devoted little County," he lamented bitterly. "The rebels were crowing everywhere and felt confident that ere another twelve-month had lapsed the Independence of the Southern Confederacy would be peaceably acknowledged and we Tennesseans that had enlisted in the Federal Army, together with all our natural kinfolk that were Union in sentiment would be forced to seek an asylum north of Mason and Dixon's line."[21]

As the war progressed, Woodcock's characterizations of Confederates as cowardly, barbarous, and treasonous increased, especially when contrasted with the Unionist civilians on whom they preyed. A furlough at the end of 1863 exposed him to Confederate guerrillas, whom he scorned as criminals, "rogues," and "desperadoes." He also came to damn the Copperheads as no better than the traitorous Rebels. After the war, he railed against political opponents in the Democratic Party by calling them "traitors" and "unwhipped Rebels."[22]

Officers played an additional, crucial role in preserving Woodcock's morale. He deeply admired Henson, especially after the captain invited Woodcock to share his tent while the young soldier recovered from measles. Henson's resignation left Woodcock dismayed, especially when new officers began to exhibit seeming pettiness. He especially wondered why Capt. William T. Bryan seemed to dislike him. Yet, in the end, he grew to admire them as well. He especially praised his regiment's lieutenant colonel, George H. Cram, as *"an officer and a gentleman,"* while Maj. J. H. Grider "was the soul of courage" if "a man of no great military acquirements." He grew closest to Lt. Turner Hestand, his immediate superior. The much-admired Hestand died at Jonesboro, much to the men's dismay. In the end, competency mattered, but courage and fair dealing with the men meant more.[23]

Generals seemed more distant, yet even they helped buoy Woodcock's morale at times. He described John Pope as "a splendid looking man," and praised Maj. Gen. William S. Rosecrans "for his magnamity [*sic*] and careful consideration for those under his control." Rosecrans's occasional visits did much to cheer Woodcock and his comrades, but, in the end, his defeat at Chickamauga allowed them to see him go without great regret. Maj. Gen. William Tecumseh Sherman fared better in the end; Woodcock praised his ingenuity and intelligence. They met twice and spoke once, on Pine Mountain, Georgia. Sherman's informality and willingness to talk tactics with a lieutenant made a lasting mark. In contrast, incomprehensible decisions and battlefield defeats often led Woodcock to question other commanders, notably Maj. Gen. Don Carlos Buell for his inexplicable behavior during the Perryville Campaign and the brigade commander, Brig. Gen. Frederick Knefler, for his rash actions at Jonesboro. Such incidents negatively affected morale.[24]

Several other, relatively incidental factors, all familiar to those versed in soldier literature, helped sustain Woodcock's morale. Mail from home cheered him, except when it brought bad news. He subconsciously revealed a clue to his mind-set when he admitted to dreaming romantically that he was a knight-errant, protecting a lady from a "rude suitor." The support he received from Unionist civilians, though now muted, continued to inspire. Surprisingly, given that, after the war, Woodcock would become one of Tennessee's leading Baptist laymen and the treasurer of the state Baptist Convention and Mission Board, he rarely alluded to religion. His faith was a postwar affair.[25]

In the end, however, these motivating elements could sustain Woodcock and the balance of the Ninth Kentucky only so much. In 1864, Congress passed the Veteran Volunteer Act. Men willing to reenlist received distinctive insignia, a bounty, and a furlough. Units with 75 percent participation could also retain their integrity as Veteran Volunteer regiments. The legislation created "considerable excitement" in the Ninth Kentucky, yet, in the end, "it never got a right start among our boys." Woodcock continued: "Had I been healthy at the time I expect I should have attempted to induce Co. B to 'go veterans[.]' I also expect my efforts would *not* have been crowned with success." It is worth noting that, once he recovered his health, Woodcock still refused to reenlist, for reasons left unexplained. One suspects that he already envisioned a political career.[26]

Ultimately, only 106 of the regiment's 417 remaining soldiers reenlisted, most ending up in the Twenty-third Kentucky Veteran Volunteer Infantry or the Veteran Reserve Corps. These figures included only 13 men from Company B. Throughout the Atlanta Campaign, the remaining 331 "non-veterans" of the regiment, Woodcock included, complained bitterly that, as a result of their collective decision, they were denied furloughs and risked unnecessarily in battle. Matters came to a head in November 1864. Arriving in Louisville to be mustered out, the men found themselves quartered with black troops. Only timely intervention prevented a riot. While hardly definitive, the incident, when coupled with previous events, suggests that, for most of the men in the regiment, preserving the Union was their sole war aim. Unlike most Union soldiers, these Southerners never accepted emancipation or the arming of African Americans. As Chandra Manning maintains, soldiers' unwillingness to accept racial equality did not bode well for the nation's future.[27]

Combat motivation was the third and final Lynn-McPherson category, the factors that "nerved men to face extreme danger in battle."[28] A bout with measles kept Woodcock out of the Ninth Kentucky's initial action at Shiloh, and the regiment was largely inactive at Perryville. His experiences at Stones River and subsequent battles, however, suggest that several factors were important. His veteran comrades' courage during his baptism of fire near Murfreesboro both steadied and inspired him. "The boys," he remembered, "cheered each other with their voices, whooping and hollering, laughing and talking, and some *cursing* and *swearing*, but shooting all the time." Likewise, the inspiring leadership of the regimental colonel, Samuel Beatty, as well as the generals Rosecrans and Thomas L. Crittenden—notably their confidence and coolness under fire—played a major role in calming an admittedly anxious Woodcock during his first fight. Anger also played a role, especially the sight of advancing Confederate flags. Woodcock's entire battle description, and notably the obvious distortion of time, suggests the major role that adrenalin played. In contrast, Woodcock rarely mentioned ideology except as it motivated others, noting at one juncture how the dying Andrew Bray of Company B thanked God that he had fallen "for the cause of freedom and nationality."[29]

The same factors—camaraderie, leadership, anger—steeled Woodcock in subsequent battles, but so did a developing pride in his regiment and its reputation. On the second day at Chickamauga, that reputation suffered a blow when the Ninth Kentucky retreated in confusion in the face of Gen.

James Longstreet's massive assault. As defeat bore down on them, men wept while their colonel appealed to their regimental pride. Separated from the rest during the melee, Woodcock spent most of the afternoon attempting to find them, occasionally shouldering a gun with other units, but always moving on as he could, anxious to find his comrades. Regimental camaraderie again loomed as important at Missionary Ridge. Unable to join his fellow soldiers because of illness, Woodcock watched the developing battle anxiously but with confidence in his commanders' planning and personal courage. At a critical juncture, praise from Maj. Gen. Thomas J. Wood spurred the exhausted regiment to seize Confederate rifle pits and begin its ascent of the ridge. The same factors then sustained Woodcock through the Atlanta Campaign and the battles around the city. Notably absent from the memoir is any sense of fighting for ideological cause. As the enemy neared the Ninth Kentucky's lines, Woodcock simply had other things on his mind.[30]

In the end, Marcus Woodcock expressed great pride in his service and his outfit. At the end of 1864, he wrote in his diary that the regiment, "the pride of her General Command," had "done her duty": "Nobly has she stood up and done battle against the traitors to save her country." For Woodcock and many of his fellow Tennesseans, the war was, indeed, a perceived struggle of patriots against traitors, of cause, men doing their duty to preserve the Union crafted by the founding fathers. Southern Unionists, even mountaineers, were no less ideological than other Americans. But their soldiering also involved living up to family and community expectations, preserving friendships forged in battle, advancing personal ambitions, and expressing an open hatred of enemies. And few of Woodcock's comrades joined him as his personal war came to embrace emancipation and racial equality. A majority instead continued to question Lincoln's policies and support his political foes. Hatred of the Confederates and their local depredations could go only so far in maintaining Unionism during and after the war; in the end, it was an ideology not well equipped to survive the coming trials of Reconstruction and Redemption in Tennessee.[31]

Notes

1. Richard Nelson Current, *Lincoln's Loyalists: Union Soldiers from the Confederacy* (Boston: Northeastern University Press, 1992), esp. 29–60, 133–57,

195–218. Other important volumes on Southern Unionism include Daniel W. Crofts, *Reluctant Confederates: Upper South Unionists in the Secession Crisis* (Chapel Hill: University of North Carolina Press, 1989); Carl N. Degler, *The Other South: Southern Dissenters in the Nineteenth Century* (New York: Harper & Row, 1974); Noel C. Fisher, *War at Every Door: Partisan Politics and Guerrilla Violence in East Tennessee, 1860–1869* (Chapel Hill: University of North Carolina Press, 1997); John C. Inscoe and Robert C. Kenzer, eds., *Enemies of the Country: New Perspectives on Unionists in the Civil War South* (Athens: University of Georgia Press, 2001); Kenneth W. Noe and Shannon H. Wilson, eds., *The Civil War in Appalachia: Collected Essays* (Knoxville: University of Tennessee Press, 1997); Philip Shaw Paludan, *Victims: A True Story of the Civil War* (Knoxville: University of Tennessee Press, 1971); and Daniel E. Sutherland, ed., *Guerrillas, Unionists, and Violence on the Confederate Home Front* (Fayetteville: University of Arkansas Press, 1999).

2. Geoff Michael, "New Research," *Journal Junior: The Newsletter of Co. B, 9th Ky Vol Infantry* 3 (Winter 1994): 2; Muster Roll, Company B, Ninth Kentucky Volunteer Infantry, Record Group (RG) 94, National Archives and Records Administration (NARA), Washington, D.C.

3. Bell Irvin Wiley, *The Life of Johnny Reb: The Common Soldier of the Confederacy* (Indianapolis: Bobbs-Merrill, 1943), and *The Life of Billy Yank: The Common Soldier of the Union* (Indianapolis: Bobbs-Merrill, 1952). See also James M. McPherson, *For Cause and Comrades: Why Men Fought in the Civil War* (New York: Oxford University Press, 1997), 90–92, 94.

4. Michael Barton, *Goodmen: The Character of Civil War Soldiers* (University Park: Pennsylvania State University Press, 1981), 24 (quotation); Gerald Linderman, *Embattled Courage: The Experience of Combat in the American Civil War* (New York: Free Press, 1987); Paul Christopher Anderson, *Blood Image: Turner Ashby in the Civil War and the Southern Mind* (Baton Rouge: Louisiana State University Press, 2002); Stephen W. Berry III, *All That Makes a Man: Love and Ambition in the Civil War South* (New York: Oxford University Press, 2003); Kenneth S. Greenberg, *Honor and Slavery: Lies, Duels, Noses, Masks, Dressing as a Woman, Gifts, Strangers, Humanitarianism, Death, Slave Rebellions, the Proslavery Argument, Baseball, Hunting, and Gambling in the Old South* (Princeton, N.J.: Princeton University Press, 1996). See also Joseph T. Glatthaar, afterword to *The View from the Ground: Experiences of Civil War Soldiers,* ed. Aaron Sheehan-Dean (Lexington: University Press of Kentucky, 2007), 250–51; and Aaron Sheehan-Dean, "The Blue and Gray in Black and White," in Sheehan-Dean, ed., *View from the Ground,* 9–16.

5. Reid Mitchell, *Civil War Soldiers: Their Expectations and Their Experiences*

(New York: Touchstone, 1988), and *The Vacant Chair: The Northern Soldier Leaves Home* (New York: Oxford University Press, 1993); Earl J. Hess, *Liberty, Virtue, and Progress: Northerners and Their War for the Union* (New York: New York University Press, 1988), and *The Union Soldier in Battle: Enduring the Ordeal of Combat* (Lawrence: University Press of Kansas, 1997); Randall C. Jimerson, *The Private Civil War: Popular Thought during the Sectional Conflict* (Baton Rouge: Louisiana State University Press, 1988); Chandra Miller Manning, "What This Cruel War Was Over: Why Union and Confederate Soldiers Thought They Were Fighting the Civil War" (Ph.D. diss., Harvard University, 2003); McPherson, *For Cause and Comrades.*

6. Kenneth W. Noe, ed., *A Southern Boy in Blue: The Memoir of Marcus Woodcock, 9th Kentucky Infantry (U.S.A.)* (Knoxville: University of Tennessee Press, 1996), xiii–xxiv, 3–5, 301.

7. Ibid., 14, 16, 18, 301. See also Jimerson, *Private Civil War,* 30–33; and McPherson, *For Cause and Comrades,* 104, 110–14.

8. Noe, ed., *Southern Boy in Blue,* 14, 23, 149.

9. Michael, "New Research," 2; Muster Roll, Company B, Ninth Kentucky Volunteer Infantry, RG 94, NARA; Stephen V. Ash, *Middle Tennessee Society Transformed, 1860–1870: War and Peace in the Upper South* (Baton Rouge: Louisiana State University Press, 1988), 4–9; Harold G. Blankenship, *History of Macon County, Tennessee* (Tompkinsville, Ky.: Monroe County Press, 1986), 14, 65, 165, 167, 171–78; William Lynwood Montell, *Monroe County History, 1820–1970* (Tompkinsville, Ky.: Tompkinsville Lions Club, 1970), 1–2, 10, 28, 80; *The Tennessee Encyclopedia of History and Culture* (Nashville: Tennessee Historical Society and Rutledge Hill Press, 1998), 177, 471, 564–65; Noe, ed., *Southern Boy in Blue,* xiv, 7–8, 15–16. Mitchell (*Civil War Soldiers,* 15–16) notes how Southern Unionism usually was embodied in a community response.

10. Ash, *Middle Tennessee Society Transformed,* 69–78; Blankenship, *Monroe County,* 171–78; Robert F. Corlew, *Tennessee: A Short History,* 2nd ed. (Knoxville: University of Tennessee Press, 1990), 284–300; James B. Jones Jr., "'Fevers Ran High': The Civil War in the Cumberland," in *Rural Life and Culture in the Upper Cumberland,* ed. Michael E. Birdwell and W. Calvin Dickinson (Lexington: University Press of Kentucky, 2004), 73–75, 78; Merton Coulter, *The Civil War and Readjustment in Kentucky* (Chapel Hill: University of North Carolina Press, 1926), 25–56, 82–84, 87; Lowell H. Harrison, *The Civil War in Kentucky* (Lexington: University Press of Kentucky, 1975), 1–16; Noe, ed., *Southern Boy in Blue,* 10, 42–43; Montell, *Monroe County,* 28; Muster Roll, Company B, Ninth Kentucky Volunteer Infantry, RG 94, NARA.

11. Noe, ed., *Southern Boy in Blue,* 9–15.

12. Ibid., 8–15 (quotations, 8, 9, 10). Wiley (*Billy Yank,* 34–35) stresses the importance of such civilian demonstrations.

13. Noe, ed., *Southern Boy in Blue,* 12–18, 20, 43 (quotation, 12); Muster Roll, Company B, Ninth Kentucky Volunteer Infantry, RG 94, NARA.

14. Noe, ed., *Southern Boy in Blue,* xiv, 11–12, 17–20, 22–23, 308–18 (quotations, 18–19, 23). For *rage militaire,* see McPherson, *For Cause and Comrades,* 13–14.

15. Noe, ed., *Southern Boy in Blue,* 148–49, 272–73, 301 (quotations, 149, 273); McPherson, *For Cause and Comrades,* 175–78.

16. Noe, ed., *Southern Boy in Blue,* 146–47; Wiley, *Billy Yank,* 113–15.

17. Noe, ed., *Southern Boy in Blue,* 147–49 (quotations, 147–48, 149); McPherson, *For Cause and Comrades,* 117–28; Mitchell, *Civil War Soldiers,* 193–98.

18. Noe, ed., *Southern Boy in Blue,* xviii–xix, 30, 47, 146–47, 149, 272–73, 301 (quotations, 146, 147, 273, 301); *Journal Junior* 2 (Winter 1993): 3; Jimerson, *Private Civil War,* 42–49, 88–111; Chandra Manning, "A 'Vexed Question': White Union Soldiers on Slavery and Race," in Sheehan-Dean, ed., *View from the Ground,* 31–66.

19. Noe, ed., *Southern Boy in Blue,* 5.

20. Ibid., 39, 48, 51, 68, 79, 113, 137, 145, 157–58, 264, 269.

21. Wiley, *Johnny Reb,* 15–17; McPherson, *For Cause and Comrades,* 153–54; Jason Phillips, "A Brothers' War? Exploring Confederate Perceptions of the Enemy," in Sheehan-Dean, ed., *View from the Ground,* 67–90; Noe, ed., *Southern Boy in Blue,* 40–41, 42–44, 70, 74, 143, 162, 177 (quotations, 43, 43–44).

22. Noe, ed., *Southern Boy in Blue,* xviii, 54, 74, 75, 80, 89, 226, 260 (quotations, xviii, 260–61).

23. Ibid., 47, 54, 60, 66, 100. See also Linderman, *Embattled Courage,* 43–57, 229–34, 299 (quotations, 66).

24. Noe, ed., *Southern Boy in Blue,* 65, 92, 97–98, 103–4, 115, 120, 144, 220, 222, 225–27, 283, 284–85, 298–99 (quotations, 65, 115).

25. Ibid., xiv, 32, 268 (quotation, 32).

26. Ibid., 249–50, 299 (quotation, 249–50); James M. McPherson, *Battle Cry of Freedom: The Civil War Era* (New York: Oxford University Press, 1988), 719–20.

27. Noe, ed., *Southern Boy in Blue,* 299; *Journal Junior* 1 (March 1992): 7–10; Linderman, *Embattled Courage,* 261–64 (quotation, 263); Manning, "'Vexed Question,'" 48–50.

28. McPherson, *For Cause and Comrades,* 12.

29. Noe, ed., *Southern Boy in Blue,* 53, 56, 68, 103–4, 121–38 (quotations, 132, 136).

30. Ibid., 196–217, 233–40, 276–97, 298–99.

31. Ibid., 301.

"Time by the forelock"

Champ Ferguson and the Borderland Style of Warfare

Brian D. McKnight

During the Civil War, the boundary separating Tennessee and Kentucky was one of the most hotly contested regions in North America. What the Confederate States sought to defend as an international border the United States worked to prove moot. Champ Ferguson, a forty-year-old farmer, lived just north of this all-important line. Having been born and reared in Clinton County, Kentucky, Ferguson was acutely aware of his proximity to Tennessee and, like others of his region, crossed the border frequently for social and economic reasons. However, the interstate border that could be taken for granted became a much more rigid dividing line once the Civil War began. For Ferguson, like many of his borderland neighbors, the border became emblematic of the internal struggle of a people beset by war. With sometimes-mortal questions of loyalty, exhibitions of partisan violence, and a perpetual instinct for self-preservation, this man, whose first documented case of violence was in 1858, became one of the most notorious guerrilla warriors of the Civil War.

To be fair, the die was cast for Champ Ferguson to join the Confederacy from the moment Tennesseans began forming Southern armies. During the late spring of 1858, Champ, along with several of his Clinton County neighbors, sold a large herd of livestock to the Evans brothers from nearby Fentress County, Tennessee. Taking a promissory note properly notarized by several of that county's leading citizens, the Kentuckians felt confident that they would see their money. However, one of the brothers ran off with the stock, and the signers of the note claimed their signatures to be clever forgeries. Ferguson and another investor filed suit in Overton County, Tennessee, and won the case, but that money would never be collected. As Kentuckians, however, the men could take advantage of a Kentucky state law that allowed confiscation of personal property to repay a debt, so Champ and his fellows began coming into Tennessee under cover of darkness to take horses and other valuable property. However legal in Kentucky, this was simple theft in Tennessee, and, in the summer of 1858, the Evanses and several of their neighbors ambushed Ferguson at a camp meeting in Fentress County, Tennessee. In the running fight that ensued, Champ killed a county constable and was later arrested and remanded to the jail at Jamestown, Tennessee. Over the course of the next two years, Ferguson, with the help of his able attorney, Willis Scott Bledsoe, petitioned for and received extension after extension while awaiting trial at home. By the time Tennessee seceded from the Union nearly three years later, Champ had still not stood trial for the killing of the constable. During this time, fortune stepped in. When Ferguson's attorney declared himself for the Confederacy, he apparently promised his client that, with a Southern victory in the impending war, the case would be lost to history. Bolstering this theory, Ferguson noted that he was "induced to join the army on the promise that all prosecution in that case would be abandoned."[1]

Like countless other residents of the Tennessee-Kentucky borderland, Champ Ferguson awoke one morning and found himself living in an enemy's country. In mid-August 1861, Capt. John W. Tuttle of the Third Kentucky Volunteer Infantry (USA) entered Albany, Kentucky, the seat of Ferguson's home county of Clinton, and recorded the citizens' overwhelming Union sentiment. He saw "the stars and stripes gaily fluttering to the breze [sic] above the tops of the houses" and noted that more than two thousand people had turned out for the military parade through Albany's streets. That day, Champ came to town with his brother Jim to hear what the pro-Union speakers had to say. Although his legal woes had already dictated which path Champ would take, Jim listened intently to the speeches and later joined the Union army, as did their younger brother Ben. The remaining members of the family openly supported the Union cause and ostracized Champ after his commitment to the Confederacy threatened much of the family's wealth, which had been put forth to secure his bond.[2]

Calm and serious with slouched shoulders, Champ Ferguson does not look like one of the Civil War's most formidable guerrilla warriors. Courtesy of the Filson Historical Society, Louisville, Ky.

By September, the situation in Clinton County had deteriorated to the point that anyone not completely behind the cause for Union lived in fear. This put Champ clearly in the sights of his Unionist neighbors, and, in late August 1861, the pro-Union Kentuckians made their move. Meeting Ferguson on the road, a small group arrested him and set out on the road to the Federal recruiting center, Camp Dick Robinson, Kentucky. After traveling a few days, Ferguson escaped his captors on realizing that his continuing to live in Kentucky would breed more of these events. The increasingly personal nature of the war, along the borderline, affected Ferguson in much the same way that it did numerous others. For Champ, it caused him to move his family south into Tennessee, where they would live among a Confederate majority. His arrest also made him rethink his own personal safety. When captured, he was carrying only an old pepperbox revolver. From that point forward, he never traveled without formidable arms.[3]

Now that he was openly a Confederate, Ferguson began to participate actively in the war as a partisan guerrilla. Having neither military training nor a complete idea of the motives, objectives, or rules of war, he interpreted them for himself as: armies fight to kill the enemy; therefore, enemies, once identified as such, were fair targets and were to be vanquished however and whenever possible. In early November, Champ killed his first man of the war. His victim was William Frogg, a Unionist who had known Ferguson for most of his life. Invited into the house by Frogg's wife, Ferguson found the man bedridden with measles. Understanding the source of Frogg's malady as Camp Dick Robinson, the major Union recruiting depot in Kentucky, Champ matter-of-factly accused Frogg of being a member of the Union army. The ill man responded that he had visited the camp but had not joined the army. However, Ferguson was not convinced. He pulled a gun and killed Frogg in his sickbed with a five-month-old child in a crib next to him. This bloody and apparently premeditated event seems illogical, but, to Ferguson, it was perfectly reasoned. Seeing the world as black and white with no shades of gray, he considered any man who was not an ally an enemy. He even defended his apparent cowardice in shooting a bedridden and unarmed man by stating that Frogg was a bigger man than he and, if permitted to recover, would "waylay and shoot me." In Ferguson's mind, his killing of Frogg was, as he would defend several other killings, a preemptive strike. "I took time by the forelock, as people say. . . . I thought there was nothing like being in time," he said, "[because,] if we did not, we would soon find ourselves in a snare."[4]

Indeed, the borderland region became a netherworld essentially devoid of civil authority. No single event illustrates this point better than Ferguson's behavior on December 2, 1861, when he stood in front of the Clinton County courthouse and stole a man's horse while calling him "a God-damned Lincolnite" and imploring him to show himself so Ferguson could kill him. With the owner safely out of sight, Ferguson mounted the animal and rode out of town en route to the Wood farm.[5]

Reuben Wood had been one of Champ's oldest friends, the one who, indeed, had been credited with keeping rogues from shooting him on his arrest for killing the constable in 1858. However, that history did not matter to Champ. He met Wood on the road and asked, "I suppose you have been to Camp Robinson." When Wood answered affirmatively, Ferguson berated him for several minutes before pulling his gun. The man begged

Ferguson and reminded him of their friendship, asking, "Has there ever been any misunderstanding between us?" Ferguson responded coldly, "No, Reuben, you have always treated me like a gentleman, but you have been to Camp Robinson, and I intend to kill you." With that, Ferguson shot Wood in the abdomen, but the sixty-year-old man stayed upright. Clutching his coat around him, Wood ran around the corner of the house and then inside. There, in the darkened room, he grabbed a hatchet and lay in wait next to the door he had entered, expecting Ferguson to follow him. However, Champ came in the front, but still could not see Wood because of the darkness of the room. When Ferguson came close, Wood attacked him with the hatchet, and the two men ended up on a bed with Wood and his hatchet on top and getting the best of Champ and his revolver. Knocking the gun out of Champ's hand, Wood struck him in the head several times before being forced off by one of the guerrilla's companions. For the next several days, the dying Wood told and retold his story, and, for weeks afterward, Ferguson sported a bandage.[6]

By the end of 1861, Ferguson had cultivated such a brutal reputation that he could no longer spend any considerable time in his home state of Kentucky. He and his family now lived near Sparta, in White County, Tennessee, and his operations began taking on a more dangerous tone as he had sown seeds of retribution among the Unionists of Clinton County and those family members left behind by his violence. For the remainder of the conflict, he was pursued, not only by the Union army, but also by the sons of the men he had killed.

The new year brought about a change in the nature of the war along the Tennessee-Kentucky border. In January, Confederate forces suffered a serious defeat at Mill Springs, forcing them to abandon Kentucky. Ferguson too began to change. His assaults had already begun to include robbery, but, with the banishment of the Confederate army from south-central Kentucky, any activity that might serve to weaken or even inconvenience the Union and its supporters became part of the borderland war.

Although desperation often drove these partisan acts, they usually had a great impact on the local population by undermining civil authority. During the Civil War, enemies both in uniform and in civilian clothing burned numerous borderland courthouses. In other cases, tax rolls and other official documents were ceremoniously dumped into the street and set afire for all to see. Apart from the more formalized assaults on local government, crimes against individuals in the forms of violence and theft also became popular as the border region became more of a no-man's-land. Ultimately, such behavior did little to change the face of the war and made no noticeable impact on the outcome, but it did tear at the fabric of society—so much so that, in the months that followed the close of the war, numerous Kentucky counties petitioned the state government to call out the militia. In Harlan County, Kentucky, one citizen wrote: "Gurillas [*sic*] has nearly laid waste to the county by pillaging, plundering, and robbing and . . . are all well armed and men of the worst character and the Civil Authorities cannot apprehend them." Even John Hunt Morgan, who had enjoyed widespread celebrity and enduring respect for much of the Civil War, sank to bank robbery toward the end of his military operations.[7]

The turmoil that resulted from local guerrilla operations caused the rise of a core of opposition. In Ferguson's area of operation, several men rose to prominence as the defenders of Unionism and those who subscribed to it. Most notable was Champ's brother Jim, who had joined the Union army and served as a scout into his home region until he was killed in an ambush in December 1861. A second brother, Ben, espoused the cause of Union, although he did not join the army. Shortly after Jim's death, one of Champ's closest associates shot Ben in the shoulder during a dispute. Curiously, at least to modern sensibilities, Champ remained close with his pro-Confederate friend and expressed little concern for his wounded pro-Union brother.[8]

Such activities smack of what modern readers might call terrorism. Champ Ferguson clearly operated on instinct over evidence and grew famous for his preventive killings. When he "took time by the forelock," he did so with the paranoid expectation that his victim would have eventually turned on and tried to kill him. He also understood that his fierce reputation could become a formidable weapon because he knew that the same fear that he felt early in the war as a Confederate living in Unionist Clinton County, Kentucky, existed among Unionists in Middle Tennessee. Champ also knew that his violent activities would spawn retributive action and that he, as a guerrilla, could thrive only within a region in flux. Neither a military theorist nor a deep thinker, Ferguson had the two great talents of the successful guerrilla: common sense and caution.

Perhaps the best-known example of violent Unionist opposition came in the form of David Beatty. "Tinker Dave," as he was commonly

known, was one of the best-known Unionist guerrillas in the region and
Ferguson's greatest nemesis. These wartime enemies seemed committed to
killing each other during the war and, in at least one case, came together
with deadly results. Through the random shots and attempted ambushes,
Champ and Dave finally came together late in the war when Champ and
several men caught Tinker Dave alone and took him prisoner, although
Dave did effect an escape, albeit one in which he was seriously wounded.[9]

Understanding that the key to controlling any border region was to
control the hearts and minds of its inhabitants, several anti-Confederate
writers began producing tracts aimed at shoring up local Unionism while
advertising the brutality of the war along the border to politicians and
generals far removed from the area. James A. Brents, a former major in the
Union army who left the service early in the war, wrote of his experiences
in *The Patriots and Guerillas of East Tennessee and Kentucky*. Another
local Unionist, J. D. Hale, took on Champ directly. Writing two tracts
specifically aimed at revealing the deeds of this nefarious character, Hale
hoped to throw light on the brutal nature of the borderland war while
bringing pressure to bear on its greatest Confederate practitioner.[10]

The second year of the war offered hope to the partisan bands of the
Cumberland region. In early March 1862, men representing the local
Unionist and Confederate bands met in Monroe, Tennessee, to negotiate a
compromise that would, they hoped, close the irregular warfare pervading
the region. Some of the Southern sympathizers suggested the compromise
by stating "to the Union citizens about Monroe, that horse stealing, and
raiding about, was a bad business" and proposing "putting a stop to it."
Gathering together, both sides agreed with the assessment and promised
that armed partisans would not invade the counties of Clinton, Kentucky,
and Overton, Tennessee. James Beatty, the son of Tinker Dave, remembered that the "arrangement was for both parties to go home, lay down
their arms, and go to work." More directly: "The Home Guard was not to
pester the [Confederate] soldiers, and we were to be protected, all faring
alike." Despite the hope that the Upper Cumberland might enjoy some
level of stability and security, the compromise did not last long. Although
his friends had forged the deal, the Confederate captain James McHenry,
a man with whom Ferguson often rode, refused to abide by it. Only days
after the attempt at peace, McHenry and his men undermined the deal
by raiding Clinton County. John Capps, a Confederate soldier, confirmed

that Confederates in the region knew about the compromise and added: "We got it into our head to believe that the union men hadn't went by it." His simple explanation: "I was a rebel."[11]

With the compromise dead and Federal troops pulling out of the region, the level of security for Unionist citizens fell to an unprecedented low. As depredations became daily occurrences, letters pleading for help began pouring into the offices of any authority that might be able to help restore order. J. D. Hale wrote to Senator Andrew Johnson complaining of the local conditions. Fortuitously for the hopeful Unionists, Johnson's political rise coincided with the increased strife along the border, and, in his first speech as military governor of Tennessee, he devoted much of his attention to the fast-growing guerrilla problem, promising "a terrible accountability" if "their depredations are not stopped." A letter to Johnson from Isaac Reneau, a minister of the Disciples of Christ, placed Champ at the forefront of the guerrilla problem in the borderland region. At the bottom of the correspondence, the governor wrote: "Reward to be offered for man . . . Champ Ferguson."[12]

Although Ferguson made no statement for the historical record regarding his newfound fame, his actions suggested a man who was comfortable with his rising importance. Over the coming months, he continued to prosecute his uniquely bloody form of warfare and added the knife to his trusty gun as a tool of the trade. Fighting in periodic small battles and skirmishes alongside Capt. Oliver Hamilton's band, he also found time for robbery and intimidation.

In an April 1862 raid into Clinton County, Kentucky, Ferguson and his men found Henry Johnson at home. Ferguson expected that Johnson, a Unionist whose son was active in the area's anti-Confederate circle, was knowledgeable about several items of Ferguson's that had been stolen. Riding up in front of the man, Ferguson drew his pistol and demanded that he either have the property returned or pay its value. While at the Johnson place, Ferguson's men spotted Johnson's Unionist son fleeing through a distant field. Firing at the younger Johnson, they forced him to jump off a low cliff along the Wolf River. When Ferguson's men rode to the edge, they could see that the fall had injured Johnson, and they climbed down to the riverbank to finish the job. Farther up the road, they had the good fortune to catch the Union captain John Morrison at home. Despite their hitting Morrison with two bullets and sending him into the woods on foot, he eluded capture that night. Pheroba Hale, the wife of Champ's nemesis Jonathan Hale, also had a visit from Ferguson during which he and his men strolled through her house taking what they wanted.

On his way out of Kentucky that evening, Ferguson did something that would go far to ensure his bloody reputation. Meeting an armed rider after dark, Champ and his men were surprised to see that a young member of the Unionist home guard had ridden directly into their midst. Sixteen-year-old Fount Zachary immediately turned his gun over to Ferguson's men when he realized his error, and Champ leveled his weapon and shot the boy. Champ then dismounted with his knife in hand and stabbed the now either dead or dying Zachary in the chest.[13] The killing of such a young person pushed Champ's growing reputation closer to that of a bandit, particularly with the exaggerations that followed during the retellings. One young Union woman recorded in her diary that Champ had killed several men and "cut one in twain," removing the man's "intrails and throwing them on a log near by."[14] Several days afterward, the news of the raid had made it as far as Nashville. The *Daily Nashville Union* reported that Ferguson had taken "a promising little boy, twelve years old, by the name of Zachary" out of his sick bed and that, while held by two guerrillas, "a third cut his abdomen wide open."[15] If Ferguson was not already fully vilified in Union circles, such coverage could certainly ensure that end.

Col. Frank Wolford's First Kentucky Cavalry (USA) had been sent out of Clinton County only a few weeks before. However, with a recent order having come down to proceed to Nashville, the colonel thought it wise to revisit the county en route to his assignment. With nearly three hundred of Wolford's men entering Albany, the Union citizens were again free to speak their minds, and they began supplying Wolford with information about the principals. They pointed him south toward Livingston, Tennessee, and, as he moved closer, he gained more information about Champ Ferguson's whereabouts. On securing Livingston, Wolford gathered a squad to attack Ferguson's camp, estimated to be four miles south of town. As the small group milled about waiting for their ranks to fill, two more Union soldiers rode up to join the expedition. After a few minutes, the two mounted men began slowly moving off when one of the Union men yelled to his comrades: "Catch them or shoot them . . . it is Champe Ferguson." Immediately thrust into a race for his life, Champ left his comrade behind as a prisoner of the Federals and galloped off hoping to escape. Weathering several shots in his direction, Ferguson saw his chance, leaped off his horse, and fled on foot through some dense underbrush.[16]

By early May, Ferguson was back in Kentucky riding with his former attorney, Scott Bledsoe, on what can be considered an advance scout for John Hunt Morgan's planned invasion of the Bluegrass State. Entering Kentucky several days ahead of Morgan's scheduled arrival, Ferguson and Bledsoe used their available time to continue prosecuting their violent regional war.[17] Morgan's embarrassing defeat at Lebanon, Tennessee, further slowed his advance, but, within days of the setback, he had regrouped his men and moved into Kentucky. By the time Morgan approached Bowling Green, Ferguson stepped back and turned the lead over to Morgan, who had more experience operating in a broader strategic capacity. For the next four weeks, Champ and his men rode along with Morgan on the guerrilla's first extended tour of official military duty.[18] However, his scout with Morgan proved successful in that it taught him an important lesson by allowing him to operate, however briefly, within the realm of traditional military channels. Also, Ferguson now had a well-respected and militarily legitimate advocate in Morgan, who, Champ expected, could serve him within the army the same way he served Morgan outside it.

Although Ferguson could have officially joined the Confederate army and instantly gained legitimacy, he consciously chose to maintain his independence, which caused some more traditional soldiers considerable concern. Basil Duke, John Hunt Morgan's brother-in-law and resident martinet, first met Ferguson in July 1862. Duke, having heard many fantastic stories about the man he faced, took time to "impress upon him the necessity of observing—while with us—the rules of civilized warfare." The poorly educated Ferguson reassured him: "Why Colonel Duke, I've got sense." Then, with his curiosity getting the best of him, Duke inquired of Ferguson the number of men he had killed. Innocently, Ferguson told him: "I ain't killed nigh as many men as they say I have; folks has lied about me powerful. I ain't killed but thirty-two men since this war commenced."[19]

Whether Ferguson intended it or not, he may have been granted a commission at some point early in the war. During Ferguson's postwar trial, Gen. Joe Wheeler testified that, typically, the Confederacy did not grant officer commissions specifically to cavalrymen but assumed the commander of any cavalry force to be part of the army when a company was raised and a muster roll submitted.[20] John Hunt Morgan's brother

Richard spoke of Ferguson as a commissioned officer when he wrote early in the war: "Capt Ferguson has now reported in accordance with your order which I sent him some time since." Unimpressed with Ferguson's preference for "roaming where he has been for some time under the pretext of trying to capture Tinker Dave . . . to steal horses & Negroes & sell them," he asked his brother: "If you can do so I would much prefer that you assign [them to] some other Co."[21]

Many years later, Basil Duke contradicted Richard Morgan when he commented: "Ferguson could hardly be called a bushwhacker, although in his methods he much resembled them." His men were "very daring fighters" and, "although not enlisted in the Confederate service, were intensely attached to Ferguson and sworn to aid the Southern cause." Duke respected the fact that, "while Ferguson undertook many expeditions on his own private account and acknowledged no obedience to Confederate orders generally," he behaved properly while serving with him and "strictly obeyed commands and abstained from evil practices."[22]

Bushwhacking, although not possessing a universal definition within Civil War circles, was the most fearsome of ambushes but universally frowned on by professional and semiprofessional soldiers. Hidden among undergrowth, or lying along the tops of low ridges overlooking frequented roads, sharpshooters would take their rifles and draw down on enemies traveling either alone or in small groups. Once the bushwhacker fired, he fled, leaving the terrorized party to guess from whence the shot came. In an area such as the Appalachian Mountains, this was the most common way for the average citizen to participate in the war. Ferguson was no bushwhacker, however. He chose not to sneak and avoid detection, nor did he make any real attempt to hide his identity or motives. Ferguson rode as a partisan and guerrilla, standing somewhere between the common bushwhacker and the mustered soldier.

In late 1862, Champ took advantage of the Confederacy's invasion of Kentucky to act more aggressively in his own personal war. On one raid in particular, his motivations and tactics come together to help explain his view of the Civil War. Early one morning in October, he and his men stopped at a farm where they proceeded to kill three men. While two were shot to death, the third had been knifed by Ferguson in fulfillment of an earlier promise to "cut your throat with this knife."[23] However, the personal nature of this killing was enhanced by mutilation. Having stabbed the man to death, Ferguson apparently then cut a cornstalk and planted it in one of the wounds for visual effect. Despite this disturbing turn of events, Ferguson recalled the incident and matter-of-factly dismissed it as an act of self-defense. "I killed men to get them out of the way, only; I took no pleasure in torturing them." He explained: "Delk had been pursuing me a long time, and knew the only way to save my life, was to kill him, and I did it."[24] Ferguson would claim self-defense several times during his bloody career.

By late December, the Confederate invasion of Kentucky was over, and the Southern army had retreated into Tennessee. Knowing that William Rosecrans was readying his Union army for a counteroffensive, Braxton Bragg ordered John Hunt Morgan to reenter Kentucky and operate behind enemy lines.[25] Again using Champ Ferguson and his men to guide them through the mountain passes into central Kentucky, Morgan's cavalry embarked on its Christmas Raid. With his primary target being Rosecrans's lifeline, the Louisville and Nashville Railroad, Morgan's men spent the coming two weeks destroying more than twenty-two hundred feet of bridges, thirty-five miles of track, and many depots, water towers, and army stores.[26]

While Morgan operated against the Union army, Ferguson took the opportunity to return to the prosecution of his personal war. Once the Confederate force made it through the mountains, he asked for permission to take two companies of Morgan's men to search out area guerrillas. Morgan agreed, and Champ took off in search of Elam Huddleston, one of the region's most steadfast Unionists. Shortly before midnight on December 31, 1862, Ferguson and his men quietly encircled the Huddleston house.[27] Moses Huddleston, Elam's brother and a private in the Union army, awoke to see Ferguson glaring at him through a window. "Damn you, we've got you now," Champ screamed. The terrified occupants grabbed their guns, ran upstairs to the second floor, and began peppering the darkness with shots. While the Huddlestons fired out the windows, some of Ferguson's men sneaked close enough to the house to set fires, hoping to drive out the occupants with either flames or smoke. After about an hour of exchanging shots, Elam Huddleston was hit and severely wounded. Hoping to save his brother's life, Moses offered to surrender, and one of Morgan's captains who had ridden along with Ferguson assured the man that they would not be harmed if they would throw down their weapons and exit the house.

John Weatherred remembered that Champ "broke in the door and rushing upstairs and came dragging Capt. E. Huddleston down the stairs and out in the yard." Once outside, Champ pulled his pistol and killed the man.[28]

Leaving Huddleston's place, the small column, guided by the captured Moses Huddleston, moved toward the Rufus Dowdy farm. Although Rufus Dowdy was not home that night, his two brothers, Allen and Peter Zachary, who were Union soldiers, were there. Pushing the door in, the Confederates poured into the small room where the men were sleeping. Terrified, one of the soldiers grabbed his pistol and fired at Champ from point-blank range, narrowly missing the guerrilla leader. A fierce hand-to-hand fight ensued during which one of the Union soldiers was shot as he tried to make his escape out the front door and the other ran out into the front yard with Champ stabbing him along the way. That night, both Zachary brothers died at the hands of Ferguson and his men, only six months after Ferguson had killed their father and younger brother in a similar night attack on the home.[29]

When Ferguson and Morgan returned to Tennessee, the guerrilla receded into his surroundings until the summer. In July, however, Morgan embarked on his ill-fated Ohio Raid. However, Champ Ferguson was fortuitously absent from this expedition, which would, ultimately, result in the capture of Morgan and hundreds of his men. Later, during his court-martial, Champ admitted that he and Morgan had a falling out on the eve of the raid because "he took forty of my men and I was left with only a small force."[30] Although Ferguson had found a military patron in Morgan, he was not willing to allow that relationship to infringe on his own personal war. Since he had moved out of Kentucky early in the war, Ferguson had made his home on Calfkiller Creek, between Sparta and Monterey, in White County, Tennessee. From that location, he could leave the relative safety of home to pursue his activities elsewhere, but, in August 1863, the war visited him.

At daylight on August 9, men of Col. George Dibrell's Eighth Tennessee Cavalry (CSA) located Union soldiers under Col. Robert Minty just north of Sparta. Dibrell's men had been camped on his farm at the time, and, as the battle broke out, the surprised Confederates retreated to a small hill overlooking the only local bridge across Wild Cat Creek. The Battle of Wild Cat Creek, or Meredith's Mill, was a rousing Confederate success on several fronts. Dibrell's men rebuffed three attempts by a Union force twice its size to cross the creek, and once Minty pulled part of his men away to ford the stream in a flanking movement. Having done his damage, Dibrell pulled his men back into town, where they enjoyed a breakfast cooked by the women of Sparta. Sharing in the celebration that day was Champ Ferguson, who had arrived during the heat of the battle leading a collection of his own men and townsmen.[31] It seems that, since Ferguson had lost his connection with Morgan, he was now trying to foster one with another legitimately commissioned commander.

The new year of 1864 saw Ferguson's elevation to the level of a Union priority. Although the politicians in Nashville had known his name for some time, the generals Ulysses Grant and George Thomas were beginning to take note of his activities. On January 4, Col. Thomas Harrison and two hundred men of the Eighth Indiana followed the Calfkiller River into Sparta. After a five-day expedition filled with small skirmishes, Harrison left the area with a handful of prisoners, but no guerrilla leaders.[32] The next Union commander into White County was Col. William Stokes. "Wild Bill of the Hills" led two hundred of his men from the Fifth Tennessee Cavalry up the Calfkiller, camping near Ferguson's house, and into Sparta. By the end of the expedition, his men had killed "17 of the worst men in the country," and "took 12 prisoners, and captured about 20 horses and mules." In closing, Stokes assured his headquarters: "It will take some time and continued scouting to break up these bands, but . . . no time will be lost and no effort spared to rid the country of them."[33]

Almost immediately on the departure of the initial Union expeditions, Champ Ferguson emerged from the hills with vengeance on his mind. On February 13, he and his men fought with a group of the Union partisan Rufus Dowdy's men in Fentress County, killing "three, four, or five." From that small fight, Ferguson's men rode on and found more enemies only a mile away. Finding three prominent Unionists at a nearby farm, Ferguson killed two, while the other was escorted away, presumably to his death.[34] One witness recalled that Ferguson chillingly made Dallas Beatty, the son of Champ's nemesis Tinker Dave Beatty, look down the barrel of the gun and asked if he would like to eat the powder just before he fired.[35]

Within days, Ferguson and the other partisan bands were back in the vicinity of Sparta, followed closely by Colonel Stokes. Now commanding six companies of the Fifth Tennessee Cavalry, Stokes moved into town and quartered his men in Sparta's deserted houses. Having "barricaded the streets strongly, and fortified around my artillery," the colonel was prepared to comb the guerrillas out of White County. This task would not be easy, however, as Stokes reported: "The country is infested with a great number of rebel soldiers." Additionally, he noted that the guerrillas had virtually stopped their plundering, instead turning their attention and efforts toward Federal soldiers venturing into the countryside in search of food and forage.[36]

At this time, Col. John Hughs, a man with whom Ferguson often worked, commanded around six hundred Confederates equipped with excellent arms taken during one of their raids into Kentucky. On February 22, some of his troopers got an opportunity to meet their enemy. Stokes had sent two companies up the Calfkiller River through the Dug Hill community of White County on a scouting operation. W. B. Hyder recalled that Ferguson and Hughs divided their force and sent the men into the bushes, where they lay in wait for the approaching Federals. When a young captain led his men into "this Narrow Place between the River and the hill," the Confederates blocked the road in front and behind. Trapped by a much larger force with only sixty men of his own, Hyder suggested that the captain entertain the idea of surrendering but deferred when he saw "their [sic] would be no quarters showed." Completely trapped, he ordered his men to "bust through the Rebel Ranks as it was nothing but Death anyway."[37]

The Battle of Dug Hill,[38] as it would become known, was a slaughter. With their quarry trapped in the gorge, the Confederates began cutting them to pieces from their superior positions, at one point even rolling down large rocks and throwing smaller ones on the men of the Fifth Tennessee.[39] That day, Hughs counted forty-seven of the enemy killed, thirteen wounded, and four taken prisoner, while he lost only two men wounded.[40] Hyder remembered: "The Rebels then Cut the throats of the Boys from Ear to Ear. It was every Man for him selfe." By the next day, Stokes clearly saw the completeness of his defeat. He reported that all six of his officers and forty-five men had made it through the hills back to town.[41] Hyder offered more detail: "They took to the Woods and Brush . . . Scattered all over the Neighborhood and worked they [their] way Back to Sparta sum of them changing their Clothes for Citizens Clothes in order to git on to Sparta."[42] The Battle of Dug Hill, although numerically small and strategically insignificant, illustrated to the Federal army that the guerrilla menace would not cease to exist in the Cumberland region despite the other Union successes throughout Tennessee.

On March 11, Hughs and Ferguson met another Federal force near the location of the Battle of Dug Hill. That day, Ferguson sustained a serious wound. An ecstatic *Nashville Daily Union* reported on March 29, 1864, that he had been "shot through the abdomen and mortally wounded and at first secreted in a cave." The information originated from a local physician who dressed the wounds and was later found and questioned by Colonel Stokes. W. B. Hyder, who was probably on the scene during the battle, wrote: "Old Champ charged up and on their Horses fired out all of their shots from their pistals[.] But the boys in the Blue held to their trees and stumps and Champ fell Back out of Gun Shot and reloaded and here they came again hard as their horses could run yelling like wildmen came up in a few steps & Old Champ spoke in a loud coarse voice to Blackman and said Surrender or I will Kill you and Blackman hollered out to him Go to Hell God Dam you." At that point, some of the Federal soldiers fired at the guerrilla, and he "sunk down on his Saddle and turned his horse and ran off." Unaware of the extent of Ferguson's wound, Colonel Stokes called for Hyder two days later and informed him that, if Champ was seriously wounded, he would not go far and that the local doctor would probably have been called to treat him. Stokes sent Hyder "their to Night With 50 Men and take the old Doctor out and Maik him tell where Champ is and if he Refuses to tell Maik him think that you are a going to hang him." Cautioning Hyder not to "hang him till he is ded," Stokes instructed the scout that he did not want the man killed, just frightened into giving the required information.[43] After the doctor informed Hyder and the others of Ferguson's whereabouts, the men went to a cave where they only found his empty bed.[44]

By March 27, the news became more dramatic as the *Nashville Daily Union* reported that Ferguson had been killed in the fracas. The story recounted how Ferguson's men had scattered but were hunted down by the Federals: "Whenever one was taken, he was shot without ceremony." Although the newspaper claimed that Stokes did not know the wounded Ferguson's whereabouts, it reported that one of Ferguson's own men betrayed the guerrilla chieftain. Fabricating a story about a captured soldier who begged for his life and managed to broker a deal with Stokes in exchange for Ferguson, the paper reported that the turncoat informed on his captain and that the colonel quickly dispatched a scout to the appointed house. The Federals "entered and found Ferguson lying on a bed in one of the rooms, suffering from the wound received the day before." On orders from Stokes: "They immediately surrounded the bed and riddled his body with pistol balls."[45] Although premature and patently false, other reports confirming his death were published by the newspaper. Its "authentic source" validated the physician's claim of the severity of the wound, and the newspaper cheerily announced: "Union men will no more be persecuted by him."[46]

Although the Nashville newspaper could not have been more wrong about Ferguson's demise, his injury was indeed life threatening. For more than three months following the fight, Champ seemingly disappeared into thin air. The next year, he remembered being "badly wounded in one of these fights": "[I] once thought I should die, but the Lord appeared to be on my side; how long he will stay of that way of thinking, I cant tell."[47]

By summer, Champ had recovered from his life-threatening wounds and volunteered his services to the Confederate cavalryman Joe Wheeler on his raid from northern Georgia into Middle Tennessee. Retreating back into Georgia and later South Carolina with Wheeler, Champ got "into some trouble with some of the guard" and was arrested. On his release, Wheeler attached him to the command of Col. George Dibrell.[48]

In early October, Ferguson reunited with Dibrell at Saltville, Virginia, where numerous small Confederate commands had congregated in an attempt to stop the raid of the Union cavalry commander Stephen Burbridge on the Confederacy's most important saltworks. On the morning of October 2, 1864, the battle began with George Dibrell's Tennesseans, including Champ Ferguson, facing part of the Fifth U.S. Colored Cavalry. After a day of Federal advances, the battle ended by 5:00 P.M., when the Union cavalry began to run out of ammunition. The two sides settled in for the evening with the Federals preparing for a nighttime retreat and the Confederates anticipating a second attack the next morning.

Early the next morning, the sounds of battle were gone, and so was the remainder of Burbridge's command. George Dallas Mosgrove would witness the beginning of a new fight. On waking, he "heard a shot, then another and another until the firing swelled to the volume of . . . a skirmish line." Asking whether the enemy had returned, and being told that it had not, Mosgrove made his way toward the sound of the firing. Finding himself in front of Robertson's and Dibrell's positions, he realized: "The Tennesseans were killing negroes. . . . They were shooting every wounded Negro they could find."[49] Edward O. Guerrant echoed and expanded on Mosgrove's story: "Scouts were sent, & went all over the field, and the continued ring of the rifle, sung the death knell of many a poor Negro who was unfortunate enough not be killed yesterday." He added: "Our men took no Negro prisoners. Great numbers of them were killed yesterday & today."[50]

Although no individual soldier was named in the aforementioned accounts, at Ferguson's trial in the summer of 1865, Henry Shocker of the Twelfth Ohio Cavalry placed the defendant on the field as an active participant in the slaughter. He recalled: "I saw the prisoner [Ferguson] in the morning pointing his revolver down at the prisoners laying on the field." Understanding what was taking place, Shocker, who had been wounded the previous evening, crawled out of the path of the slowly approaching Ferguson. Keeping quiet, and probably feigning death, he heard Champ ask his friend Crawford Henselwood "what he was doing there? And why he came down there to fight with the damned niggers." With that, Ferguson pulled out his pistol and asked Henselwood: "Where will you have it, in the back or in the face?" Henselwood, now begging for his life, could not sway Ferguson. Having heard such pleas many times before, Champ shot the wounded trooper in midplea.[51]

Still playing dead, Shocker felt Ferguson walk past him and watched him go to a small log building nearby that was serving as a hospital. For several minutes, Shocker lost sight of Ferguson, and, when two harmless-looking Confederates came near, the wounded Union soldier asked them if they would take him into the hospital. As the two soldiers neared the building with Shocker, Ferguson came out with two black soldiers. "Wait and see what he does with them," commented one of the men. Shocker testified that Champ took the men several yards away and killed them with a revolver. He then returned to the hospital and took two more, whom he killed in a similar way.[52]

More insightful was Lt. George Carter's account. Carter's Eleventh Michigan Cavalry was separated from the Fifth U.S. Colored Cavalry on the battlefield by the Twelfth Ohio, but, on the morning following the fight, the lieutenant "saw some colored soldiers killed, eight or nine of them." Recalling that all the Federals on the field were now prisoners and no longer armed, Carter claimed that he then saw several of the prisoners killed. The men doing the killing confused Carter: "I couldn't tell whether or not citizens or soldiers did the killing of the prisoners, as all seemed to be dressed alike." Unsurprisingly, the profound breakdown of discipline and command within Confederate ranks that morning was also noted. Carter did not "know that anybody had command" and recalled: "They all appeared to be commanding themselves."[53]

Another eyewitness to the events at the makeshift hospital offered similar testimony. William H. Gardner had been a surgeon in the Thirtieth Kentucky Infantry (USA). Either captured by the enemy or left behind by his unit to treat wounded Federals, Gardner was inside the Confederate hospital working when "Ferguson came there with several armed men." The guerrilla then "took 5 men, privates, wounded (Negroes), and shot them."[54]

Ferguson was not finished with the Saltville fight. Long after dark on the night of October 7, four days after the battlefield killings, Ferguson and several others ascended the stairs of Wiley Hall on the campus of Emory and Henry College. The building had been converted to a hospital and was by that time serving wounded prisoners from Saltville. Orange Sells, a member of the Twelfth Ohio Cavalry, recalled three men bursting into his room. With one holding a candle and the others carrying revolvers, they were clearly looking for someone specific. After looking at each prisoner's face, one of the men said, "There are none of them here," and left the room. Within seconds, Sells heard gunfire in the room next door, and a black soldier wrapped in a sheet ran frantically into his room.[55] Apparently still angered by his experience fighting black troops, Ferguson had found two wounded black soldiers on the second floor and shot them in their beds.[56]

If a single person could be credited with sending Ferguson to the gallows, it would be Elza Smith. A lieutenant in the Thirteenth Kentucky Cavalry (USA), Smith, a cousin of Ferguson's first wife, hailed from Clinton County, Kentucky. About 4:00 P.M. the day after Ferguson came to the hospital and killed the two black soldiers he returned. Normally, guards would be stationed in each stairwell to prevent escape attempts, but, after the previous night's excitement, they were also on the lookout for vigilantes. Attempting to climb one of the stairs, Ferguson was stopped by a Confederate guard. Dr. James B. Murfree, a Tennessean who was assigned to the hospital at Emory and Henry College, remembered that, when the guard told Ferguson and the others that they could not go upstairs, the guerrilla replied that "they would go up the steps in spite of him." Undeterred, the guard leveled his gun on the small group and warned them not to advance. Without knowing it, the guard, whom Murfree colorfully described as "an Irishman . . . as brave as Julius Caesar," had accomplished a rare feat by forcing Champ Ferguson to back down. Ferguson, still wanting to go upstairs, but not badly enough to get shot, changed his tack. Leaving the Irish guard, he and his men walked to the other end of the building, where they climbed a different stairwell over the protestations of a less committed guard.[57]

On the third floor, Champ found the man for whom he was looking. The "badly wounded and perfectly helpless" Lieutenant Smith was lying in a bed in a room with two other ailing prisoners. Though seriously wounded, Smith recognized Ferguson and asked, "Champ, is that you?" Without a word, Ferguson approached the bed while pulling up a gun with one hand and hitting the breech with the other. Asking, "Smith, do you see this?" while leveling the weapon on the soldier, Smith begged, "Champ! For God's sake, don't shoot me here." Pushing the muzzle of the gun to within a foot of Smith's head, Ferguson pulled the trigger three times before it finally fired. Orange Sells, a soldier in the Twelfth Ohio Cavalry, was in the room when Ferguson entered and watched as Ferguson and another man inspected the wound to make sure that it was mortal before they left.[58]

Although Confederate authorities wished to prosecute Champ for the hospital killings, his illegitimate status also presented formidable problems. Milton P. Jarrigan, the judge advocate in Abingdon, Virginia, wrote a month later naming Ferguson and William Hildreth as the two central figures in the Emory and Henry murders but judged that "a military court has no jurisdiction over Ferguson and Hildreth." Unimpressed, Brig. Gen. John C. Vaughn replied: "The outrage committed at Emory Hospital . . . demands the punishment of the offenders." On his own investigation, Vaughn informed Jarrigan: "Those charged by name left this Dept with [Gen. John S.] Williams' command which returned to Genl Hood's army shortly after this act was perpetrated." In closing, Vaughn wrote: "I respectfully urge that the men Ferguson and Hildreth be arrested and sent to Abingdon for trial."[59] Angry, and embarrassed by the killing of an unarmed and wounded enemy officer, the Confederate major general John C.

Breckinridge ordered the arrest of Ferguson and Hildreth, demanding that they return to his department to face justice. On February 8, 1865, they reported to jail at Wytheville, Virginia, where they would remain, awaiting trial, until the waning days of the Confederacy.[60] During Ferguson's and Hildreth's two-month imprisonment, Breckinridge wrestled with his duty as an army officer and as a protector of the Southern cause. He devoted all the time he could to the investigation of the happenings at Emory and Henry but was also wrapped up in the unfolding drama of the war's final weeks. Seeking answers from Wheeler, he asked the cavalry commander the question that would ultimately decide Ferguson's fate: Under whose authority had Ferguson raised his company?

The answer to this plaguing question would not be simple. Responding to both Breckinridge and the court that tried Ferguson later that year, Wheeler claimed to understand that Edmund Kirby Smith had initially allowed the guerrilla to form his band and operate along the Tennessee-Kentucky border. It appears that Ferguson's legitimacy within Confederate circles was assumed, and only under close scrutiny, such as that of Judge Advocate Jarrigan in Abingdon, did Champ's unofficial status reveal itself.

On April 5, as Robert E. Lee's tattered army was retreating across southside Virginia, hoping to reach the railroad at Danville, Brig. Gen. John Echols ordered Ferguson's release from jail.[61] With the Confederacy's hope quickly fading, Echols likely considered dealing with such mundane business counterproductive in light of the state of the nation. Joseph Wheeler, who had been apprised of Ferguson's release, credited the difficulty of securing witnesses against the guerrilla as being another factor motivating Echols.[62]

From his release in early April through much of the month, Ferguson's whereabouts are unknown. Although Echols had turned him loose with orders to return to Wheeler, the guerrilla would not have had enough time to travel from Wytheville to Georgia or South Carolina, rejoin the fight, and make it back to Middle Tennessee by late April. It is more likely that Ferguson either heard of the Army of Northern Virginia's demise and returned home or, having become jaded by his arrest and imprisonment, had no intention of returning to the field. Whatever his reason, by late April, Champ Ferguson was back in the Cumberland region and still acting as if at war.

Standing tall, straight, and proud, Ferguson dominates this photograph taken at
the request of his guard, the men of the Ninth Michigan Infantry. Courtesy of
the Bentley Historical Library, University of Michigan.

Harper's Weekly covered Ferguson's trial and subsequent execution throughout
the fall of 1865.

Champ spent the month of April and much of May alternately rebuilding his burned-out house on Calfkiller Creek and hunting for longtime enemies. Toward the end of April, he and another man caught Dave Beatty near Jamestown, Tennessee, but the partisan escaped his captors and received life-threatening wounds.[63] Within a few days, Ferguson and several others rode to the Van "Bug" Duvall farm, where the infamous guerrilla killed his last man.[64] That same day, Gen. George Thomas authorized his subordinate commanders to publish surrender terms for independent bands in the newspapers.[65]

While Thomas was offering liberal terms to the mass of Upper Cumberland partisans, Ferguson was an exception to the policy. At the point Thomas ordered the publication of the terms of surrender, Ferguson had already fought his last fight. Therefore, those terms would embrace all participants who agreed to avoid partisan activities from then forward, which Ferguson evidently did. However, when news of Ferguson's post-Appomattox, but presurrender, attacks reached Thomas, the general made the guerrilla an exception to the rule and refused his surrender under the terms offered to the others. On May 16, Thomas's subordinate general, Lovell Rousseau, made the decision a matter of public record when he declared: "Champ Ferguson and his gang of cut-throats having refused to surrender are denounced as outlaws, and the military forces of this district will deal with and treat them accordingly."[66]

By the end of May, Champ Ferguson had been arrested and remanded to prison in Nashville to await his trial. Beginning on July 3, the proceedings lasted until September 18. During that time, the prosecution had seated dozens of witnesses, while the defense managed only a handful of friendly voices. It took only a few hours for the military commission to arrive at its verdict, and, on October 10, the court announced that Ferguson had been convicted on fifty-three counts of murder and sentenced to hang for his crimes. At 10:00 A.M. on October 20, 1865, Champ Ferguson climbed the steps of the gallows and was executed, thus ending the bloodiest single career of the Civil War.[67]

Notes

This essay is an abridgement of my forthcoming biography of Champ Ferguson.

1. *Nashville Dispatch,* August 19, 1865; J. A. Brents, *The Patriots and Guerillas of East Tennessee and Kentucky* (New York: J. A. Brents, 1863; reprint, Danville: Kentucky Jayhawker, 2001), 21–22; J. D. Hale, *Champ Furguson: The Border Rebel, and Thief, Robber, and Murderer* (Cincinnati: privately printed, 1864), 3–4; Albert R. Hogue, *Mark Twain's Obedstown and Knobs of Tennessee: A History of Jamestown and Fentress County, Tennessee* (Jamestown, Tenn.: Cumberland, 1950), 58, and *History of Fentress County, Tennessee* (Baltimore: Regional, 1975), 35; Thomas Davidson Mays, "Cumberland Blood: Champ Ferguson's Civil War" (Ph.D. diss., Texas Christian University, 1996), 23; *Nashville Daily Press and Times,* July 13, 1865.

2. Hambleton Tapp and James C. Klotter, eds., *The Union, the Civil War, and John W. Tuttle: A Kentucky Captain's Account* (Frankfort: Kentucky Historical Society, 1980), 1–2; Hogue, *Mark Twain's Obedstown and Knobs of Tennessee,* 58; Mays, "Cumberland Blood," 23.

3. Brents, *Patriots and Guerillas,* 22; *Nashville Daily Press,* September 19, 1865; Albert W. Schroeder Jr., "Writings of a Tennessee Unionist," *Tennessee Historical Quarterly* 9 (September 1950): 250; R. R. Hancock, *Hancock's Diary; or, A History of the Second Tennessee Confederate Cavalry* (Nashville: Brandon, 1887), 36–37; Mays, "Cumberland Blood," 41; L. W. Duvall Testimony, August 7, 1865, Proceedings of the Trial of Champ Ferguson, Record Group 153, Records of the Office of the Judge Advocate General (Army), 1792–1981, Court Martial Case Files, Textual Archives Services Division, National Archives and Records Administration, Washington, D.C. (hereafter cited as NARA-Trial); and Alvin C. Piles Testimony, July 26, 1865, NARA-Trial.

4. Esther Ann Frogg Testimony, August 2, 1865, NARA-Trial; Isaac T. Reneau to Gov. A. Johnson, March 31, 1861, Military Governor Andrew Johnson Papers, 1862–1865, Manuscripts and Archives Section, Tennessee State Library and Archives, Nashville (hereafter cited as TSLA-Johnson); *Nashville Union,* October 21, 1865.

5. P. A. Hale Testimony, August 12, 1865, NARA-Trial.

6. Miss Elizabeth Wood Testimony, August 4, 1865, NARA-Trial; Robert W. Wood Testimony, August 5, 1865, NARA-Trial; Brents, *Patriots and Guerillas,* 23; Isaac T. Reneau to Gov. A. Johnson, March 31, 1861, TSLA-Johnson; Lucinda Hatfield Statement, n.d., and Rufus Dowdy Statement, n.d., both in J. D. Hale, *Sketches of Scenes in the Career of Champ Furguson and His Lieutenant* (n.p.: n.p., 1870), 18–19.

7. James W. Orr, *Recollections of the War between the States, 1861–1865* (n.p.: n.p., 1909), 13; Bonnie Ball, "Impact of the Civil War upon the Southwestern

Corner of Virginia," *Historical Sketches of Southwest Virginia* 15 (March 1982): 3; Robert Perry, *Jack May's War: Colonel Andrew Jackson May and the Civil War in Eastern Kentucky, East Tennessee, and Southwest Virginia* (Johnson City, Tenn.: Overmountain, 1998), 64; Unknown to W. H. Hays, Esq., May 23, 1865, in "Harlan County Battalion and Reports," *Harlan County Footprints* 1, no. 4 (n.d.): 134; and James A. Ramage, *Rebel Raider: The Life of General John Hunt Morgan* (Lexington: University Press of Kentucky, 1986), 218, 220.

8. Brents, *Patriots and Guerillas*, 31; and Mays, "Cumberland Blood," 61.

9. Brents, *Patriots and Guerillas*, 30; Eastham Tarrant, *The Wild Riders of the First Kentucky Cavalry: A History of the Regiment, in the Great War of the Rebellion, 1861–1865* (Lexington, Ky.: Henry Clay Press, 1969), 57; Mays, "Cumberland Blood," 61, 173–74; *Nashville Dispatch,* July 21, 1865; Thurman Sensing, *Champ Ferguson: Confederate Guerrilla* (Nashville: Vanderbilt University Press, 1942), 76; David Beatty Testimony, July 20, 1865, NARA-Trial.

10. Brents, *Patriots and Guerillas*, 12–14; Tarrant, *Wild Riders,* 21; J. D. Hale, *Champ Furguson: A Sketch of the War in East Tennessee Detailing Some of the Leading Spirits of the Rebellion* (Cincinnati: privately printed, 1862), and *The Border Rebel,* 3–4.

11. Winburne W. Goodpasture Testimony, August 22, 1865, NARA-Trial; Undated Statement signed by John J. McDonald, John Boles, Sen., H. Stover, and John Winingham, in Hale, *Sketches of Scenes,* 7–8; James Beatty Testimony, August 9, 1865, NARA-Trial; Marion Johnson Testimony, August 9, 1865, NARA-Trial; Hale, *A Sketch of the War,* 8. Goodpasture (Testimony, August 22, 1865) and Rufus Dowdy (Testimony, August 26, 1865, NARA-Trial) confirmed that McHenry broke the accord within days of its adoption. Other interesting statements regarding the compromise effort can be found in Hale, *Sketches and Scenes,* 7–10; and John A. Capps Testimony, August 21, 1865, NARA-Trial.

12. Jonathan D. Hale to Honorable Andrew Johnson, December 16, 1861, in *The Papers of Andrew Johnson*, vol. 5, *1861–1862,* ed. Leroy P. Graf and Ralph W. Haskins (Knoxville: University of Tennessee Press, 1976), 61; Speech to Davidson County Citizens, March 22, 1862, in ibid., 5:237; and Isaac T. Reneau to Gov. A. Johnson, March 31, 1861, in ibid., 5:257–58.

13. Esther A. Jackson Testimony, July 28, 1865, NARA-Trial; Rufus Dowdy Testimony, August 24, 1865, NARA-Trial; A. F. Capps Testimony, August 2, 1865, NARA-Trial; and Brents, *Patriots and Guerillas,* 25.

14. Schroeder, "Writings of a Tennessee Unionist," 257.

15. *Daily Nashville Union,* April 19, 1862.

16. Tarrant, *Wild Riders,* 76–79.

17. Hogue, *History of Fentress County, Tennessee,* 35.

18. Basil W. Duke, *History of Morgan's Cavalry* (Cincinnati: Miami Printing & Publishing Co., 1867), 165–66; Ramage, *Rebel Raider,* 85–87; and *Richmond Enquirer,* May 22, 1862.

19. Basil W. Duke, *The Civil War Reminiscences of General Basil W. Duke, C.S.A.* (1911; reprint, New York: Cooper Square, 2001), 123–24.

20. *Nashville Dispatch,* August 25, 26, 1865.

21. R. C. M. to Dr. Johny, May 4, 1863, John Hunt Morgan Papers, Southern Historical Collection, Manuscripts Department, Wilson Library, University of North Carolina at Chapel Hill (hereafter cited as SHC-Morgan).

22. Duke, *Reminiscences,* 123.

23. John Huff Testimony, August 10, 1865, NARA-Trial.

24. *Nashville Union,* October 21, 1865.

25. Ramage, *Rebel Raider,* 137.

26. Ibid.; Grady McWhiney, *Braxton Bragg and Confederate Defeat,* 2 vols. (New York: Columbia University Press, 1969–1991), 1:341; Duke, *History of Morgan's Cavalry,* 325–42; Thomas Lawrence Connelly, *Autumn of Glory: The Army of Tennessee, 1863–1865* (Baton Rouge: Louisiana State University, 1971), 29.

27. Wartime Diary of John Weatherred, copy held privately by Mr. Jack Masters, Gallatin, Tenn.

28. Moses Huddleston Testimony, July 27, 1865, NARA-Trial; Wartime Diary of John Weatherred.

29. Sarah Dowdy Testimony, July 28, 1865, NARA-Trial; Moses Huddleston Testimony, July 27, 1865, NARA-Trial.

30. *Nashville Dispatch,* August 19, 1865.

31. Report of Col. George G. Dibrell, August 18, 1865, in U.S. War Department, *War of the Rebellion: A Compilation of the Official Records of the Union and Confederate Armies, 1861–1865* (hereafter cited as *OR*) (Washington, D.C.: U.S. Government Printing Office, 1880–1901), ser. 1, vol. 23, pt. 1, pp. 847–48; Report of Col. Robert H. G. Minty, August 11, 1863, in ibid., ser. 1, vol. 23, pt. 1, pp. 846–47.

32. Report of Col. Thomas J. Harrison, January 14, 1864, in ibid., ser. 1, vol. 32, pt. 1, pp. 65–66.

33. Report of Col. William B. Stokes, February 2, 1864, in ibid., ser. 1, vol. 32, pt. 1, pp. 162–63.

34. Daniel W. Garrett Testimony, July 22, 1865, NARA-Trial; Isham Richards Testimony, July 22, 1865, NARA-Trial; Captain Rufus Dowdy Testimony, August 24, 1865, NARA-Trial.

35. Confession of Columbus German, July 3, 1866, J. D. Hale Papers, Wright Room Research Library, Historical Society of Cheshire County, Keene, N.H.

36. Report of Col. William B. Stokes, February 24, 1864, in *OR,* ser. 1, vol. 32, pt. 1, p. 416.

37. W. B. Hyder Recollections, Special Collections, Angelo and Jennette Volpe Library and Media Center, Tennessee Technological University, Cookeville, Tennessee (hereafter cited as TTU-Hyder).

38. The Battle of Dug Hill is sometimes called the Battle of the Calfkiller.

39. Betty Jane Dudney, "Civil War in White County, Tennessee, 1861–1865" (M.A. thesis, Tennessee Technological University, 1985), 35–36; Monroe Seals, *History of White County, Tennessee* (Spartanburg, S.C.: Reprint Co., 1982), 71–72; Lewis A. Lawson, *Wheeler's Last Raid* (Greenwood, Fla.: Penkevill, 1986), 248–49.

40. James T. Siburt, "Colonel John M. Hughs: Brigade Commander and Confederate Guerrilla," *Tennessee Historical Quarterly* 51 (Summer 1992): 90.

41. Report of Col. William B. Stokes, February 24, 1864, in *OR,* ser. 1, vol. 32, pt. 1, p. 416.

42. W. B. Hyder Recollections, TTU-Hyder.

43. Ibid.

44. *Nashville Daily Union,* March 29, 1864.

45. *Nashville Daily Union,* March 27, 1864.

46. *Nashville Daily Union,* April 1, 1864.

47. *Nashville Union,* October 21, 1865.

48. General Joseph Wheeler Testimony, August 28, 1865, NARA-Trial.

49. George Dallas Mosgrove, *Kentucky Cavaliers in Dixie: Reminiscences of a Confederate Cavalryman* (Jackson, Tenn.: McCowart-Mercer, 1957; reprint, Lincoln: University of Nebraska Press, 1999), 206.

50. William C. Davis and Meredith L. Swentor, eds., *Bluegrass Confederate: The Headquarters Diary of Edward O. Guerrant* (Baton Rouge: Louisiana State University Press, 1999), 546–47.

51. *Nashville Dispatch,* August 2, 1865.

52. *Nashville Dispatch,* August 2, 1865.

53. William C. Davis, "Massacre at Saltville," *Civil War Times Illustrated,* February 1971, 45.

54. Report of Surg. William H. Gardner, October 26, 1864, in *OR,* ser. 1, vol. 39, pt. 1, pp. 554–55.

55. Orange Sells Testimony, August 12, 1865, NARA-Trial.

56. Report of Surg. William H. Gardner, October 26, 1864, in *OR,* ser. 1, vol. 39, pt. 1, pp. 554–55; Milton P. Jarrigan, November 8, 1864, MIAC Endorsements on Letters, Department of East Tennessee, 1862–1864, chap. 8, vol. 357, War Department Collection of Confederate States of America Records, National

Archives and Records Administration, Washington, D.C. (hereafter cited as NARA–MIAC Endorsements).

57. "Dr. Murfree Meets Champ Ferguson," *Rutherford County Historical Society* (Winter 1973): 15–19.

58. W. W. Stringfield, "The Champ Ferguson Affair," *Emory and Henry Era* 17, no. 6 (May 1914): 300–302; R. N. Price, *Holston Methodism: From Its Origin to the Present Time* (Nashville: Publishing House of the Methodist Episcopal Church, South, 1913), 396–99; Orange Sells Testimony, August 12, 1865, NARA-Trial; Milton P. Jarrigan, November 8, 1865, NARA–MIAC Endorsements.

59. Milton P. Jarrigan, November 8, 1865, NARA–MIAC Endorsements.

60. Document O, NARA-Trial.

61. Ibid.

62. Joseph Wheeler Testimony, August 28, 1865, NARA-Trial.

63. *Nashville Dispatch,* July 21, 1865; Mays, "Cumberland Blood," 173–74; Sensing, *Champ Ferguson,* 76; David Beatty Testimony, July 20, 1865, NARA-Trial.

64. L. W. Duvall Testimony, August 7, 1865, NARA-Trial; Martin Hurt Testimony, August 8, 1865, NARA-Trial.

65. Document H, NARA-Trial; Mays, "Cumberland Blood," 176.

66. H. C. Whittemore to Major-General Milroy, May 16, 1865, in *OR,* ser. 1, vol. 49, pt. 2, p. 806; Mays, "Cumberland Blood," 177; *New York Herald,* May 19, 1865.

67. Your Son Robert Johnson to Dear Father, May 31, 1865, in *The Papers of Andrew Johnson,* vol. 8, *May–August 1865,* ed. Paul H. Bergeron (Knoxville: University of Tennessee Press, 1989), 155–56; David Beatty Testimony, July 21, 1865, NARA-Trial; Nancy Kogier Testimony, August 5, 1865, NARA-Trial; A. F. Capps Testimony, August 2, 1865, NARA-Trial; John A. Capps Testimony, August 21, 1865, NARA-Trial; Winburn Goodpasture Testimony, August 22, 1865, NARA-Trial; *Nashville Daily Press and Times,* September 19, 1865; *Nashville Dispatch,* October 20, 21, 1865.

"I shoot the men and burn their houses"

Home Fires in the Line of Fire

Michael R. Bradley

When the Civil War began, both Northerners and Southerners believed that they were the victims of aggression. The bombardment of Fort Sumter was to the North a clear example of Southern belligerence. The South considered itself under attack as early as 1854 when conflict arose in Kansas and the use of violence to end slavery became acceptable to certain parties in the North. Indeed, John Brown's raid on the U.S. arsenal at Harpers Ferry in October 1859, with the intent of inciting a slave rebellion, and the acclaim of Brown as a martyr by some Northerners increased this sentiment. For Tennesseans, the idea that one side had attacked the other became the overriding factor when the voters cast their ballots on the issue of secession. In February 1861, this feeling was restrained by the possibility of peaceful separation between the sections; however, in June 1861, when another vote was held, the war had begun, and the only choice for Tennesseans was whom to join in attacking whom.

Public speeches by civic leaders and newspaper editorials in both the North and the South in 1861 called for retaliation against the aggressors, and the men who went to war in 1861 saw vengeance as a reasonable action to be used against the other side. Because the war was fought primarily in the South, this section would feel the hard hand of war more than the North. When organized armies met on the battlefield, luck, numbers, and skill might bring victory, but the opportunity for retribution was limited by the ability of the other army to defend itself. The civilian population was not able to shield itself effectively, and the desire for revenge against the society that had attacked the Union was directed at them. Civilians took what steps they could to strike back, often resorting to guerrilla warfare.

While it is appropriate for students of history to focus on the issues that moved governments to go to war, they must not neglect the motives that induced men to take up arms. Their reasons may well be different from those of the governments involved, at least in the beginning of the conflict. Indeed, in the years 1861–1865, and continuing to 1877, soldiers talked much about retribution. This clearly was the intention of many of the war's participants, and Tennessee was one location where intent became action. This emphasis on the settling of scores contradicts the popular notion that the Civil War was a gentlemen's war in which civilians were seldom molested. This claim also challenges the veracity of Abraham Lincoln's statement in his Second Inaugural Address that the U.S. government held "malice toward none." In truth, there was a great deal of malice toward the South in the hearts of many Northerners, for, in their minds, the South had initiated the war. This antipathy began to show itself almost as soon as the first Union soldiers set foot on Southern soil, and it continued until the last left at the end of Reconstruction. As early as 1861 and 1862, Northern enlisted men and low-ranking officers implemented a hard-war policy that sought to punish the Southern populace. By 1863, it was accepted as official policy endorsed by the White House and the War Department and carried out by the military forces of the United States. Thus, the economic infrastructure of the South, including homes and farms, was considered a valid military target. Civilian deaths, therefore, became inevitable. The home fires were in the line of fire.

Although there was some contact between civilians and Union forces in Tennessee as campaigns evolved, most Tennesseans would not find themselves near a battlefield or in the path of major troop movements. For the majority of the state's residents, contact with Union soldiers was limited to small foraging parties or garrisons posted along the railroads. Discipline was lax in these small units, especially among those engaged in foraging. Northern troops behind the front lines were generally under the command of the provost marshal general. Documents detailing their actions are not a part of the *Official Records of the War of the Rebellion* but, rather, contained in a separate collection called *Provost Marshal Records of the United States Army.* Sadly, these records have been largely neglected by historians.

The duties of the provost troops during the war included seeking out spies, capturing deserters, and arresting civilians suspected of disloyalty; investigating the theft or misuse of government property; controlling travel in the military zone by issuing passes and monitoring government transportation; maintaining the records of military parolees and those who took the oath of allegiance. Each army post had a provost officer who, in addition to carrying out these duties, could also convene military commissions to try cases involving violations of military orders, departures from the laws of war, and other offenses that arose under military jurisdiction. Since most of Tennessee was under martial law, the provost marshal handled all disputes that normally would have gone before a civil court. These included disagreements over property boundaries, ownership of livestock, fair market value of property, and disturbances of the peace. But the provosts also found themselves dealing with issues of rape, arson, robbery, and murder as well as with the activities of Confederate cavalry units and guerrillas operating behind Union lines.

In 1862, the Union Army of the Cumberland moved into Middle Tennessee following the victories of General U. S. Grant at Forts Henry and Donelson. The commander of this force, Gen. Don Carlos Buell, was dedicated to restoring the Union, an objective that Lincoln declared to be his primary focus in the early days of the war. The conciliatory attitude that Buell adopted toward secessionists alienated the commander from many of his troops who had come South to punish the Rebels.[1] One Union commander, Gen. John Pope, disagreed with the Buell's gentle approach, a position that he made clear in the behavior he allowed his men to pursue. Pope's dedication to hard-war policies in West Tennessee won the approval of Secretary of War Edwin Stanton and of Abraham Lincoln, who brought Pope east to command Federal forces in Virginia. In that theater, Pope made himself notorious by allowing his men to live off the land, take hostages, force civilians to labor for the army, and deport all those who refused to take the oath of allegiance, women and children included. This policy continued until Pope was soundly defeated at Second Manassas in the summer of 1862.

The Union advance in Middle Tennessee led to the occupation of the village of Wartrace in Bedford County, an area noted for Unionist sentiment. By the late spring of 1862, however, the Unionist citizens of Wartrace had filed a complaint with Buell alleging that numerous robberies had been committed by Northern troops, that homes were routinely looted, and that several women, both black and white, had been raped. The final straw that sparked the complaint was the attempted gang rape of the wife and daughter of the leading Unionist in the town, which was frustrated by the intervention of several male citizens. While these events were transpiring in Middle Tennessee, the western part of the state was being tormented by Col. Charles Jennison's Seventh Kansas. The actions of Jennison's Jayhawks were characterized by one Union officer as nothing short of "banditry, brutality, and cold-blooded murder."[2]

In all Union-occupied areas of Tennessee, one response of the Confederate population was the organization of guerrilla bands. The prewar militia system provided a base for the organization of such bands since the men in each community had some rudimentary knowledge of military drill and military organization. Conscription had not yet been implemented, which left at home many able-bodied men who had seen no need to volunteer in 1861 but who now confronted the obvious need to defend their homes. Soon, Union boats carrying supplies along the rivers were being shot at whenever the channel brought them close to shore, forage parties were bushwhacked, marching columns were ambushed, and railroads were sabotaged. The rural nature of Tennessee gave guerrillas plenty of room in which to roam, while knowledge of the local countryside provided them a significant advantage. Union forces routinely retaliated against the local civilian population where the attack occurred, thus creating more guerrillas since those harmed by the retaliatory strikes often sought revenge. When the pro-Union elements of the population became involved, a true civil war ensued, leaving a bitterness that lasted for decades.

In the autumn of 1862, Gen. Braxton Bragg led a Confederate army through Tennessee in his invasion of Kentucky. This move forced the Union general Buell to withdraw most of his troops north to confront the Rebels. As the Federal troops retreated, local guerrillas sprang into action. The Union retreat through Lincoln and Rutherford counties saw men lost to guerrillas every day. These partisan bands took no prisoners, or, if they did, they held them only long enough to reach a place where they could kill them at their leisure. Retaliation from the Northern troops followed as a matter of course. Charles Anderson, a former vice president of the

Nashville and Chattanooga Railroad, recalled that, when Buell's troops passed his home at Anderson's Station near Murfreesboro, they burned his house, barns, and other outbuildings. The troops had first looted Anderson's home, then took the portraits of his parents outside and ran sabers through them. Embittered by this destruction, Anderson decided to support the Confederate cause and joined the staff of General Nathan Bedford Forrest.[3]

On occasion, guerrillas joined together in large bands and served alongside regular Confederate troops in some military operation. Adam R. Johnson and T. G. Woodward participated in an effort to capture Clarksville, Tennessee, from Union forces. The Rebels even threatened the town of Dover, a major Union supply base. The Confederates, however, were unable to hold Clarksville in the face of an advance by Federal troops.[4]

It was during this time that Ellis Harper began to make life miserable for Northern forces around the "twin tunnels" on the Louisville and Nashville Railroad near Gallatin, eventually earning for himself the reputation of a fierce opponent of the Union and a dauntless guerrilla. Harper had enlisted in Company I, Thirtieth Tennessee Infantry, on November 22, 1861. His regiment made up part of the garrison of Fort Donelson when it surrendered in February 1862. A prisoner of war, Harper was sent to Camp Butler, Illinois, but escaped soon after. On returning to his home in Sumner County, he found C. A. Peddicord organizing a company of scouts. This service appealed to Harper, and soon he had raised his own band to fight within the organizational structure that Peddicord had established. When Peddicord and many of his men were captured, Harper became the leading partisan commander in the area north of Nashville. His career would last for the duration of the war.

In mid- to late 1862, civil life deteriorated in the Confederacy as more and more territory came under Federal occupation. The North's official policy of conciliation was being questioned by the actions of the men in the ranks who had frequent contact with recalcitrant Southerners. Their desire for vengeance was reinforced by Confederate battlefield successes, which erased many of the gains made by the Union earlier in the year. Devastation of civilian property became widespread, and the organization of partisan units increased. The Union general James Negley complained of guerrillas around Columbia, Tennessee, while other bands sprang up near Union-occupied Fort Donelson, Memphis, and in the Jackson Purchase area of western Kentucky. The Union general Grenville Dodge reported from Trenton, Tennessee, that all nine hundred cavalrymen under his command were busy chasing guerrillas who "were determined to give us work."[5]

Late autumn and early winter of 1862 were relatively quiet in Tennessee. Home fires burned peacefully, while the major armies maneuvered and fought in Kentucky. However, when these armies returned to Middle Tennessee to confront each other along the banks of Stones River, the civilian population again experienced the hardships associated with civil war. As the Union Army of the Cumberland and the Confederate Army of Tennessee fought to a tactical draw at Murfreesboro in the last days of the year, Confederate cavalry under Gens. Nathan Bedford Forrest, John Hunt Morgan, and Earl Van Dorn devastated Union supply lines in West and Middle Tennessee as well as in north Mississippi. Inspired by these raids, Southern civilians sought ways to participate in the war effort. One of these civilians was Mrs. Clara Judd, the widow of the Episcopal rector of Winchester, Tennessee. Judd's parents lived in Minnesota, but her adult children were employed by a Confederate government factory in Atlanta. Learning of a projected Confederate cavalry raid in her area, Judd traveled to Louisville, Kentucky, where she purchased a sock-knitting machine. She returned to Tennessee with the machine and was intentionally captured during the raid. The knitting machine was then forwarded to Atlanta, where it was copied by machinists working for the Confederate quartermaster department. Judd was later apprehended by Union authorities and was tried before a military commission. She was sentenced and imprisoned at Camp Butler, where she remained for the duration of the war.[6]

The tedium of winter encampment caused a waning of discipline in Northern ranks. Foraging parties became more disorderly and often turned into robbing expeditions. Such actions brought the soldiers some excitement but also increased the hardship on civilians, sparking an increase in guerrilla activity. The inability of Andrew Johnson, the military governor of the state, to establish a functioning civil government only exacerbated the situation.

The beginning of the Vicksburg Campaign left West Tennessee as a secondary theater of operations while Gen. William Rosecrans and the Army of the Cumberland struggled to amass supplies and men before moving against Braxton Bragg. The success of Rosecrans in clearing Middle Tennessee of large bodies of organized Confederates increased resistance by Confederate guerrillas.

While foraging, Rosecrans's soldiers often found opportunities to exhibit their contempt for Southern civilians. On July 8, 1863, the general noted that stragglers had been committing robberies and that quartermasters were foraging in violation of army regulations. He reminded his corps commanders that "disloyalty does not forfeit the rights of humanity." At the same time, Chief of Staff James A. Garfield reported that "the lawlessness of our soldiers on foraging parties will make bushwhackers faster than any other thing."[7] These words proved to be prophetic.

The presence of the Federal army following the successful summer campaigns of 1863 created an opportunity for Tennessee Unionists to enlist in Union army units. One such unit was the Fifth Tennessee Cavalry, USA, sometimes referred to as the First Middle Tennessee Cavalry. As early as August 1863, the Union general W. C. Whitaker, commanding the First Division, Granger's Corps, Army of the Cumberland, noted that the "cavalry of Colonel Galbraith, the 5th Tennessee, is giving me excessive trouble, and worrying and plundering throughout the country whenever they go out. They are under no control or discipline at all as far as I can learn. Several instances have come to my attention of their insulting females."[8]

Such actions escalated the conflict with the guerrillas. Over a period of four weeks during the winter of 1863–1864, five men—William Lemmons, Cyrus Lee Cathey, Jesse B. Neeren, Thomas R. West, and Benjamin West—attacked Union supporters and soldiers near Boons Hill, Tennessee, a few miles west of Fayetteville. In this foray, the guerrilla band killed Irwin C. McLean, a Unionist citizen, and robbed him of his valuables. On the same day, another pro-Union man, Samuel J. Wakefield, was killed. Guerrillas also struck near Shelbyville, killing William White, a citizen, and Grey Hyde, a member of the Fifth Tennessee. William Smith, another trooper in the Fifth, escaped with his life but lost his horse and weapons. Newcomb Thompson, another Unionist, lost several mules in the same attack. On January 15, 1864, this same band attacked a Union foraging party consisting of two wagons and a small escort of soldiers. They drove off the escort, captured and burned the wagons, and made off with the horses. These guerrillas were captured in February, sentenced to death, and executed on June 17, 1864.[9]

At the same time, only a few miles away another band of guerrillas led by Burton Tolley assaulted Federal forage wagons near the village of Mulberry. On December 26, a foraging party of ten wagons and a guard of seventy men were sent to collect foodstuffs from local farmers. The officer in charge divided the wagons and guards into several parties on reaching his objective in order to speed up the expedition. One of the wagons and four men became separated from the others by a distance of approximately two hundred yards. They were subsequently bushwhacked by insurgents, who captured the soldiers, the wagon, and the horses. The guerrillas then retreated to a safe location near the Elk River, where they executed three of the soldiers. The survivor returned to his command with the story of what had happened.[10] The army sent a detachment of mounted soldiers to Mulberry, but they returned empty-handed, for the guerrillas had taken to the hills. Since the guerrillas could not be caught, the soldiers arrested John Tolley, the father of the local insurgent leader, Thomas Baley, Dr. Philander Whitier, and Newton Whitier, even though none of these men was thought to have had anything to do with the attack.[11] Frustrated, Union general George Thomas sent another detachment to Mulberry with instructions to seize $30,000 worth of property, to be used to indemnify the families of the dead Union soldiers. This mission was carried out, though the residents of the community filed a complaint that $60,000 had actually been taken.[12] In current dollars, over $2,400,000 worth of money, livestock, and household goods was removed from a town of only 150 people, leaving the residents destitute.

Such actions led Gen. Alpheus Williams, one of the Union heroes of Gettysburg and now in Tennessee with Slocum's Corps of the Army of the Potomac, to comment in a letter to his daughter: "The making of fortunes I do not understand. I could have made one here if I had consented to have sold my self-respect and the good name of my children to the third and fourth generation."[13] Gen. Lovell Rousseau wrote in an official report dated December 31, 1863: "From impressments, legal and illegal, and from thefts, there are very few horses, mules, or oxen left on the farms, and those that are left are almost worthless. . . . Every mounted regiment that goes through the country takes what it pleases of stock, &c. . . . Between the loyal and the disloyal no discrimination is made. Unless an order be made preventing future impressments and protecting the farmers little or no crops will be produced."[14] With the end of the war nowhere in sight,

Tennessee's civilian population was already facing famine. The destitution of civilians in towns and cities caused the Union authorities to fear outbreaks of rioting, which would require troops to put down. This became one motive for setting up relief efforts in many towns where Federal garrisons were located. Such efforts existed in Nashville and other places in Tennessee.[15] However, this control of the population's daily bread was also a method of controlling behavior and punishing those suspected of continuing to harbor pro-Confederate sympathies. Shelbyville, Tennessee, was considered to be a loyal town, having even earned the title "Little Boston." But, Lt. Col. P. H. Sturdevant, acting provost of the town, deemed the politics of some of the women to be disloyal. The colonel recommended that Mrs. R. W. Wallace, Misses V. and M. Matthews, and Miss Selica Whitthorn be denied access to the commissary and that their rations be stopped. General Slocum, commanding the Twelfth Army Corps, which occupied the area at the time, agreed with this suggestion and denied these women food.[16]

Soldiers serving in regular Confederate military units at times engaged in irregular warfare. One of the most effective opponents of Union occupation was John M. Hughs, a major in the Twenty-fifth Tennessee Infantry. Wounded at Murfreesboro in December 1862, he had been at home recovering from his injuries when Union forces occupied the area where his home was located. While home in the late summer of 1863, he organized recruits and other convalescing soldiers and began a campaign to disrupt Union garrisons in Tennessee and Kentucky. In the fall of that year, Hughs attacked Glasgow, Monticello, and Scottsville, Kentucky, before falling back into Tennessee, where he attacked Livingston, defeating the Thirteenth Kentucky Cavalry, USA. Although Hughs was a commissioned Confederate officer, Union authorities declared him an outlaw and threatened to hang him if captured. This did not happen, however, for he defeated all those sent against him, including the First Tennessee Cavalry, led by the son of Parson Brownlow, and the Fifth Tennessee, commanded by Colonel Galbraith and Lieutenant Colonel Stokes. By April 1864, this successful band of raiders left the mountains of Tennessee to rejoin the Confederate Army of Tennessee at Dalton, Georgia, taking with them ninety-five new recruits who were fully armed, and leaving thirty-five hundred arms in the hands of guerrillas.[17]

One of the high-ranking Union officers who enthusiastically embraced the hard-war policy toward Southern civilians was Gen. Eleazer A. Paine. An 1839 graduate of West Point, Paine had resigned from the army to practice law and had become active in politics in Illinois. He had been commissioned a brigadier of volunteers and had been placed in command at Cairo, Illinois. He saw combat at New Madrid, Island No. 10, and at Corinth. During his time at Cairo, Paine had gained a reputation as a "hanging officer" after he had ordered that, for every one of his men killed by guerrillas, two Confederate prisoners would be hanged. Because many in the Cairo area sympathized with the Confederacy, Paine exercised strict control of the civilian population.[18] In the winter of 1863–1864, keeping with the general practice of U.S. Army officers commanding posts well behind the battle lines, Paine instituted a hard-war policy in an attempt to suppress guerrilla activity. Following a guerrilla attack in which the bridge across Goose Creek was destroyed, a fifteen-year-old boy, Lafayette Hughes, was arrested on suspicion of participating in the bridge's destruction and executed. Seventeen-year-old Fleming Sanders was arrested and confined to the town jail for several weeks before being taken out of town some five miles and summarily executed.[19] A soldier in Paine's command wrote his sister: "We made a number of them bite the dust and we burned a lot of houses and distilleries."[20] A few days later, an entire company went to the house of a suspected disloyal citizen about fifteen miles from Gallatin. The man was taken into the yard and executed in the presence of his wife and children. The house was then burned, leaving the widow and three children destitute. Despite the lack of evidence regarding the man's disloyalty, Paine approved of the act, saying: "It served the damned son of a bitch right."[21]

This merciless attitude extended to military prisoners as well. Gen. John Hunt Morgan made life miserable for Union commanders in upper Tennessee and Kentucky, so much so that Union authorities were determined to eliminate the threat. Just before Christmas 1863, members of the Seventy-first Ohio, part of Paine's command, executed a lieutenant and seven enlisted men from Morgan's command who had been captured.[22] Weary of war, the Confederate soldier Alfred T. Dalton returned home and professed his willingness to take the oath of allegiance to the United States. Before he could take the oath, however, Paine had him arrested at his home and executed on the spot. The same day, another young man, about sixteen years old, was given a drumhead trial in Gallatin and hanged that evening. Only a few days later, a Confederate soldier was removed from the post stockade and taken out of town on "a worn out horse." Given a five-minute head start, the soldier was pursued by Union soldiers on fresh horses until caught, whereupon he was murdered. Members of Paine's own staff and their wives participated in the chase.[23]

These acts were not unknown to Paine's superior officers. Indeed, Gen. Ulysses Grant, the senior U.S. officer in the western theater, commented that Paine was "entirely unfit to command a post," but he issued no orders restraining his actions or punishing him for violating the rules of war.[24] Instead, Paine was transferred to Tullahoma to protect the Nashville and Chattanooga Railroad, which supplied Sherman's move into Georgia. In Tullahoma, Paine continued his harsh treatment of the civilian population. Maj. Gen. Robert Milroy, Paine's commanding officer, wrote to his wife:

General Paine has had about two hundred guerrillas shot since he has been stationed here. It is not often that his men bring in any that they capture, and if they do, and Paine ascertains them to be guerillas beyond a doubt he orders them quietly walked outside the pickets and shot and no report is made of the matter and nothing is said about it. Two of them have been shot that way since I come here. I would not have known anything of it had I not happened on their dead bodies in riding out.[25]

While General Paine was on his way to Tullahoma, Gen. Nathan Bedford Forrest was leading his cavalry north from Mississippi in a raid that would reach the banks of the Ohio River. During the raid, a confrontation between Confederates and U.S. provost troops occurred, creating a controversy that echoes in Civil War history to this day. As Forrest completed his incursion into West Tennessee, it was reported to him that the Union troops at Fort Pillow had been "robbing people of their horses, mules, beef cattle, beds, plate, wearing apparel, money and every possible movable article of value, besides venting upon the wives and daughters of Southern soldiers the most opprobrious and obscene epithets, with more than one extreme outrage upon the persons of these victims of their hate and lust."[26] When Forrest arrived at Fort Pillow, he found it occupied by members of the Sixth U.S. Colored Heavy Artillery. After spending most of April 12 maneuvering against the fortified position and calling on the garrison to surrender, a demand that was refused, Forrest ordered an assault. The garrison of approximately 600 suffered 280 casualties. Immediately, Union authorities claimed that there had been a massacre of those who had surrendered. Confederates denied reports that there had been a surrender and maintained that the garrison had attempted to escape. Some things are seen quite clearly through the clouds of controversy that still surround the event—after two years of vengeful warfare, human life was a cheap commodity in Tennessee; retribution had become commonplace.[27]

As the spring of 1864 progressed, the Nashville and Chattanooga Railroad became an important supply line for Sherman's campaign against Atlanta. Every day, several trains loaded with military equipment and provisions left Nashville for Chattanooga. Recognizing the vulnerability of Sherman's lines of communication, Confederate guerrillas swarmed the railroad. Although Sherman could forage for provisions if forced to do so, he had to rely on the railroad for munitions and equipment. The railroad bridges across the Duck, Elk, and Tennessee rivers and the twenty-two-hundred-foot-long tunnel at Cowan were heavily guarded and safe from guerrilla attacks, but smaller bridges, culverts, and water tanks were easy targets. In an effort to prevent guerrilla attacks, the Federals forbade any civilian to live within eight hundred yards of the railroad except in villages and towns garrisoned by the Union army. Union authorities ordered all houses, farm buildings, fences, trees, and brush within this zone burned and anyone found in the cleared area shot on sight. Attacks persisted despite these measures.

Into this situation came the Union provost commander Maj. Gen. Robert H. Milroy. A native of Indiana, Milroy was a man frustrated in his desire to be a soldier. He had sought unsuccessfully admission to West Point and had been forced to delay his education until he enrolled in the Norwich Military University in Vermont at the age of twenty-four. He raised a regiment for service in the war with Mexico but arrived at the front too late to see any action. During the 1850s, he became an abolitionist and an early supporter of Abraham Lincoln. In 1861, he raised the first regiment from Indiana and served as its colonel. Assigned to western Virginia, Milroy participated in some of the early Union successes there but was promoted beyond his level of competence in early 1862. He was soundly drubbed by Stonewall Jackson in his Valley Campaign, was outperformed at Second Manassas, and was trounced by Richard Ewell at Winchester, Virginia, in the summer of 1863. A court-martial ruled that Milroy had made poor decisions at Winchester but found that he had not disobeyed any orders, so he was merely sent to the rear instead of being dismissed from the service. Using his political connections, Milroy received command of an occupied area and was sent to Tullahoma.

Soon after Milroy took command in Tullahoma, Robert Blackwell, a former sheriff and Confederate guerrilla, raided the nearby town of Shelbyville. Bottling up the small Union garrison in the fortified railroad depot, Blackwell and his nearly three-hundred-strong guerrilla band stripped the town of military supplies and looted the sutlers doing business with the U.S. forces. In an attempt to learn where Blackwell had his lair, Milroy sent Gen. Eleazar Paine to Fayetteville in Lincoln County on June 15, 1864, to collect information. Paine planned to seize hostages and announce that the men would be shot by 3:00 P.M. unless citizens provided information about Blackwell. His deadline having passed, Paine took the locals Thomas Massey, William Pickett, Franklin Burroughs, and Dr. J. W. Miller a short distance up the road from the county courthouse and ordered them shot. Dr. Miller was released by a sympathetic lieutenant who recognized him as a fellow Mason. John R. Massey, Thomas's older brother, rode up to Paine just before the killings took place and volunteered to take the place of his younger sibling. Paine accepted the offer and then had the three men executed. He left their bodies lying in the road to serve as an example to other civilians.[28]

On September 27, Blackwell struck back. With eleven men, he entered Shelbyville, surrounded the Union garrison of twenty-one men, and convinced them to surrender. The captives were taken south a few miles to Fayetteville and there were divided into two groups. Paroling several of the "more respectable" men, the guerrillas took those remaining who had been identified either as deserters from the Confederate army or native Tennesseans to the top of Wells Hill and executed them. A note was affixed to the breast of each man that read: "Remember Massey."[29]

Along the Nashville and Louisville Railroad, guerrillas led by Ellis Harper continued to harass Union soldiers. Like all guerrillas, Harper depended on the support and cooperation of the civilians in the area where he operated. If support was not forthcoming, silence at least was required. Harvey Travelstead of Simpson County, Kentucky, just above the Tennessee state line, informed Union authorities of some of Harper's movements. Learning of this betrayal, Harper and a few of his men went to the Smyrna Cumberland Presbyterian Church where Travelstead was attending services. They took him outside and killed him. At about the same time, Harper went to the home of Hensley Harris near Pilot Knob in Simpson County to impress on him the need for silence. Harris refused to open the door, so Harper, or one of his men, fired through the door, killing Harris's three-year-old son. Enraged, Harris armed himself and ran out the door, only to be shot down. Although severely wounded in the encounter, Harris was nursed back to health by his slaves and his wife. He survived the war and went on to serve in the Kentucky legislature in the postwar years.[30]

In response to these and similar acts, the Union provost, Brig. Gen. Stephen G. Burbridge, issued orders that, "whenever an unarmed Union citizen is murdered, four guerrillas will be selected from the prisoners in the hands of the military authorities, and publicly shot to death in the most convenient place near the scene of the outrage." On August 25, 1864, the *Louisville Journal* reported:

Charles Clary, Lieutenant of the 12th Kentucky Cavalry, who with a detail of ten men, on the morning of the 20th left the city in charge of four guerrillas taken from the Military Prison, with orders to proceed to Franklin, Kentucky, and there execute them in retaliation for the murder of Union citizens, reports to Col. Fairleigh that he has returned to Louisville, having faithfully obeyed his orders. He states that he arrived in Franklin at two o'clock P.M. and found Lieutenant Adams there with a detachment of twenty men from the 26th Kentucky Volunteers. Soon after he received a dispatch from headquarters in Louisville, directing him to defer the execution of J. H. Cave until further orders. At 6 o'clock in the evening he ordered the two remaining prisoners, J. Bloom and W. B. McClasson, to prepare to meet their doom. Both refused to make any confessions. McClasson claimed that he was innocent of any crime. Bloom was morose and spoke but little. . . . The Lieutenant placed Bloom on one side of the courthouse and McClasson on the other. Both of the doomed men appeared calm and collected. . . . The order was given to fire and the report of musketry rang clear and startling upon the air. The two prisoners fell forward, bloody corpses.[31]

As bloodthirsty as Harper's actions had been, those of the provost were scarcely less so. Neither of the men executed had been part of Harper's guerrilla band; indeed, J. H. Bloom was a member of Company I, Fifteenth

Tennessee Infantry, and McClasson was enlisted in Company E, Second Kentucky Cavalry. J. H. Cave was a member of Company B, First Kentucky Cavalry, and was said to have been granted a reprieve because he was a Mason.[32]

The social chaos in the closing months of the war is reflected in the lists of "disloyal" persons turned in to the provost in every garrison town occupied by the Union army. The atrocities committed by both sides embittered local populations, prompting neighbors to turn against neighbors to seek revenge for wrongs both real and imagined. Much of this violence stemmed from Tennesseans' divided loyalties, for pro-Union sentiment was found across the state, not merely in East Tennessee. Some of the hard feelings predated the war and reflected disagreements over property boundaries or other civil issues. Sometimes people were labeled *disloyal* simply because they were competitors in the same occupation. The informants knew that, for the most part, an accusation of disloyalty was enough to prompt Union authorities to act.

The example of Moses Pittman of Franklin County, Tennessee, illustrates this. In December 1864, Pittman sent to Gen. Robert Milroy a list containing the names of fifty-eight of his neighbors, male and female, whom Pittman charged with various acts of disloyalty. Milroy remarked that these people should have their farm buildings and houses destroyed and that many of them should be shot on sight.[33] This became the basis of official action on January 7, 1865, when Milroy issued orders to Capt. William H. Lewis, Company A, Forty-second Missouri Volunteers, directing him to seek out these individuals, seize any of their property deemed useful to the military, destroy their homes and private possessions, and execute several who had been identified as guerrillas. A list of names was provided.[34]

Copies of these orders were sent up the line to departmental headquarters and were forwarded from there to the War Department in Washington. There they were reviewed by the secretary of war and by the president of the United States. It is important to note that no orders ever came back down the chain of command from Washington ordering that these killings cease. Occasional attempts to restrain Union officers and men were weak and ineffective. Thus, one could argue that the policy of targeting civilians in Tennessee, and throughout the South, had implicit approval from the highest levels of the U.S. government. Without extensive further study of the provost records, it cannot be estimated how many civilians in the Confederacy were killed, but the number is no doubt large. While the actions of Confederates who committed atrocities have long been the subject of historical discussion, the killings of Southern civilians by Union troops has largely been ignored. Yet the evidence of such killings was recorded by those who ordered the executions and is preserved in the archives of the U.S. government.

For Tennesseans, the Civil War was an uncivil experience. Both Union and Confederate supporters committed violent acts against each other. Atrocities committed against Tennessee's civilian population by the Union army and its Union supporters only reinforced the feeling among the Southern populace that they were under attack, thus creating a burning desire for revenge. When they sought retribution, the cycle of vengeance escalated. The result was that, by the end of the military conflict in 1865, Tennessee was left in a state of social chaos. That chaos did not cease when the Confederate armies surrendered. Indeed, Reconstruction was a continuation of the wartime cycle of vengeance and should be understood as the final act of that cycle.

Notes

The quotation used as this essay's title is taken from Maj. Gen. Robert Milroy, USA, to his wife, Tullahoma, Tenn., May 5, 1864, cited in Michael R. Bradley, *With Blood and Fire: Behind Union Lines in Middle Tennessee, 1863–65* (Shippensburg, Pa.: Burd Street, 2003), xvi. Original copies of the Milroy letters are in the Renssaler Public Library, Renssaler, Ind., and can also be viewed at www.cwrc.org.

1. Larry J. Daniel, *Days of Glory: The Army of the Cumberland, 1861–1865* (Baton Rouge: Louisiana State University Press, 2004), 99–100.

2. Union Provost Marshal Records (UPM), File of Two or More Citizens, Microfilm Collection (MC) 416, roll 23, National Archives, Washington, D.C.; Stephen Z. Starr, *Jennison's Jayhawkers: A Civil War Cavalry Regiment and Its Commander* (Baton Rouge: Louisiana State University Press, 1973), 167.

3. Michael R. Bradley, *Nathan Bedford Forrest's Escort and Staff* (Gretna, La.: Pelican, 2006), 35.

4. Daniel, *Days of Glory*, 106; Benjamin Franklin Cooling, *Fort Donelson's Legacy: War and Society in Kentucky and Tennessee, 1862–1863* (Knoxville: University of Tennessee Press, 1997), 94–95.

5. Cooling, *Fort Donelson's Legacy,* 75.

6. Michael R. Bradley, *With Blood and Fire: Behind Union Lines in Middle Tennessee, 1863–65* (Shippensburg, Pa.: Burd Street, 2003), 25–27. This is the only book available that is based solely on the official records of the U.S. provost marshal troops.

7. U.S. War Department, *The War of the Rebellion: A Compilation of the Official Records of the Union and Confederate Armies, 1861–1865* (hereafter cited as *OR*), 70 vols. in 128 pts. (Washington, D.C.: U.S. Government Printing Office, 1880–1901), ser. 1, vol. 23, pt. 1, pp. 521, 525; Michael R. Bradley, *Tullahoma: The 1863 Campaign for Control of Middle Tennessee* (Shippensburg, Pa.: Burd Street, 2000), 90.

8. *Tennesseans in the Civil War: A Military History of Confederate and Union Units with Available Rosters of Personnel,* 2 vols. (Nashville: Civil War Centennial Commission, 1964–1965), 1:331.

9. UPM, MC 416, rolls 34–35.

10. *OR,* ser. 1, vol. 31, pt. 1, pp. 623–24.

11. UPM, MC 416, roll 26.

12. *OR,* ser. 1, vol. 32, pt. 2, pp. 37–38; UPM, MC 345, roll 131.

13. Milo M. Quaife, ed., *From the Cannon's Mouth: The Civil War Letters of General Alpheus Williams* (Detroit: Wayne State University Press, 1959), 297.

14. *OR,* ser. 1, vol. 58, pt. 1, p. 269.

15. Stephen V. Ash, *When the Yankees Came: Conflict and Chaos in the Occupied South, 1861–1865* (Chapel Hill: University of North Carolina Press, 1995), 82.

16. UPM, MC 416, roll 28.

17. *OR,* ser. 1, vol. 30, pt. 4, p. 144; vol. 31, pt. 1, p. 575; vol. 31, pt. 3, pp. 469, 591; and vol. 32, pt. 1, pp. 55, 416.

18. Walter T. Durham, *Rebellion Revisited: A History of Sumner County, Tennessee, from 1861 to 1870* (Gallatin, Tenn.: Sumner County Museum Association, 1982), 112–13.

19. *Nashville Dispatch,* October 14, 1864, cited in ibid., 163.

20. Arthur H. DeRosier et al., eds., *Through the South with a Union Soldier* (Johnson City: East Tennessee State University, Research Advisory Council, 1969), 56ff.

21. *Louisville Daily Journal,* November 12, 1864, cited in Durham, *Rebellion Revisited,* 164.

22. *OR,* ser. 2, vol. 7, pt. 1, p. 792.

23. Durham, *Rebellion Revisited,* 189–90. Durham quotes from the diary of Alice Williamson, a young woman living in Gallatin at the time of these events.

24. Ibid., 187.

25. Robert Milroy to Mary Milroy, November 15, 1864, cited in Bradley, *With Blood and Fire,* xix.

26. Thomas Jordan and J. P. Pryor, *The Campaigns of Lieut.-Gen. N. B. Forrest* (Dayton, Ohio: Morningside Bookshop, 1977), 422.

27. The identity of the units in the Fort Pillow garrison can be readily established by referencing any of the biographies of Nathan Bedford Forrest. The number of men in the garrison and the number of casualties vary, so I have used a figure that represents a rough average for both the numbers present and the numbers killed and wounded.

28. Bradley, *With Blood and Fire,* 76–79; *Fayetteville Observer,* April 6, 1915, April 6, 1919.

29. Bradley, *With Blood and Fire,* 80–82; UPM, MC 416, roll 27.

30. See the Harris and Travelstead papers in the archives of the Simpson County, Ky., Historical Society.

31. *Louisville Journal,* August 25, 1864.

32. Stewart Cruickshank, "Terror in the Bluegrass," *The Lost Cause: Journal of the Kentucky Division, Sons of Confederate Veterans* 22, no. 2 (Summer 2004): unpaginated.

33. UPM, MC 416, roll 46.

34. The order reads:

Sir: You will proceed to the residences of the persons herein named and deal with them in accordance with the following instructions. In all cases where the residences of the persons are ordered to be destroyed you will observe the following previous to setting them on fire. You will first search the houses and premises to see if they have any articles belonging to the U.S. Govt or that are contraband of war, which you will bring away in case any are found. Also all or any of the following articles that may be found belonging to the aforesaid persons.

First All horses, hogs, sheep, cattle, and any other animals or articles of whatever description that may be valuable to the U.S. Govt especially those that are valuable to the Quartermaster, Commissary and Hospital Department.

Second All stoves and stovepipes of whatever description and all kitchen utensils, Queens ware, beds, bedding, knives, forks & etc also all chairs, sofas, sociable lounges and everything of the character of household furniture.

Third All windows, sash, glass, looking glasses, carpets, & etc.

Fourth Every article of household furniture which you do not bring with you must be destroyed or burned with the house.

Fifth All barns, stables, smoke houses, or any other outbuilding of any description whatsoever or any building or article that could possible be of any benefit or comfort to Rebels or Bushwhackers their friends or any person aiding, abetting, or sympathizing with Rebels, Bushwhackers & etc which could be used for subsistence for man or beast will be destroyed and burned.

Sixth All animals forage or other articles brought in by you will be turned over to Lieut J. W. Raymond AAQm on this Staff to be subject to the order of Maj Genl Milroy to be disposed of as he may think proper, taking a receipt therefore from Lieut Raymond.

Seventh The train accompanying will be subject to your orders, together with all the persons connected with it, whether soldiers or civilians and you will cause any of them who may be guilty of committing depredations upon Loyal citizens or their property to be arrested and you will not your-self suffer those under your Command to commit any trespass, or do any damage to Persons or property except those specified in this order.

Eighth You will burn the houses of the following named persons, take any of the articles named above that they may have, together with all forage and grains belonging to them that you can bring away which may be useful to the U.S. govt for military purposes or otherwise and will give no receipt of any kind whatsoever. [Seven names follow this section of the order.]

Ninth The following persons will be shot in addition to suffering in the manner prescribed in paragraph #8. [Four names appear in this section of the order.]

Tenth The following persons have committed murder and if caught will be hung to the first tree in front of their door and be allowed to hang there for an indefinite period. You will assure yourself that they are dead before leaving them also if at their residence they will be stripped of everything as per the above instructions and then burned. If Willis Taylor is caught he will be turned over to Moses Pittman and he will be allowed to kill him. (UPM, MC 416, roll 50)

The implications of paragraph 10 are chilling. If a person is hanged with a hangman's noose, the fall snaps the third cervical vertebra, and death is instantaneous. People are left to hang for "an indefinite period" because they have been hanged with a slip knot and left to strangle to death. This slow, agonizing process was being witnessed by the wives and children of the victim since the execution was happening at "the first tree in front of their door." Neither was this the only instance of such vengeance. On February 7, 1865, Milroy issued identical orders listing eighteen persons under paragraph 8, and thirty-four persons were ordered executed without trial under paragraph 9. Similar orders are to be found in virtually every area controlled by a Union provost officer in Tennessee. See UPM, MC 416, roll 50.

Freedom Is Better Than Slavery

Black Families and Soldiers in Civil War Kentucky

Marion B. Lucas

In the late 1850s, many of Kentucky's blacks were aware of the growing antagonism between the North and the South, the role of slavery in the controversy, and the potential impact on their lives. A few, both free and slave, fearing the worst, fled north of the Ohio River at the first opportunity. By 1860, others, aware of the association of Abraham Lincoln's presidential campaign with the antislavery movement, eagerly waited for and talked openly of anticipated freedom. After the election, rumors of imminent emancipation continued to spread, and, in one area of central Kentucky, slaves became convinced that they would be freed on March 1, 1861.[1]

Gradually, as the Southern states seceded and hostilities began, news of the war spread throughout the black community. Rumors abounded of one side's successes only to be contradicted shortly thereafter. All the while, masters assured their slaves that, whatever the outcome, they would remain bondsmen. Of those early war years, one slave later wrote: "We did not know what to believe."[2]

Life became more complicated and uncertain for most Kentucky blacks during the early stages of the Civil War. Many freemen complained that the war offered racists an opportunity to harass the black community. Whites threatened to enforce laws that authorized prison sentences for freemen who left the state and returned, and Northern freemen who ventured into the commonwealth occasionally landed in jail, charged with being runaways. These false arrests usually took months to rectify.[3]

Harassment by law officers was a major problem for all blacks in the early days of the conflict. In some cities and counties, the authorities systematically searched the premises of blacks, confiscating weapons. Louisville blacks increasingly claimed that they had "no redress" against police officers who, in the middle of the night, invaded their homes. The home guard forced blacks off the streets, sometimes administering harsh punishments for those without passes. Independent or so-called abolition congregations occasionally fell under suspicion, resulting in the interruption of religious meetings. Authorities, including the military, frequently used vagrancy laws to retard the movement of blacks, and runaways arriving from the South or escaping north from the commonwealth experienced no relaxation of the fugitive slave laws. Meanwhile, bondsmanship, including hiring out and the slave trade, continued.[4]

Changing conditions caused by the hostilities created new opportunities for a few bondsmen. The war brought higher wages for skilled laborers, and several black entrepreneurs were credited with having "grown rich" during the conflict. In some areas of the economy, blacks also found whites more willing to labor alongside them, and there was a noticeable decline in white hostility toward black mechanics. Some black observers also noticed a reduction in cruel treatment.[5]

Still other blacks took advantage of the volatile conditions to challenge the slave system. Those suspected of violating the slave code found it easier, especially in urban areas, to evade detection by hiding in the black community. Whites increasingly noticed a change in the work patterns of hired slaves and that bondsmen seemed less inclined to obey orders. One of the most unusual demonstrations of black hostility to the slave system occurred at New Castle in December 1861. After getting off work one night, a group of about fifty slaves marched through the streets, frequently tarrying in front of the homes of pro-Southern whites, "singing political songs and shouting for Lincoln." The demonstration lasted until midnight.[6]

The arrival of Federal troops in Kentucky provided many slaves with their first real opportunity to challenge involuntary servitude. Troops had scarcely appeared before blacks entered the military camps. Friendship with Federal troops and employment opportunities with the military further enticed slaves to flee their bondage. Some soldiers encouraged slaves to run away, while others, seeking to escape the hard work of camp duty, simply hired local bondsmen to perform tasks. Once troops and slaves mutually realized what each offered the other, bondsmen entered Federal camps in increasing numbers. What began as a trickle of slaves into Union camps during the summer of 1861 swelled to a steady stream by the year's end. Soon, almost every regiment employed at least a half dozen fugitives who lived in camp.[7]

This early flow of slaves into Union lines created enormous problems for the Union army, both practical and political. Once troops filled their labor requirements, they had no use for additional slaves or their families. Unfortunately, the employment of a few bondsmen opened a floodgate the troops could not close. From the military's point of view, the presence of fugitives increased logistic problems and exacerbated relations with Kentucky's white leaders. This situation was complicated further during the first two years of war by the absence of a consistent Federal policy for handling fugitives who entered Union lines. Thus, generals reacted individually to the influx of blacks, a situation that resulted in difficult times for many fugitives. On taking command in Kentucky, Brig. Gen. William T. Sherman, for example, ordered his subordinates in October 1861 to surrender runaways according to federal and commonwealth laws if owners claimed them. When his inquiries brought "no instructions" from Washington regarding policy, Sherman decided in November to ignore the issue of refugees. "We have nothing to do with them at all," he instructed a subordinate, "and you should not let them take refuge in camp."[8]

A year later, officers operating in Kentucky still had no instructions regarding the increasing number of fugitives in camp. In August 1862, the commander at Columbus prohibited slave women from entering his lines, while his counterpart at Bowling Green followed a policy that excluded all bondsmen. During 1862, some officers regularly allowed slave owners to enter their camps to remove bondsmen, while other officers received severe reprimands for similar actions. Maj. Gen. Gordon Granger, harassed by Kentuckians who hoped to retrieve fugitives, called the situation "embarrassing," and, in November 1862, he begged Maj. Gen. Henry W. Halleck to develop a "definite policy." Unfortunately, conflicting orders regarding the treatment of fugitives in Union camps continued through the summer of 1864.[9]

The attitudes of Federal troops toward fugitives entering Union lines further complicated the situation. While few were abolitionists, most were observing slavery for the first time on entering Kentucky, and, in general, they did not like what they saw. Slaves entering camps related stories of severe abuse from "Rebel" owners and frequently won the sympathy of troops. Masters often alienated soldiers when they appeared at camps and threatened to whip or shoot fugitives who resisted returning to slavery. Such actions caused many lower-echelon officers and their troops to become hesitant about returning runaways to their owners.[10]

During the summer and fall of 1862, as the number of slaves fleeing to Union lines increased dramatically, three conditions combined to transform this growing migration into a serious problem. The first was the impressment of large numbers of blacks, free and slave, by both the Confederate and the Union armies for military labor. Wherever the two armies went, they impressed black laborers, disrupting families, and creating refugees. During 1861, the Confederates impressed thousands of slaves to work on defensive positions from Columbus on the Mississippi River to Mill Springs in the east. By early 1862, fugitives entered Union lines with horror stories resulting from Confederate impressment. Those lucky enough to escape fled north to Union lines. The less fortunate were sold south.[11]

As soon as the Union army entered Kentucky, it began impressing slaves, initially seeking the slaves of those deemed disloyal. As the Union military effort intensified, Federal officers began impressing slaves without regard for ownership, a policy that provoked severe criticism from some Unionists. After March 1862, Union officers regularly impressed hundreds of slaves throughout the state to build roads, to cut timber for building new bridges and repairing old ones, to chop wood for fueling railway engines, and to labor on Federal riverboats. Some of these slaves never returned to their owners.[12]

The events surrounding the invasion of Kentucky by the Confederate general Braxton Bragg and Maj. Gen. Edmund Kirby Smith during the summer and fall of 1862 greatly increased impressment and the refugee problem. Unsure of the destination of Confederate forces, authorities in Ohio River cities scrambled desperately to build fortifications. In Louisville, officials drafted more than a thousand slaves and freemen for the "spade and shovel brigade," forcing them to work around the clock. During the crisis, the provost marshal combed the town for laborers, picking up blacks found on the streets, emptying the jails and workhouses, and snatching them at all hours of the night from their homes. Estimates of the total number of blacks and whites working on the fortification ran as high as ten thousand.[13]

In northern Kentucky, not enough blacks were available to dig the entrenchments needed to protect Cincinnati. Consequently, authorities impressed large numbers of Cincinnati's free blacks. City police, who had a history of harassing freemen, rounded up blacks wherever they found them, dragging them without explanation from their homes, places of employment, and the streets. Policemen drove some eleven hundred freemen to a holding pen where they were caged like animals, unable to inform loved ones of their whereabouts. As the freemen dug entrenchments on the section of the line from Alexandria Road to Newport Turnpike and Licking River in Kentucky, Union soldiers periodically appeared, selected workers from among the freemen, and marched them off at bayonet point to become regimental cooks and servants. Many wondered whether they would ever see their homes again.

The circumstances were partially rectified when Maj. Gen. Lew Wallace learned of these injustices and appointed the Cincinnati judge William M. Dickson to take command of the impressed workers. Dickson selected a staff, organized the "Black Brigade," freed those workers taken by Union regiments, and ordered his men back to their Cincinnati homes to secure clothes and supplies. When the military crisis ended, Dickson gave the Cincinnati freemen credit for building most of northern Kentucky's defenses.[14]

In the midst of the Confederate invasion of Kentucky, President Abraham Lincoln on September 22, 1862, issued his preliminary Emancipation Proclamation, followed by the final notice on January 1, 1863. Even though the action legally did not affect Kentucky, Lincoln had created a second condition that encouraged slaves to flee from their owners. White Kentuckians bitterly denounced the president, and the state legislature rejected the document. But, once the proclamation was generally known, slaves became less hesitant to enter Federal lines, and many Union officers, in turn, became indifferent to whether an impressed slave's owner was a Union or a Confederate sympathizer.[15]

Ultimately, impressed blacks and refugees performed most of the labor that supported the Federal war machine in Kentucky. From impressment, it was also only a short step to recruiting blacks as soldiers, the third and most important condition that resulted in the influx of slaves into Union lines. The federal government had rejected offers of free blacks to enlist at the outbreak of the war, and Lincoln assured slaveholders in 1861 that the war would not affect the "peculiar institution." The need for troops, however, forced the president in December 1862 to authorize the use of black troops, but, fearing the adverse reaction of Kentuckians, he exempted the Bluegrass State.[16]

By mid-1863, when the federal government began actively recruiting blacks, but before Lincoln authorized recruitment in the commonwealth, many Kentucky slaves enlisted at Union recruiting stations outside the state. They hurried by the thousands to Union camps in Tennessee or crossed the Ohio River to join the army on free soil. Evansville, Indiana, located within a few miles of one of Kentucky's largest slave centers, was a convenient destination for slaves enlisting in the west, and Cincinnati, which offered a bounty of four hundred dollars, drew many recruits from the northern counties. In addition, Northern states sent recruiting agents into Kentucky to entice blacks to join their units. Long after recruiting was legal in the commonwealth, southern Indiana officials reported, groups of "five to ten" Kentucky slaves regularly passed through their district on their way to fill draft quotas in Northern states.[17]

Lincoln made his first move toward enrolling Kentucky blacks into the Union army in early 1863 when he authorized a census of blacks between the ages of eighteen and forty-five. The enumeration of freemen—there were only 1,650 of draft age—became public during the summer, eliciting protests from many whites and several Federal commanders. Lincoln continued to promise Governor Thomas E. Bramlette, as late as the fall of 1863, that no commonwealth slaves would be recruited, but, with a Federal manpower shortage and the availability of 40,285 draft-age Kentucky slaves, more discerning whites realized that the enlistment of blacks could no longer be delayed. Reluctantly, Bramlette in March 1864 acquiesced in the recruitment of blacks, but only to fill deficits created by the failure of whites to meet the state's draft quota.[18]

In March 1864, when the recruitment of blacks began in earnest, Kentucky continued to be a special case. The federal government promised to maintain strict control over recruiting procedures by enrolling only those free blacks and slaves who applied. Loyal owners received certificates guaranteeing compensation of up to three hundred dollars a recruit and assurances that recruits would be taken to rendezvous camps "outside of the State."[19]

A few whites recognized that recruiting blacks was the death knell of slavery and tried to minimize their losses. Concluding that their slaves would ultimately enter the army, these owners decided to enroll their bondsmen to help fill Kentucky's draft quota and, thereby, establish a bounty claim. As owners, they received the bounties due slave enlistees until July 1864, when the government decided that bondsmen who volunteered would receive the bounty, a promise not always honored.[20]

Whites also used slave enlistments to escape the draft themselves. Many Kentuckians simply enlisted their slaves at the local recruiting office with little or no payment of money to the bondsmen, while others promised slave substitutes cash they never received. In some instances, however, owners paid slaves premium prices for taking their places in the military. During the final year of war, the practice of buying and selling blacks as substitutes for whites was common.[21]

Federal authorities mistakenly believed that their moderate policy would mollify white hostility to black recruiting. Echoing the attitude of the legislature, Col. Frank L. Wolford, a Kentucky cavalry officer, protested so vehemently that he received a dishonorable discharge from the Union army. Recruiting officers in every district of the state encountered opposition from fellow recruiters and from large segments of the white population, virtually thwarting the March 1864 call for black troops.[22]

Faced with the failure of black recruitment in Kentucky, the federal government during June and July 1864 initiated a vigorous effort to ensure its success. Adj. Gen. Lorenzo Thomas, charged with raising black troops for the Union army, began enrolling all able-bodied slaves, "regardless of the wishes of their owners." The government garrisoned military camps to receive and protect these recruits in major towns and cities. Anyone who interfered with black recruiting was promptly arrested.[23]

The offer of Federal protection for slave volunteers provided many Kentucky bondsmen with their first viable opportunity to flee slavery. They responded by the thousands in order to achieve their freedom. Volunteers frequently told company clerks at Federal camps that they enlisted "to be free" or "for liberty." Joining the army also provided an opportunity to make a statement regarding their manhood—their worth as a human being. As soldiers, they might fight alongside whites as equals while simultaneously delivering a death blow to the hated system of involuntary servitude. Those who received volunteer bounties might also improve their potential for land ownership, independence, and a better life after the war. Others viewed the military as an adventure, and many Kentucky slaves experienced their first knowledge of the "outside world" in Federal blue.[24]

The large slaveholding region of central Kentucky—Fayette and surrounding counties—proved to be one of the best recruiting zones for the Union army. Volunteers flowed into Lexington from all directions during June 1864. They arrived from Bourbon County by the trainload, and one large Mercer County contingency of recruits marched through the streets of Lexington shouting their support for the Union. Slave recruits quickly filled the draft quota of Jessamine County, and, in nearby Madison County, slaves ran off in droves to join the army. Boyle County slaves "thronged" into the Danville enlistment office the first day it opened. On being formed into squads, they marched off toward Camp Nelson, a recruiting center located on the Kentucky River in southern Jessamine County. Slaves in Marion County volunteered in such numbers that authorities closed the recruiting office until they had processed the mass of enlistees.[25]

In western Kentucky, slaves also volunteered in large numbers. "Cheerful" recruits, some no more than fifteen years old, journeyed to Louisville to enlist, often having walked long distances. Marching through the streets of Louisville, the new enlistees on one occasion demonstrated their hostility to slavery by singing songs such as "John Brown." Blacks entered the recruiting office at Bowling Green by the score, with three hundred arriving from surrounding counties in one month. When recruiting slowed in September 1864, the army opened additional recruiting offices to absorb recruits from the large slaveholding counties of western Kentucky. Slaves also demonstrated "enthusiasm" for military service in the counties surrounding Owensboro and Henderson, joining in large numbers. Brisk enlistment also continued west of the Cumberland River. By July 1, about two hundred recruits had joined regiments at Paducah, and another six hundred men drilled at Smithland and Columbus.[26]

Most slaves who ran off to join the military slipped quietly away from their cabins as opportunities arose. G. W. Buckner remembered being awakened late at night by his mother, who whispered for him to tell his uncles "good-bye." The startled child opened his eyes to see four of his uncles leaving to join the army, "the light of adventure shining" on their faces. George Conrad did not get to wish his father farewell. His father and thirteen other slaves disappeared one night shortly after the Union army began recruiting blacks. Of the group, only Conrad's father returned after the war.[27]

Ironically, the first violence that many black volunteers experienced came, not from the Southern armies, but from local whites. Recruits leaving Boyle County were "pretty severely injured" by a mob of angry whites, and, when they arrived "grievously dispirited" at Camp Nelson, the post commander "refused to accept them." In the Lebanon area, "certain persons" detained a group of about seventeen recruits under false pretenses, releasing them after administering a hundred lashes to each man, and, in Green, Taylor, and Adair counties, gangs whipped volunteers whenever they caught them. On one occasion, Hancock County volunteers had to be locked in the jail to protect them from an angry mob, some of whom were Kentucky white recruits.[28]

Additional complications in recruiting blacks occurred when former owners appeared at recruiting offices and Federal camps shortly after the volunteers arrived, hoping to reclaim their slaves. Federal commanders, either hostile to black recruiting or unsure of government policy, frequently forced slaves to return to their masters. Some owners attempted to entice recruits into returning home by taking their wives or girlfriends to Federal camps, alternately promising the enlistees a better life if they returned home and threatening retribution against loved ones if they refused. After a Bourbon County slaveholder convinced a Cynthiana recruiter that he should be allowed to converse with his slaves, the master talked one of the six into returning home, apparently to assure food for his family. Within four hours after Elijah P. Marrs and his band of recruits reached Louisville, their owners arrived "hunting their slaves," eventually reclaiming one underage volunteer. The provost marshal of Boyle County, in cooperation with a number of slaveholders, personally went to Camp Nelson and attempted to persuade twenty recruits to return to slavery. The post commander intervened, but one recruit went home with his owner.[29]

Not all blacks rushed to the Federal barricades. A few fled the state to avoid military service, and some free blacks bought substitutes. Most slaves who hesitated to enlist expressed concern for their families' well-being since many slaveholders threatened retaliation against the loved ones of volunteers. The federal government naively reassured potential enlistees by telling them that their masters were honor "bound" to take care of families of volunteers. Government policy was equally unrealistic regarding the fate of those slaves rejected for military service. Though a few entered "invalid" or labor regiments, in most instances the government forced those "unfit for service" to return to their masters.[30]

These and other circumstances combined to turn the spring 1864 flood of recruits into a late summer trickle. Consequently, General Thomas concluded that it would require "armed parties passing through the counties," impressing slaves, to enroll the quantity of troops needed. Indeed, a policy of impressment of all available black men already existed in some areas of Kentucky. As early as February 1864, black troops operating out of Clarksville, Tennessee, began impressing slaves in southern Kentucky, and troops from west of the Cumberland River, where forcible induction of bondsmen had begun some months earlier, impressed slaves as far east as Henderson County in June 1864. By September, units of black troops scoured the countryside, impressing blacks wherever they found them. The violence and bloodshed associated with the impressment of slaves caused bitter complaints from white Kentuckians.[31]

The forcible induction of blacks continued for the remainder of the Civil War. Squads of both black and white troops roamed Kentucky's cities and counties in search of recruits. While most slaves viewed recruiters as liberators, others saw them as press gangs. When a Henderson-area slave complained that, for health reasons, he did not want to enlist, the white Union officer reportedly shouted: "Take this damned nigger to the jail." Given that option, blacks usually concluded, as one former slave put it: "I would rather enlist than be put in jail."[32]

The trickle of slaves fleeing into Union lines that began in the summer and fall of 1862 grew steadily after 1863, and, when slave recruits entered Federal lines, in many cases their families followed. "This morning Henry was missing and my favorite saddle horse Mack!" a Logan County minister wrote in July 1863. "I suppose he is aiming for some of the Yankee camps." Six months later, the same observer reported that "thousands" of slaves were enlisting and "thousands more" fleeing to Federal encampments.[33]

Increasingly, slaves fled in family groups. Susan, a Henry County slave, escaped with all her children in May 1864 after the men had run off. Abram, Bob, Jeff, George, Ellen, Dolly, William, Ida, Nicholas, and Lucy, all trusted Logan County slaves, fled a month later. With their few clothes, a wagon, a carriage, two horses, and two mules belonging to their owner, the slaves, along with about twenty area bondsmen, set out for a Union camp in Clarksville, Tennessee. Hotly pursued and overtaken, a few fugitives escaped by abandoning the caravan. Of those recaptured, several fell under the lash, and others were hired out in Louisville. In early March 1865, the promulgation of a Federal law freeing the wives and children of soldiers also increased the number of slave families entering Union camps. Mary Fields, whose husband was in the Union army, "left to-day" with her daughters, Eliza and Mildred, "being free under the law," a Louisville diarist wrote in March 1865, and a week later her slave Ed enlisted, freeing his wife Patsy and their sons Coleman and William. An unknown number of female slaves married soldiers for the sole purpose of freeing themselves and their children.[34]

Taken altogether, the events beginning in 1862 with the impressment of slave labor and culminating in the forced induction of bondsmen into the army and the fleeing of their families to Federal camps during 1864–1865 removed large numbers of slaves from Kentucky farms. Those who remained developed more independence, causing their owners to view them as increasingly intractable. A Bourbon County master believed local slaves to be "insubordinate" and unwilling to work after 1863, and, a year later, a Fayette County observer found the slaves "no longer humble" but "restless, impertinent, and discontented." In 1864, a Louisville newspaper lamented that slaves in many Ohio River counties could no longer "be controlled by their masters." A Logan County farmer observed that, by 1865, many of the slaves in southern Kentucky were also "refusing to work." Those who offered slaves financial incentives usually fared better than those who tried to maintain the status quo. Slaves on a Lexington farm accepted their owner's 1863 offer of fifteen dollars a month wages and remained on the farm throughout the war. Peter Bruner worked for wages during one period of the war, demanding payment at the end of each day, and later, in 1863, agreed to farm and chop wood for his master for half the profits he produced.[35]

After 1863, the realization that slavery was doomed led thoughtful whites to contemplate the future without it. Robert Anderson's conversation with his owner was probably typical of thousands of exchanges between masters and slaves across Kentucky as the war drew to a close. After thinking "for some time" about fleeing to the army, the twenty-one-year-old Anderson made up his mind in 1864. "I went to my old master and talked it over with him. At first he was angry," Anderson wrote in his memoirs, but "then he told me I would have to decide for myself what I wanted to do. . . . He seemed to sense the fact that the slavery of the past was over, and that a new era was opening for all. We had quite a talk, and parted friends." Another owner, tormented over having to pursue his fleeing bondsmen, secretly hoped that they would make good their escape, thus absolving him of any "responsibility."[36]

The federal government estimated that 71 percent, or all but about sixty-five thousand, of Kentucky's slaves were legally freed by March 1865, though all had not left their former owners. The result of this decline in black laborers was the near collapse of Kentucky's agriculture by 1864–1865. Tobacco production had dropped 57 percent, wheat 63 percent, barley 15 percent, and the hemp crop four-fifths. The assessed value of slaves, which stood at $107,494,527 in 1860, decreased to $34,179,246 in 1864, a decline of 68 percent. A year later, slave property was valued at only $7,224,851. Though slavery did not officially end until December 1865, it was essentially destroyed by March of that year.[37]

One of the saddest tragedies of this mass movement of slave families was that many suffered greatly after entering Union lines. Federal authorities were generally as unprepared and as unwilling to receive refugees after 1863 as they had been in 1861 and 1862. When hundreds of relatives followed recruits to Fort Anderson in Paducah, they soon encountered starvation and hostile military commanders who ordered that women, children, and the ill, infirm, and aged be "returned to their masters." Only the direct disobedience of that order by Col. H. W. Barry forced the government to reverse its policy. In late 1864, the Union adjutant general Lorenzo Thomas officially approved Barry's policy of caring for refugees, but many continued to suffer from exposure and hunger for the duration of the war. Similar tribulations of hunger, poor housing, unsanitary conditions, and hatefulness greeted families of recruits at Bowling Green, Munfordville, and Louisa.[38]

The treatment of refugees at Camp Nelson was, unfortunately, all too typical. During the summer and fall of 1864, relatives of central Kentucky recruits lined the roads leading to Camp Nelson, swelling to thousands the number of black refugees seeking refuge there. On arriving, they found a hostile post commander, Brig. Gen. Speed S. Fry, who rejected any responsibility for feeding or sheltering refugees. Fry promptly ordered the return of all those unfit for military service—women, children, the elderly, the ill—to their owners, promising that "the lash" awaited any refugee who returned to Camp Nelson.[39]

Nevertheless, women and children, expelled from their homes by unfriendly owners or urged to come to Camp Nelson by their soldier-husbands, continued to arrive, but Fry's policy of harassment did not abate. When three women expelled from camp returned, Fry had them bound and whipped as an example for all. Reports also spread of "men, women, and children, tied together," guarded by Union soldiers, awaiting their masters to claim them. Still others told of squads of soldiers "hunting slaves" throughout the camp, "returning them to their masters." A slave girl employed as a cook at the camp hospital, arrested and held for her master on Fry's orders, "begged" to be shot rather than sent back into slavery. A band of sympathetic soldiers who heard her pleas eventually rescued the girl, successfully preventing her return.[40]

The shortage of food, shelter, clothing, and health care among refugees at Camp Nelson created some of the worst living conditions of the Civil War. Women were forced to compete for the few jobs available as cooks and washerwomen in order to keep their loved ones alive. Extended families lived in small tents, crude huts, and shanties built from scrap material. "Nowhere in the whole range of my observation of misfortune and misery occasioned by the war," a U.S. Sanitary Commission worker wrote, "have I seen any cases which appealed so strongly to the sympathies of the benevolent as those congregated in the contraband camp at Camp Nelson." Despite an appalling death rate, refugees continued to arrive, and they continued to die. General Fry periodically swept the camp with troops, harassing refugees out of his lines, only to see them return. To solve the recurring problem, Fry decided to expel those refugees living inside Camp Nelson and destroy their shantytown in order to prevent their return. Early on the morning of November 23, 1864, a bitterly cold day when the temperature remained below freezing, warmly clad soldiers of the provost guard drove four hundred raggedly clothed women and children, including the sick, from their huts into "the wintry blast."[41]

Joseph Miller, a Lincoln County recruit and former slave, described what happened to his wife and four children. Early in the morning, an armed guard rousted his family from his tent. The officer in charge ordered Miller's wife and children to get into a wagon. Miller protested, saying his family was poorly clothed, that his young son was deathly ill. The officer in charge rejected Miller's pleas and threatened to "shoot the last one of them" if they did not get into the wagon. That night Miller found his family in an African American church near Nicholasville. His family, "shivering with cold and famished with hunger," had been unable to get near the fire. His son, Miller lamented, was dead. Sadly, 102 of the 400 refugees driven from Camp Nelson died from exposure.[42]

Only the efforts of religious humanitarians and Northern philanthropic organizations prevented Camp Nelson from becoming an even greater disaster for refugees. These friends of the refugees worked to ameliorate some of the worst conditions, protesting the government's policy at every opportunity. It was not, however, until accounts of the Camp Nelson expulsion in November reached the Northern press that their protests had a significant impact. On December 15, 1864, Gen. Lorenzo Thomas announced a new policy to provide shelter and rations for families of recruits in all rendezvous camps.[43]

Refugees also flocked into Louisville. By the autumn of 1864, a large refugee camp, consisting mostly of women and children, occupied ten acres of land on Broadway near the outskirts of the city. Its inhabitants, as at other camps, survived the harsh conditions in abandoned buildings, shanties they constructed, and discarded army tents. Though Union authorities provided some sustenance for the refugees as early as 1862 and Northern freedmen's aid organizations donated clothes, fuel, and other assistance, women and children perished by the hundreds from pestilence and disease. City officials did nothing to alleviate the suffering of these poor or sick blacks, with the single exception of isolating those with contagious diseases.[44]

Louisville's black benevolent societies played a vital role in easing the plight of the city's refugees. During the war, the Fifth Street Baptist Church established a "Colored Soldiers' Aid Society" to assist both recruits and their families. At society meetings, speakers, sometimes from the North, exhorted the people to raise recruits while contributing money to sustain their families. The black ladies of Louisville also sponsored fairs and benefits to raise money, clothes, fuel, and furniture for destitute refugees. Contributions from local black businessmen supplemented out-of-state donations.[45]

In late 1864, when the federal government began playing a more active role in assisting refugees, Rev. Thomas James, a vigorous fifty-eight-year-old New York freeman who worked among Louisville's black soldiers and refugees for the American Missionary Association, assumed charge of the refugee camp. James built a refugee home that provided "temporary assistance" while he worked on the overall problem of permanent lodging for Louisville's black homeless. Under James's leadership, strict rules to govern the morals and movement of refugees were set up and the first school established for their children.[46]

James, controversial from almost his first day in Louisville, clashed with the city's white leaders and with local black ministers such as Henry Adams, who believed the Northerner pushed too hard. Proslavery whites were particularly hostile to James. During his first eighteen months in Louisville, death threats forced James to post nightly guards at his door. On one occasion, he narrowly escaped injury when his guards fled as a band of men attacked his apartment. Later, when he headed the refugee camp, James refused to light candles in his apartment, fearing bushwhackers. Before his departure from Louisville, a blow from an assailant wielding a metal bar left his right arm paralyzed.[47]

When slaves entered the Union army, recruiting officers completed an enlistment form that indicated their occupation, physical condition, and company assignment. At their enlistment, only 329 of the 20,905 black recruits failed to list an occupation. Though slaves went into camp with a variety of backgrounds, experiences, and skills, more than 97 percent listed their occupations as farmers or laborers. The remaining 3 percent were artisans, servants, draymen, wagoners, and teamsters. Only 5 recruits claimed the ministry as their profession, and 3 had held jobs as clerks.[48]

Medical examinations of black recruits by army physicians indicated that, in general, they were healthy. Dr. E. P. Buckner's records, the most extensive of any examiner, were typical. A white Covington physician, Buckner administered about sixteen hundred physicals to black Kentucky recruits. He believed relatively "nutritious" diets had produced men with such "full" chests, "powerful" muscles, and "finely developed" physiques.

During examinations, the inductees expressed, Buckner indicated, few complaints about their "livers, stomachs, bowels, kidneys, or bladders," and he found tuberculosis "comparatively rare." In addition, he found few instances of heart disease. Evidence of fractures was *"uncommon,"* and he found his subjects' teeth "nearly always *perfect.*" Overall, Buckner concluded that Kentucky blacks entering the Union army were healthy and fit for service.[49]

Kentucky's black troops were organized into all-black units—designated U.S. Colored Troops—commanded by whites and a small number of black noncommissioned officers. The rapid growth of these units forced a frantic search for officers. As quickly as whites passed officer examination boards in Lexington, Nashville, and elsewhere, they hurried off to command the newly created regiments. It is impossible to determine the exact number of black Kentuckians who joined the Union army since some who enlisted outside the commonwealth may not have been credited to the state. By July 1864, the government estimated that 16,000 had volunteered and anticipated an additional 4,000 recruits within a month. Eventually, the army reported a total of 23,703 black Kentucky troops, an impressive 56.5 percent of the 41,935 eligible slaves and freemen between the ages of eighteen and forty-five. Kentucky provided about 13 percent of the 178,895 black Union troops.[50]

Black regiments served in a number of theaters outside the commonwealth. The Sixth U.S. Colored Cavalry Regiment and the 116th U.S. Colored Infantry Regiment, both organized at Camp Nelson, took part in the siege of Petersburg, Virginia, and the Fourth U.S. Colored Heavy Artillery Regiment, organized at Columbus, saw duty in northwestern Tennessee. The One Hundredth U.S. Colored Infantry, a regiment commanded by Col. Reuben D. Mussey, participated in the Nashville Campaign. The Eighth U.S. Colored Heavy Artillery Regiment spent most of its tour of duty in the Paducah area, where it had organized in April 1864, and the Twelfth U.S. Colored Heavy Artillery Regiment operated in south-central Kentucky. Colonel Mussey's One Hundredth Infantry also campaigned in central Kentucky, and the 108th U.S. Colored Infantry garrisoned at Owensboro. Kentucky mustered at least twenty-three regiments, but some were never at full strength.[51]

For many people, entering the military was often a traumatic experience, and blacks proved no exception. Elijah P. Marrs's first night in the barracks made him wish he "had never heard of the war." After induction, Marrs and his fellow recruits marched to Taylor Barracks on Third Street in Louisville, where they received uniforms, weapons, bunks, and company assignments. That night, as Marrs slept on the top bunk, the recruit in the middle, sleeping with a cocked revolver in his bed, accidentally discharged his weapon, killing the man on the lowest bunk. Recruits promptly descended on the dead soldier, stealing his three hundred dollars substitute fee. During the few hours Marrs actually slept the remainder of that night, he experienced "horrible" dreams. Reveille awakened him to a new day and soon to a new attitude. When an officer called his name and he stepped forward for his rations, he "felt freedom" in his "bones," and he thought to himself: "Pshaw! . . . This is better than slavery."[52]

Kentucky's black recruits spent most of their time in camp engaged in purely routine activities. They did little marching to or from battle and even less fighting. Those who took few or no interests with them into the military suffered most from boredom, but, for the energetic recruit, military life offered many opportunities. The deeply religious usually wasted little time in locating fellow believers, a place to worship, and a willing preacher. Rev. Sandy Bullitt preached to his Simpsonville friends on their third night in the Louisville barracks, and, at Camp Nelson, it seemed to one observer that preachers kept the dining hall busy almost nightly and on Sundays from "sunrise to taps." The saintly Elijah P. Marrs found devout Christian friends wherever he went. On one occasion when Marrs was stationed in Bowling Green, a soldier he had never seen before walked up to him and said: "You look like a Christian." Marrs greeted the stranger warmly and expressed his concern over the absence of religious fervor among his fellow black soldiers. Shortly thereafter, with the permission of his captain, Marrs and his new friend, Swift Johnson, led "a glorious prayer meeting" in the barracks.[53]

One of the first thoughts of many soldiers on getting settled in camp was to inform their loved ones of the events that had transpired in their lives since leaving home. For many illiterate blacks, this meant finding someone to write letters for them. Humphrey, a former Madison County slave stationed at Camp Nelson, found a friend to write letters for him on a weekly basis. Humphrey described the army as a better life than slavery, and the money he regularly sent his family impressed them. Eventually, friends and relatives arrived at Camp Nelson to observe for themselves.

After several visits, Humphrey's father, Alfred, concluded that his son was right, and he informed his owner of his intention to enlist at Camp Nelson. Letter-writing white ministers, such as John G. Fee, performed a very important service for black soldiers at Camp Nelson. One army chaplain wrote 150 letters to soldiers' families in a single month, and Elijah P. Marrs, known as "that little fellow from Shelby County" who could write, was surrounded nightly "by a number of men, each waiting his turn to have a letter written home."[54]

Military camp also offered black soldiers an opportunity to improve their minds, their bodies, and, occasionally, their pocketbooks. Many black troops wanted to acquire an education, a desire not ignored by missionary associations. By November 1864, thirteen volunteer missionaries were teaching classes at Camp Nelson, and countless numbers of individual soldiers, both black and white, took it on themselves to teach reading and writing to blacks at Federal encampments. Black troops also attended classes to improve their musical talents. Camp Nelson authorities provided instruction in drums, the fife, and the bugle for members of the field marching band, and there were glee clubs for troops, with occasional classes in vocal music. Time always seemed to be available for recreation of various sorts around camp. Soldiers played games, engaged in wrestling matches, held regimental picnics, and, of course, used weekend passes to "visit the ladies." Soldiers could also make extra money in their spare time. When passing through Nicholasville, the men in Marrs's company earned a few dollars by guarding a circus.[55]

Black volunteer societies helped relieve the suffering of soldiers by supplementing the inadequate nursing services of the federal government. The Soldiers' Aid Society of Louisville's Green Street Baptist Church, led by churchwomen, cared for sick and wounded black soldiers brought to hospitals in Louisville and New Albany, Indiana. Society members also visited the barracks of black troops, caring for the sick, and providing for the needy. The Colored Soldiers' Aid Society of the Fifth Street Baptist Church engaged in similar work. The Louisville Colored Ladies' Soldiers' Aid Society, which held most of its meetings in Methodist churches, also raised money to assist sick and disabled black soldiers and their families. Other Louisville groups that aided wounded and disabled soldiers and assisted their families included the "Sons and Daughters of the Morning" and the "Daughters of Zion."[56]

Though assigned to artillery, cavalry, and infantry units, black troops were viewed by most white officers as primarily "hewers of wood and drawers of water." The federal government recognized as early as June 1864 that abuse of blacks existed in Kentucky and ordered that black recruits receive only "their fair share" of labor assignments, but observers noted that, regardless of the number of white troops available, blacks performed the hardest work. Four days after joining the army in Louisville, Elijah P. Marrs was ordered to take a squad of men to clear off several lots at Tenth and Broadway streets. Marrs's first thought on receiving orders from a "white man" to perform manual labor was probably similar to that of thousands of black volunteers: "Is my condition any better now than before I entered the army?" Nevertheless, he marched off with his labor detail, believing that the army provided a step toward freedom, but, like so many of his black friends, he longed for the day when no one could order him to "come and go."[57]

Literate blacks, or those with special skills, possessed the best opportunities for assignment to leadership positions in the Union army. When officers learned that Elijah P. Marrs could read and write, they made him third duty sergeant of Company L, Twelfth U.S. Colored Heavy Artillery Regiment, and later, temporarily, regimental quartermaster sergeant. His brother, Henry C. Marrs, became orderly sergeant for another company and, eventually, sergeant major. Peter Bruner, attached to Company C, Twelfth U.S. Colored Heavy Artillery Regiment, spent most of his time as a laborer, but he later served in the base hospital as a nurse, a position that usually went to troops recovering from illness. The vast majority of black troops in the field, in addition to recruiting slaves, served as pickets or as guards.[58]

Wherever they served in Kentucky, black troops more often than not encountered hostility from whites, both civilians and soldiers. Treatment of the Fifth and Sixth U.S. Colored Cavalry regiments was typical. Harassment of these units began at Camp Nelson as they were being formed. Racial epithets were commonly hurled at black soldiers, but they were also victims of beatings and murder. One officer at Camp Nelson, commenting on the long-standing hostility directed at black troops, stated that "rarely a day passed" without a violent attack on one of his men.[59]

The Fifth and Sixth U.S. Colored cavalries were part of a larger force that marched east out of Camp Nelson in late 1864 to attack the Confederates at Saltville, Virginia. The insults, taunts, and ridicule from their fellow white soldiers began almost immediately. Along the march, black soldiers quietly endured the humiliation of having their hats knocked off and their horses stolen and verbal charges that they were cowards who would run away at the first sound of enemy fire. On the day of the attack, October 2, 1864, the Union commander, who had 4,000 troops, put into battle only 2,500 men, 400 of whom were from black regiments. The Rebels defended a mountainside position, strongly protected by log and rock breastworks. The Union soldiers fought to within fifty yards of the first Confederate line when the order to charge was given. The black troops "rushed upon the works with a yell and after a desperate struggle carried the entire line killing and wounding a large number of the enemy and capturing some prisoners." Unable to penetrate the second Confederate line, and hampered by heavy casualties, the Union forces withdrew. In an engagement that gained nothing, 114 black troops and 4 of their officers fell dead or wounded, and most remained overnight on the battlefield. The next morning, in one of the more horrifying atrocities of the Civil War, Confederate soldiers systematically executed about a hundred of the wounded and captured Federal troops, most of whom were black. Those wounded black troops who had reached Federal lines after the battle suffered grievously during the Union army's retreat since no one wanted to be left behind. But, according to their commanding officer, none scoffed at the black troops as they returned to Kentucky.[60]

Most whites went into the Civil War with the assumption that blacks were incapable of becoming soldiers. This concept stemmed from the widely held view that blacks were, in every way, inferior. Though blacks had a long history of standing by their Kentucky owners in the Indian wars, and though tales of their heroism were well known, the nineteenth-century white mind found it difficult—indeed, impossible—to transfer such heroism to black troops fighting an organized battle in the Civil War.

Though few whites changed their opinions regarding black equality during the war, black troops produced a mild revolution in some minds. One physician, after observing blacks in combat, declared that the black man "possesses courage sufficient to make him an effective soldier, no person acquainted with him can deny. Let his officers inform him that he has a right to do a thing desired, and that the officers want it done, and he will do it if it be possible for bravery, determination, and physical manhood to accomplish."[61]

White officers who fought with black troops in Kentucky, however grudgingly, usually came to respect their willingness to fight and die for the Union cause. Stephen Jocelyn, a first lieutenant in the 115th U.S. Colored Infantry Regiment, stationed in Bowling Green, admitted that Kentucky's black troops "fight well." A battalion commander with the Sixth U.S. Colored Cavalry Regiment was slightly more liberal in his praise. His battalion, about 300 men, attacked about 350 Confederate cavalrymen near Marion in January 1865. The black troops, in their first engagement of the war, "charged over open ground and did not fire a gun until within thirty yards of the rebels," driving the enemy back about a half mile, the officer reported. The officers who led the black troops into battle at Saltville, Virginia, also had praise for their soldiering. General S. G. Burbridge spoke highly of the gallantry of the Fifth U.S. Colored Cavalry Regiment, stating that it performed "better" than any other troops on the battlefield while absorbing the "principal loss." Finally, the rate of volunteering among blacks of military age in Kentucky, a standard that will probably never be surpassed, testifies to both their desire for freedom and their courage.[62]

The Civil War further complicated the lives of Kentucky blacks. Harassment and harsh treatment increased, but most slaves eventually realized how much they stood to benefit from a Union victory and bided their time. It is significant that, when the first viable opportunity occurred for large numbers to escape slavery, Kentucky's bondsmen left their masters by the thousands, entering Union camps, and volunteering for the Union army. Unfortunately, those seeking refugee status within Union lines frequently met with rebuff or, on entering Federal camps, discrimination and abuse. Those who became soldiers sometimes watched helplessly as their families suffered and died in refugee camps, and they frequently endured the indignity of discrimination within the military as they fought to end slavery. Nevertheless, black civilians and soldiers, convinced that their new status was better than slavery, contributed more than their share of the physical labor and much of the military power that ran the Federal war machine in Kentucky. Out of their effort came victory and, eventually, freedom of a sort. For those blacks who survived the horrors of slavery and civil war, many battles were yet to be fought and won before they would enjoy the most basic freedoms guaranteed by the U.S. Constitution that Kentucky whites had so long possessed.

Notes

1. W. H. Gibson, *Historical Sketch of the Progress of the Colored Race, in Louisville, Ky.* (Louisville, Ky.: Bradley & Gilbert, 1897), 41–42; Victor B. Howard, *Black Liberation in Kentucky: Emancipation and Freedom, 1862–1884* (Lexington: University Press of Kentucky, 1983), 4; Harry Smith, *Fifty Years of Slavery in the United States of America* (Grand Rapids: West Michigan Printing Co., 1891), 116; Isaac Johnson, *Slavery Days in Old Kentucky* (Ogdensburg, N.Y.: n.p., 1901), 36; Anna Dicken to Henry, February 10, 1861, Dicken-Troutman-Balke Family Papers, Special Collections, University of Kentucky, Lexington.

2. Smith, *Fifty Years of Slavery,* 116; Robert Anderson, *From Slavery to Affluence: Memoirs of Robert Anderson, Ex-Slave* (Hemingford, Nebr.: Hemingford Ledger, 1927), 42; Johnson, *Slavery Days,* 36; Norman R. Yetman, ed., *Voices from Slavery* (New York: Holt, Rinehart & Winston, 1970), 137–38; James William Massie, *America: The Origin of Her Present Conflict . . .* (1864; reprint, Miami, Fla.: Mnemosyn, 1969), 266; Elijah P. Marrs, *Life and History of the Rev. Elijah P. Marrs, First Pastor of Beargrass Baptist Church, and Author* (Louisville, Ky.: Bradley & Gilbert, 1885), 17.

3. John W. Blassingame, ed., *Slave Testimony: Plantation Life in the Antebellum South,* rev. ed. (New York: Oxford University Press, 1979), 385–86; *National Anti-Slavery Standard* (New York), March 19, 1864; Ira Berlin, "The Structure of the Free Negro Caste in the Antebellum United States," in *The Southern Common People: Studies in Nineteenth Century Social History,* ed. Edward Magdol and Jon L. Wakelyn (Westport, Conn.: Greenwood, 1980), 65.

4. Lewis W. McKee and Lydia K. Bond, *A History of Anderson County* (Frankfort, Ky.: Roberts Printing Co., 1936), 63; Blassingame, ed., *Slave Testimony,* 385, 387; Gibson, *Historical Sketch,* 49; Richard L. Troutman, ed., *The Heavens Are Weeping: The Diaries of George Richard Browder, 1852–1886* (Grand Rapids, Mich.: Zondervan, 1987), 175; *AME Christian Recorder,* April 5, 1862; *National Anti-Slavery Standard,* March 19, 1864; *Lexington, Ky., Observer and Reporter,* April 2, 1864; Herbert G. Gutman, *The Black Family in Slavery and Freedom, 1750–1925* (New York: Pantheon, 1976), 378; U.S. War Department, *The War of the Rebellion: A Compilation of the Official Records of the Union and Confederate Armies, 1861–1865* (hereafter cited as *OR*), 70 vols. in 128 pts. (Washington, D.C.: U.S. Government Printing Office, 1880–1901), ser. 1, vol. 20, pt. 2, p. 68; Howard, *Black Liberation,* 44.

5. Blassingame, ed., *Slave Testimony,* 390, 632; *National Anti-Slavery Stan-*

dard, April 8, 1865; Berlin, "Free Negro Caste," 65; Gibson, *Historical Sketch,* 49; Howard, *Black Liberation,* 91.

6. Blassingame, ed., *Slave Testimony,* 385; *AME Christian Recorder,* June 3, 1865; Anna Dicken Troutman to Henry, January 26, 1861, and to Mother, April 3, 1863, Dicken-Troutman-Balke Family Papers; Troutman, ed., *The Heavens Are Weeping,* 141, 171; *New York Tribune,* January 23, 1862; *Cincinnati Daily Gazette,* November 23, 1861.

7. Howard, *Black Liberation,* 14; *OR,* ser. 2, vol. 1, p. 776.

8. General Orders No. 9, October 22, 1862, The Negro in the Military Service of the United States, 1639–1886 (hereafter cited as NIMS), National Archives (NA), Washington, D.C., microfilm 858, roll 1, frames 428, 431, 455, 699; *OR,* ser. 2, vol. 1, p. 777. Eventually, all slaves who entered Union lines were designated as "contraband."

9. Howard, *Black Liberation,* 108–9, 114; *Paris, Ky., Western Citizen,* March 28, 1862; *OR,* ser. 1, vol. 20, pt. 2, p. 91, ser. 2, vol. 1, p. 809, and ser. 3, vol. 4, pp. 501–2; General Orders No. 27, March 21, 1862, and No. 9, October 22, 1862, Brig. Gen. Q. A. Gillmore to Maj. Gen. Gordon Grainger, December 11, 1862, NIMS, NA, roll 1, frames 480, 696–97, 699; Adj. Gen. Lorenzo Thomas to Col. S. G. Hicks, July 25, 1864, ibid., roll 3, frame 432; Ira Berlin et al., eds., *The Black Military Experience,* vol. 1, ser. 2, of *Freedom: A Documentary History of Emancipation, 1861–1867, Selected from the Holdings of the National Archives* (Cambridge: Cambridge University Press, 1982), 263.

10. Howard, *Black Liberation,* 13, 14, 16, 23, 39.

11. *New York Tribune,* January 23, 1862; M. B. Morton, *Kentuckians Are Different* (Louisville, Ky.: Standard, 1938), 16–17.

12. Howard, *Black Liberation,* 45–46, 50; Mary Julia Neal, ed., *The Journal of Eldress Nancy Kept at the South Union, Kentucky, Shaker Colony August 15, 1861–September 4, 1864* (Nashville: Parthenon, 1963), 186; *National Anti-Slavery Standard,* July 11, 1863; Frances Dallam Peter Diary, October 10, 1863, Evans Family Papers, Special Collections, University of Kentucky, Lexington; Troutman, ed., *The Heavens Are Weeping,* 169–70.

13. Howard, *Black Liberation,* 44; Gibson, *Historical Sketch,* 47; Robert Emmett McDowell, *City of Conflict: Louisville in the Civil War, 1861–1865* (Louisville, Ky.: Louisville Civil War Round Table, 1962), 83–84; *AME Christian Recorder,* September 27, 1862.

14. Edgar A. Toppin, "Humbly They Served: The Black Brigade in the Defense of Cincinnati," *Journal of Negro History* 48 (1963): 84–88; Vernon L. Volpe, "Squirrel Hunting for the Union: The Defense of Cincinnati in 1862," *Civil War History* 33 (1987): 244–45.

15. Howard, *Black Liberation*, 34, 36, 46, 50.

16. *National Anti-Slavery Standard,* July 11, 1863; Peter Diary, October 10, 1863, Evans Family Papers; *OR,* ser. 3, vol. 4, pp. 921–22; John David Smith and William Cooper Jr., eds., *Window on the War: Frances Dallam Peter Civil War Diary* (Lexington, Ky.: Lexington–Fayette County Historical Commission, 1976), 43; John David Smith, "The Recruitment of Negro Soldiers in Kentucky, 1863–1865," *Register of the Kentucky Historical Society* 72 (1974): 374; M. A. Harris to Riley Handy, January 2, 1973, Harris Small Collection, Department of Library Special Collections, Manuscripts, Western Kentucky University, Bowling Green; Johnson, *Slavery Days,* 36–38.

17. Gutman, *Black Family,* 368; Howard, *Black Liberation,* 51–52, 66–67; *OR,* ser. 3, vol. 4, pp. 59–60, 559, 733, 768; Gibson, *Historical Sketch,* 47–48; Federal Writers Project (FWP), Works Progress Administration (WPA), *Military History of Kentucky* (Frankfort, Ky.: Printed by the State Journal, 1939), 203–4. The federal government estimated that nine hundred black Kentuckians enlisted at Gallatin and one thousand at Evansville. The often-quoted figure in Lewis Collins, *History of Kentucky: By the Late Lewis Collins, Revised, Enlarged Four-Fold, and Brought Down to the Year 1874, by His Son, Richard H. Collins,* 2 vols. (1874; reprint, Frankfort: Kentucky Historical Society, 1966), 1:136, placing Kentucky black enlistees in other states at twelve thousand seems too high.

18. Supt. of Census Joseph C. G. Kennedy to Sec. of Interior J. P. Usher, February 11, 1863, NIMS, NA, roll 2, frame 37; Maj. W. H. Sidell to Col. James B. Fry, March 14, 1864, ibid., roll 3, frames 135–36; *OR,* ser. 3, vol. 3, pp. 416, 418–19, and vol. 4, p. 177; Smith, "Negro Soldiers in Kentucky," 383–84; Howard, *Black Liberation,* 57. Federal draft problems in Kentucky were complicated by the number of residents who joined the Confederate army.

19. *OR,* ser. 3, vol. 3, pp. 1174–75, 1178–79, and vol. 4, pp. 233–34, 248–49; General Orders No. 34, April 18, 1864, District of Kentucky, Records of the U.S. Army Continental Commands, Record Group (RG) 393, NA, Washington, D.C.

20. Capt. William C. Grier to Fry, April 10, 1864, Records of the Provost Marshal General's Bureau, 1863–1866 (hereafter cited as PMGB), RG 110, NA; Prov. Mar. to Sidell, March 16, 1864, NIMS, NA, roll 3, frame 145; Howard, *Black Liberation,* 58, 64n, 68; Gutman, *Black Family,* 368; *New York Times,* March 13, 1865; Ira Berlin et al., eds., *The Destruction of Slavery,* vol. 1, ser. 1, of *Freedom: A Documentary History of Emancipation, 1861–1867, Selected from the Holdings of the National Archives of the United States* (New York: Cambridge University Press, 1985), 616.

21. Gutman, *Black Family,* 368; Jonathan Truman Dorris and John Cabell Chenault, *Old Cane Springs: A Story of the War between the States in Madison*

County, Kentucky (Louisville, Ky.: Standard Printing Co., 1937), 122; *Louisville Daily Courier,* March 3, 1866; Stephen Jocelyn, *Mostly Alkali: A Biography* (Caldwell, Idaho: Caxton, 1953), 34; Howard, *Black Liberation,* 68, 73; *New York Times,* March 13, 1865; Fry to Sidell, May 14, 1864, Telegrams Received, Asst. Prov. Mar. for Kentucky, PMGB, RG 110, NA; Smith, "Negro Soldiers in Kentucky," 387; *OR,* ser. 3, vol. 4, p. 559. According to J. H. Baxter, comp., *Statistics, Medical and Anthropological . . . ,* 2 vols. (Washington, D.C.: U.S. Government Printing Office, 1875), 1:372, slave owners sometimes attempted to enroll elderly or ill slaves as substitutes.

22. E. Merton Coulter, *The Civil War and Readjustment in Kentucky* (1926; reprint, Gloucester, Mass.: Peter Smith, 1966), 199–200, 206–7; *Kentucky House Journal, 1863–1864* (Frankfort, Ky.: George D. Prentice, State Printer, 1865), 397, 466, 579; *OR,* ser. 3, vol. 4, pp. 177–79; John W. Blassingame, "The Recruitment of Colored Troops in Kentucky, Maryland and Missouri, 1863–1865," *Historian* 29 (1967): 542–43.

23. *OR,* ser. 3, vol. 4, pp. 429–30, 548; Maj. Gen. S. G. Burbridge to Sidell, May 13, 1864, Telegrams Received, Asst. Prov. Mar. for Kentucky, PMGB, RG 110, NA.

24. Johnson, *Slavery Days,* 36; *American Missionary* 9 (1865): 121; Smith, "Negro Soldiers in Kentucky," 390; Blassingame, "Colored Troops," 544.

25. Collins, *History,* 1:134; Gutman, *Black Family,* 368–69; Smith, "Negro Soldiers in Kentucky," 384–85; Capt. Thomas H. Moore to Sidell, May 12, 24, 1864, and Capt. James M. Fidler to Sidell, May 16, 1864, Telegrams Received, Asst. Pro. Mar. for Kentucky, PMGB, RG 110, NA; Dorris and Chenault, *Old Cane Springs,* 123; Howard, *Black Liberation,* 63; Col. R. D. Mussey to C. W. Foster, June 2, 1864, Letters Received, Colored Troops Division, Records of the Adjutant General's Office (hereafter cited as CTD, RAGO), RG 94, NA; J. S. Newberry, *The U.S. Sanitary Commission in the Valley of the Mississippi, during the War of the Rebellion, 1861–1866* (Cleveland: Fairbanks, Benedict, 1871), 520; Tri-Monthly Report of Business and General Transactions, May 1864, Asst. Prov. Mar. for Kentucky, PMGB, RG 110, NA; Berlin et al., eds., *Destruction of Slavery,* 607.

26. S. E. Smith, ed., *History of the Anti-Separate Coach Movement . . .* (Evansville, Ind.: National Afro-American Journal and Directory Publishing Co., [1874]), 173; J. W. Gibson and W. H. Crogman, *The Colored American: From Slavery to Honorable Citizenship* (Atlanta: J. L. Nicholas, 1906), 552; *National Anti-Slavery Standard,* June 18, 1864; Thomas to Townsend, April 25, 1865, NIMS, NA, roll 4, frame 118; Henry A. Ford and Kate Ford, *History of the Ohio Falls Cities and Their Counties, with Illustrations and Biographical Sketches,* 2 vols. (Cleveland: L. A. Williams, 1882), 1:329; S. M. Starling to Daughters [Mary and Anna], June

19, 1864, Lewis-Starling Collection, Department of Library Special Collections, Manuscripts, Western Kentucky University, Bowling Green; Capt. A. G. Hobson to Brig. Gen. James B. Fry, August 4, 1864, NIMS, NA, roll 3, frame 458; Jocelyn, *Mostly Alkali,* 30–34; Capt. J. R. Grissom to Fry, June 1, 1865, NIMS, NA, roll 4, frame 151; Smith, "Negro Soldiers in Kentucky," 384–85; *History of Daviess County, Kentucky . . .* (Chicago: Inter-State Publishing Co., 1893), 168–69; OR, ser. 3, vol. 4, p. 501; Col. C. H. Adams to Brig. Gen. J. P. Hawkins, September 28, 1863, NIMS, NA, roll 2, frame 584; Thomas to Townsend, April 25, 1865, NIMS, NA, roll 4, frame 118.

27. George P. Rawick, ed., *The American Slave: A Composite Biography,* 19 vols. (1941; reprint, Westport, Conn.: Greenwood, 1972), 6:30, 7:39–41.

28. Mussey to Foster, June 2, 1864, Letters Received, CTD, RAGO, RG 94, NA; Newberry, *Sanitary Commission,* 520; *National Anti-Slavery Standard,* July 9, 1864; Fidler to Fry, May 31, 1864, NIMS, NA, roll 3, frame 314; Fidler to Sidell, June 15, 1865, NIMS, NA, roll 4, frames 161–64; Berlin et al., eds., *Black Military Experience,* 259.

29. *Lexington, Ky., Observer and Reporter,* July 16, 1864; OR, ser. 3, vol. 4, p. 501; Thomas Hood and S. W. Bostwick, *Report of the Commissioners of Investigation of Colored Refugees in Kentucky, Tennessee, and Alabama,* December 28, 1864, Senate Executive Document 28, ser. 1209, 38th Cong., 2nd Sess. (Washington, D.C.: U.S. Government Printing Office, 1865), 17; Newberry, *Sanitary Commission,* 521–24; Rawick, ed., *The American Slave,* 7:40; Marrs, *Life,* 20; Berlin et al., eds., *Destruction of Slavery,* 610.

30. OR, ser. 3, vol. 4, pp. 210, 422, 474; Troutman, ed., *The Heavens Are Weeping,* 186; Howard, *Black Liberation,* 79, 111, 116; Blassingame, "Colored Troops," 539; *Lexington, Ky., Observer and Reporter,* July 16, 1864.

31. Smith, "Negro Soldiers in Kentucky," 385; OR, ser. 3, vol. 4, pp. 429, 501; George Browder Diary, February 27, 1864, September 5, 1864, Department of Library Special Collections, Manuscripts, Western Kentucky University, Bowling Green; E. L. Starling, *History of Henderson and Henderson County, Ky.* (Henderson, Ky.: n.p., 1887), 227–31; FWP, WPA, *Military History of Kentucky,* 209; *National Anti-Slavery Standard,* June 18, 1864. Browder recorded as early as September 11, 1862, that Federal troops had "seized" a Logan County slave, "strapped a gun on him," and ridden off.

32. *National Anti-Slavery Standard,* June 18, 1864; Troutman, ed., *The Heavens Are Weeping,* 170, 184, 189; Smith, "Negro Soldiers in Kentucky," 385–86; Berlin et al., eds., *Black Military Experience,* 273–74; Howard, *Black Liberation,* 73; *New York Times,* March 1, 1865; Ford and Ford, *Ohio Falls Cities,* 329; Gutman, *Black Family,* 368.

33. Troutman, ed., *The Heavens Are Weeping,* 160, 171, 174; Neal, ed., *Eldress Nancy,* 186.

34. Gutman, *Black Family,* 370; George D. Dicken to Anna and Frank [Troutman], May 24, 1864, Dicken-Troutman-Balke Family Papers; Hood and Bostwick, *Report of the Commissioners of Investigation of Colored Refugees,* 17; *National Anti-Slavery Standard,* June 18, 1864; Troutman, ed., *The Heavens Are Weeping,* 179; Berlin et al., eds., *Black Military Experience,* 275–76; Howard Miller Diary, March 20, 1865, Manuscript Collection, Filson Historical Society, Louisville; William Pratt Diary, vol. 3, April 1, 1865, 5 vols., Special Collections, University of Kentucky, Lexington; Thomas James, *The Autobiography of Rev. Thomas James* (1887; reprint, Rochester, N.Y.: Rochester Public Library, 1975), 24; John M. Palmer, *Personal Recollections of John M. Palmer: The Story of an Earnest Life* (Cincinnati: Robert Clarke, 1901), 233; *New York Times,* March 13, 1865.

35. Troutman, ed., *The Heavens Are Weeping,* 131, 156, 194; Howard, *Black Liberation,* 16, 91, 93; Anna Dicken Troutman to Mother, April 3, 1863, Dicken-Troutman-Balke Family Papers; Peter Diary, January 27, 1864, Evans Family Papers; Peter Bruner, *A Slave's Adventures toward Freedom; Not Fiction, but the True Story of a Struggle* (Oxford, Ohio: privately printed, 1918), 41; *National Anti-Slavery Standard,* June 18, 1864.

36. Troutman, ed., *The Heavens Are Weeping,* 171, 179; Neal, ed., *Eldress Nancy,* 199; Peter Diary, January 27, 1864, Evans Family Papers; Anderson, *From Slavery to Affluence,* 43; John Egerton, *Generations: An American Family* (Lexington: University Press of Kentucky, 1983), 54, 57.

37. Ross A. Webb, *Kentucky in the Reconstruction Era* (Lexington: University Press of Kentucky, 1979), 39; *Frankfort, Ky., Commonwealth,* April 28, 1865; Howard, *Black Liberation,* 71, 79, 82; Mary Sudman Donovan, "Kentucky Law Regarding the Negro, 1865–1877" (M.A. thesis, University of Louisville, 1967), 13. Lowell H. Harrison (*The Civil War in Kentucky* [Lexington: University Press of Kentucky, 1975], 101–2) points out that a rise in prices partially offset some of the losses in production.

38. Berlin et al., eds., *Black Military Experience,* 262; *National Anti-Slavery Standard,* March 28, 1863; Howard, *Black Liberation,* 113, 117.

39. Pratt Diary, vol. 3, July 4, 1864, Special Collections, University of Kentucky, Lexington; Newberry, *Sanitary Commission,* 385; *National Anti-Slavery Standard,* June 18, 1864.

40. Berlin et al., eds., *Black Military Experience,* 270; Newberry, *Sanitary Commission,* 527; *National Anti-Slavery Standard,* June 18, 1864; *The Liberator,* June 24, December 9, 1864.

41. Newberry, *Sanitary Commission*, 527–28; Gutman, *Black Family*, 372; *Liberator*, December 9, 1864.

42. Berlin et al., eds., *Black Military Experience*, 270–71.

43. *Sanitary Reporter* 2 (September 1864): 61; General Orders No. 29, December 15, 1864, NIMS, NA, roll 3, frame 567.

44. *Louisville Daily Union Press*, January 28, 1865; James, *Autobiography*, 21; Howard, *Black Liberation*, 110; Blassingame, ed., *Slave Testimony*, 385.

45. Minutes, Fifth Street Baptist Church, vol. 1, February 7, 1865, Fifth Street Baptist Church, Louisville; *Daily Union Press*, January 7, 16, 1865.

46. James, *Autobiography*, 21, 32; Gutman, *Black Family*, 376n.

47. James, *Autobiography*, 22–23, 26–28. James claimed that ministers like Adams "were ready to do the bidding of their [white] masters," but Adams and his friends no doubt believed that the Northerner would one day depart Louisville, as he eventually did, leaving them to an unpleasant fate that he had helped create.

48. Gutman, *Black Family*, 367–68. For a sample of slave enlistment declarations, see "Coleman Family Business Transactions and Correspondence," folder 162, Evans Family Papers.

49. Baxter, comp., *Statistics, Medical and Anthropological*, 1:364, 368–70, 372, 379, 382, 384, 386, 505, 510. Physicians who examined blacks entering the military in Kentucky summarized their findings in reports written between May and August 1865. The reports, between one and nine pages each, are generally couched in racist terms, but they contain an extremely valuable historical record. For a complete analysis of the physical condition of the commonwealth's black soldiers, see John David Smith, "Kentucky Civil War Recruits: A Medical Profile," *Medical History* 24 (1980): 185–96; and, more generally, Michael Anthony Cooke, "The Health of Blacks during Reconstruction, 1862–1870" (Ph.D. diss., University of Maryland, 1983), 37–43, 50–51, 123–25.

50. *OR*, ser. 3, vol. 4, pp. 542, 733, 921, 1018, 1270; Kennedy to Usher, February 11, 1863, NIMS, NA, roll 2, frame 37; Smith, "Negro Soldiers in Kentucky," 389. The 1867 report of the Kentucky adjutant general placed 25,438 black enlistees in fifteen infantry, two cavalry, and four artillery regiments. See *Kentucky's Black Heritage* . . . (Frankfort: Kentucky Commission on Human Rights, 1971), 30.

51. *Official Army Register of the Volunteer Force of the United States Army for the Years 1861, '62, '63, '64, '65*, 8 vols. (Washington, D.C.: U.S. Government Printing Office, 1865–1867), 8:332, 338, 341; Joseph T. Wilson, *The Black Phalanx: A History of the Negro Soldiers of the United States in the Wars of 1775–1812, 1861–'65* (Hartford, Conn.: American Publishing Co., 1888), 464–65, 476–78;

Special War Order No. 29, May 3, 1865, NIMS, NA, roll 4, frame 132; *OR*, ser. 3, vol. 4, pp. 1017–18.

52. Marrs, *Life*, 21–22.

53. Ibid., 24–26, 32, 59–60; Newberry, *Sanitary Commission*, 524–26.

54. Dorris and Chenault, *Old Cane Springs*, 122–23; Howard, *Black Liberation*, 11–12; Berlin et al., eds., *Black Military Experience*, 630; Marrs, *Life*, 23.

55. *American Missionary* 8 (1864): 262–63; John G. Fee to M. E. Strieby, March 7, 1865, microfilm no. 44106, American Missionary Association Archives, Amistad Research Center, Tulane University; Howard, *Black Liberation*, 65; Marrs, *Life*, 28, 65–66; *OR*, ser. 3, vol. 4, p. 460.

56. Minutes, Green Street Baptist Church, vol. 1, November 23, 1864, Church Library, Green Street Baptist Church, Louisville; *Louisville Daily Union Press*, January 7, 9, 17, 19, February 7, 1865, microfilm, University of Louisville Archives; Thomas James to George Whipple, February 10, 1865, AMA; *New York Times*, March 13, 1865; *Sanitary Reporter* 2 (September 1864): 61.

57. *OR*, ser. 3, vol. 4, pp. 431, 921–22; Marrs, *Life*, 25.

58. Marrs, *Life*, 23, 27, 37, 61–63, 67, 73, 75; *Official Army Register*, 8:304; H. C. Weeden, *Weeden's History of the Colored People of Louisville* (Louisville, Ky.: privately printed, 1897), 10; Newberry, *Sanitary Commission*, 526; Bruner, *A Slave's Adventures*, 43–44; *OR*, ser. 3, vol. 4, pp. 451, 469; Troutman, ed., *The Heavens Are Weeping*, 184; Mussey to Foster, June 12, 1864, NIMS, NA, roll 3, frame 893.

59. Smith, "Negro Soldiers in Kentucky," 388; Newberry, *Sanitary Commission*, 521; *Louisville Daily Union Press*, April 11, 1865.

60. Thomas to Secretary of War E. M. Stanton, October 10, 1864, and Col. James S. Brisbin to Thomas, October 20, 1864, NIMS, NA, roll 3, frames 1097, 1099–1101; James C. Klotter, *The Breckinridges of Kentucky* (Lexington: University Press of Kentucky, 1986), 127–28.

61. Baxter, comp., *Statistics, Medical and Anthropological*, 1:368.

62. Jocelyn, *Mostly Alkali*, 27–28, 45; Thomas to Stanton, October 10, 1864, January 1, 1865, NIMS, NA, roll 3, frames 1097, 1200.

A Long Way from Freedom

Camp Nelson Refugees

Richard D. Sears

Dictionaries define *refugees* as people displaced from their *country* by war, persecution, famine, or disaster. But clearly the term is applied to those homeless or imperiled within their own nation. It is also used to describe groups that are simply not where they are *supposed* to be. In practice, refugees are the people, sometimes quite helpless, who have suddenly become an unexpected and unwanted responsibility within a purview—the system or, let us say, the military camp—where some alien authority, not necessarily of a different nationality, must respond. Nobody wants *them* here, but *we* are responsible for them: the classic us/them relationship.

In looking at the history of refugees at Camp Nelson, Kentucky, one is struck with the constant unpreparedness of the people in charge; over a period of years, there was never enough food, there were never enough shoes, shelters were not ready, and so on. There were always too many refugees, new problems, and fresh devastation. Of course, the conditions that produce refugees, in our own time as during the Civil War, are never totally predictable. War, as we have learned (or failed to learn) over and over, is never completely controllable, never conveniently manageable; disease and disaster and the weather are frighteningly beyond our power to shape to our own ends. Wherever and whenever refugees arrive, they are almost always unexpected, hence not prepared for, thus doomed to suffer more than is really necessary, if only someone had known. It is difficult to be prepared for one expected emergency, impossible to be ready for multiple emergencies continuing over a period of years. But attitudes of those in command also contributed substantially to the refugee problem, as we shall see. Both overt racism and class prejudice led to unnecessary human suffering in ways that may remind us of the refugee problem in our own day.

In any case, Camp Nelson in performance always lagged behind the plans for its use, which changed drastically from time to time. It operated with three major consecutive functions: as an immense supply depot (pronounced a failure by no less an authority than Ulysses S. Grant himself), as a recruiting station for Kentucky's black soldiers, and as a refugee camp. In all of these areas, the camp was virtually overwhelmed by the demands of unexpected circumstances and by the numbers of people involved.

Beginning in the spring of 1863, Camp Nelson was constructed as a military supply depot and way station for the Union army. In the first capacity, it was supposed to provide all the materiel for the troops invading East Tennessee, from central Kentucky south to Knoxville. In the latter capacity, as a temporary campsite, a haven of safety from the war itself, an oasis, a welcome center, it became the hub of almost incessant activity—coming and going, a busy, bustling place, prosperous and impressive with its many new buildings, its waterworks, its Soldiers' Home, its hospitals, its stores, its herds of horses and mules, its hundreds of workers, and its thousands of soldiers, its constantly shifting population as big as a small city. With all this and even some luxuries—running water in some of the buildings, a fountain and flower gardens—it must have been, in many respects, an attractive place.

But, even at the height of the camp's operation as a supply depot, the Union soldiers who depended on it were short of shoes (literally hundreds of documents mention some portion of the population—soldiers or various refugee groups—who were inadequately shod), short of rations, short of blankets. Frequently, the camp had more than adequate supplies but simply could not deliver them because of the weather, the bad roads, the mountains that had to be crossed to reach the needy troops—in effect, because of the very poor or absent planning that established the campsite in the first place.

Long before it became an official refugee home for African Americans, Camp Nelson already had a pattern of "delivery" problems. It was a massive operation, covering a vast territory, heavily equipped, yet ill prepared, immensely complicated, and tangled in red tape from beginning to end. An order from Washington, perfectly feasible on paper, might emerge as totally unworkable on the ground at Camp Nelson. At the height of black recruitment at the camp, according to a typical report, men were "flocking in by hundreds—far beyond the ability of the provost-marshal to attend to them—to enlist."[1] Once the enlistment of Kentucky slave men began, anyone might have predicted that the camp would be flooded with refugees, with the families of the soldiers, just as military camps had already been in other parts of the country. But the pressure and stress of the recruitment period prevented camp officials from making any preparations for a new class of refugees. And flocks of them would soon follow, in a humanitarian crisis that was actually never solved.

Camp Nelson was in large part designed by circumstances over which people had no control. It was built piecemeal as its functions changed, failed, disappeared, and changed again. Its original design did not include any provision for use as a refugee camp. Nevertheless, two major populations of refugees would seek shelter there; one group was white and the other black. The white Appalachians, mostly from East Tennessee, and the African Americans, mostly wives and children of Kentucky's black soldiers, shared many conditions of suffering: starvation, nakedness, poverty, homelessness, disease, and the constant threat of death. They did not, however, share race, citizenship, or civil rights.

These two groups of refugees at Camp Nelson during the Civil War were never counted together. The total number of refugees was never announced at any point because it was always changing, sometimes from day to day. Hundreds died. Some people came into camp, then left and did not return; some were hiding there and unwilling to be counted; others were expelled and came back again and again. Therefore, it is impossible to do anything but estimate how many refugees passed through the camp. The high point of an actual count was 3,060 (black women and children) right before October 2, 1865,[2] but slaves from out of state, older black men (nonsoldiers) from Kentucky, and white refugees were not included. A report about Appalachian refugees at Camp Nelson stated that "in the aggregate they amounted to thousands."[3] A very conservative estimate then: at one time or another more than 5,000 individual refugees (and surely a great many more) were in the camp system.

The Appalachian refugees were the lowest of the low socially; the reports of their behavior by authorities who had to care for them were scathing. Of the denizens of Camp Nelson, they were considered the most quarrelsome, least cooperative, dirtiest, and most barbarous. They needed everything: food, clothing, shelter, medical treatment; they lacked work, education, manners, and gratitude. But many of them were transitory visitors to the camp. They could and did move on; their passage to some point north was sponsored and paid for by the military and the Sanitary Commission. For example, a commission official reported: "On the 20th of February [1864] . . . I was enabled to shelter about forty refugees from East Tennessee, who, after two or three days spent in preparation for entering the world at Cincinnati, went on their way thither rejoicing."[4]

The later refugees—African American women and children—presented a different range of problems. They also needed food, clothing, shelter, and medical care, but they had no social mobility because they were black; they could not go "on their way thither [anywhere] rejoicing" or otherwise. They could not move on and out into the larger world; they could not go wherever they wanted to go or—more accurately—where someone in command wanted to send them. They were black: they were not citizens, they were slaves. However destitute the East Tennesseans might be—and they were sometimes said to be more needy than their African American counterparts—they were free to go anywhere in the country, settle anywhere, seek work anywhere. None of that was true for black people, whether they were free or enslaved. And the East Tennesseans were not illegal; they were legitimate refugees. They had rights somewhere.

This treatment of the refugee experience at Camp Nelson is divided into four sections corresponding to the history of the site itself. As I have said, Camp Nelson functioned in three major ways that developed consecutively: as an army supply depot, as a recruiting station for black soldiers, and as a refugee camp. These functions disappeared in the same order, and Camp Nelson's existence as an agency of the federal government ended when the refugee camp was closed three years after the operation had begun. The first period opens with the establishment of the campsite in April 1863 and lasts until Camp Nelson was officially recognized as the primary recruitment center for Kentucky's black soldiers exactly one year later. During that period, the camp was basically a supply depot, with its fortunes, activities, and reputation tied to actual warfare in East Tennessee. The refugees of this time were mostly Appalachians (although they were not yet called that) fleeing a war zone.

The second period, beginning in April 1864, included the heyday of the enlistment of black soldiers; it was also the period when Kentucky slave women and children began arriving at the camp in great numbers. At that time, these refugees from bondage were illegal. Since Kentucky was a loyal state, slavery was still protected there by the U.S. Constitution. The wives and children of enlisted black soldiers were not freed by the Emancipation Proclamation, and they were not freed by the recruitment process in the state; they were the property of loyal citizens, many of whom were leaders in the government and in the military. Because the black women and children were not legitimate refugees (not *contrabands*, to use the term then current), they were periodically evicted from Camp Nelson. Continuous enlistment and repeated expulsion were the keynote activities of this period.

The third period opens in November 1864, with the expulsion of four hundred slave women and children in freezing weather. Many of them died, suffering was intense, and the whole terrible episode became public knowledge across the country, virtually while it was still happening. Almost immediately, an official Colored Refugee Home, promoted strongly by Rev. John G. Fee and Capt. Theron E. Hall, but motivated by public outcry, was established at Camp Nelson. From January 1865, Kentucky slave women and children (but not older black men) became legal refugees, or contrabands. Shelters, amid some controversy (the two founders, Fee and Hall, disagreed about whether the refugees should live in dormitories or cottages), were built for them, rations supplied, medical treatment provided—and they died by the hundreds. Shortly after becoming legal refugees, they were legally freed.

The activities of the Freedmen's Bureau, which took control of Camp Nelson on October 6, 1865, defined the fourth and last period of refugee life there. Since the bureau was intent on closing all military installations where refugees had gathered and dispersing all assembled populations of former slaves, its tenure at Camp Nelson was a time of dissolution; everything that had been built up, everything that was provided, had to disappear. In a way, this particular era was the most tragic of all.

The final section of this essay deals with the aftermath of the refugee experience at Camp Nelson. It investigates some crucial, simple, questions: Where did they go, and what did they do? What happened to the former refugees when the refuge was gone?

Appalachian Refugees and Others
(April 1863–April 1864)

Camp Nelson first attracted refugees simply because soldiers were there. The presence of Union troops promised safety to many people from East Tennessee and southeastern Kentucky, refugees who had lived with "hostile armies in their midst since the opening of the war" and then found themselves trapped within enemy territory.[5] As a matter of fact, all residents of Camp Nelson were spared actual battle conditions while they remained there. The site was never attacked. Fortified in an excellent position, it remained a safe haven, even though its occupants dreaded violence that did not materialize (John Hunt Morgan and his raiders were expected but never arrived). Unfortunately, the dangers of Camp Nelson were very real, although they did not involve cannon fire.

Among the earliest refugees was a group of contrabands, slaves who were legally free because their owners were Confederates from states in rebellion. These were refugees from Tennessee, Alabama, and other points south who followed the Union army north into Kentucky. As early as June 1863, some had arrived in the state, where they were liable to be imprisoned and resold into slavery.[6] Southern contrabands soon found their way to Camp Nelson, where they were safe. Although all Kentucky slaves were evicted from the camp over and over again, the former slaves from Tennessee and elsewhere were legally exempt and allowed to stay.

The largest group of refugees in Camp Nelson before the recruitment of blacks consisted of whites from East Tennessee. When it became clear that the Union army under the command of Gen. Ambrose E. Burnside would leave the Knoxville region, loyal citizens who had been liberated from Confederate rule were stricken. They knew the Rebels would regain the territory and feared that, as Union sympathizers, they would suffer even more than before their temporary rescue. "The terror in East Tennessee, when it became known that they were likely to be abandoned, was something fearful."[7] People swarmed north by the thousands. All along the escape route, food was scarce because the ill-equipped soldiers had been forced to pillage.[8] At his home in Berea, "near the great road leading into eastern Tennessee through Cumberland Gap," John G. Fee observed the soldiers who passed, the government trains, guerrilla bands, and then "flocks of women and children in most destitute condition on their way to some other part of the state or to the free states."[9]

Many found shelter at Camp Nelson, squarely on the route of the Union soldiers coming back from Tennessee: "Nearly every Quartermaster's train brought more or less families from their poverty-stricken homes into the camp. . . . The refugees were in many instances compelled to leave their homes and all they possessed to save their lives, while the majority started for this 'city of refuge' because their fathers, husbands and brothers were in the army, and no men were left to afford them protection and provide [for] them." The initial reception for these refugees was very hospitable, although Camp Nelson had never been intended for a refugee camp. They were given shelter and rations, an officer was appointed whose sole duty was to care for them, a surgeon and hospital were designated for them, and they had easy access to "the seat of authority." Government authorities expressed their desire to provide for these people, who were "refugees by necessity of their fidelity and loyalty," and "to relieve the sufferings which had thereby been occasioned."[10]

Families "willing and able to go North" were housed in the Soldiers' Home, the most well-appointed, comfortable lodging in the camp. These people were unable to go on without help, but help was provided generously. In addition to food and lodging, they were given "clothing, Government transportation, all necessary information, and a man to attend them to the cars [trains] and render such assistance as was required."[11]

After February 1864, some Appalachian refugees were provided with rooms and cabins that had once been part of a large plantation situated within the camp, but the displaced persons were so numerous that many families simply squatted where they could, scattering to various areas of the camp. Wherever they were located, they were under the care of the Sanitary Commission, which drew rations for them and delivered the food to their doors: "During the winter months the delivery of their fuel required five or six days per month, and was attended with much labor."[12]

Once they discovered that officials at Camp Nelson would take care of them, the Appalachian refugees, it is reported, "became as dependent and troublesome as children, and still more unmanageable." They made incessant demands; every day they asked for labor to be done that "they were quite as well able to perform themselves." They were "listless," "unambitious," "almost imbecile," with "their moral character in an undeveloped state." They fought constantly among themselves. Feuds developed or continued, and the refugees found their "sole employment and enjoyment . . . in strife and hostilities," engaging in "pitched battles, when the violence and obscenity of their tongues failed to produce the desired effect." Sometimes, quarreling was the only communication between several families living under the same roof. Their incessant fighting could be stopped only by separating them in the camp itself or sending them off to the North, where jobs were readily available: "A career of honorable independence was opened to all who were willing to work in almost any part of the North." But they would not go: they were unwilling to be separated from one another. "Like all such people," said the Sanitary Commission report, "ignorant and helpless, with little self-reliance and no enterprise, they herded together like sheep or savages, and were distrustful of strangers even to [the point of] hostility."[13]

The final account of the Sanitary Commission pronounced this judgment on them: "It was very sad to find these poor people thus disgracing their inevitable poverty and helplessness, and converting the solicitude of friends into comparative disgust."[14]

So they stayed on and on, still cared for by Sanitary Commission workers, who grew to disrespect them, and grudgingly sustained by the Union army. But they had forfeited the sympathy of the authorities. The later masses of black refugees received a great deal of attention, favorable and unfavorable, from officials in the camp, military brass, missionaries, and reporters throughout the United States as well as from Camp Nelson's letter writers, but the Appalachian refugees went almost unmentioned.[15] Attention simply shifted from them. They became an ordinary, unpleasant, insoluble problem, whereas the extraordinary one was the other throng of refugees.

Black Recruitment and Illegal Refugees (April 1864–November 1864)

Enlistment of slaves into the Union army began very late for Kentucky, two years after black soldiers from other states were first recruited. The Lincoln administration had been reluctant to offend loyal, slaveholding

Kentucky, the most important of all the border states in a military sense, and the most exposed. But, in the spring of 1864, full-scale recruitment began, eventuating in the most unrestricted policy. By June 1864, any black man who presented himself at a recruiting station could be enlisted, whether he was slave or free, with or without the knowledge and consent of his owner.

Two enormous groundswells of response developed simultaneously. Suddenly, the black men of Kentucky demonstrated their eagerness and determination to enlist, immediately proving that the Union army's gain in manpower from the new policy would be significant. And, just as suddenly, "loyal," slaveholding Kentuckians demonstrated, even to the point of disloyalty or treason, their absolute opposition to the recruitment of their property.

White Kentuckians resisted the recruitment of black Kentuckians with all their strength and with remarkable malice. According to an official report addressed to Edwin Stanton, the secretary of war: "Slaves escaping from their masters with a view of entering the military service were waylaid, beaten, maimed, and often murdered."[16] Two men who wanted to enlist had their left ears cut off.[17] Near Camp Nelson, one recruit was murdered, and "two [more] were fastened to trees in the woods and flayed alive."[18] Beatings were routine. After a large number of black men had already been recruited at Camp Nelson, John G. Fee reported that surgeons who examined the first three thousand soldiers found that "three out of five bore on their bodies marks of cruelty."[19]

Some of the first black refugees from Kentucky were men who came to enlist and were turned down because of age or unfitness. Once a black man went out to join the army, he could not easily go back to his former life since any slave returning to his master after attempting to enlist was likely to suffer severe punishment. Some of the "old men" continually listed among Camp Nelson's refugee population were among those who came to the camp expecting to be soldiers.[20]

In spite of the manifold difficulties in their way, slaves responded to the call to arms in great numbers; in approximately a year, more than half the eligible black men in Kentucky joined the Union army. As in all states where slave men were enlisted, their wives and children and other dependents followed them to recruiting centers and pressed to stay near them at training camps. Villages of contrabands had sprung up in Tennessee, Mississippi, Louisiana, and so on; it was much the same in Kentucky, except that the women and children were still the property of their masters.

When slaves arrived at the camp, they were frequently treated like runaways and driven out of camp to be reclaimed by their owners. At first, camp officials cooperated completely with slaveholders, notifying them of times when their slaves would be placed outside the lines and available to be captured. According to an account provided to the *National Anti-Slavery Standard* by an informant from Camp Nelson, it was an "almost daily occurrence for a squad of men to be employed in hunting slaves, and returning them to their masters. I have seen a Colonel of a regiment riding at the rear of a slave gang composed of men, women, and children, tied together, and guarded by men in the uniform of U.S. soldiers."[21]

Slaveholders, deprived of the services of their male property, sometimes confined and restrained their remaining slaves and often punished slave soldiers by proxy, humiliating, beating, and torturing their wives. Dozens of affidavits testify to the atrocities that slave owners committed against African American women in Kentucky during this period. One example—unfortunately, very typical—of testimony taken from slave women at Camp Nelson should suffice:

When my husband was killed [at the Salt Works in Virginia] my master whipped me severely saying my husband had gone into the army to fight against white folks[; so] my master would let me know that I was foolish to let my husband go. He would "take it out of my back," he would "kill me by pi[e]cemeal," and he hoped "that the last one of the nigger soldiers would be killed." He whipped me twice after that, using similar expressions. The last whipping he gave me he took me into the kitchen, tied my hands, tore all my clothes off until I was entirely naked, bent me down, placed my head between his knees, then whipped me most unmercifully until my back was lacerated all over, the blood oozing out in several places so that I could not wear my underclothes without their becoming saturated with blood. The marks are still visible on my back. On this and other occasions my master whipped me for no other cause than my husband having enlisted. When he had whipped me he said, "Never mind, God damn you, when I am done with you tomorrow you never will live no more."

She ran off to Camp Nelson with her baby, leaving four of her children behind; she wanted to go back for them, she said, but she was afraid to "go near [her] master knowing he would whip [her] again."[22]

After hundreds of women and children had assembled at Camp Nelson, John G. Fee gave an overview—derived from their own accounts of themselves—of their initial condition: "As counted a few days since, there were within this Camp, seven hundred and fifty three women and children. Of this number, one hundred and fifty say they were cruelly treated on account of their husbands enlisting, and three hundred and ten say they were driven off 'from home.' Three were so horribly lacerated that the military authorities after examinations by surgeons sent them to Cincinnati."[23] The majority of slave owners, as Fee noted, did not hang on to their slaves but "punished" the black soldiers in an alternative way, by turning their wives and children out, refusing to support them, sometimes tearing their cabins down around them, putting them out on the road without clothing, without shoes, without food. These people, too, fled to Camp Nelson.

The problem of prostitution began with white women. Some women of "bad character" were thrown out of camp, returned the next day, and were put in the military prison, given ten lashes, and then expelled from the camp again under escort.[24] One order (there were many) concerning these women stipulated: "Any negro woman here without authority will be arrested and sent beyond the lines, and informed that if they return, the lash awaits them."[25] The next month (June 1864), "a bevy of women and children," specifically designated as "colored," were found to be "engaged in lewd business annoying everything and everybody in the vicinity." The provost marshal was ordered "to place the whole kit beyond the lines for five (5) miles"; they were to be warned "not to return on pain of being imprisoned."[26]

On July 12, 1864, General Orders No. 4 included the following provision:

The law authorizing the enlistment of colored troops has only reference to the able bodied negroes capable of bearing arms, and not to old men, the infirm, or women and children. Accordingly, none but able bodied men will be received at the various camps designated for their reception, all others will be encouraged to remain at their respective homes, where, under the state laws, their masters are bound to take care of them, and those who may have been received at Camp Nelson will be sent to their homes. This letter is necessary as many cases of disease have made their appearance among both sexes, of such a nature as to require their removal beyond the limits of the camp. Furthermore all of this class of persons are required to assist in securing the crops now suffering in many cases for the want of labor.[27]

Guards "stationed at all the openings in the fortifications" were ordered "not to allow negro women and children or lewd white women to enter the Camp." They made it clear that soldiers and whores had to be kept separate. The same order specified that soldiers were to be permitted to pass outside the lines only at certain points, "except when sent out on duty, or by special permit."[28]

The idea that some black women in the camp were spreading sexually transmitted diseases was part of the early rationale for ousting all of them. Another reason was also mentioned in General Orders No. 4: with the slave men in the army, only the women and children were left to harvest the crops. The recruitment of black soldiers could not be allowed to diminish Camp Nelson's food supply.

The status of Kentucky slave women and children was determined, not simply by law, but by people's attitudes toward them. Some people—especially the missionaries, but some of the military as well—wanted to welcome them as legitimate refugees because they clearly needed refuge. Others wanted them cleared out of the way because they impeded troop movements, caused extra work, necessitated extra supplies and expense, and so on. But they could not be stopped from coming into the camp no matter what anyone thought of them. Various generals issued stern orders to keep them out, and they got in anyway. They were kicked out, and they came back. The wives and children wanted to be with the men, who also insisted that the safety of their families be guaranteed, and both men and women were desperate to escape the evils of slavery, which was probably more brutal now than it had ever been, lashing out in its death throes.

Slaves were running from intense suffering, but it was clear that Union military officials usually did not understand that. They expected black women to cooperate and go home willingly. At one point, a group of women and children were offered passes for all "that desired to return home." The officer reporting seemed surprised that "not one among two hundred (200)" wanted to go. Some were willing to move outside the lines and try to "shift for themselves." But, said the officer, "they are laboring under the impression that they will be killed by their masters if they return and can not be assured to the contrary."[29] Ironically, the officer may have been the person laboring under a false impression.

On June 20, Brig. Gen. Burbridge ordered the establishment of "a contraband camp at Camp Nelson [because] the women and children [could not] be left to starve."[30] Ten days later, the same man conveyed Adjutant General Lorenzo Thomas's countermanding order "to discourage as far as possible negro women and children coming into Camp," although those who came had to be provided for.[31] Thomas wrote to the secretary of war on July 3, expressing his view that, "in this State, where slavery exists, I conceive I have only to do with those who can be put into the army."[32] This was very far from being the case, however. An order on the same day commanded: "Only able bodied Negroes of lawful age who express a desire to enter the U.S. service shall hereafter be permitted to enter this Camp, and any old men, women or children shall under no pretense whatever be allowed to pass the line of Pickets at this Post."[33] After a few days, an order was issued "that all negro women and children & men in camp unfit for the service will be delivered to their owners, the delivery to commence on Monday next and continue from day to day until all are sent off."[34] Nevertheless, some days later, when General Thomas himself visited the camp, he found "a number of old men, women, and children" whom, he reported, "I decided should be sent to their homes, as in this State, where slavery exists, I am only authorized under the law to take able-bodied men for soldiers. They, too, are needed to secure the crops, which we shall certainly require for the army."[35] The order "that all negro women and children & men in camp unfit for the service will be delivered to their owners" was repeated over and over.[36]

At various times in the summer and autumn of 1864, the women and children at Camp Nelson and its subdepots were driven out. On June 18, Col. Andrew H. Clark cited "standing orders" that directed "all negroes that are found in camp without authority from their owners to be placed beyond the lines." On July 6, Speed S. Fry ordered that "all negro women and children & men in camp unfit for service [should] be delivered to their owners." On July 16, Lorenzo Thomas found at the camp "a number of old men, women, and children, which . . . should be sent to their homes." On August 13, General Burbridge ordered "that all women children & men unemployed in Camp Nelson be expelled." All the Kentucky black women in the camp were sent out by General Orders No. 19 on August 23. "All negro women and children, except those who have written permits from these Head Qtrs, to remain within the limits of this Camp," were expelled on September 19. Moving beyond Camp Nelson, the orders were sent to subdepots; for example, on October 29, the commander of Point Burnside was ordered by the commander of Camp Nelson: "Preparatory to the Regiments moving you will turn out of Camp all Negro women and children."[37]

For months the orders continued, repetitive, frequently in exactly the same words, and for months it could easily be observed that women, children, and old men were still staying at Camp Nelson and still arriving. Again and again, an official expulsion would be announced, and then it would be observed that women, children, and old men were still there or there again. Perhaps this situation would have continued to the end of the war if the temperature had not been below freezing from November 23 through November 25, 1864.

Expulsion and an Official Refugee Home (November 23, 1864–October 1865)

In late November 1864, Camp Nelson was in the midst of the furor of its last military assignment, the preparation for Stoneman's Raid in Virginia. Regiments were coming and going, horses and mules had to be procured, and forage had to be provided. Many military leaders were out of patience with the refugees, who created many difficulties in an environment that had not been designed for them. The plan was to sweep them out of the way. No one seemed to have time to notice the weather. But it was most important to get all the illegals out of the camp as quickly as possible so that the soldiers could devote themselves entirely to important business.

The tragic expulsion of November 1864 was the last official action of this sort. It was an inhumane blunder on the part of the Union army, with soldiers at Camp Nelson *following orders* to expel four hundred slave women and children—inadequately clothed, frequently without shoes, without shelter, without food, and already sick—in spite of the fact that the temperature was, unexpectedly, below freezing. A black soldier named Joseph Miller described the incident in an affidavit dated November 26, 1864:

I was a slave of George Miller of Lincoln County, Ky. I have always resided in Kentucky and am now a Soldier in the service of the United States. I belong to Company I 124 U.S.C. Inft now Stationed at Camp Nelson Ky. When I came to Camp for the purpose of enlisting about the middle of October 1864 my wife and children came with me because my master said that if I enlisted he would not maintain them and I knew they would be abused by him when I left. I had then four children, ages respectively ten nine seven and four years. On my presenting myself as a recruit I was told by the Lieut. in command to take my family into a tent within the limits of the Camp. My wife and family occupied this tent by the express permission of the aforementioned Officer and never received any notice to leave until Tuesday November 22nd when a mounted guard gave my wife notice that she and her children must leave Camp before early morning. This was about six o'clock at night. My little boy about seven years of age had been very sick and was slowly recovering. My wife had no place to go and so remained until morning. About eight o'clock Wednesday morning November 23rd a mounted guard came to my tent and ordered my wife and children out of Camp. The morning was bitter cold. It was freezing hard. I was certain that it would Kill my sick child to take him out in the cold. I told the man in charge of the guard that it would be the death of my boy I told him that my wife and children had no place to go and I told him that I was a Soldier of the United States. He told me that it did not make any difference he had orders to take all out of Camp. He told my wife and family that if they did not get up into the wagon which he had he would shoot the last one of them. On being thus threatened my wife and children went into the wagon. My wife carried her sick child in her arms. When they left the tent the wind was blowing hard and cold and having had to leave much of our clothing when we left our master, my wife with her little ones was poorly clad. I followed them as far as the lines. I had no Knowledge where they were taking them. At night I went in search of my family. I found them at Nicholasville about six miles from Camp. They were in an old meeting house belonging to the colored people. The building was very cold having only one fire. My wife and children could not get near the fire, because of the number of colored people huddled together by the soldiers. I found my wife and children shivering with cold and famished with hunger. They had not recieved a morsel of food during the whole day. My boy was dead. He died directly after getting down from the wagon. I know he was killed by exposure to the inclement weather. I had to return to Camp that night, so I left my family in the meeting house and walked back. I had walked there. I travelled in all twelve miles. Next morning I walked to Nicholasville. I dug a grave myself and buried my own child. I left my family in the Meeting house—where they still remain.[38]

Every member of the Miller family died at Camp Nelson between December 17, 1864, and January 6, 1865. The father was the last to die.[39]

John Vetters, an American Missionary Association worker, reported what he saw before, during, and immediately after the expulsion:

I was in Camp Nelson on the 22nd day of last November. It was a bitter cold day; the wind was blowing quite hard and many of the women and children were driven from the Camp. I counted six or eight wagon loads of these women & children being driven away on Thursday or Friday. When they were expelled their huts were destroyed and in some instances before the inmates got out. The work of destruction commenced on Saturday Nov 26th. I went to Nicholasville to inquire into the condition of the outcasts. I found that one hundred or more had taken shelter in the woods, having been driven from a meeting house in which they had taken refuge. I saw some in the town in a very destitute condition. . . . On reaching Nicholasville on Sunday Nov. 27th I found that those who had gone to the woods had been scattered by the storm of the previous night and those we found were without food. I . . . saw that they were entirely destitute, some were sick. I learned that several had died. On Saturday Dec. 3rd I went to Lexington to ascertain the condition of some of the women and children who having been driven from the Camp had taken refuge there. I found fourteen in an old shed, doorless and floorless, sitting around a stick of burning wood with no food or bedding. One woman was apparently overcome by exposure and another had given birth to a child in that place. Among those around the fire was a boy evidently near death, whom on the following morning I found dead. I believe he died through exposure and want. In another old building I found about half a dozen sick without even the necessaries of life. . . . One woman had been so pressed with hunger as to offer her child for sale in the City to obtain bread. I brought a number of the sick with me to Camp in an Ambulance.[40]

The November expulsion, resulting in many deaths and great suffering, climaxed the period of illegal refugees and almost overnight initiated a new phase of the refugee experience. The incident was reported in the New York papers almost as soon as it happened, and the whole terrible episode became public knowledge across the country. Suddenly, Camp Nelson was notorious. The federal government moved quickly to deal with the humanitarian crisis—and the bad press. Immediately after reports of the expulsion hit the headlines, military commanders ordered that all the people who had been kicked out should be found and restored to camp, then that all black refugees, legal or not, be accepted into camp. Soon, the camp became the site for an official Colored Refugee Home, and, very soon afterward, all wives and children of Kentucky's black soldiers became free: "The General commanding [Major General Palmer] announces to the colored men of Kentucky that by an act of Congress passed on the 3d day of March, 1865, the wives and children of all colored men who have heretofore enlisted, or may hereafter enlist, in the military service of the Government, are made free."[41] And again, as if in atonement, the camp was ordered to accept any slaves who arrived, whether qualified for freedom or not. Although it brought about a significant change in policy and, perhaps, a more humane or at least more informed attitude about the plight of slave refugees, the November expulsion must be acknowledged as one of the darkest incidents in the history of Kentucky, much less of Camp Nelson.

On the basis of the hardships and tragedies that this incident caused, and through the combined efforts of Rev. John G. Fee and Capt. Theron E. Hall, an official, government-sponsored Colored Refugee Home at Camp Nelson was established, with new buildings erected under the supervision of Captain Hall.[42] Thousands of slaves took advantage of this opportunity to escape the savage persecution that they were suffering at the hands of their masters.

From disease and death, however, they were not safe. Even as more refugees assembled, they grew sick and died, especially the children. Because average Kentucky slaveholders had owned only a few slaves, most of the black refugees had never been exposed to common communicable diseases. In fact, most of them had probably never been in a large crowd of people before. Beyond that, many of the refugees had been starved, beaten, and half frozen; their lives had been in turmoil for months.

A report concerning the women and children in the Refugee Home, giving statistics for every five-day period from April 11 through July 16, reveals the full extent of the disaster. During the months covered, the number of women at the camp increased steadily from 728 to 1,408; the number of children increased from 813 to 1,392. The number arriving far exceeded the number being discharged, but by a figure much larger than might be expected because there were so many deaths; 969 women arrived, and 196 were discharged, while 1,030 children arrived, and 105 were discharged. The death statistics were staggering: in a period of approximately three months, 103 women and 409 children died.[43]

Although many military officials and most of the doctors and missionaries tried to help, the high mortality continued for the entire duration of the Refugee Home's operation. In the month of February 1865, "the population of the colored refugee camp was about eight hundred women and children, of whom four hundred were sick." Mrs. John Christopher of Louisville, an aid worker at the camp, visited the refugee hospital and reported: "I found the poor people huddled together in rags and dirt. The wards were full of human wretchedness. I found poor women dying, amidst filth and suffering, for the simplest food, within twenty steps of the superintendent's office."[44]

On February 21, 1865, John G. Fee wrote an account of the suffering he was observing at Camp Nelson:

There is yet much distress & mortality. Out of 400 cast out [during the November expulsion] about 250 came back into camp. Of this number just one hundred and two have died in consequence of being exposed to cold and then herded together into Barracks, until better buildings could be prepared! The buildings now prepared, though somewhat artistic and well *meant,* are not suitable for women and children. With 150 persons in one building, noise, disease, and death rage. Oh, the suffering incident to Slavery! Today as I looked upon the sick and dead—little ones—I was completely overcome and wept for the poor sufferers.[45]

An absolutely opposing view of the refugee situation at Camp Nelson, but one that was widely held, was expressed by a local doctor, C. Graham, M.D., of Crab Orchard, who wrote to Abraham Lincoln on July 24, 1865, with the express purpose of informing the president "of the state of things in Kentucky":

The servants, being seduced from their happy homes by the pledge of free papers at Camp Nelson, assemble in such numbers as to render their condition uncomfortable and unhealthy; so much so that the fatality amongst those deluded creatures has been sadly and notoriously great. Mothers, becoming wearied with the toil of their children and scarce of food, often neglect them till they perish, while others throw them into the ponds around Camp Nelson, from which many have been taken. Disease of every kind, *Private* and public, seems to be rife in their ranks, and the time is fast coming when, if not checked, the loafing vagrants and filthy lepers will die off like sheep with the rot. The worst feature about this Camp Nelson business is, that the blacks have taken up the idea that their free papers is to enable them to live the remainder of their lives without work, and that the Government will support them, at the expense and labor of the white man.[46]

The suffering at the Colored Refugee Home was intense and terrible, but, according to a Sanitary Commission report, the Appalachian refugees "were even more wretched and more pitiable than the 'contrabands'":[47] "They received less than one-third of the amount of food furnished *per capita* to the colored refugees. From the 1st of February, 1865, a large ration was issued to colored women and children, while the white received the substance of only one meal per day. Fuel was continued to the colored, but discontinued to the sickly white people. Good buildings were erected for the negroes, while the white refugees remained in old log huts and miserable, dilapidated places." Government policy "made suitable provision for the poor and unfortunate without regard to race or color," and discrimination was forbidden. But the people who were so intent on helping the former slave refugees, "from a narrow and unreasoning sympathy" for "the colored race, allowed themselves to be unfeeling and unjust to the women and children of their own color." Camp officials were ordered to treat the two refugee groups—characterized as "equally deserving and equally destitute and wretched"—exactly the same, but the orders were apparently ignored by "the officers having local authority at Camp Nelson." The brief period of favoritism for slave refugees—through no fault of their own—had tragic consequences for their free white counterparts. The Appalachian refugees were afflicted with smallpox and measles. A hospital for "eruptive diseases" was established for them, but "death made many seizures among them, as one group of about sixty graves, and others located according to family inclination, plainly indicate[d]."[48]

In the brief period when the Colored Refugee Home was in operation—less than a year—various administrators, commandants, superintendents, missionaries, teachers, aid workers, and others fought with one another about who should get food, what kind of shelters should be provided, which group was in charge of which function; the quarrels about who should do what and who had the authority to do something else were seemingly endless. Many organizations vied for power at Camp Nelson, quite often ignoring the people who were dying while bureaucrats conducted a free-for-all of their own.

In the meantime, many actions were taken that were quite effective and stabilizing. Schools that had been established from the very beginning of black recruitment operated at their optimum level during this period. In spite of the inroads of illness and death, six hundred black children learned to read in the schools that John G. Fee had founded.[49] Everyone was not sick; many black people found themselves for the first time in a sympathetic, supportive community where hardships could be dealt with more effectively. They liked living together. They appreciated being saved from their torturing, barbaric masters. And, of course, they were very enthusiastic about having their food and shelter supplied to them until they could support themselves. In spite of everything, some aspects of the lives of black refugees during this interval—the only time when everybody in the camp was legal—were happy.

A letter from William A. Warfield, Sergeant in Company D, 119th United States Colored Infantry, dated July 7, 1865, and published in the *Weekly Anglo-African* on July 22, 1865, fervently described what he saw as the dawning of a new day:

This is an age of wonders, and not the least among them is the celebration of the Fourth of July at Camp Nelson, Ky., by the colored people. To see so many thousands, who a year ago were slaves, congregate in the heart of a slave State and celebrate the day sacred to the cause of freedom, "with none to molest or make afraid," was a grand spectacle. It was the first time we have ever been permitted to celebrate the Nation's Day. . . . The people gathered in from far and near. With several regiments of colored soldiers, with the thousands at the Refugee Home, and with the many [visitors?] from different parts of the country, the numbers swelled to many thousands. Such an assemblage of colored people on the "sacred soil of Kentucky" was never before beheld.

The exercises consisted in martial music, songs, speeches, and declamations, with an interlude of a good dinner. The first part of the exercises were performed by the colored people themselves. The school-girls took an active part in the singing and recitations. Speeches, pointed and witty, were made by several colored speakers. In the afternoon, toasts were given and responded to in well-timed and effective remarks. Almost boundless enthusiasm prevailed throughout.[50]

Former slaves, 13,332 of them, were issued freedom papers at Camp Nelson.[51]

Freedmen's Bureau (October 6, 1865–March 14, 1866)

The activities of the Freedmen's Bureau define the last period of refugee life at Camp Nelson. Since the bureau was intent on closing all military installations where black refugees had gathered and dispersing all assembled populations of former slaves, its tenure at the camp was a time of dissolution.

When the war ended in April 1865, elements of Camp Nelson immediately started to disappear. The soldiers went first, leaving only a token military presence at the camp, then withdrawing altogether. The missionaries were next: the teachers and aid workers departed for other assignments. But the refugees stayed.

On June 26, 1865, Gen. Clinton B. Fisk took office as assistant commissioner of the Freedmen's Bureau for Tennessee and Kentucky, and Royal Estabrook ("R. E.") Farwell, the bureau's special agent, designated superintendent of the refugee camp at Camp Nelson, was charged with the monumental task of breaking up the camp.[52] By October 6, 1865, the week before Farwell's arrival, all but one of the camps in Kentucky and Tennessee had already been closed.[53] Only Camp Nelson, the final challenge, remained. Fisk had already decided "to cease offering rations." According to official policy, closing the camps and denying food to those people living within former camps would "[force] the idle to work or starve."[54]

Even before Farwell's assignment began, the Bureau had been reducing the numbers of women and children in the camp. A volunteer named Annie Hager, for example, relocated 450 refugees from Camp Nelson to various points in Ohio (Urbana, Mechanicsburg, Landau, Xenia, among others), serving as their guardian and escort to homes and work in communities that had agreed to receive them.[55]

But Hager's people were only a small percentage of thousands who had to be turned out of the camp. Farwell had been expected to accomplish the task in days or at most weeks, but it stretched on for months, in order to be "consistent with humanity."[56] Some of the people scheduled to depart from Camp Nelson were not allowed on the trains; Farwell had to fight to force the railroads to transport them. By federal law, he was ordered to get the people away, yet he could find no means for them to travel.

Variety of housing: barracks, tents, and huts. Photograph from a book of plates taken by G. W. Foster and Co.: *Photographic Views of Camp Nelson and Vicinity* (Lexington, Ky.: Government Office, Print, 1864).

Street scene in the refugee camp. Photograph from a book of plates taken by G. W. Foster and Co.: *Photographic Views of Camp Nelson and Vicinity* (Lexington, Ky.: Government Office, Print, 1864).

Refugees lined up outside their barrack-style building. Photograph from a book of plates taken by G. W. Foster and Co.: *Photographic Views of Camp Nelson and Vicinity* (Lexington, Ky.: Government Office, Print, 1864).

Farwell assembled the black refugees on October 16, 1865, to make the official announcement that the camp was closing permanently:

They were willing and ready to strike their tents and move on, [he said,] but the blinding tears that filled their eyes and coursed down their cheeks showed [it] was no light thing, and well they might think so, for some of them, knowing that the camp must soon be closed had previously sought the old home in order if *possible* to bring away some dear child they had left behind, hoping that when the hour for closing the camp should come they might be ready to cross the Ohio and be forever beyond the lash of the tyrant: but what a reception! They were hunted and driven from the old home like savage beasts. Their masters were firing at them with their rifles. Wives of Soldiers who have been freed by act of Congress cannot get their children and even their own freedom is contested at every step.[57]

Farwell was ordered to make life at the camp so unpleasant that the people would gladly leave; government rations were reduced to beans and split peas.[58] And still many refugees stayed. Buildings had to be torn down around them to induce some to depart.

Eventually, inevitably, but only with great difficulty and constant suffering, the camp was almost emptied. Some refugees struck off on their own; some dealt with their former owners and returned to situations frighteningly like slavery; many migrated to big cities, Cincinnati especially; some were settled in small towns in Indiana and Ohio. Some families and individual soldiers accepted John G. Fee's invitation to join an experimental colony at Berea, Kentucky, where they could buy land, attend an integrated school and church, and live on a basis of equality with white neighbors. Some were impressed into work gangs, much against their will, and shipped to a plantation in Mississippi. It was said that black people on this journey were to be "free" workers.[59] Farwell requested that a guardian be appointed for one hundred orphans who remained but needed to be sent somewhere.[60] The largest group of refugees left Camp Nelson by the grimmest possible route: the road to the cemetery.

Some refugees remained where the camp had been, protesting that they could take care of themselves. A few—superannuated, blind, lame, feebleminded, or insane—were simply abandoned.

Months behind his original schedule, Farwell filed his last Camp Nelson report on March 14, 1866.[61] From that day forward, no official refuge for freedmen existed in Kentucky. At the site of the former Colored Refugee Home, the black people remaining became the inhabitants of a small village known first as Ariel, then as Hall, or merely Camp Nelson.[62]

Notes

Full-scale documentation for every point and a fuller account of virtually every incident recounted in this essay can be found in Richard D. Sears, *Camp Nelson, Kentucky: A Civil War History* (Lexington: University Press of Kentucky, 2002).

1. U.S. War Department, *The War of the Rebellion: A Compilation of the Official Records of the Union and Confederate Armies, 1861–1865* (hereafter cited as *OR*), 70 vols. in 128 pts. (Washington, D.C.: U.S. Government Printing Office, 1880–1901), ser. 1, vol. 39, pt. 2, p. 81.

2. John G. Fee to George Whipple, October 2, 1865, American Missionary Association Archives (AMAA) 44223–27, Amistead Research Center, Tulane University; also in *American Missionary* 9, no. 11 (November 1865): 246–47.

3. John Strong Newberry, *The U.S. Sanitary Commission in the Valley of the Mississippi during the War of the Rebellion, 1861–1866* (Cleveland: Fairbanks,

Benedict, 1871), 529–31. In the hundreds of documents about Camp Nelson, this is the only one that suggests any total number for Appalachian refugees. Unfortunately, the statement is worded very ambiguously: it could mean that smaller numbers of refugees were present at particular times but that, added together, they "amounted to thousands."

4. Thomas Butler to Dr. J. S. Newberry, in Newberry, *Sanitary Commission,* 380–82.

5. Reports of Maj. Gen. John G. Foster, December 14, 1863, *OR,* ser. 1, vol. 31, pt. 1, pp. 282–83.

6. G. P. Reiley to John G. Fee, June 17, 1863, AMAA 43974–77.

7. Jacob Dolson Cox, *Military Reminiscences of the Civil War,* vol. 1, *April 1861–November 1863* (New York: Scribner's, 1900), 542.

8. Reports of Maj. Gen. John G. Foster, Dec. 14, 1863, *OR,* ser. 1, vol. 31, pt. 1, pp. 282–83.

9. Fee to S. S. Jocelyn, May 11, 1864, AMAA 43996. Rev. John G. Fee—the founder of Berea, Kentucky, Berea College, Union Church in Berea, and many other churches in Kentucky, including the one in Camp Nelson—played an immensely important role in the history of Camp Nelson. As the leader of the American Missionary Association workers in the camp, he founded schools for soldiers, women, and children while the war was still going on and established Ariel Academy at the site of Camp Nelson after the war was over. He sponsored the settlement of a black community by buying land at Camp Nelson and reselling it to African Americans, former refugees who wanted to live there.

10. Newberry, *Sanitary Commission,* 529–31.

11. Ibid., 531–33.

12. Ibid.

13. Ibid.

14. Ibid.

15. The white Appalachian refugees at Camp Nelson have been the best-kept secret of its history. They continued to be a presence at the camp until its official closing as a military post in 1865. Throughout the period when black refugees were flocking to the camp, white refugees were arriving as well, although very few contemporary sources mention them.

16. *OR,* ser. 1, vol. 39, pt. 2, pp. 212–14.

17. James M. Fidler to J. B. Fry, May 31, 1864, in Elon A. Woodward, ed., *The Negro in the Military Service of the United States: A Compilation of the Official Records, State Papers, Historical Extracts, Relating to His Military Status and Service, from the North American Colonies* (hereafter cited as *NIMSUS*), 7 vols. (typescript, 1888), 4:2600, Record Group (RG) 84, National Archives (NA), Washington, D.C.

18. Newberry, *Sanitary Commission,* 520.

19. John G. Fee to George Whipple, February 8, 1865, AMAA 44079–82.

20. Elderly black men at Camp Nelson never had legal status as refugees, for obvious reasons. They could never be wives or children of soldiers.

21. *National Anti-Slavery Standard,* June 18, 1864. The informant was almost certainly Capt. Theron E. Hall.

22. Affidavit of Patsey Leach, March 25, 1865, M999, roll 7, frames 668–69, Bureau of Refugees, Freedman, and Abandoned Lands (BRFL), RG 105, NA.

23. Fee to Whipple, February 8, 1865, AMAA 44079–82.

24. George A. Hanaford to John McQueen, May 26, 1864, vol. 107, p. 25, entry 902, pt. 4, RG 393, NA.

25. *National Anti-Slavery Standard,* June 18, 1864.

26. Hanaford to McQueen, June 17, 1864, vol. 107, p. 234, entry 902, pt. 4, RG 393, NA.

27. General Orders No. 4, July 12, 1864, vol. 111/256, p. 54, General Orders, November 1863–May 1865, entry 905, Camp Nelson, Ky., 1863–66, pt. 4, RG 393, NA.

28. Orders, September 3, 1864, vol. 111/256, p. 84, General Orders, November 1863–May 1865, entry 905, Camp Nelson, Ky., 1863–66, pt. 4, RG 393, NA.

29. George A. Hanaford to J. Bates Dickson, July 6, 1864, vol. 107, p. 370, entry 902, pt. 4, RG 393, NA.

30. J. Bates Dickson to T. E. Hall, June 20, 1864, vol. 62/117, 119, p. 74, Telegrams Sent, January 1864–February 1865, entry 2168, Department of Kentucky, pt. 1, RG 393, NA.

31. J. Bates Dickson to Thomas D. Sedgewick, June 30, 1864, vol. 62/117, 119, p. 99, Telegrams Sent, January 1864–February 1865, entry 2168, Department of Kentucky, pt. 1, RG 393, NA.

32. *OR,* ser. 3, vol. 4, pp. 467–68.

33. George A. Hanaford, Order from Speed S. Fry, July 3, 1864, vol. 107, p. 354, entry 902, pt. 4, RG 393, NA.

34. Speed S. Fry to George A. Hanaford, July 6, 1864, vol. 112/258, p. 24, Telegrams Sent and Received, June 1864–February 1865, entry 904, Camp Nelson, Ky., 1863–66, pt. 4, RG 393, NA.

35. *OR,* ser. 3, vol. 4, pp. 501–2.

36. Speed S. Fry to Hanaford, July 6, 1864, vol. 112/258, p. 24, Telegrams Sent and Received, June 1864–February 1865, entry 904, Camp Nelson, Ky., 1863–66, pt. 4, RG 393, NA.

37. Clark to Dickson, June 18, 1864, p. 129, entry 902, pt. 4, RG 393, NA; Fry to Hanaford, July 6, 1864, p. 24, entry 904, pt. 4, RG 393, NA; Thomas to Stanton, July 16, 1864, *OR,* ser. 3, vol. 4, pp. 501–2; Hamilton to Fry, August 13, 1864, p. 46, entry 904, pt. 4, RG 393, NA; General Orders No. 19, August 23, 1864, p. 78, entry

904, pt. 4, RG 393, NA; General Orders No. 23, September 16, 1864, p. 87, entry
905, pt. 4, RG 393, NA; Sedgewick to Andrew J. Hogan, October 29, 1864, p. 191,
entry 904, pt. 4, RG 393, NA. In all these cases, the orders applied to Kentucky
slave women, not those from Tennessee and other states.

38. Affidavit of Joseph Miller, November 26, 1864, M999, roll 7, frames
682–84, BRFL, RG 105, NA.

39. Affidavit of Albert A. Livermore, June 26, 1865, M999, roll 7, frames
680–81, BRFL, RG 105, NA.

40. Affidavit of John Vetter, December 16, 1864, M999, roll 7, frames 673–75,
BRFL, RG 105, NA; also filed in Camp Nelson, box 720, Consolidated Corre-
spondence File, 1794–1915, entry 225, Records of the Office of the Quartermaster
General, RG 92, NA.

41. General Orders No. 10, March 12, 1865, printed leaflet in *NIMSUS*,
6:3597; also transcribed in *OR*, ser. 1, vol. 49, pt. 1, p. 904.

42. Captain Theron E. Hall, the quartermaster for Camp Nelson, a native
of Massachusetts, was one of the most influential people there; throughout his
career at the camp, he was active on behalf of black soldiers, their wives, and their
children, reporting their hardships to the public, lobbying on their behalf, working constantly to provide shelter and aid for refugees. It was he who reported the
expulsion of slave women and children in November 1864, in an impassioned article published in the *New York Tribune* and William Lloyd Garrison's *Liberator*.

43. Report by Lester Williams, Superintendent of the Refugee Home, n.d.
(but after July 11, 1865), M999, roll 6, frame 1040, BRFL, RG 105, NA.

44. Newberry, *Sanitary Commission*, 526–29.

45. John G. Fee to Lewis Tappan, February 21, 1865, AMAA 44091–92.

46. C. Graham to Abraham Lincoln, July 24, 1865, in Ira Berlin, Barbara J.
Fields, Thavolia Glymph, Joseph P. Reidy, and Leslie S. Rowland, eds., *The Destruction of Slavery*, vol. 1, ser. 1, of *Freedom: A Documentary History of Emancipation, 1861–1867, Selected from the Holdings of the National Archives of the
United States* (Cambridge: Cambridge University Press, 1985), 626.

47. Having been freed, Kentucky's former slaves were, of course, contrabands.

48. Newberry, *Sanitary Commission*, 529–36.

49. John G. Fee to George Whipple, October 2, 1865, AMAA 44223–27; also
in *American Missionary* 9, no. 11 (November 1865): 246–47.

50. Quoted in Edwin S. Redkey, ed., *A Grand Army of Black Men: Letters
from African-American Soldiers in the Union Army, 1861–1865* (New York: Cambridge University Press, 1992), 187–88.

51. Frederick H. Bierbower to Clinton B. Fisk, February 13, 1866, M999, roll
9, frames 611–13, BRFL, RG 105, NA.

52. Royal Estabrook Farwell (always "R. E." in the records) was a civilian

appointee to the Freedmen's Bureau. Ill health had disqualified him for military service, but he joined "the Christian Commission to . . . relieve the hardship and sufferings of the Union Army." His work in this capacity led to his appointment to the bureau. He was born in Harvard, Massachusetts, October 1, 1841, a descendant of a family that had settled in Concord, Massachusetts, by 1638. William Richard Cutter, ed., *Historic Homes and Places and Genealogical and Personal Memoirs Relating to the Families of Middlesex County, Massachusetts,* 4 vols. (New York: Lewis Historical Publishing Co., 1908), 1:277–78.

53. Farwell had been employed previously by the bureau in Tennessee; in August 1865, e.g., he was instructed to break up the camp at Clarksville "at the earliest possible day." Cochrane to Farwell, August 29, 1865, M999, roll 4, frame 718, BRFL, RG 105, NA.

54. George R. Bentley, *A History of the Freedmen's Bureau* (New York: Octagon, 1970), 77.

55. Account of Hager, M999, roll 10, frames 351–55, BRFL, RG 105, NA.

56. In a letter to John G. Fee, the bureau chief Clinton B. Fisk said that his instructions from Washington were to break up the camp "at the earliest possible day consistent with humanity." Fisk to Fee, August 4, 1865, AMAA 44174–75.

57. R. E. Farwell to Clinton B. Fisk, October 16, 1865, M999, roll 7, frames 282–85, BRFL, RG 105, NA.

58. Ibid., January 8, 1866, M999, roll 7, frames 404–5, BRFL, RG 105, NA.

59. Ibid., December 22, 1865, M999, roll 7, frames 373–78, BRFL, RG 105, NA.

60. Ibid., November 29, 1865, M999, roll 7, frames 309–10, BRFL, RG 105, NA.

61. Ibid., March 14, 1866, M999, roll 9, frame 1674, BRFL, RG 105, NA.

62. A church and school founded by Fee both remained in operation at Camp Nelson for decades, into the beginning of the twentieth century.

"Not much a friend to traiters no matter how beautiful"

The Union Military and Confederate Women in Civil War Kentucky

Kristen L. Streater

The divisive nature of the Civil War in Kentucky presented unique challenges for the Union military authorities trying to prevent the state from joining the Confederacy. While most of the state's civilian population threw its support behind the Union, a strong, vocal, and active group of Confederate sympathizers competed for the state's loyalties. As did Union women, Kentucky's Confederate women played important roles in sustaining the Rebel cause through their traditional domestic activities like sewing and provisioning. However, in the context of a civil war, such support was politicized by both the Confederate women themselves and their Union military opponents. As the Union military gained control over the state, its policies and responses toward the "she-Rebels" in Kentucky reflected this domestic politicization.

As the war began, Union officials were keenly aware of Kentucky's precarious status in the conflict. While not wanting to be overly aggressive in its treatment of civilians, the Union nonetheless would not tolerate behavior that would promote the rebellion. Early policy reflected an attempt to balance public relations with a need to control the population. In the fall of 1861, Gen. John Anderson, Department of the Cumberland, ordered: "No one will be arrested for mere opinion's sake. All peaceable citizens of whatever opinion will be protected if they do not engage in giving aid in any manner to the enemies of our country."[1] A subsequent order from Anderson urged the civil and military authorities "not to make any arrests except when the parties are attempting to join the rebels or are engaged in giving aid or information to them, and in all cases the evidence must be such as will convict them before a court of justice."[2] From his headquarters in Washington, D.C., Gen. George B. McClellan explained to Gen. Don Carlos Buell, the commander of the Department of the Ohio: "It is the desire of the Government to avoid unnecessary irritation by causeless arrests and persecutions of individuals. Where there is good reason to believe that persons are actually giving aid, comfort or information to the enemy it is of course necessary to arrest them. . . . It should be our constant aim to make it apparent to all that their property, their comfort and their personal safety will be best preserved by adhering to the cause of the Union."[3] The elaboration of military policy demonstrated a Union politicization of the home front and outlined the manner in which the Union military would respond to Confederate women's transgressions. Women were the group most likely to offer aid and comfort to the Union's enemy as they were at home and such activities fell within their traditional gender duties. The politicization came when the military made these activities susceptible to arrest and punishment. In the context of a civil war, the Union army understood Confederate women, in their traditional domestic roles, to be as politically motivated as the soldiers in the field of battle. To secure the state for the Union, the military would work to eliminate all support of the rebellion by showing the Confederates that "their property, their comfort and their personal safety" were at stake because of their Confederate loyalties.

Once the Union military had secured control over much of the state by 1862, the authorities began to tighten their policies toward rebellious civilians. Much of their focus turned toward Confederate women's public display of their political devotions. Needing to quell any anti-Union sentiment, Unionists now attached consequences to such demonstrations. The Unionist Frances Peter noted the new treatment at a Louisville concert in 1862. One night, Confederate women "flirted out of the room" when the band played Union songs, but these women paid for their protest the next night. When the manager announced the playing of "national airs," he warned: "All those who were too much opposed to the Government to listen to them had now an opportunity to leave. As on the previous night, a number of ladies got up and flirted out of the room, but at the door they were met by the Provost Guard who marched them off to jail."[4] Clearly a shock for these women, the moment of public embarrassment would, Unionists hoped, make others think twice about their own rebellious sentiments. When Gen. Jeremiah T. Boyle assumed command over the state in 1862, he "intensified the campaign against dissenters, arresting innumerable persons for their opinions and presumed sympathies with the rebellion." As the most prevalent home-front supporters of the rebellion, Confederate women especially fell under the scope of his examination. By several accounts, Boyle "ordered that a prison be set up at Newport [south of Cincinnati] for the incarceration of 'disloyal' women, who were required to sew clothes for Union soldiers."[5] By requiring them to provision their enemies, Boyle's policy attempted to depoliticize the Confederate women, who had otherwise sewn for their own men. If women insisted on active support of the Confederacy, Boyle's prison in Newport assured them that their comfort and, perhaps, their personal safety would be jeopardized. Mrs. M. M. Givens of Cynthiana faced such a threat when she protested a Union soldier taking her horse. According to her account of the incident: "My indignation knew no bounds. . . . When the soldier was ordered to lead the horse away, I defied him to touch the horse or me. 'You would look pretty if I put you up behind one of these soldiers,' said Major Brocht, 'and took you to Newport barracks to sew on soldiers' clothes.' 'I would not do it,' I replied; 'you could not force me to.' At the same time feeling pride that I had sewed on 'butternut jeans' more than once."[6] Givens recognized the political implications of the soldier's threat yet was able to maintain her defiance since the consequence of her devotion was just the loss of a horse. However, other women faced weightier choices. Lizzie Hardin of Harrodsburg related the story of a sixteen-year-old girl who had been arrested and whose captors "had threatened to send her to Newport Barracks, where there were none but men, and make her sew for the Yankee soldiers. She held out until they put her on the cars, when the terror of her situation overcame her, and she told them she would rather sacrifice her conscience and take the oath than sacrifice her health sewing for the Yankees."[7] For this young woman, personal well-being triumphed over political devotion.

Further depoliticization of Confederate women came as the Union monitored women's visits to Confederate prisoners of war in military prisons in the state. Women were frequent visitors at military prisons, looking to offer emotional support and physical comforts to their men.

For instance, in Cynthiana, Kentucky, a group of women sewed two pair of pants for a Confederate soldier in prison. As a bonus, they "put some tobacco in the pockets. He wrote a note of thanks back thanking them for the pants for 'my rear was almost exposed,' but expressed the most joy for the hidden surprise of tobacco."[8] In another instance, as the Union escorted a group of Rebel prisoners through Kentucky, a group of secessionist women "tried to get to talk to the prisoners and brought them things to eat and flowers &c."[9] These Confederate women understood such provisioning as a way of expanding their domestic duties into the public realm to demonstrate their patriotism.[10] However, Union authorities interpreted such activities as a means of sustaining the rebellion. New pants, a plug of tobacco, a friendly face, and home-cooked food would be enough for many Confederate soldiers to renew their willingness to continue the fight.

Under General Boyle's command, these interactions between Confederate women and soldiers were severely limited. One Union assistant adjutant general asked the Louisville provost marshal: "Has it always been customary for secessionists to send victuals to the prisoners?"[11] The immediate reply was no, and this was followed by Special Orders No. 18, issued by General Boyle on July 20, 1862: "No victuals or delicacies will be permitted to be furnished Military Prisoners by secessionist sympathizers and all such prisoners will be restricted to prison fare. Requests and similar favors will be strictly excluded. Newspapers and all publications and letters referring to current political matters will be strictly kept from the prisoners. Anyone attempting to convey any prisoner clandestinely or openly any of the articles herein proscribed will be immediately arrested and lodged in the Military Prison."[12]

Encouragement of the rebellion was not permitted in any form. Any visitor the Union guards did allow was required to have an official pass,[13] and a loyalty oath to the Union had to be sworn before a pass would be issued. In the Louisville provost marshal records from 1863, one entry noted: "Some ladies came to obtain papers to visit the Military Prison but being unwilling to take the oath of allegiance were refused. While living in our midst they must be true citizens or no privileges will be granted them. They begin to think the Pro. Mar'l a very stern ruler and not much a friend to traiters [sic] no matter how beautiful."[14] Not only had the Union literally repoliticized Confederate women with the oath; the authorities had also stripped them of the once-protective garb of gender. The war eliminated the cultural assumption "that before she was an enemy, she was a woman, and more than that, a lady."[15] Kentucky Confederate women felt that they could use this perceived immunity to express their politics in otherwise traditional ways.[16] In a civil war, even pretty women were a threat.

By 1863, the Union began issuing more orders that specifically addressed Confederate women's support for the rebellion. In that year, the commander of the Department of the Ohio issued General Orders No. 24:

The following articles of war are published for the information of all concerned;

and all officers in the military service of the United States, in the Department of the Ohio, are enjoined to arrest all persons guilty of their violation, without regard to age, sex or condition. . . .

ART. 56. "Whosoever shall relieve the enemy with money, victuals, or ammunition, or shall knowingly harbor or protect an enemy, shall suffer death, or such other punishment as shall be ordered by the sentence of a court martial."

When Gen. Ambrose Burnside assumed command of the same department, he followed up this order with his own General Orders No. 38: "All persons within our lines who harbor, protect, conceal, feed, clothe, or in any way aid the enemies of our country" would "be tried as spies or traitors; and if convicted, will suffer death." Burnside reasserted: "The habit of declaring sympathies for the enemy will no longer be tolerated in this department. Persons committing such offenses will be at once arrested, with a view to being tried as above stated, or sent beyond our lines into the lines of their friends."[17] No longer were traitors defined only as men who fought against the government on the field of battle; the official definition now included women on the home front. By 1864, the warning to Confederate women was clear. U.S. Chief of Staff Henry W. Halleck's order to Gen. Stephen G. Burbridge in Lexington declaring martial law in Kentucky stated: "Any attempt at rebellion in Kentucky must be put down with a strong hand, and traitors must be punished without regard to their rank or sex."[18]

With such definitive orders, Union investigations of Confederate women's activities increased. Union records reveal that numerous Kentucky women were under close observation for any evidence of Confederate sympathies. A group of six women, all living north of Maysville,

Kentucky, on Hurricane Creek, were reported as being "rebel sympathizer," "disloyal," or "cannot be trusted."[19] The provost marshal in Louisville
issued an order "that a shrewd detective be sent to watch the movements
of Miss Callie Lambertson at Planters Hotel."[20] Gen. William T. Sherman
asked Lt. Col. Thomas Fairleigh to report on the activities of "a woman
by the name of Louise Oyster alias Coline alias Goodwin supposed to be
a rebel spy . . . reported to be in Louisville at the City Hotel."[21] A friend
of Susan Grigsby's wrote: "We have a rumor that arrests are to be made
to-day—of both gentlemen and ladies—we think it is a false one, thus far
are not trying to hide."[22] Lizzie Hardin dismissed all warnings of potential
arrests in Harrodsburg. Concern came to her from family and friends
alike; two friends came "to warn us," one of the Hardin slaves "begged us
to save ourselves by flight," and even "Grandma begged us to hush [about
laughing about the rumors] for 'we might talk about such things until they
became true.'"[23] Such rumors even reached Louisville, where Cora Hume
had heard that her mother would be arrested for "wav[ing] her scarf at
our prisoners up in the 4th story [of the military prison]."[24] Ultimately,
arrests came. As Mary Wallace's cousin reported from Louisville: "They
are beginning to arrest ladies here now. Three or four ladies have been
ordered south by the 18th of this month."[25] In light of the new reality, some
women chose to be guarded in their actions and words. Susan Grigsby's
cousin Libby was cautious about the tone and content of her letter, stating:
"Well better not write our thoughts, I for one have been maddened too
often by my letters being opened, but found nothing in them to arrest
me for."[26] Other women remained defiant. Indeed, Ellen Wallace's disgust
with the Union only grew with the installment of martial law. In 1864, she
commented: "I was perfectly shocked this evening when Mr. Wallace told
me . . . that no one was allowed to speak against [Abraham] Lincoln or his
infamous administration. I cannot believe that the free born people of this
land will submit to the rule of a low cowardly tyrant."[27]

Outrage over the arrests abounded. Rev. George Browder, in a moment of atypical anger, noted: "Heard today that Miss Almeda Mason had
been sentenced & sent off to the military prison at Johnson's I[sland] to be
confined during the war—for the crime of yielding to the dictates of common humanity & writing a letter to her brother in the rebel army! Genl
Burnsides [sic] infamous order 38 can be enforced against helpless women
in Ky!"[28] In a clearly pro-Confederate state history, the author described

the distressing times for Kentucky's Confederate women: "Women whose children, brothers, and husbands were in the Confederate army, or dead on its battle-fields, were naturally given to uttering much treason in their speech; but it was a pitiable sight to see the power of the Federal government turned against these helpless sufferers."[29]

As "helpless" as Confederate women appeared or portrayed themselves to be, their successful support of the rebellion was great enough to warrant the arrests. Whether through symbolic or real actions, women's disloyalty would not be tolerated in Union-held Kentucky. In a letter to her family, Maria Holyoke, a Unionist, conveyed her need for justice when confronted by a Confederate's rebellious behavior: "I trust that all traitors will in the end be punished and 'our flag' will again wave over a prosperous and happy country. How would it make you feel to see a young lady tear the American flag from its staff and whipe [*sic*] her feet on it[?] . . . Yet such things occur here, in loyal Kentucky."[30] To Unionists' relief, justice prevailed in such cases: Lillie Parker was arrested for "distroying [*sic*] the American Flag"; similarly, Mary Burk was arrested for "taring [*sic*] down the American Flag."[31] Many Unionists found women who were vocal opponents of the Union to be particularly heinous and deserving of punishment. In the 1864 case of Jennie Mann of Louisville, one witness gave the following description: "The language used by her was so disloyal as to have the blood of ever [*sic*] true and loyal man boil. Such as that she wished The President was dead and that nothing would please her better and she hoped that Jeff Davis would soon be in Washington as President of the United States. That she would rather have murder on her soul than to have a Brother in the Federal Army and many other abusive and disloyal epithets."[32] More overt actions also warranted punishment. Lewis Collins recorded that, in the summer of 1863, "a number of females [were] arrested at Demossville, Pendleton co., and some other points, to be sent South. They are regarded as dangerous to the U.S. government."[33] "Dangerous" women lost the privilege of remaining in their homes under Union protection. In a January 1864 report from Louisville, Prov. Mar. Stephen Jones noted that, while the recapture of two escaped Confederate officers merited praise, attention needed to be paid to the women at whose home the arrests were made. Jones reported: "I am assured that Mrs. Lightcap and her family, consisting of her two daughters and her niece Miss L. L. Howard were aware of the character of the parties they harbored. They have all been violent and demonstrative rebels, have manifested their sympathy openly with rebel prisoners while marching through the streets and were impertinent and defiant to the officers who arrested the rebel officers. I respectfully recommend they be sent beyond the Federal lines."[34] A directive later came that Mrs. Lightcap and her daughters "be required to take the oath of allegiance, and give paroles of honor to remain north of the Ohio River during the War, to be sent through the lines should they fail to comply."[35] In securing the state for the Union, military authorities had to remain vigilant in their depoliticization of the Kentucky Confederate home front.

Generally, the Union military arrested Confederate women for a variety of causes linked to supporting the rebellion. The records of the McLean Barracks in Cincinnati offer several examples of Kentucky women who were incarcerated there for disloyal behavior. In 1863, charges against Mrs. Minerva Rees of Cynthiana, Kentucky, included "aiding and abetting the Rebels." The specifics of Rees's arrest state that she was twice detained "while in male attire . . . for carrying messages destined for Southern friends past the Union road guards."[36] The McLean Barracks also housed Mrs. Emily Vaughn of Boone County, Kentucky, for "communicating with Rebels beyond our lines," and Amanda Cook of Morgan County, Kentucky, faced charges of spying.[37] The Louisville military commander, Col. M. Mundy, requested assistance in the detainment of Mrs. Mattie Patterson, of Louisville, who was arrested in 1863 on charges of spying. Mundy's concern was that "since her imprisonment she has given birth to a child and now she had been turned from the Jeffersonville Prison when they refuse to keep her." With "no place to confine her here," Mundy sent her to the McLean Barracks, whose records also noted that she was confined there through July and August 1863. On September 1, 1863, General Rosecrans sent word of his willingness to "remit the sentence against Mrs. Mattie Patterson on conditions that she return to her friends [in northern Illinois] and that [she] has give[n] bonds with sufficient security for her future good behavior."[38]

The Union paid particular attention to those who supported Confederate guerrillas. The nature of guerrilla warfare increased the reliance on civilian support by the Confederacy; thus, the Union's need to suppress Confederate home-front support also increased. Union authorities began targeting women who supported the Kentucky-raised Confederate cavalry general John Hunt Morgan and his men. In the summer of 1862, Morgan and his men rode through Lizzie Hardin's hometown of Harrodsburg, Kentucky. As the parade of Confederate heroes rode by, Hardin, her mother, and her sister patriotically waved their handkerchiefs in support of the Rebels' cause. She thought nothing of the possible consequences. In fact, she remarked: "I was not much afraid of being arrested for they [the Union authorities] had not yet ventured upon such enormity in Harrodsburg as taking women to prison for talking and if I had done anything worse they did not know it."[39] However, General Boyle had determined to suppress home-front enthusiasm, and, in July, 1862, these orders caught up with the Hardin women, Union military authorities arresting them and sending them to prison in Louisville.[40]

While under interrogation, Hardin persistently asserted her rights. She noted: "In the course of my remarks, I occasionally digressed to express an abstract opinion as to the relative merits of Yankees and Southerners. Also as to the right of the former to drive native-born Kentuckians from their homes."[41] With such self-righteousness and bold expression, the Hardin women failed to grasp the logic that the severity of their crime was owing to Morgan's status as a guerrilla; they reasoned that, since Union women could salute Union troops, Confederate sympathizers should hold the same privilege.[42] Union authorities felt otherwise; support like the Hardins' would only encourage Confederate war efforts generally and perpetuate the hero worship of Morgan and his tactics.[43] Found guilty of treason, the Hardins could take the loyalty oath to the Union and return home, be jailed, or be exiled to Confederate lines. While devotion to the Confederate cause prevented them from swearing the oath, Hardin's Aunt Lucinda pled with General Boyle to release the women into her custody. She assured him that "the slightest verbal promise not to interfere with 'the government' would be as binding as an oath." Boyle, however, was unimpressed and replied: "The women think they will rule Kentucky, but I will show them they can't do it while I am military governor."[44] The divisive nature of the war in Kentucky had made women's actions significant. In their attempt to lend emotional support to the rebellion, Confederate women in Kentucky were manipulating gender conventions for political ends. Union authorities had to eliminate these gender conventions among the enemy to be successful in the war. If exposing Confederate women to the harsh realities of political consequences for their actions facilitated the war's end, then the arrests like the Hardins' were warranted. As for the Hardin menace, Boyle sent Lizzie, her mother, and her sister into exile from Kentucky, and they spent the remainder of the war as refugees roaming throughout the deep South.[45]

Guarding against the effects of Morgan supporters continued through 1863, as the guerrilla again raided Kentucky and invaded Indiana and Ohio. Union lieutenant colonel J. N. Styles reported "two women soliciting subscriptions for the benefit of John Hunt Morgan gang[;] one of them boasting of 'our late success.'" The provost marshal instructed Styles "to notify the women referred that no such demonstrations will be tolerated in this war."[46] Any praise of Morgan had to be silenced. In 1864, Gen. Stephen G. Burbridge ordered Louisville's provost marshal to "take whatever steps may be necessary to prevent the circulation in this city of Mrs. Sallie Rochester Ford's Book entitled 'Romance and Raids of Morgan and his Men.'"[47] Even after the Morgan threat was eliminated, Confederate guerrillas remained active in the state through 1865, continuing to rely on sympathetic women for support and assistance. Union tolerance for this remained low even as the war drew to a close, and records indicate that numerous women were arrested from late 1864 through 1865: on November 10, 1864, Olivia H. Park of Bath County was arrested "for aiding and abetting guerrillas"; Elise Jones of Warren County, Kentucky, was arrested in Bowling Green in February, 1865, for "aiding Guerrillas"; and Rachel Carter, Nancy Ann Downs, and Sarah A. Stevens, all of Mt. Sterling, Kentucky, were arrested on April 20, 1865, on charges of "Harboring Guerrillas."[48] The details of such assistance come to light in the cases of Miss Hutchinson and Mrs. Wilson, both of Louisville. In a sworn affidavit, John C. Gorin noted that, when the captain of his regiment had escaped, he received clothes and money from Hutchinson and so on his own escape he too sought Hutchinson. She offered him five dollars and referred him to other sympathetic citizens in the area. Gorin then went "to Mrs. Wilson for help as an escaped rebel Prisoner in company with a federal Soldier who she thought was a rebel soldier[.] She gave me 2 pr. Drawers, 3 Shirts One Pr Pants and one Hat and gave me a note to Mr. Charley Miller for money."[49] This provisioning, even as the war had all but ended, spoke to the lingering importance of Confederate women in sustaining elements of the rebellion.

Finally, Confederate women's ability to communicate with their men in the military was of particular concern for Union authorities. Women's letters to their loved ones on the battlefield were often filled with what seemed like innocuous information about daily life and surroundings; however, if those descriptions included remarks about Union troops, the potential for security leaks was too great to go unchecked. Frances Peter presented a case in point concerning Mrs. Joel Higgins. According to one report: "One of the principal things against her was a letter she wrote to her sons, in which she invited them back. Said now was the time for them to come, that the Federals had more sick in the hospitals than men in the field. That now was the time for retaliation . . . [for the] twelve noble Southern men [who] had been murdered in cold blood the night before."[50] The seriousness of this woman's actions was manifold. First, reporting on Union troop strength to her Confederate sons counted as treason. Second, her desire for violent revenge for the deaths of other Confederates in the state spoke to her continued support of the rebellion, which Union authorities knew had to be quelled. Following her detainment, authorities determined that her punishment would be either exile to the South or a trial, where she would be hanged if convicted.[51]

The Union desire was to remove such a potential threat completely. Several cases demonstrated the danger to the Union cause in Kentucky that the wives of Confederate officers still living in the state posed. One was the case of Mrs. Marible, who was found, on returning from a visit to her Rebel husband, to have begun "reporting favorably of the conditions of Dixie abusing the U.S. Government and doing what she can to encourage rebellion."[52] Another case was that of Mrs. L. Mumfort of Oldham County, Kentucky. Union authorities had not only "detected [her] in the act of carrying provisions to two escaped rebel prisoners, concealed near her home," but also found her to have been "in constant communication with her husband [a Confederate soldier fighting in Virginia]" and to have been "a violent & defiant rebel since the war began." Asst. Adj. Gen. Stephen Jones remarked: "An example among this class of women in Ky is greatly needed. I have the honor to recommend that she be sent through the lines in Eastern Ky or in East Tenn."[53] Authorities did finally catch up with Mrs. Mary Faulkner Hoffman for "passing through Confederate lines" to visit her husband in Georgia. Earlier in the war, her Confederate sympathies led her covertly to feed and supply Confederate soldiers in Union-occupied Cynthiana. After giving the soldiers "'Yankee' overcoats and pepper-box pistols for protection," she guided them out of town to rejoin their troops.[54] When Hoffman was initially brought to Louisville, the provost marshal, Lt. Col. Henry Dent, forwarded her papers to General Boyle and then remarked: "Having no place suitable for her, I respectfully request instructions."[55]

Indeed, exile was often the course of action taken for many families of Confederate soldiers in Kentucky. The authorities ordered numerous women and children out of the state simply for their relationship to a Confederate soldier or officer. Col. M. Mundy, the commander in Louisville in 1863, reflected on the value of such policy:

The encumbering of the rebels from Ky with their family, would be certain to induce reflection, which is the first step towards repentance. While they know that their wives and children are safe and comfortable under the good government they are striving to destroy like reckless spendthrifts they plunge on in their evil cause; but send their families to risk the jeopardy they are helping to make and most of them will soon begin the debate in their own minds upon this important question: "While I am trying to help my southern neighbors to their rights what am I doing with those of my own family?" and but few of them are so insane as not to stop the ruin they would work upon themselves. I am not an advocate for the punishment of women for the wrongs of their husbands; but the lives of our thousands of soldiers are to be considered before the personal comforts of rebels' wives.[56]

Union authorities came to understand the hypocrisy behind the Kentucky Confederate women's expectation of protection from a government that they and their soldiers were trying to undermine. Familial associations frequently warranted the loss of property and the comforts of home.

From a set of Louisville military records we can see that, between May 1863 and November 1864, ten women were notified by the Union authorities "to make preparations to be sent to your husband within the Confederate lines." Not only did these women lose their homes; they also were limited in the amount of personal property they could take with them. These women were allowed "to carry one trunk not to exceed in weight one hundred pounds containing your personal apparel and one trunk of like dimensions containing the clothing of your children. . . . You will

also be allowed to carry money with you to the amount of One Thousand
. . . Dollars for your personal expenses." The authorities also issued a final
warning: "You will not be allowed to return during the war under penalty
of being considered and treated as a spy."[57] Once a threat was eliminated,
the Union did not want it returned. At least one Confederate navy officer's
wife recognized and accepted the Union's interpretation of the threat of
Confederate families in the state. In her request for a pass to join her husband in Richmond, Virginia, Mrs. Bernard Pratt of Louisville "offer[ed] to
pledge her honor not to carry to the rebels any information, & to remain
in the rebel lines . . . during the continuance of the rebellion."[58]

Even if the Union did not remove Confederate women from the state,
evidence of disloyalty could also cause them to lose their property. Much
of the value of the Kentucky home front was its use as a supply line for
friend and enemy alike. Often, in the constant need to resupply Union soldiers in the state, officers would take provisions from Confederate homes,
reinforcing the association between disloyalty and loss of property. Major
General Burbridge ordered one of his officers in Munfordsville, Kentucky,
to "press houses from rebel citizens in the different counties in your district
to mount the 48th and 26th Ky [Regiments]. Let the pressing be done by
commissioned officers and the receipts show that the parties are disloyal."[59]
Even without orders from officers, Union soldiers frequently ransacked
Confederate homes for provisions. Josephine Covington, a Confederate,
noted that, when the Union occupied her hometown of Bowling Green,
the soldiers "went from garret to cellar, . . . insulting persons in them,
particularly those of southern proclivities in the lowest manner. . . . They
broke into the houses stealing every thing that they could possibly use,
even taking womens and childrens clothes to send to their own families
as they said."[60]

As the need for hospital space became urgent, orders were issued to
take possession of homes to convert.[61] Not only would a woman lose her
privacy, but she and her family would be exposed to the diseased and unsanitary conditions that came with army medical care at the time. Dr. F.
Meacham, a surgeon stationed in Lexington, informed his commander:
"We have at present twelve cases of Small Pox, and the number is increasing daily. . . . There is a house on the Richmond pike three miles from
the city owned by the wife of the Rebel Gen'l Preston which is very well
addapted [*sic*] for [housing the smallpox cases]. Col. King will seize the

house if authorized."[62] Threats to a woman's property were often enough to sway her professed loyalties. On October 6, 1862, the provost marshal in Paducah, Kentucky, noted: "Mrs. Adams . . . applied to me for relief [sic] about her home. . . . On examination of her I found her to be a violent Rebel[,] and [she] declared she will not take the oath if she rots, That she illuminated her home . . . on the 'Bull Run' victory—I promised her to send for her and to take her property if she refused to take the oath." The threat and her need for Union protection of her property worked; Mrs. Adams swore the oath on October 9, 1862.[63]

The evolution of Union military policy toward Kentucky's Confederate women reflected the growing recognition of the importance of the home front in the Civil War. At first, when the state's loyalty was uncertain, Union commanders placed only general restrictions on the population's devotion to the Confederacy. By 1862, once the main Confederate military threat to the state had been quelled, Union authorities could more specifically target lingering Confederate sentiment. It was at this point that women's public opinions and actions took on greater significance in the fight to control the state. With the increase in guerrilla activity late in the war, the contribution that women's domestic activities made in sustaining the rebellion spurred the Union to suppress further the Confederate's efforts. Union success in Kentucky would not be complete until all elements of Confederate support were eliminated.

Support for the rebellion through domestic means was the way in which Kentucky Confederate women could be active participants in the conflict. Women on both sides transferred their traditional duties of providing for men's physical and emotional needs to their soldiers during the war. Because of the divided sympathies within the state and the Union need to retain complete control over the state, women's traditional domestic actions fell under military scrutiny. Because Confederate women supported the rebellion, they were susceptible to real consequences for their political choice, just as their soldiers were for fighting against the Union. The so-called she-Rebels faced investigations, arrests, imprisonment, and exile for their devotion to the secessionist cause. The Union military depoliticized Confederate women's domestic efforts by enacting consequences that would demonstrate that women's comfort, safety, and property were secure only if they supported the Union.

Notes

1. Assistant Adjutant-General Oliver D. Greene to J. J. Anderson, Esq., September 27, 1861, U.S. War Department, *The War of the Rebellion: A Compilation of the Official Records of the Union and Confederate Armies, 1861–1865* (hereafter cited as *OR*), 70 vols. in 128 pts. (Washington, D.C.: U.S. Government Printing Office, 1880–1901), ser. 2, vol. 2, pp. 81–82.

2. Brigadier-General John Anderson, General Orders No. 5, October 7, 1861, in *OR*, ser. 2, vol. 2, pp. 91–92. See also Edward Conrad Smith, *The Borderland in the Civil War* (New York: Macmillan, 1927), 372–73.

3. McClellan to Buell, November 12, 1861, in *OR*, ser. 2, vol. 2, p. 136.

4. Frances Peter, transcribed diary, November 6, 1862, Evans Papers: Frances (Dallam) Peter material, 72M15, box 7, folder 86, pp. 106–7, University of Kentucky (UK) Archives and Special Collections, M. I. King Library, Lexington.

5. Martha McDowell Buford Jones, *Peach Leather and Rebel Gray: Bluegrass Life and the War, 1860–1865: Farm and Social Life, Famous Horses, Tragedies of War: Diary and Letters of a Confederate Wife*, ed. Mary E. Wharton and Ellen F. Williams (Lexington, Ky.: Helicon, 1986), 90. See also Lizzie [Elizabeth Pendleton] Hardin, *The Private War of Lizzie Hardin: A Kentucky Confederate Girl's Diary of the Civil War in Kentucky, Virginia, Tennessee, Alabama, and Georgia*, ed. G. Glen Clift (Frankfort: Kentucky Historical Society, 1963), 96–97n. Several other state histories make references to Boyle's attention to Confederate women. See Lewis Collins, *History of Kentucky*, rev. ed., ed. Richard H. Collins, 2 vols. (Frankfort: Kentucky Historical Society, 1966), vol. 1; E. Merton Coulter, *Civil War and Reconstruction in Kentucky* (Gloucester, Mass.: Peter Smith, 1966); and Lowell Harrison and James C. Klotter, *A New History of Kentucky* (Lexington: University Press of Kentucky, 1997), 205–6.

6. Mrs. M. M. Givens, *Minutes of the Fourteenth Annual Convention of the Kentucky Division Daughters of the Confederacy; Held in Louisville, Kentucky, October 12, 13 and 14, 1910* (Lexington, Ky.: Press of Transylvania Printing Co., 1910), 75.

7. Hardin, *Private War*, 157. Collins also confirms this story. Only July 28, 1862, he records: "By order of Gen. Boyle, a prison prepared at Newport for 'rebel females'—where they will be required to sew for the Federal soldiers" (*History of Kentucky*, 105).

8. William A. Penn, *Rattling Spurs and Broad-Brimmed Hats: The Civil War in Cynthiana and Harrison County, Kentucky* (Midway, Ky.: Battle Grove, 1995), 150.

9. Peter, diary, September 22, 1863, UK Archives.

10. LeeAnn Whites, *The Civil War as a Crisis in Gender: Augusta, Georgia, 1860–1890* (Athens: University of Georgia Press, 1995), 57–58.

11. Captain John Boyle to Lt. Col. Dent, Louisville, July 18, 1862, National Archives (NA), Washington, D.C., Preliminary Inventory of the Records of the United States Army Continental Commands, 1821–1920, Record Group (RG) 393, pt. 4, Military Installations, 1821–81 (hereafter cited as pt. 4), Louisville, 1861–66, entry 1636, "Letters Received, 1862–65."

12. Lt. Col. Henry Dent to Capt. Dillard, July 18, 1862, NA, RG 393, pt. 4, Louisville, Ky., 1861–66, entry 1632, "Letters Sent by the Provost Marshal, Jan. 1862–Apr. 1863," vol. 220, DKy, p. 61; Brigadier General Jeremiah Boyle, Special Orders No. 18, July 20, 1862, NA, RG 393, pt. 4, Louisville, Ky., 1861–66, entry 1636, "Letters Received, 1862–65."

13. See, e.g., Maj. Selby Hamer to Capt. W. G. Dilliard, June 26, 1862, NA, RG 393, pt. 4, Louisville, Ky., 1861–66, entry 1632, "Letters Sent by the Provost Marshal, Jan. 1862–Apr. 1863," vol. 220, DKy, p. 40; Special Orders No. 14, October 3, 1863, NA, RG 393, pt. 4, entry 729, "Letters Sent, Jan.–Aug. 1862, Dec. 1862–Feb. 1864, and May 1866–June 1873," 2 of 3, vol. 142, bk. 329, DKy; Order from Brig. Gen. Boyle to Major D. C. Fitch, May 8, 1863, NA, RG 393, pt. 4, Louisville, Ky., 1861–66, entry 1636, "Letters Received, 1862–65."

14. April 19, [1863], NA, RG 393, pt. 4, Louisville, Ky., 1861–66, entry 1644, "Miscellaneous Records, 1861–65," 5 of 5, vol. 161, bk. 381, DKy, p. 9.

15. Drew Gilpin Faust, *Mothers of Invention: Women of the Slaveholding South in the American Civil War* (Chapel Hill: University of North Carolina Press, 1996), 198, 205; Victoria E. Bynum, *Unruly Women: The Politics of Social and Sexual Control in the Old South* (Chapel Hill: University of North Carolina Press, 1992), 143–44.

16. Faust, *Mothers of Invention,* 210, 214.

17. *OR,* ser. 1, vol. 23, pt. 2, p. 237. See also Newspaper Clipping, RG 393, pt. 4, entry 304, vol. 113, bk. 261, DKy.

18. Halleck to Burbridge, June 25, 1864, *OR,* ser. 1, vol. 39, pt. 2, pp. 144–45. On July 19, 1864, Abraham Lincoln issued General Orders No. 233 from the War Department in Washington, D.C., officially declaring martial law in Kentucky. See *OR,* ser. 1, vol. 39, pt. 2, p. 180.

19. NA, RG 393, pt. 1, Geographical Divisions and Departments and Military (Reconstruction) Districts (hereafter cited as pt. 1), entry 2237, "Miscellaneous Records of the Provost Marshal, 1863–66," 4 of 5, vol. 219, bk. 517, pp. 5, 28, 72, 81, 107.

20. Order from Capt. S. E. Jones, March 19, 1864, NA, RG 393, pt. 4, Louisville, Ky., 1861–66, entry 1635, "Register of Letters Received, Sept. 1861–Sept. 1863, Feb.–Oct. 1864, and Jan. 1865–Feb. 1866," 1 of 2, vol. 145, bk. 340, DKy.

21. Maj.-Gen. W. T. Sherman to Lt. Col. Thos. B. Fairleigh, August 1, 1864, NA, RG 393, pt. 4, Louisville, Ky., 1862–73, entry 739, "Special Orders Issued, Jan. 1862–June 1873," 5 of 6, vol. 152, bk. 363, DKy, p. 66.

22. H. Mepick to Susan Grigsby, August 11, 1862, Susan Preston (Shelby) Grigsby Papers, MS A.G857, folder 173, Filson Historical Society (FHS), Louisville, Ky.

23. Hardin, *Private War,* 101.

24. "War between the States Seen with 13-Year-Old Eyes in Diary of Louisvillian Still Living," *Louisville Courier-Journal,* September 20, 27, October 4, 1936, citing a January 24, 1863, diary entry of Cora Owens Hume's.

25. Cousin Hattie to Mary Hooe Wallace, May 7, 1863, Edmund T. Halsey Collection, MS A.H196, folder 32, Letters to her, 1863, FHS.

26. Libby [?] to Susan Grigsby, January 5, 1864, Susan Preston (Shelby) Grigsby Papers, MS A.G857, folder 181, FHS.

27. Ellen Kenton MaGaughey Wallace, August 16, 1864, in "Journal, 1849–1865," transcribed and annotated by James T. Killebrew (1988), in Wallace-Starling Family Diaries, 96M07, folder 1, Kentucky Historical Society, Frankfort.

28. George Browder, diary entry, June 23, 1863, in *The Heavens Are Weeping: The Diaries of George Richard Browder, 1852–1886,* ed. Richard L. Troutman (Grand Rapids, Mich.: Zondervan, 1987), 157. See also Thomas D. Clark, *A History of Kentucky,* rev. 6th ed. (Ashland: Jesse Stuart Foundation, 1988), 346.

29. N. S. [Nathanial Southgate] Shaler, *Kentucky: A Pioneer Commonwealth,* 4th ed. (Boston: Houghton, Mifflin, 1888), 348.

30. Maria Holyoke to Mother and Sister, August 16, 1861, Holyoke Family Papers, MS CH, typed copy, FHS.

31. Entry date November 21, 1863, NA, RG 393, pt. 4, Louisville, Ky., 1861–66, entry 1644, "Miscellaneous Records, 1861–65," 1 of 5, vol. 222, bk. 528, DKy; Entry date April 16, 1865, NA, RG 393, pt. 4, Louisville, Ky., 1861–65, entry 1644, "Miscellaneous Records, 1861–65," 7 of 10, vol. 228, bk. 549, DKy, 253.

32. Papers in the case of Miss Jennie Mann, Statement by Capt. W. H. Ward, October 17, 1864, NA, RG 393, pt. 1, Provost Marshal, entry 2229, "Correspondence, Affidavits, and Oaths Relating to Civilians Charged with Illegal or Disloyal Acts, 1863–65."

33. Collins, *History of Kentucky,* 123. Collins also mentions the arrests of other women on July 18, 1864. See ibid., 136.

34. Report by Stephen Jones, January 15, 1864, NA, RG 393, pt. 1, Provost Marshal, entry 2239, "Correspondence, Affidavits, and Oaths Relating to Civilians Charged with Illegal or Disloyal Acts, 1863–65," 2 of 3.

35. Directive dated February 26, 1864, NA, RG 393, pt. 4, Louisville, Ky., 1861–66, entry 1635, "Register of Letters Received, Sept. 1861–Sept. 1863, Feb.–Oct. 1864, and Jan. 1865–Feb. 1866," 1 of 2, vol. 145, bks. 338, 340, DKy.

36. U.S. War Department, Selected Records of the War Department Relating to Confederate Prisoners of War, 1861–1865, roll 97, vols. 311–17; *McLean Barracks, Cincinnati, Ohio,* Register of Prisoners and Order Books, 1863–1865, National Archives Microfilm Publications, microcopy 598 (Washington, D.C.: National Archives and Records Service, General Services Administration, 1965), located at the Kentucky State Archives, Microfilm Drawer 529, M598-0097 (hereafter cited as U.S. War Department, *McLean Barracks*); Penn, *Rattling Spurs and Broad-Brimmed Hats,* 43, 48, 175.

37. U.S. War Department, *McLean Barracks.*

38. Col. M. Mundy to Brig. Gen. Garfield, August 27, 1863, NA, RG 393, pt. 4, Louisville, Ky., 1862–73, entry 729, "Letters Sent, Jan.–Aug. 1862, Dec. 1862–Feb. 1864, and May 1866–June 1873," 2 of 3, vol. 142, bk. 329; U.S. War Department, *McLean Barracks;* Order by Major General Rosecrans, September 1, 1863, NA, RG 393, pt. 4, Louisville, Ky., 1862–73, entry 729, "Letters Sent, Jan.–Aug 1862, Dec. 1862–Feb. 1864, and May 1866–June 1873," 2 of 3, vol. 142, bk. 329.

39. Hardin, *Private War,* 96–97.

40. Ibid., 125. Collins notes on August 2, 1862: "Three ladies, of Harrodsburg, brought to Louisville by one Capt. Jack Mann, and put in the military prison" (*History of Kentucky,* 105).

41. Hardin, *Private War,* 103.

42. Ibid., 122–23.

43. James A. Ramage, *Rebel Raider: The Life of John Hunt Morgan* (Lexington: University Press of Kentucky, 1986), 64–68.

44. Hardin, *Private War,* 153.

45. Ibid., 125.

46. NA, RG 393, pt. 1, Provost Marshal, entry 2241, "Register of Letters Received and Endorsements Sent by Capt. Stephen E. Jones, Provost Marshal and Aide-de-Camp, May 1863–Dec. 1864," 1 of 2, vol. 21, pp. 102, 103.

47. Col. S. D. Rance to Major D. C. Fitch, March 19, 1864, NA, RG 393, pt. 4, Louisville, Ky., 1861–66, entry 1636, "Letters Received, 1862–65."

48. NA, RG 393, pt. 1, Provost Marshal, entry 2237, "Miscellaneous Records of the Provost Marshal, 1863–66," 5 of 5, vol. 269, bk. 509, DKy, pp. 173, 104, 28, 38, 206, respectively.

49. Affidavits in the cases of Miss Hutchinson and Mrs. Wilson, April 13, 1865, NA, RG 393, pt. 1, Provost Marshal, entry 2229, "Correspondence, Affidavits, and Oaths Relating to Civilians Charged with Illegal or Disloyal Acts, 1863–65."

50. Peter, diary, March 26, 1863, p. 174, UK Archives.

51. Ibid.

52. October 7, 1863, NA, RG 393, pt. 4, Louisville, Ky., 1861–66, entry 1637, "Register of Letters Received Relating to Prisoners, Feb. 1862–Dec. 1864," vol. 145, bk. 339.

53. Stephen E. Jones, February 1, [1864?], NA, RG 393, pt. 1, Provost Marshal, entry 2239, "Press Copies of Letters Sent by Capt. Stephen E. Jones, Provost Marshal and Aide-de-Camp, Apr. 1863–Feb. 1865," 2 of 3.

54. Penn, *Rattling Spurs and Broad-Brimmed Hats,* 43, 175.

55. Lt. Col. Henry Dent to Brig. Gen. Jeremiah Boyle, August 1, 1862, NA, RG 393, pt. 4, Louisville, Ky., 1861–66, entry 1632, "Letters Sent by the Provost Marshal, Jan. 1862–Apr. 1863," vol. 220, p. 76.

56. Col. M. Mundy to Capt. A. C. Semple, May 20, 1863, NA, RG 393, pt. 4, Louisville, Ky., 1862–73, entry 729, "Press Copies of Letters Sent, May 1863–Jan. 1866," 2 of 3, vol. 142, bk. 329, DKy.

57. Col. M. Mundy to Mrs. Charles Johnson, May 4, 1863, NA, RG 393, pt. 4, Louisville, Ky., 1862–73, entry 729, "Letters Sent, Jan.–Aug. 1862, Dec. 1862–Feb. 1864, and May 1866–June 1873," 2 of 3, vol. 142, bk. 329, DKy. See also letters dated May 4, May 5, May 13, 1863, in ibid.; Special Orders No. 111, May 18, 1863, NA, RG 393, pt. 4, Louisville, Ky., 1862–73, entry 732, "Register of Letters Received, May–Aug. 1863," vol. 149, bks. 353, 354, 356, DKy; Col. M. Mundy to Mrs. Dr. L. Blackburn, July 21, 1863, NA, RG 393, pt. 4, Louisville, Ky., 1862–73, entry 729, "Letters Sent, Jan.–Aug. 1862, Dec. 1862–Feb. 1864, and May 1866–June 1873," 2 of 3, vol. 142, bk. 329, DKy; Capt. Stephen E. Jones to Capt. C. Bates Dickson, November 16, 1864, NA, RG 393, pt. 1, Provost Marshal, entry 2239, "Press Copies of Letters Sent by Capt. Stephen E. Jones, Provost Marshal and Aide-de-Camp, Apr. 1863–Feb. 1865," 3 of 3, vol. 17, letter book C, p. 244. See also ibid., p. 74.

58. Capt. Stephen E. Jones to Capt. C. Bates Dickson, November 16, 1864, NA, RG 393, pt. 1, Provost Marshal, entry 2239, "Press Copies of Letters Sent by Capt. Stephen E. Jones, Provost Marshal and Aide-de-Camp, Apr. 1863–Feb. 1865," 3 of 3, vol. 17, letter book C, p. 244.

59. Bvt. Maj. Genl. Stephen Burbridge to Brig. Genl. Hugh Ewing, July 7, [1864?], NA, RG 393, pt. 1, General Records, entry 2168, "Telegrams Sent, Jan. 1864–Feb. 1865," 1 of 2, vol. 62, bk. 119, DKy, p. 108.

60. Josephine Covington (Wells) [Mrs. Albert Covington] to Robert Wells, March 2, 1862, MS C C, FHS.

61. Brig. Genl. Stephen Burbridge to Lt. Col. T. B. Fairleigh, June 28, [?], NA, RG 393, pt. 1, General Records, entry 2168, "Telegrams Sent, Jan. 1864–Feb. 1865," 1 of 2, vol. 62, bk. 119, DKy, p. 95; Brig. Genl. Stephen Burbridge to Lt. Col. Thomas B. Fairleigh, June 28, 1864, NA, RG 393, pt. 4, Louisville, Ky., 1862–73, entry 739, "Special Orders Issued, Jan. 1862–June 1873," 5 of 6, vol. 152, bk. 363, DKy, p. 51.

62. F. Meacham to George S. Shumard, March 10, 1864, NA, RG 393, pt. 4, Louisville, Ky., 1861–66, entry 1636, "Letters Received, 1862–65."

63. Report of J. C. Dawn, Provost Marshal, October 6, 1862, NA, RG 393, pt. 4, Paducah, Ky., 1862–65, entry 1708, "Records of the Provost Marshal, 1862–65," 2 of 2, vol. 231, bk. 558, DKy, p. 25.

Part 3

★ ★ ★

War's Impact in Kentucky and Tennessee

"My trust is still firmly fixed in God"

Alfred T. Fielder, His Christian Faith, and the Ordeal of War

Kent T. Dollar

Soldiers experienced extraordinary hardships during the Civil War. They served long stints in the army far away from hearth and home, they watched comrades fall in battle, and each soldier faced the possibility of death. The conflict tested the endurance of soldiers on both sides, and thousands sought refuge in religion and relied on God to carry on. But how did their religious faith help them persevere? What impact did their trust in God have on their courage in battle? And how was their faith affected as a result?

The example of Alfred T. Fielder, a Tennessee soldier, offers some insight into these questions. Fielder, who was forty-seven years old when the war began in April 1861, enlisted as a private in the Friendship Volunteers, Company B, Twelfth Tennessee Infantry Regiment. The unit was made up of local boys (including several of his relatives) from the vicinity of his hometown, Friendship, located in West Tennessee. By 1863, Fielder, having demonstrated his leadership abilities, was elected captain by his fellow soldiers. The regiment was soon mustered into the Army of Tennessee, where it fought for the remainder of the war.[1]

Recognizing the hazards of military service, Fielder, a longtime Christian, early in the war laid his petitions before his Heavenly Father's throne for protection for himself and his family. He realized that, while serving in the army, he was no longer in control of his own fate or that of dear ones at home, but he acknowledged God's power over such matters,

Alfred T. Fielder in 1870.
Courtesy of the Tennessee State
Library and Archives, Nashville.

and he derived great comfort and peace from his faith. Religion, therefore, consoled him and helped him endure the ordeal of war, allowing him to carry on. And, as God proved faithful in his care, Fielder's faith or trust in God was strengthened.[2]

A native of North Carolina, Fielder traveled with his wife, Isabell Tate, to West Tennessee in 1835 and settled in the town of Friendship, located in Dyer County. There, he operated a small farm on which he grew corn, wheat, and cotton. Fielder prospered as a farmer and, over time, increased his holdings, including his property in slaves; by 1860, he owned more than ten. Fielder became a respected community leader and was elected by the citizens in his district to the state legislature in 1855.[3]

Fielder was a longtime Methodist and a devout Christian. Apparently, his interest in religion began when he was a child, for his wartime diary indicates that his father and mother were faithful Christians. Nurtured by godly parents, he embraced religion at an early age and became a dedicated believer. Once he had settled in Tennessee, Fielder attended Mt. Zion Methodist Church in Friendship and served on the board of trustees, which oversaw the physical property of the church. Fielder's piety and faithfulness must have been evident to those who knew him, for members of the board of trustees were nominated by their church pastor and elected by the district's Quarterly Conference. He remained a spiritual pillar of his local church during the antebellum period. He demonstrated his devoutness in his actions as well. In 1857, he deeded two acres free of charge to the church for the construction of a new "house or place or worship . . . to preach and expand God's Holy word therein." He remained a trustee of Mt. Zion until his death in 1893.[4]

As an ardent Christian, Fielder must have recognized the inconsistency of war and his religious convictions, for did not Christ command his followers to love one another? James M. McPherson points out that devout soldiers had little difficulty justifying their participation in what they considered a war of self-defense against Northern aggression. Indeed, these men could not idly stand by and watch as their native land was desolated by invading armies. If Fielder was troubled by his participation in the war, he must have resolved early on any dilemma he may have had, for there are no references to it in his journal. He likely had little difficulty reconciling his faith and fighting in a war he considered just. In the second entry in his diary, made on July 27, 1861, the day he was sworn into Confederate service, he noted that he had "[taken] up his musket with a firm determination to use it in defence of the rights of myself and family and the Southern Confederacy." He echoed these sentiments nearly a year later when, manning the trenches surrounding Corinth, Mississippi, in May 1862, he wrote that he and other Southerners were fighting "for our homes our wives and our families and all that is sacred and all we want to be let alone[.] [O]ur enemies are fighting for conquest and plunder."[5]

Army life in the early months of the Civil War was inhospitable to men of faith. Few soldiers on either side expressed any interest in spiritual matters, religious services were held in the camps only irregularly, and the soldiers faced a multitude of temptations—a fact observed by Fielder early on. "I find there is more infidelity in the army than I had immagened," he reported in March 1862. Steven E. Woodworth concludes that camp life "during the first year or so of the war was not having a good moral and religious effect on the soldiers." He contends that many fighting men were excited initially by the novelty of army life, which could be enjoyed in relative anonymity. Historians who agree that camp life in the first months of the war was not conducive to religion include Drew Gilpin Faust, James I. Robertson, and Larry J. Daniel. Faust maintains that, early on, many prewar churchgoers, far away from hearth and home, often succumbed to the ubiquitous temptations found in camp. War "inevitably dented the faith of many Civil War participants," says Robertson. "Leaving the restraints of home and loved ones, and then cast as soldiers in a novel environment that alternated between apathy and loneliness on the one hand to excitement and danger on the other, invited a wandering from the straight and narrow." And Daniel asserts that, "because of the festive atmosphere in camp" early in the war, "a general religious indifference permeated the army." The wartime letters and diaries of Civil War chaplains confirm that, on the whole, fighting men on both sides exhibited little interest in religion at the outset of the war. As a result, many regimental chaplains resigned their positions out of frustration.[6]

Fielder was, however, determined to continue his prewar routine of attending religious services, praying, and reading his Bible once in the army. Indeed, he attended services (both morning and evening) his first Sunday in camp. He continued his religious practices in part out of habit. "As has been my custom for years I offered my devotions to almighty God before closing my eyes to sleep," he wrote in June 1862. Fielder also maintained his routine because he was a genuine Christian and cherished the relationship he had with his Heavenly Father and sought to continue it while serving in the army. His sincere attempt to persist in his religious activities tells us something, not only about his relationship with God, but also about his prewar religious commitment. Historians contend that antebellum Southern men often engaged in "worldly amusements" and that devotion to religion resided primarily in the female sphere. But Fielder's wartime experiences indicate that he, too, was intensely pious and had been prior to the war. Disturbed by the iniquitous activities of his fellow soldiers in December 1861, Fielder openly criticized their behavior: "The Cause of sobrity, virtue, and piety have comparatively few advocates in the army but as for myself though it may be unpopular—I am determined by Gods grace to advocate them all and remonstrate with those who say and act differantly." Apparently Fielder found few who took his advice, for two days later he remarked: "I further intend to talk less (because it anoys some) and think more as it may be more profit to myself and less anoyance to others." Even though his influence on others was limited, Fielder was determined to remain untarnished. He did not completely isolate himself from his comrades but chose instead to associate with other godly men in camp. During his first few weeks in the army, he joined other like-minded soldiers nearly every night in the chaplain's tent for prayer meeting.[7]

Fielder also believed that it was necessary to act piously to secure the Lord's blessing in order to prevail over the North, for he realized that God would not bless those he considered unrighteous. Indeed, his fear was that the irreligious behavior of his comrades would, instead, provoke God's wrath. He was bothered in particular by the soldiers', as well as the army's, violation of the Fourth Commandment. In December 1861, Fielder noted: "The Sabbath is but little regarded in the army[.] May God have mercy upon our rulers and our men and help them to learn righteousness . . . 'righteousness exalth a nation but sin is a reproach to any people.'" Apparently, things improved but little, for, on a Sunday in 1863, he remarked: "It is now sun set and this Sabbath day has been spent by the army in one general stir and I fear but few have thought that it is written 'Thou shalt observe the sabbath day to keep it holy.' . . . I pray God to forgive us our wrongs both national and individual." He furthermore believed that Southerners must demonstrate a firm faith in the Lord and "meet his aprobation" in order to achieve victory. In July 1863, he asserted: "Our cause is Just and will prevail, God is a Just God and if we will but trust him as we ought he will bring us off Conquerors[.] Lord help us as a nation to humble ourselves under thy mighty hand." Therefore, Fielder endeavored to remain faithful and desired that his fellow soldiers would do likewise and become pious men, which would guarantee military success.[8]

Fielder's relationship with God took on even more importance once he was in the army, for he faced many new and terrible trials. Illness, mishap, or military action could claim his life at any time. He was reminded of this when the Twelfth Tennessee participated in the effort to repel a small force of Yankees advancing on Belmont, Missouri, in November 1861. Fielder saw several of his friends fall, and he himself "felt the wind from a ball brush my left lock or whisker." The next day he confided in his journal: "Oh! how thankful to God I am that I am still spared and that I am what I am. . . . I do not remember to have ever seen a day in my life that I felt more thankful and more willing to submit to the will of providence." Fielder trusted in the Lord for his own safety, and he found peace of mind in his faith, for he, like most mid-nineteenth-century Americans, believed strongly in the providence of God. According to Lewis O. Saum, the belief in providence was the most pervasive religious theme in antebellum

America. Therefore, most Americans during this era interpreted trials as part of God's plan and resigned themselves to his will. Their belief in providence, Saum contends, also helped soldiers accept the deaths of their comrades as the inscrutable will of an all-wise Heavenly Father. Fielder's certainty that the Lord directed human events meant that God could shield him and his loved ones from harm. And, if he were to perish on the battlefield, Fielder understood that it must be the Lord's will and that there was little he could do to prevent it. Thus, he became resigned to the will of his Heavenly Father. Fielder prayed earnestly for his own protection, which eased his fears about the events going on around him. In June 1863, he wrote: "I was enabled to feel that God was still my father and friend and in my soul there was a peace the wor[l]d can neither give nor take away."[9]

Nor was Fielder able to care for his family back home. He prayed fervently throughout the conflict for God's safekeeping, not only for himself, but also for them. Thoughts of his loved ones frequently crowded his mind, particularly early in the war. After the fall of Forts Henry and Donelson in February 1862, his concern for his home in West Tennessee was evident: "For the last two or three days my mind has much run out in prayer for myself and family . . . my mind [was] much upon home my family and all my earthly possessions being between me and Lincolns army. I pray God it may not long be the case, but that the time may be near at hand when the soil of Tennessee shall not be polluted by the tread of an enemy of the Southern Cause." Although the area near his home in Friendship was not subjected to any long-term Federal occupation, both Union and Confederate soldiers frequently conducted raids and foraging expeditions in that region. Realizing that he could do little to protect his loved ones, Fielder turned the matter over to God. When called on to pray during a church service in the summer of 1862, Fielder "felt my heart much drawn out after my wife and family & friends who are now exposed to the enemy oh! that God may throw the arms of his protection around them and protect them from insult and abuse." Learning in December 1862 that Yankees had been to his farm in Friendship and had confiscated his slaves, an incensed Fielder wrote: "They are stealing our property burning our houses. . . . O Lord throw the arms of protection around my wife and family and shield them from insult and injury is my prayer." As with himself, he placed his "family & all that I possess" in God's hands and noted in his diary that, when it came to his loved ones, "my trust is still firmly fixed in God."[10]

Fielder was furthermore comforted by the fact that, if he were to fall in battle, he knew that God would take care of his family. Before departing for his command after a brief furlough home in January 1865, he confessed: "This is the day I am to start for the army of Tennessee[.] My trust is firm in God and into his hands I commit my family as into the hands of a faithful and trusty friend." He was also reassured by the thought that, if he were to die, he would see his loved ones again in the next world, where they would remain together for eternity. He wrote in the spring of 1863: "God has blessed me much of late though I have been the subject of some bodily affliction yet he has blessed my soul and I have been enabled to look by faith beyond the Jordon of death to a better and happier home in heaven when I expect to overtake many loved ones that have crossed over before me and many others who are on the way."[11]

As his words reveal, Fielder's religion consoled and sustained him during the war. The uncertainty of military life and his inability to care for his loved ones back home in West Tennessee moved Fielder to place his life and the lives of his loved ones in the hands of his "faithful and trusty friend," and he found great comfort in the thought that a sovereign and loving God directed events. Accepting that his all-wise Heavenly Father was in control of human affairs, Fielder petitioned God for his protection and gave him the credit when he was spared. And if the Lord allowed him to fall on the field of battle, then it was his will. These thoughts helped Fielder overcome any fears he may have had and strengthened his will to fight. And, when it came to death, he had no fear, for he was destined for another world—an eternal one where hardship and war could not trespass. Thus, the strength he drew from his faith had a positive impact on his courage. Earl J. Hess phrases it best: "Many soldiers clung desperately to thoughts of God while bullets flew over their heads. . . . This was the elemental role that religion played in the soldier's ability to hold on. It steadied his emotions at a critical time and provided a rock on which he based his courage." Indeed, devout Christians like Fielder made the bravest soldiers, for they held no fear of death. "Live or die I am his," confessed Fielder in the summer of 1864. The comrades of dying soldier-Christians often noted that they were at peace as death approached, for their thoughts were focused on the next world. Such thoughts reassured Fielder and helped him persevere despite the hardships he encountered, allowing him to see the war through to the end.[12]

Furthermore, Fielder's faith in God was strengthened during the war. The Lord had proved dependable time and again in protecting, not only Fielder, but also his loved ones at home, and Fielder acknowledged God's faithfulness. His gratefulness to the Lord for watching over his family was evident when, after receiving word throughout the war that his family was doing well, he attributed it to God and thanked him. He also expressed thankfulness for his own protection. After each engagement in which he fought, Fielder credited God with sparing him. Following Shiloh in April 1862, he admitted: "I . . . passed the two days of the ever memorable battle of Shiloah—the thousands that had been Killed and wounded and that I had passed through it all and was not seriously hurt my soul appeared to be almost melted within me in thankfulness to God for his preserving Care." Crediting God for sparing him at Shiloh was Fielder's acknowledgment that the Lord was answering his prayers and protecting him. God's faithfulness in preserving his life engendered in Fielder a desire to trust him further. He echoed this sentiment after surviving several more engagements. After the desperate fighting on the Union right in the Battle of Murfreesboro on December 31, 1862, Fielder wrote: "Thank God I have been spared to see the Commencement of an other year[.] Dear Lord help me to spend the future of my life more devoted than the past[;] it is my firm determination to do so." Fielder made a similar statement nearly two years later when, near Corinth, Mississippi, he visited his regiment's old encampment and "thought of the boys that were there then, many of whom have since been Killed upon the battle field, or disabled for life. . . . [T]hought of the many long and wearsome marches I had made and hard fought battles I have been in since that time and how many had been cut down by the relentless hand of death while I was still spared which caused me to thank God for his goodness and mercy towards me—I returned to my quarters I trust prepared to be a better man." Indeed, his own words testify to his deeper faith in God. Recuperating from the wounds he received during the Battle of Atlanta, Fielder noted: "I am quite feeble and have a poor apetite but my faith and trust is strong in God." The best testament to his strengthened faith, however, occurred on March 3, 1865, the day he celebrated another birthday as a soldier. The significance of the day engendered much thought and reflection. As he was preparing to leave home and rejoin his command, Fielder recorded these words in his diary: "I am 51 years of age this day—My life may be said to have been an eventful one. I have Come up through many difficulties and dangers but Gods unseen hand has protected and shielded me thus far for which I am thankful and feel in my heart willing to trust him in the future believing his grace will be sufficient for me."[13]

As Fielder relied more on God, he drew nearer to him and sought to become a better Christian. At his post as sentinel one evening at Columbus, Kentucky, in September 1861, Fielder took advantage of his time alone and spent it "much drawn out in prayer," hoping that the "morning found me a better more devoted man." This desire to improve his spiritual condition did not abate during the war. At Chattanooga, Tennessee, in the summer of 1863, he climbed Lookout Mountain for some alone time with God and remarked: "I was there thinking of the great power and wisdom of him that spoke all things into existence . . . and in comparison of which how weak, feeble and insignificant the creative man—I trust that what I have this day seen may bring about reflections that will make me a better man."[14]

As Fielder became more devout, he exhibited a greater desire to worship. Congregating with other Christians in the presence of God as well as listening to the ministers' discourses encouraged him and helped assuage his fears. Indeed, by early 1863, he was often attending several different services on Sundays. On one Sabbath day, he wrote: "I trust that I have spent this day to profit having heard three sermons and indeavered to worship the God of my fathers in sincerity." Other times, he went out of his way to worship. One Sunday in the spring of 1862, Fielder, recognizing that no church service would occur in his regiment, called on the chaplain of a nearby regiment and arranged for him to hold services in his command later that day. Traveling home in the spring of 1864, Fielder sought out congregations holding services in the towns he passed through and joined them for worship. On a Sunday in Selma, Alabama, he heard two sermons while awaiting his departure for Tennessee. And, when military operations prevented his attending formal services, he expressed his disappointment and often escaped from camp and sought a quiet, natural setting in which to worship. In November 1862 in Tullahoma, Tennessee, he recorded in his diary: "I have Just come in from a walk to the woods where I spent several hours in meditation and prayer Oh! I have thought of and prayed for dear friends at home." Fielder especially enjoyed worshipping among the clouds atop Lookout Mountain in 1863. He noted that it was "one of the best places for reflection and meditation upon nature and natures God I ever saw." His devotion to worship is further illustrated by his recording the scriptural references for the sermons he heard. This not only indicates his interest in the sermons but also likely meant that he took notes as well and meditated on the ministers' words over and again. He also regularly evaluated the ministers' discourses and criticized those he found lacking, especially when he sought comforting words. Uneasy about an impending engagement near Murfreesboro, Tennessee, in December 1862, he listened intently to a sermon delivered by his new chaplain but found it unsatisfying, for the minister "did not preach exceeding 10 minutes."[15]

Another sign of his growing devoutness was the frequency with which Fielder studied Scripture. During his first week in the army, he immersed himself in the Bible. Just days after arriving at his command, he read the three chapters in Matthew that constitute Christ's Sermon on the Mount and encourage believers to remain true to Christ's teachings even in the face of difficult circumstances. He no doubt found these verses comforting, especially after observing the moral corrosiveness of army life. Fielder continued to study Scripture throughout the war. At Columbus in January 1862, he reported that, because of the disagreeable weather, there was "little stiring about" in camp, so he spent the time reading the Bible and "read nine Chapters." Near Chattanooga, Tennessee, in August 1863, with the pickets exchanging fire continuously, he recorded in his diary: "I spent some time of this day in reading the Scriptures meditation and prayer for myself and family Kindred friends and Country yes and for my enemies." In the summer of 1864, he set out to read the Bible from beginning to end, a task that he completed in under six weeks. His Bible was so worn from use that, in March 1865, he paid to have it rebound.[16]

Fielder also grew more spiritually minded in his outlook on life as the war progressed. For one, his thoughts turned increasingly to the other world beyond the clouds. Phillip Shaw Paludan maintains that, prior to the Civil War, Americans had thought little about the afterlife, but the war's appalling carnage had touched virtually every family and, thus, had "brought death into the foreground of life." Families mourning the loss of loved ones, therefore, thought more of heaven and saw it as an eternal refuge far away from the tribulations inherent in a human existence. Fielder's comments suggest that Paludan's assertion was especially true for soldiers, for Fielder found hope in the thought of an eternal home free from earthly troubles. He wrote in June 1862: "I [feel] that this world was not my perpetual home but I was enabled to look by faith beyond the vail that skirts time from eternity where there will be no wars, no sickness, no pain, no death but . . . triumph o'er sorrow and death." In the summer of 1864, convalescing from the wounds he suffered during the Atlanta Campaign, Fielder confessed: "Last night I commenced thinking on the love of God to man and my heart was melted down in thankfulness and God [descended] to pour his love into my soul. . . . I looked forward with pleasing anticipation to a home in heaven." His references to heaven only increased as the war dragged on.[17]

Another sign of Fielder's increasing focus on religious matters was his concern about the spiritual state of the army. Fielder was disappointed by the irreligiousness of the troops early on. "I awfully fear that religion and the worship of God is on the retro[grade]," he wrote in December 1861. "May God have mercy upon our rulers and our men and help them to learn righteousness." Religious interest among the troops in the Army of Tennessee did increase, however. The discouraging retreat from Kentucky in the fall of 1862 and the bloody stalemate at Murfreesboro at year's end triggered a wave of religious fervor that swept the army during its winter quarters near Tullahoma, Tennessee. The role that longtime Christians like Fielder played in initiating the revivals is unclear. What *is* clear, however, is that, at a time when few of their comrades were interested in spiritual matters, ardent Christians like Fielder kept religious interest alive in the armies. Fielder persisted in his religious activities enthusiastically and openly, and he served as an example to those around him. Indeed, his fellow soldiers recognized his devoutness and repeatedly asked him to lead them in prayer during services, which he did willingly. After a desperate first day of fighting at the Battle of Shiloh in April 1862, Fielder led the men in his company in worship: "At the suggestion of Jas Hammons I read the 71 Psalm give out and sing two verses of the hymn Commencing 'God of my life whose gracious power' Knelt down and tried to return Thanksgiving and prayer to God." During one prayer meeting in January 1863 at Tullahoma, the chaplain asked Fielder to lead the meeting, which he did gladly. Later he recorded: "I trust good was accomplished." Fielder furthermore was determined to conduct himself morally and avoid any activity that could bring reproach to himself or to the cause of Christ. In December 1862, he noted regretfully: "I played two games of Fox & Geese

. . . last night and am sorry that I indulged even that much and intend to do so no more." Even though his influence on others was limited, he was determined to stand firm in his faith: "I this day resolve in my heart to live more prayerful and let others do as they may as for me I will still try to serve God and get to heaven." The actions of committed believers like Fielder kept religion alive in the armies, and, whether or not soldiers were interested in religion initially, they were constantly exposed to it as well as the hope and contentment it offered. The actions of these devout Christian soldiers provided fertile soil in the ranks that helped the revivals to blossom. Fielder hoped that the soldiers' interest in religion would continue and that the men would benefit spiritually from the revival services. After one service he remarked: "I pray God that [the meetings] may be to his glory and our good." The meetings continued with much fervor until the summer of 1863, when the Army of Tennessee commenced a new campaign.[18]

The army experienced another outbreak of even more intense revivals during the winter of 1863–1864 at Dalton, Georgia. Wounds he suffered in the battle for Chattanooga in November 1863 and a journey home in early 1864 to collect stragglers and enlist new recruits prevented Fielder from participating in most of these meetings, but he would certainly have been encouraged by the soldiers' religious interest, for, even late in the war, he continued to express his hope that the cause of Christ was being advanced in the army. Attending a service held by his chaplain on April 30, 1865, just days after Gen. Joseph E. Johnston surrendered the Army of Tennessee, Fielder wrote: "I trust its fruits will be seen in eternity."[19]

As Fielder grew more spiritually minded, he focused less on sectarian issues and more on worshipping God. Prior to the war, and during the first months of the conflict, Fielder, a staunch Methodist, strictly adhered to the tenets of his faith. He and his home church pastor, Rev. T. D. Harwell, had a good friendship, which they continued throughout the war. And, in 1857, Fielder even donated property for the construction of a Methodist church near his home. When an interdenominational Christian association was organized in his regiment in early 1863, Fielder refused to join. "I am a member of the M. E. C. South and am willing to [be] governed [only] by its rules," he wrote in April. Less than two months later, however, he reconsidered and admitted in his diary: "[To]Night the Christian association met and quite a number Joined it[,] myself among the number." He seldom missed the meetings and at one even read an essay on prayer he had written. He even attended the associational meetings of other regiments. Fielder's primary desire was to hear the Gospel preached regardless of the setting or the minister. Indeed, he regularly attended services held by ministers of other denominations. On a Sabbath near Augusta, Georgia, in 1865, he wrote that he had attended a Methodist service in the morning, an Episcopal church in the afternoon, and still another church that evening.[20]

Although Fielder held out hope, even late in the conflict, that the South would win the war and achieve its independence, this was not to be. He and other Southerners were forced to reconcile the defeat of the South with the belief that they held early in the war that God was on their side. Confederate Christians accepted defeat because they interpreted it as the inscrutable will of a providential God. Although initially they held a firm belief that God favored the Confederate cause, military setbacks cast doubt on that conviction. Although soldier-Christians maintained the belief that the Lord would intervene at the appropriate time, they sought an explanation for the defeats. The South's surrender, however, ended all hope of divine intervention and forced Christians in that region to reconcile their faith with the defeat of the Confederacy. Southern Christians concluded that God refused to intervene on their behalf because they were undeserving of his favor. Although tens of thousands of Confederates had made professions of faith during the revivals and became God-fearing soldiers, Christians maintained that Southerners as a whole had turned away from the Lord. Indeed, they believed that many had exhibited a lack of faith in God, placing their trust instead in Confederate military leaders. The Southern people, they insisted, were not worthy of God's blessing. Moreover, Christian soldiers believed that, if God, in his infinite wisdom, allowed the defeat of the South, they must accept it as part of his plan. Southerners took great comfort from Hebrews 12:6—"For whom the Lord loveth he chasteneth"—and believed that the Lord's chastisement was preparing them for something greater. Realizing that God's will might be contrary his own, Fielder expressed his willingness to yield to the Almighty's infinite wisdom.[21]

Direct evidence about Fielder's spiritual life after the war is lacking. He discontinued his diary shortly after arriving home, and no postwar correspondence exists. What little evidence does exist provides only a glimpse of his postwar life.

Fielder surrendered with Gen. Joseph E. Johnston's Army of Tennessee in April 1865 and soon thereafter received his parole. He made his way home to Friendship, Tennessee, reaching there on Friday, May 26. After his arrival, he commented: "I felt in my heart to thank God I was at home once more."[22]

Fielder's strengthened relationship with God carried over into the postwar era. Once home, he eagerly resumed his religious routine. Indeed, his first Sunday back he attended both morning and evening services at Mt. Zion Methodist Church and noted that he hoped he had spent the day "profitably." In all likelihood, he faithfully attended church each Sunday thereafter. He returned to his duties as a trustee of Mt. Zion and played an integral part in its operation. During this time, he placed immense importance on furthering the cause of Christ. In 1868, he and others chartered a new Methodist church in Friendship. Whether he became an active member of the Friendship church is uncertain. It is clear, however, that he continued his affiliation with Mt. Zion, for, in 1889, he gave a half acre to the church for a cemetery, and he is listed as a trustee in the deed. He furthermore served as a lay delegate to the Dyersburg District Conference during the late 1880s and early 1890s. Alfred Fielder died August 1, 1893, and was buried in the Mt. Zion cemetery he helped establish.[23]

Military service brought distress and difficulties unmatched by anything Fielder had seen in his civilian life. He responded to the hardships he faced by relying on his religious faith, in which he found sanctuary and sustenance. Fielder believed that God controlled human affairs, and he trusted him to protect himself and his family. And, as God proved faithful time and again, Fielder's faith or trust in him grew. Furthermore, Fielder believed that, if it was God's will that he should fall, he would take up residence in heaven, where he would be reunited with loved ones—a fact that he took comfort in. In heaven, he would live in eternal peace and happiness. Reassured by these thoughts, Fielder exhibited courage despite the possibility of his death, and he demonstrated a willingness to fight to the end. His relationship with his Maker also benefited from his wartime experiences. It became more meaningful and grew stronger as he faced new trials and tribulations. He also thought increasingly of spiritual matters and of heaven. His increased spiritual-mindedness can be seen in the concern he expressed for his comrades in arms and his frequent references to heaven. In short, his religious faith had a positive influence on his military service, and his wartime experiences had a positive impact on his faith. Indeed, Alfred T. Fielder went to war in 1861 relying on his faith to get him through the ordeal, and he emerged from the conflict a more committed Christian and the better man he had sought to become.

Notes

This essay is an expansion of a topic first mentioned in Kent T. Dollar, *Soldiers of the Cross: Confederate Soldier-Christians and the Impact of War on Their Faith* (Macon, Ga.: Mercer University Press, 2005).

1. Ann York Franklin, ed., *The Civil War Diaries of Capt. Alfred Tyler Fielder, 12th Tennessee Regiment Infantry, Company B, 1861–1865* (Louisville, Ky.: privately printed, 1996), 1, 7, 152, 189–90, 248; Compiled Service Records, Twelfth Tennessee Infantry, National Archives (NA), Washington, D.C.

2. "A battlefield offers the extreme challenge to the belief that man can control his fate," writes James McPherson. "Rain, shells and bullets fall on the just and unjust alike" (*For Cause and Comrades: Why Men Fought in the Civil War* [New York: Oxford University Press, 1997], 62).

3. Franklin, ed., *Fielder Diaries*, 248; *History of Tennessee from the Earliest Time to the Present; Together with an Historical and a Biographical Sketch of Gibson, Obion, Dyer, Weakley and Lake Counties* (hereafter cited as *History of Dyer County*) (Nashville: Goodspeed, 1887), 842, 845; Eighth Census, 1860, Manuscript Returns of Productions of Agriculture, Dyer County, Tennessee, 59; Seventh Census, 1850, Manuscript Returns of Productions of Agriculture, Dyer County, Tennessee, 801; Seventh Census, 1850, Manuscript Returns of Slaves, Dyer County, Tennessee, 886; Eighth Census, 1860, Manuscript Returns of Slaves, Dyer County, Tennessee, 207, NA; *History of Tennessee from the Earliest Time to the Present; Together with an Historical and a Biographical Sketch of Lauderdale, Tipton, Haywood and Crockett Counties* (Nashville: Goodspeed, 1887), 837; Nancy C. Wallace, ed., *History of Friendship, Tennessee, 1824–1986* (n.p., n.d.), 43, Tennessee State Library and Archives, Nashville; Robert M. McBride and Dan M. Robison, *Biographical Directory of the Tennessee General Assembly,* 2 vols. (Nashville: Tennessee State Library and Archives and the Tennessee Historical Commission, 1979), 2:1031–32.

4. Franklin, ed., *Fielder Diaries*, 21, 24, 46–47, 114, 160–61, 164; *The Doctrines and Disciplines of the Methodist Episcopal Church* (New York: Nelson & Phillips, 1876), 215; Susanna W. Fielder and Alfred T. Fielder to A. W. Swift and

Others, April 4, 1857, Deed Book L, 350, Register of Deeds Office, Dyer County, Dyersburg, Tenn.; *The History of the Mt. Zion Methodist Church* (n.p., n.d.), 1, Mary Alice Badget Personal Papers, Friendship, Tenn.

5. McPherson, *For Cause and Comrades,* 71–72; Franklin, ed., *Fielder Diaries,* 1, 26, 41, 52, 98, 124, 127, 135. For more on how Christian soldiers reconciled their participation in the war and their Christian faith, see McPherson, *For Cause and Comrades,* 21–29, 71–74; Steven E. Woodworth, *While God Is Marching On: The Religious World of Civil War Soldiers* (Lawrence: University Press of Kansas, 2001), 128–32; and Kent T. Dollar, *Soldiers of the Cross: Confederate Soldier-Christians and the Impact of War on Their Faith* (Macon, Ga.: Mercer University Press, 2005), 53–64.

6. Franklin, ed., *Fielder Diaries,* 41; Woodworth, *While God Is Marching On,* 175–89; Bell I. Wiley, *The Life of Johnny Reb: The Common Soldier of the Confederacy* (Baton Rouge: Louisiana State University Press, 1943), 175; Drew Gilpin Faust, "Christian Soldiers: The Meaning of Revivalism in the Confederate Army," *Journal of Southern History* 53 (February 1987): 68; James I. Robertson, *Soldiers Blue and Gray* (Columbia: University of South Carolina Press, 1988), 172–73; and Larry J. Daniel, *Soldiering in the Army of Tennessee* (Chapel Hill: University of North Carolina Press, 1991), 115. Woodworth does admit, however, that many soldiers struggled to remain faithful followers of Christ despite the difficult conditions in camp. For more on these committed Christians, see Woodworth, *While God Is Marching On,* 175–90; and Dollar, *Soldiers of the Cross,* 52–98. Chaplains who commented on the irreligious nature of the soldiers early in the war include the Confederate chaplains Nicholas A. Davis and Pere Louis-Hippolyte Gache and the Northern chaplain Louis N. Beaudry. See Donald E. Everett, ed., *Chaplain Davis and Hood's Texas Brigade* (San Antonio, Tex.: Principia Press of Trinity University, 1962; reprint, Baton Rouge: Louisiana State University Press, 1999), 2; Cornelius M. Buckley, ed. and trans., *A Frenchman, a Chaplain, a Rebel: The War Letters of Pere Louis-Hippolyte Gache, S.J.* (Chicago: Loyola University Press, 1981), 48; and Richard E. Beaudry, ed., *War Journal of Louis N. Beaudry, Fifth New York Cavalry: The Diary of a Union Chaplain, Commencing February 16, 1863* (Jefferson, N.C.: McFarland, 1996), 7–9.

7. Franklin, ed., *Fielder Diaries,* 1–8, 18, 24–25, 35, 56, 92, 110, 121, 134, 136–37, 148, 151, 163, 165, 169; Anne C. Loveland, *Southern Evangelicals and the Social Order, 1800–1860* (Baton Rouge: Louisiana State University Press, 1980), 2, 8, 13–16, 93, 97, 103; Drew Gilpin Faust, *Mothers of Invention: Women of the Slaveholding South in the American Civil War* (Chapel Hill: University of North Carolina Press, 1996), 180. See also Donald G. Mathews, *Religion in the Old South* (Chicago: University of Chicago Press, 1977), 101–3, 109, 111–13, 115, 120–23;

John B. Boles, "Evangelical Protestantism in the Old South: From Religious Dissent to Cultural Dominance," in *Religion in the South*, ed. Charles Reagan Wilson (Jackson: University Press of Mississippi, 1985), 32–33; Orville V. Burton, *In My Father's House Are Many Mansions: Family and Community in Edgefield, South Carolina* (Chapel Hill: University of North Carolina Press, 1985), 114–15, 131–34, 138–40, 145–46. Scholars are, however, beginning to challenge this stereotype of men in the Old South. Peter Carmichael, e.g., contends that the "popular, but one-dimensional image of Southern youth as lazy, immoral, and hotheaded overlooks the changing nature of what it meant to be a young man in the slave South." Southern manliness was not static, but evolving, asserts Carmichael, and a generation of young Virginians was reshaping what it meant to be manly. They were drawn in particular to the ideal of the Christian gentleman, a man of feeling and faith. See Peter S. Carmichael, *The Last Generation: Young Virginians in Peace, War, and Reunion* (Chapel Hill: University of North Carolina Press, 2005), 6, 11, 58–88, 244n, 245n. See also Stephen W. Berry, *All That Makes a Man: Love and Ambition in the Civil War South* (New York: Oxford University Press, 2003), 9–13, 90–94, 115–16, and passim. For more on the thoughts and activities of religious soldiers in the first months of the conflict, see Kent T. Dollar, "Strangers in a Strange Land: Christian Soldiers in the Early Months of the Civil War," in *The View from the Ground: Experiences of Civil War Soldiers*, ed. Aaron Sheehan-Dean (Lexington: University Press of Kentucky, 2007), 145–69.

    8. Franklin, ed., *Fielder Diaries*, 22–23, 127–28. According to Steven Woodworth and Gardiner Shattuck, many Confederates feared that God would allow their defeat if they proved unworthy. See Woodworth, *While God Is Marching On*, 126–27; and Gardiner H. Shattuck, *A Shield and Hiding Place: The Religious Life of the Civil War Armies* (Macon, Ga.: Mercer University Press, 1987), 106.

    9. Franklin, ed., *Fielder Diaries*, 15–16, 121; Christopher Losson, *Tennessee's Forgotten Warriors* (Knoxville: University of Tennessee Press, 1989), 33–35; U.S. War Department, *The War of the Rebellion: A Compilation of the Official Records of the Union and Confederate Armies, 1861–1865*, 70 vols. in 128 pts. (Washington, D.C.: U.S. Government Printing Office, 1880–1901), ser. 1, vol. 3, pp. 306–10; Lewis O. Saum, *The Popular Mood of Pre-Civil War America* (Westport, Conn.: Greenwood, 1980), 3–17.

    10. Franklin, ed., *Fielder Diaries*, 35, 59, 62–63, 94; *History of Dyer County*, 847.

    11. Franklin, ed., *Fielder Diaries*, 111, 214. Lewis Saum maintains that, for mid-nineteenth-century Americans, death represented "an escape from the world's sadness, an end to the pilgrimage through spiritual and bodily hostility. It meant the passage to that realm where parting is no more" (*Popular Mood of Pre-Civil War America*, 103–4).

12. Earl J. Hess, *Union Soldier in Battle: Enduring the Ordeal of Combat* (Lawrence: University Press of Kansas, 1997), 103–4; Franklin, ed., *Fielder Diaries*, 191; Woodworth, *While God Is Marching On*, 244. The topic of religion's impact on soldiers' combat motivation and courage has attracted the interest of historians. Samuel J. Watson points out that soldiers' religious faith had a positive impact on their combat performance, for it "enabled men to control their fear" ("Religion and Combat Motivation in the Confederate Armies," *Journal of Military History* 58 [January 1994]: 34–36, 52–55). McPherson goes even further and asserts: "[The] heightened religiosity helped to prevent the collapse of both armies during the terrible carnage of 1864, but was a particularly potent force in the Confederacy. It may not be an exaggeration to say that the revivals of 1863–64 enabled Confederate armies to prolong the war into 1865" (*For Cause and Comrades*, 75).

13. Franklin, ed., *Fielder Diaries*, 7, 24, 32, 34, 36, 44, 63, 100, 107, 134, 191, 207, 219. On March 3, 1863, Fielder celebrated his second birthday in the ranks. It prompted this remark: "I am 49 years of age and feel thankful to God for his preserving Care. Oh! the dangers through which I have come[,] so many have died who set out in life since I have lived[.] Lord help me to live more religious than I have ever done" (ibid., 108).

14. Ibid., 8, 130. Fielder expressed his desire to become a more devout Christian several times throughout the war. See ibid., 59, 100, 105, 108, 111, 121, 137, 168.

15. Ibid., 50, 88, 95, 104, 130, 169–70.

16. Ibid., 1–2, 28–29, 135, 197, 220. Christ's Sermon on the Mount is in Matthew, chaps. 5–7. Fielder also read other religious books he borrowed from his chaplain. See ibid., 33, 58.

17. Phillip Shaw Paludan, *A People's Contest: The Union and the Civil War, 1861–1865* (New York: Harper & Row, 1988), 365–68; Franklin, ed., *Fielder Diaries*, 55–56, 194. For Fielder's other references to heaven, see ibid., 21, 101, 110–11, 137, 168.

18. Franklin, ed., *Fielder Diaries*, 21–22, 25, 43, 102–24, 148, 164; Woodworth, *While God Is Marching On*, 212, 232. For other times Fielder led a service or prayer, see Franklin, ed., *Fielder Diaries*, 3, 55, 59–60, 63. In Psalm 71, David seeks God's refuge and deliverance. For a description of the revivals that swept the Army of Tennessee, see Shattuck, *A Shield and Hiding Place*, 100; and Daniel, *Soldiering in the Army of Tennessee*, 116–17.

19. Franklin, ed., *Fielder Diaries*, 152–62, 169–79, 230.

20. Ibid., 114, 121, 136–37, 148, 219, and passim. The chaplain in Fielder's regiment for much of the war was a Baptist, and Fielder, although a Methodist,

regularly attended his services. See John W. Brinsfield et al., eds., *Faith in the Fight: Civil War Chaplains* (Mechanicsburg, Pa.: Stackpole, 2003), 213.

21. Franklin, ed., *Fielder Diaries*, 53, 139, 153. Many Southern fighting men maintained the belief late in the war that God could and would deliver to the South ultimate victory. For more on this, see Jason Phillips, "Religious Belief and Troop Motivation: 'For the Smiles of My Blessed Saviour,'" in *Virginia's Civil War,* ed. Peter Wallenstein and Bertram Wyatt-Brown (Charlottesville: University of Virginia Press, 2005), 101–13. For more on how Northern and Southern Christians viewed military reverses and the war in general, see Woodworth, *While God Is Marching On,* 94–137. For more on Southern Christians' attempts to reconcile defeats (including the defeat of the South) and God's will, see Shattuck, *A Shield and Hiding Place,* 40, 100, 102, 108–9, 113; Woodworth, *While God Is Marching On,* 270–86; Daniel W. Stowell, *Rebuilding Zion: The Religious Reconstruction of the South, 1863–1877* (New York: Oxford University Press, 1998), 5, 33–44, and "Stonewall Jackson and the Providence of God," in *Religion and the American Civil War,* ed. Randall M. Miller, Harry S. Stout, and Charles Reagan Wilson (New York: Oxford University Press, 1998), 197–202; Eugene D. Genovese, *A Consuming Fire: The Fall of the Confederacy in the Mind of the White Christian South* (Athens: University of Georgia Press, 1998), passim; Dollar, *Soldiers of the Cross,* 177–222; Charles Reagan Wilson, introduction to Miller, Stout, and Wilson, eds., *Religion and the American Civil War,* 10; and Paul Harvey, "'Yankee Faith' and Southern Redemption," in ibid., 175. Many Christian soldiers concluded that defeat was consistent with the will of God. See Shattuck, *A Shield and Hiding Place,* 40, 109.

22. Compiled Service Records, Twelfth Tennessee Infantry, NA; Franklin, ed., *Fielder Diaries,* 235.

23. Franklin, ed., *Fielder Diaries,* 235–36, 248; Pearl Dunagon, Elizabeth Kirby, and Virginia Kirby, *The History of Friendship Methodist Church* (n.p., n.d.), 1, Friendship Methodist Church, Friendship, Tenn.; *History of the Mt. Zion Methodist Church,* 1; Dyersburg District Conference Journal, May 24, 1889, May 29, 1891, May 24, 1892, McIver's Grant Public Library, Dyersburg, Tenn.

An Interrupted Life

Colonel Sidney Smith Stanton

W. Calvin Dickinson

Civil War historians often paint with a broad brush, devoting little attention to individual soldiers and the impact of the war on their lives. But hundreds of thousands of individuals put their civilian lives on hold to serve in the Civil War armies. Many of these men perished during the four-year-long conflict, never to return home and realize their prewar promise. Tennessean Sidney Smith Stanton was one such individual. The ninth child of a large family, Stanton accomplished a great deal in the middle of the nineteenth century, especially in politics. But his promising political career ended with his service and death in the Civil War. His contemporaries lauded his service both before and during the war, and postwar eulogies lamented the loss of Stanton as a soldier and a statesman. By offering a brief glimpse into Stanton's life, this essay attempts to humanize one Civil War participant.

The Stanton family was among the early settlers of the Upper Cumberland region. Champion Stanton and his wife, Sallie (Sarah) Lindsey Stanton, both born in the 1780s in Virginia, settled in Jackson County, Tennessee, in the 1820s. By 1832, Stanton had built a log house on Martin's Creek and owned at least 125 acres to support his large family.[1] His wife gave birth to eleven children, seven boys and four girls.

Sidney was born in Jackson County in 1829, and he attended school there, maybe Montpelier Academy near Gainesboro. There is also speculation that he studied law in Lebanon. Although no personal letters of Stan-

Col. Sidney S. Stanton. Courtesy *Mc-Minnville (Tenn.) Southern Standard.*

ton's exist, his official letters and reports in the *Official Records* indicate that he was a highly literate person. The grammar, syntax, and spelling in his writings are superb.

Sidney married Martha Apple about 1857 and began practicing law in Carthage, moving back to Jackson County, and hanging out his shingle in Gainesboro.[2] One early author claimed: "His fame as a brilliant and logical orator had spread throughout the upper Cumberland district, and before he was 25 he was lionized."[3]

Stanton joined the Whig rather than the Democratic Party in the 1850s, just as that party was dividing between its Northern and Southern factions. Winfield Scott, the Whig presidential candidate in 1852, carried Tennessee by fewer than two thousand votes, the last time that a Whig candidate would win the state.

The American Party resulted from the decline of the Whigs; it became the second party in Tennessee for a short time, its members expressing dissatisfaction with the large number of immigrants and Catholics who were entering the nation. Stanton's thoughts concerning this particular issue are unknown; he may have harbored strong feelings, or maybe he was just following the leaders of his party.

In the 1855 congressional campaign in the "mountain district," Stanton supported the American Party candidate, Gen. William Cullom, against the incumbent, Col. John H. Savage, a Democrat. While Stanton was making a speech in support of Cullom in McMinnville, Savage called him a liar. Stanton immediately challenged Savage to a duel, a practice that had long been illegal in Tennessee. Efforts at reconciliation failed, and the two principals practiced their skills with pistols. Savage enjoyed a formidable reputation as a duelist, and Stanton possessed no experience. Balie Peyton took Stanton to his mansion in Gallatin to teach him the skill of shooting. The duel was finally aborted by Savage's apology, which rescued the political careers of both men (convicted duelists could not hold public office) and maybe saved the life of one of them.[4]

William G. Brownlow and Andrew Jackson Donelson led the American Party in Tennessee, and Stanton was among their followers. In 1857, the party chose Robert Hatton of Wilson County as its gubernatorial candidate, and Stanton ran for the General Assembly on the ticket. Isham G. Harris, a Democrat, defeated Hatton, but Stanton won a legislative seat, representing Jackson County. Two years later, he won a seat in the Senate, representing Jackson, Macon, and White counties; Harris was the successful candidate for governor again.

By 1860, Governor Harris was the leader of a vocal minority in the state that advocated secession. Senator Stanton adamantly opposed the idea. He and other former Whigs formed the Constitutional Union Party and nominated Tennessean John Bell for the presidency, and Stanton served as a presidential elector in his behalf. Balie Peyton, Thomas A. R. Nelson, and Horace Maynard joined Stanton in the campaign for Bell and national union. Bell carried only Tennessee and two other states in the election.

In January 1861 a special session of the General Assembly convened to consider a secession convention. The body called for a vote of the people, and in February Tennesseans rejected the idea of a secession convention; only West Tennessee favored the idea. Stanton campaigned against a convention, supposedly stumping the state from border to border. On April

14, Stanton attended a meeting of the Union Party in Carthage. There, he was appointed to a committee charged with drafting resolutions. The second resolution complimented Congressman W. B. Stokes for "unflinching devotion to the union of these States."[5] Later that week, John Bell called for the preservation of the Union.

On April 25, after the battle at Fort Sumter, Governor Harris called a second special session. After Fort Sumter and President Lincoln's call for seventy-five thousand volunteers to put down the rebellion, the mood in Middle Tennessee had changed drastically, and the lawmakers' actions reflected a more bellicose sentiment. On April 26, Senator Payne offered a resolution "to prepare a plan for separating the State of Tennessee from the States of the Union." Stanton immediately offered a second resolution that "the Governor of this State be . . . authorized to make contracts to ration and subsist the military forces of the State."[6]

On May 6, the lawmakers drafted a "Declaration of Independence" and put it before Tennessee voters for approval on June 8. Stanton voted for the declaration; only four senators voted no.[7] On May 9, Stanton, a member of the Joint Select Committee, signed a "Legislative Address to the People of Tennessee."[8]

Stanton was now in sympathy with secession, and in the 1861 General Assembly he led the effort to align Tennessee with the Confederacy. On June 28, Tennessee accepted the "Permanent Constitution of the Confederate States." Stanton also sponsored other measures related to establishing a military force for the state.[9] The legislature presented Stanton with an engraved gold-headed cane in appreciation for his leadership in the body. Lt. Col. R. C. Sanders later said of his friend: "His prospects for success as a lawyer and a politician at the breaking out of the war were of the most flattering character."[10]

In July, Sidney Stanton returned to the Upper Cumberland to pursue the Confederate cause in the military. At Livingston, he enlisted as a private in Company F, Twenty-fifth Tennessee Infantry. He recruited several companies of men from Putnam, Jackson, Overton, and White counties, totaling about eleven hundred "large, brave, and stalwart men."[11] In August, the regiment elected Stanton colonel instead of George Dibrell; Dibrell became lieutenant colonel.

The regiment trained for about three months at Camp Myers in Overton County until October 1861. The Twenty-fifth Tennessee skirmished with home guards and Federal troops along the Kentucky border, making one raid into Albany to capture arms and ammunition. This action was intended to provide safety for Overton County citizens, who were worried about attacks from the Federal troops in Kentucky.

The Twenty-fifth Regiment left Tennessee for Kentucky in October 1861, moving along the Tennessee-Kentucky border toward Camp Beech Grove near Mill Springs and Fishing Creek. Near Tompkinsville they burned camps of the home guards, "including Fraims, the Mud camps, the Moore camp, and the Burkesville camp, and also the Albany camp."[12] Gen. S. B. Buckner complimented Stanton on the actions of his regiment during the march: "Your dispatch is received and contains very satisfactory intelligence. Please compliment your troops on their good conduct. I doubt not, from the manner in which they have already borne themselves, that their campaign will be a successful one."[13]

The unit was to be part of Gen. Albert Sidney Johnston's army. Johnston was recognized as one of the nation's most capable generals, and Stanton was pleased to be under his command. Brig. Gen. Felix Zollicoffer requested control of the Twenty-fifth Tennessee, a move Stanton opposed. When Zollicoffer complained about Stanton's fierce opposition, Stanton wrote Johnston asking for clarification regarding his status and the composition of his troops: "We are proud to be under your command and will cheerfully obey all your orders strictly. . . . I hope at least that if your last order (which I have not yet seen) does not define the nature and extent of my command, that you will soon forward to me such information in that regard as you may think proper."[14] The regiment had at this time about 683 men on duty, out of 949 on the regiment roll, and Zollicoffer desperately wanted such a force. He may have heard of the unit's success on its march to Kentucky. The general was advised in November that Stanton would be under his command.

Stanton then complained to General Johnston that his regiment was ill equipped. He explained that his soldiers each had only about four rounds of cartridges: "It will be indispensably necessary that about 12,000 musket cartridges and 5,000 rifle cartridges be sent at once from Nashville to my regiment. . . . We have no Government wagons at all and have to hire and press into the service ox and all other sorts of inferior teams."[15] In addition, the regiment had not been paid for months: "My regiment, although mustered into service more than three months ago, has not received a dime's pay, neither officers nor privates, and their clothes (only one suit each) are well-night [*sic*] worn out (inferior at first). They have but one light, small blanket, each, weather getting cold, no money to clothe themselves with; . . . I hope you will see that they are soon to be visited with means of relief."[16]

No record exists to indicate whether Stanton's requests were satisfied, but, on November 15, the Twenty-fifth Tennessee Regiment arrived at Camp Beech Grove near Mill Springs, Kentucky. Two months later, the regiment was engaged in the Battle of Mill Springs (or Fishing Creek) against Gen. George Thomas's ten-thousand-man army. On January 19, Gen. George Crittenden's poorly equipped force of about sixty-five hundred troops attacked the larger Union force. Stanton's regiment of General Zollicoffer's brigade was in the first line of attack. Conditions were miserable. Poor visibility owing to the early hour and a driving rain along with inadequate training slowed the Confederate assault. Chaos and confusion reigned on the battlefield. The Confederate Fifteenth Mississippi Regiment mistook the Union Fourth Kentucky Regiment for a Rebel unit. General Zollicoffer also mistook the Fourth Kentucky for a Confederate outfit, and he was killed instantly by Union fire. Colonel Stanton suffered a severe wound in his arm, but he continued to lead the charge until Zollicoffer was killed. The Confederate left flank began to crumble with Zollicoffer's death, and Stanton led a counterattack to gain time for the other forces to regroup and recover Zollicoffer's body. By ten o'clock, the entire Confederate line had collapsed and fallen back to Camp Beech Grove, abandoning cannon, animals, food supplies, and wounded men. The dismal retreat under General Crittenden terminated in Gainesboro, Tennessee, eighty-five miles south. In addition to Stanton's wounded arm, the Twenty-fifth Regiment had suffered fifty-five casualties; the entire Confederate army had about three hundred killed and wounded. Although Stanton and his men had acted courageously and fought bravely in their first major action, the results of their efforts were disheartening. The reasons for this Confederate disaster were numerous and are not the topic of this essay. Stanton's reaction to this catastrophe is unknown, but the losses must have weighed heavily on him.

In February 1862, the Twenty-fifth Tennessee moved to Livingston, then to Murfreesboro. As the Battle of Shiloh was shaping up, Stanton's regiment was ordered into Mississippi to guard a railroad out of Corinth. The Twenty-fifth took no direct part at Shiloh, the first major bloodbath of the western theater.

Mississippi was perhaps the low point of Stanton's military career. In an engagement on Farmington Road on May 28, the Twenty-fifth Tennessee Regiment was under the command of Gen. Patrick Cleburne in Gen. P. G. T. Beauregard's army. The Twenty-fifth was repeatedly ordered to advance in this action, but, according to Cleburne, Stanton failed to comply. Stanton suffered no disciplinary action except Cleburne's rebuke.[17] The regiment moved to Tupelo in the summer, and there Stanton engaged in a dispute with the brigade commander, Gen. John Marmaduke, concerning a matter of discipline. The details of the disagreement are not known, but Stanton was ordered to the rear by the general. Stanton's fellow officer R. C. Sanders later said: "If he had a fault as a military man, . . . he was too kind-hearted to impose discipline upon his inferior officers and privates."[18] The altercation resulted in Stanton's and Sanders's resignations from the Twenty-fifth Tennessee Regiment.

Returning to his home in Tennessee, Stanton soon became restless. Gen. Braxton Bragg's Confederate army passed through White, Putnam, and Jackson counties on its way to Kentucky during the summer and autumn of 1862, prompting Stanton to act. In December, he went to McMinnville in Warren County to organize a new regiment, the Eighty-fourth Tennessee Infantry. Men from Smith, Warren, DeKalb, Overton, and Putnam counties made up the unit. Lt. Col. R. C. Sanders and Capt. W. Gooch Smith, Stanton's colleagues from the Twenty-fifth Tennessee, became his field officers in the Eighty-fourth. They had also resigned from the Twenty-fifth because of disagreements concerning discipline.

With very little training, the Eighty-fourth joined the Army of Tennessee on December 29 and became part of Gen. D. S. Donelson's brigade. Within the next twelve hours, the Battle of Murfreesboro (Stones River) began. General Bragg's outnumbered army was positioned on both sides of Stones River north of Murfreesboro. The Union general William S. Rosecrans's sizable army was advancing south from Nashville. Stanton's Eighty-fourth was positioned on the left flank of Bragg's army west of the river, where the attack against Rosecrans would take place.

Preparing frantically for the conflict, Stanton "drilled the regiment all day Tuesday, on the field, under the enemy's shells, and likewise Wednesday morning until the battle opened."[19] Because of its lack of training and experience, the Eighty-fourth acted in support of Captain Carnes's battery during the battle; however, in the middle of combat, the unit was directed to support Colonel Savage's Sixteenth Tennessee Regiment as it moved up to "the brick house."

At one critical point in the battle, Confederate troops were driven behind Stanton's regiment and began reforming. On receiving orders, Stanton moved forward to protect these units. He advanced some five hundred yards to a bend in the Stones River and halted on a bluff. Savage's regiment and the Twelfth Tennessee joined him, and there they waited for orders. Stanton's report indicated that his regiment "showed marked coolness and courage all the while, as they were under heavy shelling for a great portion of three days, and showed no fear or excitement. They kept good order and never scattered."[20] On the night of January 3, the Confederate army began withdrawing from Murfreesboro to assume strong positions along the Duck River.

Trouble once again visited Stanton after Murfreesboro. After the battle, he was ordered to the rear under arrest "on account of a personal difficulty or fight with a staff officer."[21] No additional details about this dispute are available, but this was the third altercation that Stanton had with a fellow officer. Lack of information prevents me from concluding any character traits or flaws of the colonel. Stanton was not disciplined after any of his three altercations, so we can conclude that none was serious.

Stanton rejoined his regiment, which was now in Shelbyville. The War Department ruled that the Eighty-fourth Regiment had been illegally organized, and, on March 8, 1863, the unit was consolidated with the Twenty-eighth Tennessee Regiment; Stanton was elected colonel of the consolidated regiment. Soldiers of the Twenty-eighth were men from Cumberland, Overton, Putnam, Wilson, Jackson, Smith, and White counties. The regiment had fought at Fishing Creek and Shiloh with Stanton's Twenty-fifth Tennessee.

In the summer of 1863, the regiment moved to Chattanooga with General Bragg's army. Bragg was forced out of Chattanooga in early September by General Rosecrans's threatened envelopment of the city; then Bragg failed on three attempts to attack and defeat portions of Rosecrans's army. By September 18, Rosecrans had concentrated his army on Chicamauga

Creek south of Chattanooga. The Federals had about fifty-eight thousand troops positioned against about sixty-six thousand Confederates.

On September 19, Bragg attacked. Confederates, including Stanton's regiment, crossed Chicamauga Creek in the morning and by noon were attacking the breastworks of the enemy: "My brave boys fired promptly at the command and moved forward a few paces, when they were ordered to fire and load lying down." After an hour, the regiment retreated about fifty yards, then moved forward again. Observing that the Federals were moving on the left flank, the Twenty-eighth received orders to counter this advance: "By this last movement the men were more fully exposed to the deadly fire of the enemy, and we were ordered to retire."[22]

Not reported by the colonel in his description of the battle to General Wright was an account of his own bravery. When the Twenty-eighth wavered and began its first retreat, Stanton "rushed to the front on horseback, seized the standard of the colors, and bearing them to the front, shouted for his men to follow, which they did in the most gallant manner, regaining the ground they had lost."[23] Stanton's flag was "riddled with ball," pierced more than thirty times. This addendum was signed by fourteen of Stanton's officers. As a result of this report, Colonel Stanton was cited for unusual bravery by General Cheatham.

Chickamauga was a tactical victory for the Confederacy, but the cost was frightful. Bragg had lost at least 28 percent of his troops, with about eighteen thousand casualties in the two-day battle. Six of the Confederate brigade commanders were killed or wounded. Stanton's regiment suffered a total loss of eighty-five—seventy wounded and fifteen dead.[24]

In November, the battle-hardened Twenty-eighth Tennessee was back in Chattanooga defending Missionary Ridge with Bragg's army. Gen. U. S. Grant was in command of the Federal troops. On November 25, Grant's troops moved in three sections against Bragg's forty thousand men on the ridge. The Union general George Thomas's troops in the center won the battle. Stanton's regiment "received orders to take position on high hill below the bridges, . . . to hold said hill as long as possible." The colonel did not report any action on that hill, and he received orders to evacuate about 11 P.M. In the retreat, Stanton was part of Gen. Lucius Polk's brigade, which covered the withdrawal.[25] Bragg lost sixty-seven thousand in the battle; Stanton had two or three slightly wounded. He commented that his men were "bold and fearless, willing to measure steel with the enemy."[26]

The Army of Tennessee now began its long and bloody retreat toward Atlanta. The hurried, chaotic nature of the movement was indicated by the fact that Stanton was four months late writing his report on the Battle of Missionary Ridge. The regiment wintered in Dalton, Georgia, although it journeyed to Demopolis, Alabama, and Atlanta during that period.

Resaca was the first battle of General Sherman's Atlanta Campaign, and it was the last battle for Colonel Stanton. Sherman attacked Joseph Johnston's troops near Resaca on May 14, 1864. The Oostanuala River was the point of contention in the battle. The crucial point was the Federals crossing the river near Calhoun, south of the Rebel forces.

Stanton's regiment was in the heat of the battle. Capt. W. L. Woods was wounded, a ball entering his mouth and shattering one side of his jaw-bone. A ball entered below the right ear of Lieutenant Rogers and exited near his left eye. Both men lived to fight again. Stanton was not so lucky. On May 14, he was standing on a log directing a line of skirmishers when a piece of shell struck his head.[27] His burial place is unknown, although the General Assembly directory lists the cemetery at "Colhoune" (Calhoun) as the site.[28] Lt. George Dillon of the Eighteenth Tennessee Regiment noted that Stanton's death was mourned by the entire army. Another of Stanton's fellow officers commented: "It was a sad and depressing sight to see this good man and gallant soldier drop to his death."[29] About 450 other Confederates died in the battle.

During his long career in the Confederate military, Sidney Stanton fought in six major battles. He was always cited for bravery, never for cowardice or indecisiveness. Fourteen officers signed for him a commendation for bravery on the battlefield at Chickamauga. He was respected by the men in his commands, as he was by his peers in the officer corps. Stanton served in three regiments, and he was elected commanding colonel in each of them. He must have possessed a strong personality and leadership qualities that inspired confidence.

Although on three occasions he had altercations with fellow officers, he was not disciplined on any occasion. As noted above, these disputations were in the heat of battle, so they may have been misunderstandings. They also may indicate an independence of mind, a trait not encouraged in the military.

Sidney Smith Stanton, like thousands of other soldiers, never returned home after the Civil War. A promising political figure in the antebellum period, he was denied the opportunity to live the life he was supposed to live. Although it cannot be known what he might have accomplished had he survived the war, his political skills might have carried him far. Indeed, his political constituents had hoped that he would return to Tennessee after the war and run for governor. Stanton's abilities are perhaps best summed up by his friend, Lt. Col. R. C. Sanders: "Col. Sidney Smith Stanton was a man of talent and genius not surpassed by any man in the state. . . . He possessed every quality of mind and soul necessary to endear him to the people—warmhearted and generous to a fault."[30]

Notes

1. Richard F. Cooke, "Putnam County Survey Book, 1825–1839," Survey No. 325, Survey No. 520, photocopy, Tennessee Room, Putnam County Library, Cookeville, Tenn.

2. Some have suggested that Stanton's home was in Putnam or Smith County, but he represented Jackson County in the House and Jackson, Macon, and White counties in the Senate. So he lived in Jackson County. His family is listed in Jackson County in the 1860 census.

3. Earnest H. Boyd, "Col. Sidney S. Stanton," special to the *Nashville Banner,* n.d., available through the Nashville public library.

4. After Cullom was defeated by Savage in the election, he was appointed clerk of the U.S. House of Representatives. Cullom invited Stanton to accompany him to Washington as his assistant. There Stanton learned valuable lessons in politics, oratory, and lawmaking.

5. *Republican Banner and Nashville Whig,* April 14, 1861. This was the same day that the firing on Fort Sumter was reported in the newspaper.

6. *Senate Journal of the Second Extra Session of the 33rd General Assembly* (1861), 14, Tennessee State Library and Archives, Nashville.

7. *Republican Banner and Nashville Whig,* May 8, 1861. The *Banner* reported a meeting in Jackson County on April 27 that had commended Senator Stanton and Representative Kenner for "their devotion to Southern rights" (*Republican Banner and Nashville Whig,* May 4, 1861).

8. *Senate Journal,* 83–91.

9. Ibid., 75, 156–57.

10. R. C. Sanders, "Twenty-fifth Tennessee Infantry," in *Military Annals of Tennessee: Confederate, First Series, Embracing a Review of Military Operations, with Regimental Histories and Memorial Rolls,* ed. John B. Lindsley (Nashville: J. M. Lindsley, 1886), 406.

11. Ibid., 401.

12. U.S. War Department, *The War of the Rebellion: A Compilation of the Official Records of the Union and Confederate Armies, 1861–1865* (hereafter cited as *OR*), 70 vols. in 128 pts. (Washington, D.C.: U.S. Government Printing Office, 1880–1901), ser. 1, vol. 52, pt. 2, pp. 182–83.

13. Ibid.

14. Ibid.

15. Ibid.

16. Ibid.

17. *Tennesseans in the Civil War: A Military History of Confederate and Union Units with Available Rosters of Personnel,* 2 vols. (Nashville: Civil War Centennial Commission, 1964–1965), 1:227.

18. Sanders, "Twenty-fifth Tennessee Infantry," 406. Sanders, Stanton's lieutenant colonel, said that Stanton was "entirely exculpated from the charges" of Marmaduke. Ibid., 405.

19. *OR,* ser. 1, vol. 20, pt. 1, pp. 720–21.

20. Ibid.

21. Ibid.

22. *OR,* ser. 1, vol. 30, pt. 2, pp. 125–27.

23. Ibid., 80, 125–27.

24. Maj. W. G. Smith reported a loss of 230 men killed and wounded. Smith "received a severe shock from the bursting of a shell, his horse being shot from under him." See *Military Annals of Tennessee,* 430.

25. *OR,* ser. 1, vol. 31, pt. 2, pp. 714–15.

26. Ibid.

27. 1st Lt. Spencer B. Talley, Twenty-eighth Regiment, "Memoirs, from Dalton to Atlanta," pt. 4, www.tennessee-scv.org/talleyA.html. Lieutenant Colonel Sanders said that Stanton "was shot through the breast and fell dead upon the field." See *Military Annals of Tennessee,* 405.

28. Robert M. McBride and Dan M. Robison, *Biographical Directory of the Tennessee General Assembly,* 6 vols. (Nashville: Tennessee State Library and Archives, 1975–1991), 1:694. Lieutenant Colonel Sanders agreed that Stanton "was buried in the cemetery at Calhoun, Georgia." See *Military Annals of Tennessee,* 405. It has also been suggested that he was buried in Resaca or Griffin, Georgia. His widow was reportedly too impoverished to bring his body back to Tennessee. His son Sidney Saunders traveled to Resaca in 1917 looking for his father's grave but could not find it.

29. Talley, "Memoirs, from Dalton to Atlanta."

30. Sanders, "Twenty-fifth Tennessee Infantry," 405–6. Martha Apple Stan-

ton remarried John C. Smith. She died in 1905 at age sixty-nine and is buried in the Granville Cemetery. One of the three Stanton children, Sidney Saunders was raised by the colonel's brother Layton. Sidney Saunders became a well-known and respected merchant in Cookeville. He died in 1932. Little is known of the other children, Bascom and Alma.

The Failure of Restoration

Wartime Reconstruction in Tennessee, 1862–1865

Jonathan M. Atkins

Tennessee's experience under a Confederate state government proved short. In June 1861, voters approved the state's "Declaration of Independence" and membership in the Confederacy. Only eight months later, after the surrender of Fort Donelson to the Union general Ulysses S. Grant on February 16, 1862, the state government abandoned Nashville just before the Confederate army evacuated the city. While Gen. Don Carlos Buell's army followed up Grant's victory and occupied the capital, the Tennessee General Assembly reconvened in Memphis. With additional Union forces moving into West Tennessee, however, lawmakers and state officials scattered. On March 20, Tennessee's Confederate legislature adjourned for good. Confederate troops continued to occupy East Tennessee for another eighteen months, but, throughout the state, civilian government collapsed.

The disintegration of Confederate authority in Tennessee presented President Abraham Lincoln with an opportunity to establish the process for a state's readmission to the Union. He had declared the restoration of the seceded states to the Union to be the purpose of the war. But how reunion would be carried out and whether the president or Congress would be ultimately responsible for ensuring a state's loyalty were questions for which there were no simple answers. To Lincoln, restoring pro-Union governments in the rebellious states appeared the most straightforward way to accomplish the war's objective. Taking the initiative, he moved to secure a quick restoration of Tennessee's civil government, one led by elected officials who accepted the authority of the U.S. Constitution. Restoring Union authority in Tennessee could provide a model for the readmission of all the Confederate states, a model that might convince the enemy to accept the president's generosity and give up the fight.

Lincoln approached reunion convinced that the mass of the white population in Tennessee and the other Confederate states remained, at heart, loyal to the Union. Secession had occurred because an extremist minority took advantage of the political controversy over slavery's expansion into new territories. Demonizing the Republican Party, Southern "Fire-Eaters" had used emotional and demagogic charges after the 1860 presidential election to persuade the loyal majority that Lincoln's administration would attack slavery and Southern rights. Once the South saw the folly of its attempt to win independence and recognized that his presidency would not threaten slavery in the states, Lincoln believed, the majority would be willing to assert itself and bring the states back under Union authority.[1]

From this viewpoint, Lincoln considered Tennessee ripe for reunion. The state appeared to have a particularly strong Unionist base on which to rebuild its government. It was one of the few Southern states where the antebellum Whig Party remained influential; during the secession crisis, most Southern Whigs had been either Unionists or the most reluctant to secede. In the 1860 presidential election, Tennessee had cast its electoral votes for the former Whig John Bell, the candidate of the Constitutional Union Party. Following the secession of the Lower South states, Tennessee voters, in a referendum held in February, rejected calling their own secession convention. After the conflict at Fort Sumter, Governor Isham G. Harris played on the emotional response to the battle to whip up hostility toward the North and drive the "Declaration of Independence" through the legislature. But, in the June referendum, almost one-third of the voters still rejected disunion. Though Bell himself accepted separation, several of Tennessee's most prominent figures continued to voice their loyalty.[2] Now, with the Confederate army fleeing the state, Lincoln expected the majority to recognize its errors and join with die-hard Unionists to return the state to the Union.

To oversee this process, Lincoln turned to the Tennessee Unionist best known outside the state. On March 4, 1862—only nine days after

Nashville's occupation—he appointed Andrew Johnson the state's military governor, with the rank of brigadier general. Johnson seemed the obvious choice. During the 1850s, he served two terms as Tennessee's governor, followed by his election to the Senate in 1857. Midway through an otherwise undistinguished term, Johnson refused to resign from the Senate when Tennessee withdrew from the Union, making him the only Southern member of Congress not to go with his state. Since then, he had made a name for himself denouncing secession in the Senate and touring Ohio and Kentucky to encourage military action to liberate Tennessee. Johnson's unwavering Unionism made him a popular figure throughout the North. The Senate unanimously confirmed his appointment on March 9, and Johnson headed for Nashville commissioned to govern Tennessee "during the pleasure of the President, or until the loyal inhabitants of that state shall organize a civil government in conformity with the Constitution of the United States."[3]

Unionists in Nashville had their doubts about the new governor. Most Tennessee Unionists had been Whigs; Johnson was and remained a Democrat, and, in state politics, he had been one of the most uncompromising partisans. While they applauded his stand during the secession crisis, state Unionists knew that blustering and grandstanding characterized the governor's politics more than constructive action or bipartisan cooperation. Prior to the war, Lincoln had indicated that he would rely on Senator Johnson's recommendations when making appointments to federal offices in Tennessee, and, in the brief time he could make these recommendations, Johnson showed that he would favor fellow Democrats. Also, Johnson hailed from Greeneville in the East Tennessee mountains and had built his career condemning slaveholding "aristocrats" in the western parts of the state. The bulk of the state's potential Unionist voters likewise could be found among East Tennessee's small farmers, who had rejected disunion in the June 1861 referendum by a two-to-one margin. At present, however, East Tennessee remained under Confederate occupation. Aside from being Whigs, the Middle and West Tennessee loyalists with whom Johnson would mainly be working were a distinct minority in their home regions, often came from the ranks of slaveholding planters, and had long been irritated by Johnson's populist, antiplanter appeals. His harsh rhetoric condemning secession frightened some Unionists, who thought that Johnson's presence alone would discourage Confederates from returning to the Union fold. At worst, many feared, he might use his authority mainly to punish his enemies and advance his own political ambitions.[4]

In spite of their concerns, Unionists had no alternative but to work with Johnson. To their relief, the new governor opened his administration with an emphasis on conciliation. General Buell warned him not to expect to be "received with enthusiasm," but Johnson, like Lincoln, thought Tennessee's Confederates to be either covert Unionists or temporarily misled. Two days after his arrival in the city, he declared before a crowd in front of his hotel that he came "with no hostile purpose"; instead, he returned to Tennessee "with the olive branch in one hand and the Constitution in the other." Five days later, on March 18, he issued a proclamation explaining that, as military governor, he was to provide law and order, to protect private property, and "as speedily as may be, to restore her government to the same condition as before the existing rebellion." Over the next several weeks, he arranged a series of mass meetings in occupied towns in Middle Tennessee to encourage the population's latent Unionism to express itself. These meetings culminated at a May 12 event in Nashville chaired by the Mexican War hero and former Whig governor William B. Campbell. In a three-hour-long speech, Johnson stated that his stand for the Union with Campbell was one of the proudest moments of his life. He promised to welcome back any Confederate who pledged his loyalty, though he would still punish the "leading traitors, who have drenched the land with blood."[5]

To Johnson's disappointment, white Tennesseans did not rush to proclaim their loyalty. Instead, the governor's determination to quash treason confirmed for most that the Union army came, not as a "liberator," but as an invading force. Once in the capital, Johnson replaced the city council when its members refused to take an oath of allegiance. He then ordered the arrest of the mayor and several prominent citizens, including the former governor Neill S. Brown and Johnson's recent Senate colleague A. O. P. Nicholson. Warrants were issued to post commanders to imprison secession leaders in occupied regions elsewhere in the state. Confederate newspapers were suppressed, Bank of Tennessee officials were arrested for accepting Confederate currency, and ministers who advocated resistance were either arrested or banished to Confederate lines.[6] These actions outraged the occupied population. Prior to the new governor's arrival, Buell had adopted a lenient policy toward Nashville's population, which military commanders believed had softened the resistance. Johnson's aggression, officers complained, destroyed the foundation they had laid for renewing the public's allegiance. Military leaders probably overestimated the effect of their leniency, but the weakness of the Union cause became apparent only ten days after Johnson's and Campbell's May 12 Unionist meeting. Reluctantly, the governor agreed to go ahead with a scheduled election for a Davidson County circuit court judge. Many Unionists probably failed to vote because they assumed that the election was unauthorized, but the result nevertheless embarrassed Johnson when a pro-Confederate defeated the Unionist candidate. Johnson commissioned the winner, then arrested him for treason and installed the Unionist in his place.[7]

Just as the apparent demise of the Confederacy led many white Tennesseans to accept Union authority, the revival of the Confederacy's military prospects strengthened resistance. When Johnson assumed the governorship, the Rebel army had retreated toward Mississippi. To stop General Grant's army as it moved up the Tennessee River, Confederates launched a surprise attack near Pittsburg Landing in early April 1862. The resulting Battle of Shiloh failed to push back Grant's force, while, farther west, the Union navy established control of the Mississippi River. With the fall of Memphis on June 9, West and Middle Tennessee appeared safely in Union hands.[8] In Memphis, more than three thousand people reportedly took a loyalty oath within three weeks after the city's fall.[9] By late summer, however, Confederate cavalry raids were harassing the supposedly secure regions. One raid almost captured Johnson after he spoke at a Union rally in Murfreesboro, only thirty miles south of Nashville. Then, in August, the Confederate generals Braxton Bragg and Edmund Kirby Smith launched invasions into Kentucky from East Tennessee. By October, the Confederate offensives had stalled, but Bragg withdrew to Murfreesboro and occupied the southern portion of Middle Tennessee. Though the Kentucky Campaign had failed, the offensive revived hope for Confederate success. In areas under Union control, guerrilla resistance increased; the public, meanwhile, showed little interest in affirming loyalty to the Union.[10]

The renewed military threat worsened the already tense relations between Tennessee's military governor and the local Union command. Since his arrival, Johnson had bickered with General Buell over a number of issues, the disagreements stemming mainly from the confusion over whether the military governor or the field commander was the final authority in the state. Johnson too expected the soldiers to support his work to revive Tennessee's civil government, while Buell—a career officer who, as a major general, outranked Johnson—led his troops as part of the larger Union effort to destroy the Confederacy. Buell usually disregarded Johnson's directives. At one point, he briefly left Nashville virtually defenseless when he took his army out of the state to assist in the defense of Kentucky. Lincoln, however, most often sided with Johnson when the governor asked him to intervene in a dispute, thus strengthening Johnson's hand in the state. But, at the same time, Lincoln pressed Johnson throughout 1862 to hold elections, despite the Confederate presence in the state. "If we could somehow, get a vote of the people of Tennessee and have it result properly," the president wrote in July, "it would be worth more to us than a battle gained."[11]

Without control of the Union stronghold in East Tennessee, however, the governor could not guarantee the proper result. A late-1862 attempt to hold an election for a congressional representative from West Tennessee revealed the difficulties facing a quick restoration. Thinking the region firmly under Union control, Johnson issued a proclamation announcing that the election would be held on December 29. Confederate cavalry raids caused enough disruption to postpone the contest until early January. Although the Unionist candidate won, only about nineteen hundred voters turned out, about 10 percent of the district's voters in 1860. With so few voters, Johnson decided not to certify the results, and Congress rejected the winner's attempt to take his seat. Frustrated, Johnson informed Lincoln that he could not proceed with an election to restore civil government until the Rebel army had been completely and permanently expelled from the state.[12]

Tennessee's leading Unionists supported Johnson through the first year of his military governorship, despite their initial reservations. But, toward the year's end, their loyalty faced a new challenge as President Lincoln moved to expand the war and attack the institution of slavery. At its outset, Lincoln stressed that the purpose of the war was to preserve the Union, not to abolish slavery. As a result, early in the war he dealt carefully with the institution, hoping that its preservation might encourage Southerners to lay down their arms while avoiding giving the four slave states still in the Union any reason to join the Confederacy. By the summer of 1862, however, Lincoln became convinced that the threat of ending slavery or the prospect of slave uprisings might further the Union cause. Thus, on September 22, 1862, the president issued his preliminary Emancipation Proclamation, announcing that, on January 1, 1863, he would declare free the slaves in any state still in rebellion.[13]

Lincoln's move toward emancipation disturbed Tennessee's Unionists. None had ever called for an end to slavery. Many, in fact, had opposed secession because they believed that slavery would be better protected if Tennessee remained in the Union. They always expected Tennessee to resume its place in the Union with slavery intact. Now, since Tennessee technically still was in rebellion, the state faced the prospect of having slavery abolished by Lincoln's proclamation. To avoid this fate, in late December William B. Campbell led a movement to petition the president to exempt Tennessee from the decree. The petition convinced Lincoln that the proclamation would have a negative effect on the state, so, in the proclamation's final version, he omitted Tennessee from the list of areas in rebellion where the slaves were to be freed.[14] Emancipation nevertheless became a more pressing concern through 1863. Lincoln increasingly pressured the Union's remaining slave states to implement emancipation programs, while the open recruitment of black soldiers after the issuance of the Emancipation Proclamation further linked antislavery with Union victory. Within Tennessee, the occupying army weakened the institution when it encouraged slave insubordination, provided a refuge for runaways, and impressed slave labor. Meanwhile, African Americans themselves began to assert their political presence. During the summer, slaves and free blacks held their own public meetings and demonstrations in Nashville and Memphis to demand freedom for their people.[15]

Some Unionists, mostly exiles from East Tennessee like Governor Johnson, moved toward supporting abolition. Johnson himself was a slave owner and signed Campbell's petition to exempt Tennessee from the Emancipation Proclamation. Like the vast majority of white Americans, he accepted black inferiority and had little concern for the plight of the slaves. Still, he appeared genuinely disturbed by the war's destructiveness and the persistence of the rebellion. Since slavery provided the foundation for the wealth of the planter aristocrats he blamed for secession, he agreed that attacking slavery would weaken the Confederate military effort. Personally, too, he understood that an antislavery stance might further his chances to advance in a Republican-dominated national government. As early as April, the Nashville Union Club, which had formed in January to support the governor, called for depriving Confederates of slave property. The strength of resistance, along with his own doubts about black abilities, made Johnson hesitate to come out openly for abolition. Still, by mid-1863, he and his followers, most notably Congressman Horace Maynard and the Knoxville editor William G. Brownlow, were being referred to as *Radicals* because they warned that emancipation might become necessary if the rebellion continued.[16]

Johnson's drift toward antislavery frightened other Unionists, mainly from Middle and West Tennessee, who were coming to be called *Conservatives.* For most, their loyalty to the Union never wavered. Predominantly Whigs and slaveholders, however, they believed that keeping slavery was essential to maintaining social order. They also held firm to the belief—taken for granted before the war—that slavery's fate should be determined by a state government, not imposed by an outside mandate. The institution's survival in four Union states demonstrated for them that, in the words of the historian John Cimprich, "the best protection against federal interference with slavery was in a unionist state government."[17] Thus, led most visibly by Campbell and the former congressmen Emerson Etheridge and Balie Peyton, Conservatives now demanded the immediate establishment of a Unionist government in Tennessee. In midsummer, once Confederate forces had been pushed back from Middle Tennessee and cavalry raids in West Tennessee had temporarily halted, Conservatives urged Johnson to call a convention to reestablish the state government. When Johnson proved reluctant, fourteen Unionists published a letter on June 23, 1863, calling for local meetings to elect delegates to a convention to restore the state's connection "with the Federal Union as it stood prior to the rebellion." When the convention met on July 1, more than two hundred delegates from forty-three counties attended. Middle and West Tennesseans insisted that the convention bypass Johnson and authorize elections for state offices and congressional representatives on August 4, the scheduled date for the state elections according to the suspended state constitution.[18]

East Tennessee delegates refused to go along with a plan that could embarrass Johnson. After a bitter argument, the convention resolved to declare its support for Johnson while asking the governor to authorize the August election, but only for a state legislature. Several Conservatives remained unsatisfied, especially after Johnson refused to approve the legislative elections. Rejecting Johnson's decision, Etheridge, who in the early months of the war had gained some influence with Republicans in Washington, led an effort to hold an election for a new governor. His efforts managed to organize only two counties, which, on August 4, cast about twenty-five hundred votes to elect Campbell as the state's civil governor. Etheridge personally appealed to President Lincoln to accept the election's results and replace Johnson with Campbell, but, with so few votes cast, Lincoln had no trouble rejecting an election that clearly represented a minority's repudiation of his appointed governor.[19]

Etheridge's failed election instead convinced Johnson that more drastic measures would be needed to secure Tennessee's loyalty. Since Conservatives were willing to bypass him to prevent emancipation, he feared that, after the war, they would join with former Confederates to produce a government that would be hostile to Lincoln's administration and to East Tennessee's Unionists. When the opportunity finally came to reestablish the state government, he would have to take precautions to prevent this outcome. There now appeared to be no greater test of absolute loyalty to Lincoln's Union than unconditional acceptance of slavery's abolition, so, only two and half weeks after Etheridge's attempted election, Johnson came out openly for emancipation. In a speech delivered at Franklin, he labeled slavery a "cancer on our society" and proposed to end the institution "immediately" by adopting an amendment to the state's constitution. "The slave aristocracy had long held their feet upon [our] necks," the governor declared. "Let the era of freedom henceforth be proclaimed to the non-slaveholders of Tennessee!"[20]

Johnson's speech showed that his willingness to end slavery did not include a call for black equality. Radicals instead emphasized that slavery's end would liberate Tennessee's nonslaveholding whites and help defeat the Confederacy by destroying the institution that propped up the South's aristocracy. Also, the governor's proposal to abolish the institution was less drastic than it first appeared, for emancipation through a constitutional amendment could not come until two years after the revival of the state government: according to the suspended state constitution, an amendment required passage by two consecutive state legislatures followed by approval in a popular referendum. But Johnson and his followers were now committed to returning Tennessee to the Union as a state without slavery. For Conservatives, the dangerous implications of the Radical position became apparent a few weeks later when the governor agreed to cooperate with the army's attempts to recruit black soldiers in the state, even though he had resisted earlier recruiting efforts.[21]

The breach between Conservatives and Johnson's Radicals appeared irreparable just as the reorganization of Tennessee's government seemed imminent. In June 1863, Gen. William Rosecrans, who the previous October had succeeded Buell as the commander of Union forces in Nashville, finally moved to pursue Braxton Bragg's army, which occupied Tullahoma after the Battle of Stones River near Murfreesboro in January. Bragg retreated to Georgia, but, after his men held off Rosecrans's troops at Chickamauga, the Confederates laid siege to the Union army at Chattanooga. After General Grant replaced Rosecrans, the army broke out of the siege in November and chased Bragg's soldiers out of Tennessee. Meanwhile, Gen. Ambrose Burnside led twenty-four thousand men into East Tennessee and occupied Knoxville in September after Confederate forces abandoned the city. A small force under Gen. James Longstreet continued to harass East Tennessee until May 1864, while a brutal guerrilla conflict broke out in the mountains between Union and Confederate supporters. Nevertheless, by January 22, 1864, it appeared that all Tennessee was under Union authority for the first time since the war began.[22]

Lincoln again wasted no time pushing Johnson to act. In September, after Bragg first withdrew from Tennessee, the president reminded the governor that "not a moment should be lost" to establish a loyal government—under "such men as can be trusted for the Union" and with emancipation added to the state constitution.[23] Three months later, with the Confederacy's prospects increasingly bleak, Lincoln issued his "Proclamation of Amnesty and Reconstruction" outlining his plan for returning the Confederate states to the Union. In this proclamation, the president offered a full pardon and the restoration of all rights—except in slave property—to all Confederates who took an oath of future loyalty to the Union. High-ranking Confederate officials could not claim amnesty, but, once the oath had been taken by 10 percent of the number of the state's voters who had participated in the 1860 presidential election, Tennessee could form a new state government, which, after abolishing slavery, could ask to be represented in Congress. Lincoln hoped that his offer of amnesty might convince the remaining Confederates to give up their fight. But he still hoped that Tennessee would be one of the first states to follow his guidelines and provide a model for other rebellious states.[24]

Unionists began taking Lincoln's oath as soon as an agent from Washington arrived to administer it. Meetings in Nashville and Memphis meanwhile began calling for Johnson to implement Lincoln's plan in Tennessee. But Johnson hesitated. Like many Republicans in Congress, the governor feared that Lincoln's offer might be too lenient, and the strength of Conservative resistance to emancipation convinced him that, without further precautions, a general amnesty would leave enemies of the Union—as well as of the administration—in control of Tennessee. Thus, when he finally announced the process for reconstructing the state government, he emphasized, not amnesty, but the need to exorcise Confederate sympathy from the state. At a Union rally on January 21, 1864, the governor declared: "Treason must be made odious, [and] traitors must be punished and impoverished." Rebel leaders, he added, "ought to be hung [*sic*]." He then proposed holding elections for county officials, after which a statewide convention could schedule elections for a new government. But now Johnson called for this convention to bypass the state constitution's amendment process and formally end slavery immediately, and he indicated that those participating in elections should take a stricter oath than the one Lincoln required. Five days later, when Johnson issued a proclamation providing for elections for county judges, sheriffs, and court clerks on March 5, he stipulated that voters had to swear, not just future loyalty, but that they "ardently desire the suppression of the present insurrection and rebellion" and would "hereafter aid and assist all loyal people in the accomplishment of these results."[25]

Conservatives immediately denounced Johnson's proclamation. Most had taken Lincoln's oath at the earliest opportunity. Now, they charged, Johnson had added an illegal condition to the president's reconstruction process, mainly to keep himself and his friends in power. They were offended by the implication in Johnson's oath that they had not supported the Union from the war's beginning, while they expected the requirement to "ardently desire" the Confederacy's defeat to keep defeated Rebels from accepting reunion. Conservatives wrote to Lincoln to protest Johnson's proclamation. After meeting with Johnson in Washington in February, however, the president endorsed his governor, writing to one Nashville Unionist that he was "entirely satisfied" with Johnson's plan.[26] Most Conservatives refused to participate in the March 5 elections, but the results were respectable nonetheless. More than forty thousand votes were cast, and local government was reestablished in two-thirds of the state's counties.[27] Still, Conservative resentment remained strong. Not all the new local officers were committed to keeping Johnson's Radicals in power, and, if the governor called a state convention, his opponents would most likely dominate the meeting and reject emancipation.[28]

With uncertain support, and with the state still subject to occasional Confederate raids, Johnson continued to delay Tennessee's reconstruction. Meanwhile, he turned his attention to the upcoming presidential election. Lincoln's and Johnson's claim that Tennessee had never legally left the Union might be more widely accepted if the state participated in the election. The president's reelection would, in turn, strengthen his administration's supporters. And the election might further Johnson's personal ambitions. Major Union offensives in Virginia and Georgia appeared to have stalled, so Lincoln expected to face a strong challenge to his reelection from the likely Democratic nominee, Gen. George B. McClellan. In the spring, Lincoln apparently explored available Union Democrats as possible vice presidential candidates, whose presence on the ticket would allow Lincoln to run as a "Union Party" candidate and have more widespread support than he could as a Republican nominee. Among possible vice presidents, Johnson appeared particularly attractive. In spite of his detractors in Tennessee, the governor remained popular in the North, and Tennessee's electoral votes might be necessary to help Lincoln win a close election against McClellan. Aware that he was under consideration for the nomination, Johnson in May encouraged his supporters to select delegates to attend the Republicans' "National Union Convention" in Baltimore. Meetings in each section of the state chose a delegation committed to supporting Lincoln and Johnson. The convention welcomed Tennessee's delegates and, on June 8, nominated Johnson for the vice presidency.[29]

Johnson then moved to make sure the presidential election would be carried out in Tennessee—and that the result would support the Lincoln-Johnson ticket. The Republican/Union platform openly endorsed emancipation. Emphasizing once again their rejection of black equality, Radicals contended that ending slavery would free the South from the leadership of the slave aristocracy and benefit Southern whites more than it would blacks. Conservatives, meanwhile, organized to support

McClellan. Calling themselves the *Constitutional Union* Party to revive the moderate Unionist appeal of 1860, they rejected the contention that the war had so damaged slavery that it could not be preserved. Instead, they protested that emancipation was being forced on the state against the majority's will. The Conservatives' appeal seemed to enjoy widespread support, so Johnson took no chances. His opponents attended yet another convention on September 5, this one called to determine officially how the election should be carried out, but they walked out when the Radical majority shouted down Conservatives when they tried to speak. The remaining delegates combined legal procedure with party activism. After recommending that the election be held on November 8, they endorsed Lincoln and Johnson and proposed that voters in the election be required to take an oath opposing "all armistices or negotiations for peace with rebel arms"—a direct repudiation of McClellan's call for a negotiated peace. Three weeks later, on September 30, Johnson issued a proclamation endorsing the convention's proscriptions. Persons of "established loyalty," as determined by the governor's appointed poll workers, could vote without restrictions, but all others had to take an oath that effectively disfranchised McClellan's supporters.[30]

Conservatives again condemned Johnson's heavy-handed governance. In response, the governor promoted emancipation even more aggressively. Calling up the state militia in September, Johnson specifically enrolled blacks as soldiers and used the troops to break up a pro-McClellan meeting in October. Civilian blacks joined in putting down this meeting and, in Nashville and Memphis, held their own rallies and parades to celebrate the advent of freedom. After one Nashville torchlight parade in late October, Johnson promised marchers that he would "be your Moses, and lead you through the Red Sea of war and bondage to a fairer future of liberty and peace."[31] Frustrated with Johnson's restrictions, ten Conservatives signed a letter asking President Lincoln to intervene. Once again, however, Lincoln refused to counter Johnson's policy, so Conservatives withdrew the McClellan ticket and refused to participate in the election. In November, 86 percent of about thirty-five thousand votes were cast for Lincoln and Johnson. Nashville blacks set up a mock polling place and cast more than thirty-four hundred ballots for the Union ticket. But, with Union forces again on the offensive in Virginia and Georgia, Tennessee's votes proved unnecessary to ensure Lincoln's reelection. Congress rejected Tennessee's electoral votes because it concluded the state was still in rebellion and could not hold a legitimate election.[32]

The election had given Lincoln's administration a national endorsement, and, with his own election to the vice presidency secured, Johnson moved quickly to end slavery immediately, revive the state government, and fully reintegrate Tennessee into the Union. As the East Tennessean Oliver P. Temple later wrote, the governor wanted "to carry to Washington his own State, as a reconstructed member of this Union, and present it as a rich jewel of the nation."[33] The past year's experience showed Johnson that the best way to ensure the new government's loyalty was to exclude from the process anyone who stood in his way. Prompted by the governor, East Tennessee Radicals formed a "Union Executive Committee"; on November 12—only four days after the presidential contest—this committee issued a call for a convention in Nashville to meet on December 19. The purpose of this convention would be to select delegates who, pending voter approval, would serve in the constitutional convention that the governor had proposed the previous January. The East Tennessee committee encouraged county meetings to select delegates, but it also suggested that individuals "come upon your own personal responsibility" if public meetings could not be held. Gen. John B. Hood's ill-fated invasion of Middle Tennessee and "siege" of Nashville—the last major Confederate military action in the state—prevented the convention from meeting until after the Union army had chased Hood's forces out of the state. When the convention finally opened on January 9, more than five hundred delegates were in attendance. More than half came from fourteen counties in East Tennessee. Many came voluntarily; others came appointed by meetings with limited or questionable popular support.[34]

In spite of its unbalanced representation and large proportion of self-selected members, the delegates unexpectedly transformed the meeting into a constitutional convention. A significant number of Conservatives attended, thinking that, as announced, the assembly would limit its actions to nominating candidates for a future convention. Shortly into the proceedings, however, a core of Radicals insisted that the current meeting should itself take on the responsibility of reconstructing the state. Other Radicals hesitated to take this step, so, for three days, the delegates argued over whether they had come together as a nominating or as a constitutional convention. Governor Johnson himself broke the deadlock. In a speech to the delegates, he declared that there was no need for another convention: the Confederacy no longer threatened Tennessee, so it was time to move forward and reestablish a government. The proceedings might be irregular, he conceded, but irregularities were sometimes necessary to save the Republic.[35]

Spurred on by Johnson, the Radical majority proceeded to act as a constitutional convention. Over Conservative protests, the delegates approved two constitutional amendments, one abolishing slavery in the state, the other prohibiting the legislature from passing any laws that recognized humans as property. After declaring null and void the state's withdrawal from the Union and membership in the Confederacy as well as any acts passed by the state government while under Confederate authority, the convention scheduled elections for a new governor and state legislature on March 4, the day Johnson would be inaugurated vice president. Since the possibility of guerrilla violence and the general state of lawlessness throughout Tennessee threatened to disrupt elections in several counties, the convention composed a general ticket of candidates to serve in a new legislature; voters would be asked merely to approve the convention's nominees, more than half of whom came from among the convention's own delegates. For governor, the convention nominated East Tennessee's most notorious Unionist, William G. Brownlow, whose vindictiveness toward the Confederacy exceeded even Andrew Johnson's. Before the election, the amendment abolishing slavery and the convention's other actions would be submitted to voters for their approval in a referendum held on George Washington's birthday, February 22. But, as in the recent presidential election, the vote should be limited to known unconditional Unionists and to those who took Johnson's stringent loyalty oath.[36]

The January 1865 convention thus effectively launched a coup d'état. The meeting had seized control of the process of Tennessee's reconstruction, imposed a government on the state, excluded the influence of the governor's opponents, and disfranchised Confederates who had renounced disunion even if their participation in the rebellion had been brief or under duress. After the convention adjourned, Johnson wrote Lincoln that "the tyrants [sic] rod has been broken," and, in a proclamation formally authorizing the convention's plans, he likened Tennessee's convention to the 1787 federal convention in Philadelphia, when delegates had likewise exceeded their instructions to write the U.S. Constitution. But Conservatives charged that Tennessee's convention had been more bent on vengeance than on reconciliation. Since the meeting had no authority to propose constitutional amendments or to schedule elections, the upcoming elections, they contended, were illegal. Their experience in the recent presidential election showed them that they could expect no help from Lincoln, so Conservatives knew that boycotting the election offered the only hope to thwart the Radicals' scheme. A low turnout would show that the Radicals' convention had only limited support and might compel the president to deny a government that was clearly being forced on the state. Radicals recognized this danger and called for a large turnout. "The moral effect of a heavy poll will be great," the *Nashville Daily Union* proclaimed. "The more numerous the votes, the more readily will the state government go into peaceful operation."[37]

The results disappointed both camps. Fewer voters participated than had cast ballots in the state's stillborn presidential election just a few months before. With Conservatives boycotting, the two constitutional amendments were ratified on February 22 by a vote of 25,293–48. Ten days later, even fewer voters endorsed the convention's gubernatorial and legislative candidates by a vote of 23,352–35. The vote did not produce the resounding mandate that the Radicals had hoped for. Nevertheless, the totals in both elections were more than 16 percent of the turnout in the 1860 presidential election and, thus, met Lincoln's ten percent requirement. On February 25, right before he left Nashville to be inaugurated vice president, Johnson issued a proclamation declaring the two amendments added to the state constitution. Edward H. East, his appointed secretary of state, certified the results of the March 4 election. The new state legislature convened on April 3, and, two days later, Brownlow was inaugurated Tennessee's new governor.[38]

Civil government in Tennessee had finally been reestablished. But it had taken three years, and it would take another year for Congress formally to readmit Tennessee to the Union. Moreover, the new government enjoyed only limited popular support. In Middle and West Tennessee, even loyalists rejected its legitimacy, so outside East Tennessee it needed the presence of the Union army to uphold its authority. Lincoln's goal for a quick restoration that would aid the Union cause had failed. Under Andrew Johnson's direction, the process of reviving the government not only had done little to promote reconciliation; it left a legacy of bitterness that overshadowed the state for years. Directed by Governor Brownlow, the legislature imposed on former Confederates harsh restrictions, including disfranchisement for five years. African Americans had gained freedom from slavery, and in 1867—when Brownlow needed their support to stay in power—they received the right to vote. Neither the state nor the federal government would make a commitment to full equality, however, so freedmen were left all but defenseless when Conservatives and Confederate veterans joined together to regain control of Tennessee in 1870.[39]

The effort to return Tennessee to the Union during the war showed the depth of the gulf that separated white Southerners from the Lincoln administration. The president and his military governor had miscalculated the strength of Union sentiment in the state. The mass of the white population in Middle and West Tennessee had not been misguided or coerced: they accepted disunion because they believed that Lincoln would attack Southern institutions, especially slavery. They might have been reluctant Confederates, but, once they chose to side with the South, they needed more than an offer of amnesty to bring them back into a Union led by the Republican Party.[40] Then, Lincoln's commitment to make the end of slavery a war objective convinced disunionists that his administration intended to revolutionize social relations in the state—a prospect they had feared even before the conflict had begun. Governor Johnson faced a difficult enough task trying to construct a Unionist state government on what one Northerner described as Tennessee's "molasses and water loyalty."[41] Emancipation introduced a more daunting challenge and all but destroyed any hope that white Tennesseans would accept a government led by unconditional Unionists.

Andrew Johnson's gradual shift from conciliator to the scourge of traitors likewise complicated and embittered the process. A less controversial, ambitious, and confrontational military governor might have produced a better result, for Johnson's heavy-handed and pugnacious administration alienated Unionists who might have been brought around to accept emancipation. Lincoln likewise deserves some of the blame, for he let politics dictate his appointment of Johnson and then backed the governor's most controversial decisions. Given the degree of hostility toward emancipation, however, it is questionable whether another governor with a different approach could have produced a better result. Shortly before his death, Lincoln himself appears to have reached this conclusion. Restoration had begun as an effort to shorten the conflict, while emancipation came about as part of a larger strategy to defeat the Confederacy. But, once he moved against slavery, Lincoln committed himself to eradicating the institution from the United States. Recognizing that state governments established during the war might not support this goal, he tentatively endorsed black voting—by soldiers and the "very intelligent"—and began considering a plan for the South's military occupation.[42] Unfortunately, Lincoln would not be the one to oversee postwar Reconstruction. An assassin's bullet instead assigned that task to Andrew Johnson, who remained committed to white supremacy and, as president, showed that he had learned little from his experience in wartime Tennessee.

Notes

1. William C. Harris, *With Charity for All: Lincoln and the Restoration of the Union* (Lexington: University Press of Kentucky, 1997), 19–20.

2. Jonathan M. Atkins, *Parties, Politics, and the Sectional Conflict in Tennessee, 1832-1861* (Knoxville: University of Tennessee Press, 1997), 215–61.

3. Hans L. Trefousse, *Andrew Johnson: A Biography* (New York: Norton, 1989), 152–54.

4. Ibid., 153; Peter Maslowski, *Treason Must Be Made Odious: Military Occupation and Wartime Reconstruction in Nashville, Tennessee, 1862-65* (Millwood, N.Y.: KTO, 1978), 21–22; James Welch Patton, *Unionism and Reconstruction in Tennessee, 1860-1869* (1934; reprint, Gloucester, Mass.: Peter Smith, 1966), 30–31.

5. Trefousse, *Andrew Johnson,* 155–56; Harris, *With Charity for All,* 43–48; Maslowski, *Treason Must Be Made Odious,* 23–26.

6. Trefousse, *Andrew Johnson,* 155–57; Harris, *With Charity for All,* 45–46; Maslowski, *Treason Must Be Made Odious,* 53–57; Thomas B. Alexander, *Political Reconstruction in Tennessee* (1950; reprint, New York: Russell & Russell, 1968), 15.

7. Trefousse, *Andrew Johnson,* 156–57; Harris, *With Charity for All,* 45; Patton, *Unionism and Reconstruction in Tennessee,* 36.

8. James M. McPherson, *Battle Cry of Freedom: The Civil War Era* (New York: Oxford University Press, 1988), 405–22.

9. Harris, *With Charity for All,* 48–49.

10. McPherson, *Battle Cry of Freedom,* 511–24, 561; Stephen V. Ash, *When the Yankees Came: Conflict and Chaos in the Occupied South, 1861-1865* (Chapel Hill: University of North Carolina Press, 1995), 46–49, 69–73.

11. Maslowski, *Treason Must Be Made Odious*, 20, 24–25, 38–44; Harris, *With Charity for All*, 41, 50–54; Trefousse, *Andrew Johnson*, 157–63.

12. Maslowski, *Treason Must Be Made Odious*, 79; Patton, *Unionism and Reconstruction in Tennessee*, 38; Trefousse, *Andrew Johnson*, 161.

13. David Herbert Donald, *Lincoln* (New York: Simon & Schuster, 1995), 362–74; McPherson, *Battle Cry of Freedom*, 502–4, 557–58.

14. John Cimprich, *Slavery's End in Tennessee, 1861–1865* (Tuscaloosa: University of Alabama Press, 1985), 101; Harris, *With Charity for All*, 54–56.

15. Cimprich, *Slavery's End in Tennessee*, 19–59; Maslowski, *Treason Must Be Made Odious*, 97–102; McPherson, *Battle Cry of Freedom*, 563–65.

16. David Warren Bowen, *Andrew Johnson and the Negro* (Knoxville: University of Tennessee Press, 1989), 45–104; Maslowski, *Treason Must Be Made Odious*, 81–83; Cimprich, *Slavery's End in Tennessee*, 99. The Radical faction in wartime Tennessee should not be confused with the Radical Republican Party in Congress, which called for harsh punishment of the South and, in the words of Eric Foner, "a far-reaching transformation of Southern society" that included African American citizenship and voting. Tennessee Radicals during the war accepted emancipation and the need to exclude former Confederates from the state government, but they did not favor either black civil rights or a dramatic social transformation. See Eric Foner, *Reconstruction: America's Unfinished Revolution, 1863–1877* (New York: Harper & Row, 1988), 36–37, 51–52; and Hans L. Trefousse, *The Radical Republicans: Lincoln's Vanguard for Racial Justice* (New York: Knopf, 1969).

17. Cimprich, *Slavery's End in Tennessee*, 102.

18. Harris, *With Charity for All*, 107–8; Patton, *Unionism and Reconstruction in Tennessee*, 39–40.

19. Lonnie E. Maness, "Emerson Etheridge and the Union," *Tennessee Historical Quarterly* 48 (Summer 1989): 101–3; Patton, *Unionism and Reconstruction in Tennessee*, 41–42; Harris, *With Charity for All*, 108–9.

20. Cimprich, *Slavery's End in Tennessee*, 103; Trefousse, *Andrew Johnson*, 167–69; Bowen, *Andrew Johnson and the Negro*, 105–7.

21. Alexander, *Political Reconstruction in Tennessee*, 29; Maslowski, *Treason Must Be Made Odious*, 102–7; Cimprich, *Slavery's End in Tennessee*, 82–87.

22. Robert E. Corlew, *Tennessee: A Short History*, 2nd ed. (Knoxville: University of Tennessee Press, 1981), 311–14; McPherson, *Battle Cry of Freedom*, 667–81; Harris, *With Charity for All*, 215.

23. Harris, *With Charity for All*, 110.

24. Foner, *Reconstruction*, 35–37; Harris, *With Charity for All*, 131–33.

25. Patton, *Unionism and Reconstruction in Tennessee*, 44; Trefousse, *Andrew Johnson*, 172–73.

26. Harris, *With Charity for All,* 214.

27. Ibid., 215.

28. Ibid., 214–15; Trefousse, *Andrew Johnson,* 173–74. Johnson attempted to build on the support he expected he would have in East Tennessee by asking Thomas A. R. Nelson to revive the Greeneville Convention. This convention had met immediately after the June 1861 referendum approving Tennessee's disunion to petition the state legislature to allow East Tennessee to remain in the Union as a separate state. Nelson had presided at the convention and was authorized to call it back into session. Even though Nelson opposed emancipation, Johnson hoped that the meeting could allow East Tennessee's Unionists to voice their support for abolition and the Radicals. This strategy backfired, however. While most Unionists in East Tennessee did appear willing to support the governor, the delegates to the convention had been selected in 1861. Conservatives were, thus, a strong presence when it met in Knoxville on April 12, and their demand for compensated emancipation divided the meeting. Radicals supported immediate emancipation, and, after four days of arguing, the delegates adjourned without taking any action. See Harris, *With Charity for All,* 215–17; Thomas B. Alexander, *Thomas A. R. Nelson of East Tennessee* (Nashville: Tennessee Historical Commission, 1956), 78–87, 114–15; and Charles F. Bryan, "A Gathering of Tories: The East Tennessee Convention of 1861," *Tennessee Historical Quarterly* 39 (Winter 1980): 27–48.

29. Donald, *Lincoln,* 493–507; Trefousse, *Andrew Johnson,* 176–79; Patton, *Unionism and Reconstruction in Tennessee,* 45–46.

30. Harris, *With Charity for All,* 219–21; Trefousse, *Andrew Johnson,* 181; Cimprich, *Slavery's End in Tennessee,* 106–8.

31. Cimprich, *Slavery's End in Tennessee,* 109–13; Trefousse, *Andrew Johnson,* 183–84.

32. Harris, *With Charity for All,* 221–23; Cimprich, *Slavery's End in Tennessee,* 110–12; Maslowski, *Treason Must Be Made Odious,* 92.

33. Harris, *With Charity for All,* 223.

34. Alexander, *Political Reconstruction in Tennessee,* 16, 26–29; Harris, *With Charity for All,* 223–24; Cimprich, *Slavery's End in Tennessee,* 102, 114.

35. Trefousse, *Andrew Johnson,* 186; Harris, *With Charity for All,* 224.

36. Alexander, *Political Reconstruction in Tennessee,* 30–31; Trefousse, *Andrew Johnson,* 186; Harris, *With Charity for All,* 224–25; Maslowski, *Treason Must Be Made Odious,* 92–94; E. Merton Coulter, *William G. Brownlow: Fighting Parson of the Southern Highlands* (Chapel Hill: University of North Carolina Press, 1937), 134–348.

37. Harris, *With Charity for All,* 225–27; Alexander, *Political Reconstruction in Tennessee,* 31.

38. Patton, *Unionism and Reconstruction in Tennessee,* 29, 49–50; Coulter, *William G. Brownlow,* 261; Harris, *With Charity for All,* 227–28; Trefousse, *Andrew Johnson,* 188.

39. On Tennessee in the Reconstruction era, see Alexander, *Political Reconstruction in Tennessee;* and Patton, *Unionism and Reconstruction in Tennessee.*

40. Daniel W. Crofts, *Reluctant Confederates: Upper South Unionists in the Secession Crisis* (Chapel Hill: University of North Carolina Press, 1989).

41. Harris, *With Charity for All,* 46.

42. Donald, *Lincoln,* 580–85, 589–92.

Reconstruction Power Play

The 1867 Mayoral Election in Nashville, Tennessee

Ben H. Severance

In September 1867, the city of Nashville went through what was probably the most controversial municipal election in its history. One of several exciting episodes in Tennessee's Reconstruction, the Nashville election pitted two unforgiving opponents against one another: the Conservative incumbents, led by Mayor W. Matt Brown, and the Radical Republican challengers, backed by Governor William G. Brownlow, a man notorious for his vitriolic hatred of anything that smacked of rebellion. The respective platforms were unimportant; political power was the objective, and the election was a showdown. In their efforts to prevail, both sides insisted on election procedures that would guarantee them victory. The ensuing legal dispute resulted in a resort to armed force, the Conservatives relying on a "special" police force composed of ex-Confederate soldiers, the Radicals receiving a battalion of Tennessee State Guard, a partisan militia body created earlier in the year. Caught in the middle of this power play was the federal garrison, a presumably neutral law enforcer that was duty bound to prevent political riots. What followed was an election that nearly degenerated into a street battle.

The politics of Reconstruction in Tennessee was the politics of force. As unconditional Unionists during the Civil War, the Radicals naturally saw themselves as the only trustworthy citizens in the state. Since coming to power in early 1865, however, Governor Brownlow and his party, whose strength lay mostly in East Tennessee, exercised tenuous control over the state. A majority of Tennessee whites, either as Conservatives or as ex-Confederates, opposed Radical rule. Conservatives may have denounced secession during the war, but they also disapproved of emancipation even as they now objected to Brownlow's authoritarian style. Ex-Confederates, not surprisingly, rejected everything about the Republican makeover in the postwar South; they increasingly resorted to paramilitary politics as a means to defeat the Reconstruction process. From the numerous leftover guerrilla bands that continued to prowl the rural parts of the state to the nascent Ku Klux Klan, which commenced its night riding as early as 1866, black Tennesseans and their white Radical benefactors faced a widespread Rebel insurgency.[1]

Radicals understandably believed that their state was still within the "grasp of war." To counter these threats, the General Assembly enacted two franchise laws (June 1865 and May 1866) that deprived all ex-Confederates and many Conservatives of the right to vote. Moreover, through a third franchise law passed in February 1867, Radicals took the controversial step of bestowing suffrage on the freedmen, who invariably became Radical voters. Political activism among blacks, most notably as members of the highly politicized Union League (five chapters of this organization existed in Nashville), theoretically served to enhance the legitimacy of political Radicalism. Governor Brownlow was well aware that his dual policies of white proscription and black empowerment had ushered in a political-racial revolution. Such drastic measures required vigilant law enforcement. To this end, the governor appointed all voting registrars in the state and vested them with complete control over the electoral process. Furthermore, in February 1867, the Brownlow administration mobilized the Tennessee State Guard—essentially a standing army of about nineteen hundred men, including about five hundred blacks, virtually all of whom were loyal to the Radicals. During the gubernatorial election in August 1867, this force effectively protected the registration of black voters, ensured a relatively safe political canvass, and policed the precincts both to thwart Rebel interference and to prevent the disfranchised from voting. Despite anti-Radical charges of military despotism, Brownlow and his party won a landslide victory over their Conservative rivals.[2]

Disappointed by the outcome of the gubernatorial election, Conservatives and ex-Confederates looked for new opportunities to defy what they termed *Brownlowism* (i.e., Radical tyranny). The upcoming mayoral contest in Nashville in September seemed a good occasion to offer fresh resistance. For over a year, the Conservative-dominated city council, led by Mayor W. Matt Brown, had orchestrated an effective policy of counter-Reconstruction. Brown's anti-Radical credentials were especially impressive. As city marshal in 1862, he denounced Union occupation and publicly refused to take the oath of allegiance. After his dismissal by the military governor, Andrew Johnson, Brown's wartime activities are unclear, but he may have offered aid and comfort to Rebel guerrillas in the Nashville area. Shortly after the war, Brown won mayoral elections in 1865 and 1866, winning each time with over 70 percent of the vote. In his second term, he directly challenged Radical power over the pending creation of a metropolitan police force. In the wake of the bloody Memphis race riot of May 1866, when local authorities unabashedly sided with the Rebel mob, Governor Brownlow urged the General Assembly to transfer urban police powers in Memphis, Chattanooga, and Nashville to the executive branch. The ensuing legislation granted the governor a power over big-city law enforcement similar to what he wielded over the state's electoral machinery. Correctly surmising that any metropolitan police force would constitute another tool of Brownlowism, Mayor Brown retaliated by obtaining a legal injunction that postponed indefinitely its formation in Nashville. Forty-seven years old in 1867, Matt Brown was a person to be reckoned with.[3]

Concerned that Mayor Brown's leadership helped rally opposition throughout Tennessee, Governor Brownlow was determined to establish Radical control over the state capital and its twenty-five thousand residents. The municipal election scheduled for September 28 provided the perfect opportunity; under the franchise laws, the potential white electorate could be reduced from about four thousand to a few hundred, whereas the new black electorate would number slightly more than two thousand voters. Taking blacks' ballots for granted, a Radical victory thus seemed inevitable. Unfortunately, Radicals in the city bickered over whom to run for mayor. One faction nominated Brownlow's friend Augustus E. Alden. A Union army veteran from Minnesota, Alden had ably served the party as voting registrar for Davidson County during the recent gubernatorial election. But Alden was also a carpetbagger disliked by many native Radicals, who suspected him of unethical conduct in his business practices. A second faction preferred Abram Myers, the likable owner of a Nashville stagecoach company. Delighted by this rift, Mayor Brown sought to complicate further the political canvass. He and his Conservative followers backed yet another, albeit much smaller, Radical faction that endorsed a third candidate, H. S. Scovel, a respectable, though uninspiring, Republican moderate.[4]

The course of the mayoral election took a dramatic turn following two important events on September 7. First, President Andrew Johnson issued a new amnesty proclamation that had direct bearing on voting restrictions. Condemning what he considered the "unnecessary disqualifications, pains, penalties, confiscations, and disfranchisements" that Reconstruction had imposed over the entire South, Johnson offered a pardon to the vast majority of ex-Confederates. Presidential amnesty ostensibly invalidated the punitive aspects of Tennessee's franchise laws. Second, the nominee Abram Myers died from injuries sustained when he fell from a hotel balcony. The significance of Myers's accidental death was that, though it initially simplified the political choices in Nashville, it polarized the political atmosphere. Most Radicals, including virtually all the city's registered blacks, united behind Alden. Alarmed by this development, but encouraged by the spirit of President Johnson's amnesty plan, Mayor Brown abruptly declared his intention to conduct the municipal election in accordance with the city charter, which stipulated that only adult white males could vote and that local authorities, not registrars appointed by the governor, controlled the electoral process. In effect, the Conservatives were arguing that their city government operated like a state-chartered bank or railroad and that therefore the state franchise laws, with their much-despised provision for black suffrage, did not apply to the upcoming election. Repudiating this assertion of "municipal sovereignty," city Radicals were quick to call on the governor for help.[5]

Governor Brownlow took firm measures to defeat the Conservative challenge. First, he appointed B. J. Sheridan, a party stalwart, the new city registrar. Sheridan immediately organized a team of Radical election officials, instructing them to scrutinize the qualifications of all prospective voters. Then, on September 18, the governor proclaimed: "The franchise law is a part and parcel of the constitution, has been sustained by the supreme court of Tennessee, and all elections held in violation of said law are null and void, and of no effect whatever." Brownlow's words electrified Nashville's black community. For the next week, black Union

Leaguers marched through the streets pounding kettle drums and waving American flags, confident of victory. Prominent among their ranks were Randal Brown, who worked at an office of the Freedmen's Savings and Trust Company, and James H. Sumner, a saloon keeper who had recently served as the only African American company commander in the Tennessee State Guard. Conservatives viewed these street demonstrations with disdain. Dropping their support for the aged Scovel, a hastily assembled Conservative convention nominated Matt Brown for reelection. Three other Nashvillians soon announced their candidacies for mayor as well, one running a simple daily advertisement requesting: "You who (either white or black) please to vote for me." With six men seeking the mayoral office, some in accordance with the state franchise laws and others under the city charter, the political campaign was turning into a circus.[6]

Not a man to be trifled with, Governor Brownlow prepared for battle. On September 22, he ordered his militia commander, Gen. Joseph A. Cooper, to concentrate the Tennessee State Guard around the Nashville precincts. Anticipating such a command, Cooper had already put his soldiers in motion. In a matter of days, a battalion of six hundred militiamen was camped within the city limits, many of them at Buena Vista Springs. The ultra-Radical *Knoxville Whig* praised the Brownlow administration's decisive response. "The militia," this newspaper smugly predicted, "will quelch this incipient rebellion in Nashville."[7]

The state guard's swift arrival in Nashville was not well received by most white residents. During the previous spring and summer, when some twenty-one militia companies patrolled large sections of the state during the gubernatorial canvass, the anti-Radical press was replete with warnings about the "bloodhounds of Brownlow" and "Cooper's Bummers." But the predicted "reign of terror" never materialized as the state guard kept the peace with minimal abuse of authority. By mid-September, most of the companies had been disbanded, including those with black militiamen. Those still active—the force deployed to Nashville—comprised the very best units under the most reliable officers. Not only were Maj. John T. Robeson, Capt. Joseph H. Blackburn, Capt. William O. Rickman, Capt. Robert L. Hall, Capt. Edwin R. Hall, Capt. George W. Kirk, and Capt. William C. Holt Tennessee veterans of the Union army, but their recent experience at Reconstruction law enforcement also ably prepared them for the challenges of a disputed election. Commanding them all was Gen.

Joseph Cooper, a native of Campbell County whose exemplary conduct leading a brigade during the Atlanta Campaign and against Hood's invasion of Middle Tennessee in 1864 earned him a brevet major generalship. Cooper was also a teetotaler and a martinet who expected his officers to act responsibly. Such mature leadership would prove especially crucial during the volatile situation in Nashville, for, with Governor Brownlow frequently bedridden with poor health, Cooper possessed de facto executive authority.[8]

As his men set up camps inside the city, General Cooper sternly admonished the Conservatives not to hold any election in violation of the franchise laws. Crying that the general intended to enforce the governor's decree "by the *bullet* by the *bayonet* or by *matches*," anti-Radicals denounced the "high-swelling and blood-portending" actions of the Brownlow administration. The *Union and Dispatch* ran a lengthy editorial in which it emphasized that "the leading lawyers of the city" all considered the governor's interpretation of the law "arrant nonsense." Mayor Brown was especially vehement. On September 24, he proclaimed that the election would take place as required by the city charter, adding: "We shall hardly be deterred from the performance of that duty by any force of mere militia with which our good and quiet citizens are threatened." Furthermore, in anticipation of a "murderous assault" by the state guard, he vowed to augment the size of the city police force to three hundred men.[9]

As an armed counterforce to the militia, the municipal police was hardly imposing. The actual force consisted of about forty or fifty constables under City Marshal James H. Brantley and Capt. Robert S. Patterson, an ex-Confederate officer. In the early years of Reconstruction, the Nashville police displayed racial prejudice and partisan bias. Black residents complained of almost daily police harassment, and, in one instance, two officers nearly bludgeoned to death a black man and his wife. (To his credit, Mayor Brown cashiered those two particular officers.) During the mayoral contest, the police targeted Radical political activities. When J. P. Rexford, a carpetbagger from Michigan, made abusive remarks about the city government during a public speech on September 18, Marshal Brantley accosted the man on the street a day after the event and pummeled him to the ground with a cane. After another Radical meeting on the night of September 23, a squad from the night watch followed seven party members and then arrested them for heckling the homes of known Conservatives.

As the state militia arrived in strength, however, the city police curtailed this brand of intimidation. Fiery editorials exhorted the mayor to match the Radical military buildup by deputizing more policemen: "Let a thousand be called out if Brownlow threatens force." Although the newspapers bandied about the figure of three hundred volunteer deputies, it is unclear exactly how many extra policemen the mayor placed on duty during the election. Nevertheless, the Radical *Daily Press and Times* claimed later: "There is no doubt that a force of several thousand men many of them ex-soldiers could have been obtained."[10]

Hoping to avoid a clash of arms, the Conservatives sought alternative courses of action. In a public statement, Mayor Brown surprisingly encouraged the Radicals to hold their own election under the franchise laws. In effect, he was recommending that the city hold a dual election, with both sides refraining from any interference, and then "let the courts, the only proper arbiters, decide in the end." It was a shrewd ploy that made the Conservatives appear conciliatory. But the mayor hedged his tactics. He wrote President Andrew Johnson, explained his predicament, and then urged the commander-in-chief to use federal troops against Brownlow's militia should the latter attempt "the seizure by armed force of our City." Though sympathetic to the Conservative position, Johnson delegated the matter to the appropriate military leaders.[11]

The federal garrison in Nashville watched these developments closely. As the tension mounted, the army officers debated their proper role in the affair. Gen. Thomas Duncan, the post commander in Nashville, believed that Mayor Brown's position was "the correct one" and suggested that federal troops provide security for both elections. "For those who hold their election illegally," he reasoned, "it will only be an innocent amusement." The departmental commander, Gen. George H. Thomas, disagreed with his subordinate. For him, two competing elections guaranteed violence. Accepting Brownlow's "construction of the law," Thomas instructed Duncan to recognize only the governor's authority and to aid the state guard in enforcing the franchise laws. As a result of Mayor Brown's communication with President Johnson, however, General of the Army Ulysses S. Grant overruled Thomas and imposed new constraints on the federal troops in Nashville. Grant ordered Thomas to "go to Nashville" and personally oversee the whole affair, yet he stressed that "the military cannot set up to be judge as to which set of election judges have the right to control, but must confine their action to putting down hostile mobs." These instructions seemed to vindicate the position of Mayor Brown, who was "exceedingly pleased," for it appeared that two elections would be held after all.[12]

The Brownlow administration was indifferent to Grant's assessment. Committed to defeating the mayor's political maneuvers, branded a "Little Rebellion" by Radical newspapers and outright treason by General Cooper, the administration steadily strengthened its military hold on the city. On September 25, the state guard took possession of the city armory to prevent its "seizure by Rebels." The next day, several hundred militiamen "were on the street under arms." Flaunting the power of the state guard, Capt. William Rickman deliberately paraded his company past the capitol with "his Band playing and Colors flying." In response to the mayor's creation of a "special" police, General Cooper recalled three recently disbanded all-black militia companies for use as a reserve force. As had been the case during the gubernatorial campaign, the existence of "negro militia" produced much consternation among white Nashvillians (these particular black units were never actually reactivated, however, the crisis having passed before the men could muster). Finally, on September 27, Governor Brownlow proclaimed that "an insurrection exists in the City of Nashville" and then called on the federal garrison to render assistance in suppressing it. In the meantime, Major Robeson dispatched units to the city's ten voting districts, the militiamen cheering for Brownlow as they marched toward their destinations. Once in place, Robeson then instructed his company commanders to bivouac at the polling sites and permit only those election officials appointed by Registrar Sheridan to operate the polls. Appalled by these martial displays, Conservatives derided the militiamen as "scarce weaned, beardless bumpkins" who "looked frightened and homesick." The *Republican Banner* moved beyond caricature and rallied its readers: "We can not be intimidated and we shall not be compelled."[13]

This militant posturing convinced General Thomas that the army could not remain neutral during the election. Warning that "a collision is inevitable," he asked General Grant for clarification of the rules of engagement. Thomas contended that, if the militia and city police came to blows, the army would have to choose sides or prevent both elections altogether. But to enforce a dual election, he added, would "be a practical decision against State authority and against the franchise law." Clearly,

Thomas favored the Radicals, but Grant repeatedly ordered him not to take sides, stating that his duty was simply to "prevent conflict" and "preserve peace." After exchanging telegrams with his superior throughout the day on September 26, however, Thomas received orders that resolved his dilemma. Late that evening, Grant significantly modified his instructions to Thomas. "The military cannot be made use of to defeat the executive of a State," Grant explained. "You are not to prevent the legal State force from the execution of its orders." Thomas could now in good conscience uphold actions taken by the Tennessee State Guard. The next morning, as Brownlow was declaring a state of insurrection, the general visited Mayor Matt Brown and bluntly informed him that the army would "sustain the governor in case of collision."[14]

Mayor Brown and the city council were crestfallen at the sudden turn of events. Brown denounced Thomas's decision as a "signal and deplorable mistake," but, under pressure from several councilmen, he agreed to concede the contest to Brownlow. Alderman John Coltart alone urged the council to continue its resistance and hold an election under the city charter "at all hazards, no matter what may be the consequences." No one seconded his motion, however. General Thomas had reinforced his garrison with over one thousand men, bringing federal troop strength in Nashville to fourteen hundred. This force, combined with the six hundred militiamen of the state guard, left the city police heavily outnumbered, even if the force did muster an additional three hundred deputies. On the afternoon of September 27, Brown notified the public of the council's decision and then withdrew from the race (as did the other anti-Radical candidates). Blaming Thomas for "forcibly preventing a peaceable election," the mayor insisted that enforcing the franchise law in Nashville was "clearly illegal." In a bitter letter to President Johnson, Brown opined that the city was in "a state of organized anarchy never parallelled."[15]

Jubilant Radicals staged a huge rally on the eve of the election. White and black speakers harangued the audience well into the night. Identifying Brown's mayoralty as "a remnant of the rebellion," one politico shouted that "the great Radical Republican party would smash everything that came its way." Another speaker directed his comments to the large number of freedmen in the crowd: "Governor Brownlow says you shall vote, and has sent the glorious old Joe Cooper here to see that you do vote."

Evidently, the state guard provided security for the event, for, when an irate observer broke through the crowd shouting epithets, several militia sentries pounced on the man and dragged him away. The Conservatives canceled a counterrally of their own, apparently owing to the congestion and confusion in the streets. Instead, their news organs printed excerpts of a purportedly scientific study that equated black people to chimpanzees.[16]

In accordance with a last-minute agreement between the militia general Cooper and the army general Thomas, the state guard relinquished control of the polls to the federal garrison shortly after the election began. The militiamen returned to their nearby camps, and the army presided over a generally quiet election. Registrar Sheridan reportedly combed the streets ensuring that every black man in the city voted the Radical ticket, while a detachment of militia under Capt. Joseph Blackburn patrolled the streets on horseback, some of his men allegedly scouring the "cellars and attics" in search of surreptitious charter voting. "Martial law reigned as completely as it did during the battle of Nashville," observed the *Republican Banner*. To this Conservative newspaper, the election was little more than "military dictation" from the "unmilitary" Thomas. To other anti-Radicals, the election was a "disgusting farce" enacted by "Satan's twin brother"—Governor Brownlow. Desperate to prevent the impending Radical triumph, Mayor Brown made a final plea to General Thomas on the afternoon of September 28, asking permission to hold an election under the charter, "late as it is," or to hold one at a subsequent date. "If you, general, desire to see equal justice," the mayor chided, "you will see that we are permitted to hold such an election without the interference from the State militia." Thomas politely refused the mayor's request, reiterating that a peaceful election under the charter was impossible.[17]

In the end, the carpetbagger A. E. Alden became mayor in a landslide over his remaining opponent, H. S. Scovel, 2,423 votes to 258. Mayor Brown picked up three votes. A correspondent for the *New York Times* remarked: "The colored voters were out in considerable numbers, while the mass of whites declined to vote." Indeed, black votes accounted for all but a few hundred of Alden's total. One disgruntled Conservative accused Registrar Sheridan of permitting many nonresident blacks to cast ballots, while another aptly noted that there were "almost as many bayonets as voters in our streets." Regardless, an elated Governor Brownlow contacted state guard headquarters to express his "entire approval" of General Cooper's leadership and the militia's performance during the crisis. The *Daily Press and Times* similarly praised the militia general as a "model soldier" who "discharged his duty like a hero and patriot." That newspaper then exulted: "The moral effect of bayonets was wonderfully illustrated [throughout the mayoral contest]." The politics of force had prevailed; Radicals had taken control of the city council. But, in the sobering words of General Thomas: "How narrowly [Tennessee] escaped from a condition of War."[18]

The drama of the Nashville election did not end with the closing of the polls. With federal troops departing as quickly as they had arrived, and with the saloons reopening, Mayor Brown, the lame duck, pursued an injunction against Registrar Sheridan's certification of the election returns. On the morning of October 2, after the Radical chancellor Horace Harrison dismissed the injunction, the mayor's friends on the city council warned him that the state guard planned to "make a 'clean shuckling' of the old administration" if he remained defiant. Brown remained defiant. When Mayor-Elect Alden arrived at city hall to assume his duties, Brown barred his entrance. "I believe you to be illegally elected," he declared, "and therefore cannot surrender you the office." Alden immediately reported this to Governor Brownlow, who instructed General Cooper to use "whatever force is necessary . . . to overcome any illegal resistance." Accordingly, Cooper ordered one of his most trusted militia officers, Capt. Joseph H. Blackburn, to effect the transfer of municipal power.[19]

The anti-Radical press depicted Blackburn's confrontation with Brown as a piece of burlesque. In the late afternoon of October 2, Blackburn arrived outside city hall with about forty mounted men. At the approach of a large crowd of black and white onlookers, the militia formed a line of battle, the "ignorant young tow-heads" presenting a "horrid front." Blackburn, accompanied by a lieutenant and five enlisted men, then entered the building and, after supposedly getting lost on the third floor, found the mayor in conversation with several Conservative politicians, including Marshal Brantley. According to one witness, the militiamen "sported shockingly bad hats." As Brown feigned surprise at the arrival of this inelegant armed party, Blackburn ordered him to turn over the mayoral books and keys. When Brown asked the militia captain if he intended to use force, Blackburn, who reportedly "trembled with excitement," replied that he had orders to "take possession" of the office. Brown then demanded to see written authorization, which Blackburn produced after some hesitation. As the mayor slowly read the orders, his fellow Conservatives growled protests at the militiamen, who "manifested considerable uneasiness." Evidently satisfied with the authenticity of Blackburn's orders, Brown departed the building and addressed the multitudes in pompous style: "I have surrendered my office, but I want you to understand that I yield only to the bayonet." The whites in the crowd cheered wildly at their mayor's audacious exit, while the "shabby" detachment of militiamen and its black allies countered with a "hideous 'yi, yi.'" Leaving a squad behind to protect Mayor Alden, who apparently had been waiting outside, Blackburn and his "critter company" sauntered off toward the courthouse, where they spent the night. "Thus ended the Brownlow-Alden *coup d' etat*."[20]

Though hardly tyrannical, Augustus Alden's tenure as mayor did typify the Radicals' frustrating quest for legitimacy. One of Alden's first acts was to lift the injunction against the metropolitan police. By the end of October 1867, the new city council and Nashville's blacks enjoyed the protection of a partisan police force consisting of fifty men under Commissioner Henry Stone, a Radical politico handpicked by Governor Brownlow. Mayor Alden next implemented a whole series of social programs—a public school system, a charity hospital, a free meal program—that directly benefited the black community. To pay for it all, Alden raised taxes on the city's mostly white propertyholders and then resorted to floating bonds and borrowing money from Northern banks, all of which plunged the city deeply into debt. Critics dubbed the Radical city council "Alden's Ring." Eventually, a team of Conservative lawyers brought suit against the mayor for alleged corruption and forced the city into receivership in June 1869. So much for the "*coup d'etat*."[21]

The Nashville election is an instructive case study, not just of Brownlowism, but of the general use of military force in a peacetime political setting. Conservative newspapers howled that the whole episode was a case of "*might* overruling *right*." Radical "might" was unmistakable, but Conservative "right" was a matter of debate. Radicals denied that the use of militia constituted military usurpation. Rather, the governor had employed justifiable force against a "pestiferous rebel Mayor." Regardless, Brownlow could not have permitted such an unprecedented event as a dual election, however reasonable the idea may have seemed to people like Mayor Brown, without subverting the franchise laws and losing credibility. When Brown and his allies pressed the issue, the state guard stymied their efforts. To be sure, the federal garrison played a critical role, but its involvement mostly prevented a street battle, one in which the more numerous and better led, trained, and equipped militia would have surely routed the city police and arrested the Conservative leadership. Arguably, the aggressive use of militia risked civil violence, but, without its employment, the Conservative scheme would likely have been carried to fruition. The army certainly would not have stopped it, for, without a potential clash between militia and city police to give it a pretext for intervening, U.S. soldiers would have stayed in their barracks on September 28. Consequently, the dual election would have taken place in spite of Brownlow's decrees. Whether the Conservatives retained control of the city or merely held the Radicals at bay temporarily while the courts sorted out the confusion, the opponents of Reconstruction would have gained immeasurable political capital.[22]

All things considered, the various instruments of coercion performed commendably during the Nashville impasse. The anti-Radical press had prophesied "conflagration and massacre," but there were no serious disturbances, violent or otherwise. To be sure, the muscular presence of the state guard was certainly extraordinary, but General Cooper and his officers appreciated the gravity of the situation and exercised tight control over their enlisted men throughout the crisis. Captain Blackburn's conduct during the standoff at city hall is an especially noteworthy indicator of the state guard's disciplined behavior. The militia captain had authority to oust the mayor physically, yet he responded to Matt Brown's condescending obstinacy with politeness and restraint. Similarly, the municipal police might have provoked trouble, but it mostly steered clear of the militia. After the election, both Marshal Brantley and Captain Patterson resigned, the latter lodging an angry protest against the incoming administration. Finally, the U.S. Army also conducted itself well despite the fact that it was really just beginning to define its role as a Reconstruction peacekeeper. According to one historian, the Nashville controversy was the army's "baptism of fire in the art of preventing election disorders in a state over which it had no civil jurisdiction." To that end, the soldiers efficiently assumed security over the polls when they opened and just as smoothly departed the scene when they closed. The politicians on both sides may have engaged in bombast and hyperbole, but the three rival law enforcers—militia, police, and regulars—kept their cool.[23]

Overall, the Nashville election of 1867 exemplifies in microcosm the political struggle that was taking place throughout Tennessee. To Governor Brownlow and the Radicals, the outcome vindicated their use of force. To the Conservatives and ex-Confederates, the event was exploited as yet another instance of Radical despotism. Regardless, the power play in Nashville demonstrates that the Civil War did not really end in 1865. Although no bloodshed occurred during this particular political event, the enduring enmity produced by four years of brutal warfare was manifest to all. It was a visceral hostility that adversely affected all facets of politics during the period of Reconstruction.

Notes

The essay is a revised and expanded version of a discussion in my earlier *Tennessee's Radical Army: The State Guard and Its Role in Reconstruction, 1867–1869* (Knoxville: University of Tennessee Press, 2005), 160–66.

1. The standard histories of the period are Thomas B. Alexander, *Political Reconstruction in Tennessee* (Nashville: Vanderbilt University Press, 1950); and James W. Patton, *Unionism and Reconstruction in Tennessee, 1860–1869* (Chapel Hill: University of North Carolina Press, 1934). A fine overview is contained in Paul H. Bergeron, Stephen V. Ash, and Jeanette Keith, *Tennesseans and Their History* (Knoxville: University of Tennessee Press, 1999), 158–80. For postwar violence in the state, see Allen W. Trelease, *White Terror: The Ku Klux Klan Conspiracy and Southern Reconstruction* (Baton Rouge: Louisiana State University Press, 1971), 3–46, 175–85; and Ben H. Severance, *Tennessee's Radical Army: The State Guard and Its Role in Reconstruction, 1867–1869* (Knoxville: University of Tennessee Press, 2005).

2. Alexander, *Political Reconstruction in Tennessee*, 73–75, 104–5, 130, 149–52; E. Merton Coulter, *William G. Brownlow, Fighting Parson of the Southern Highlands* (Chapel Hill: University of North Carolina Press, 1937), 269–70, 283–87, 330–39; Eugene G. Feistman, "Radical Disfranchisement and the Restoration of Tennessee, 1865–1866," *Tennessee Historical Quarterly* 12 (1953): 140–45; *Nashville Union and Dispatch,* September 26, 1867; Severance, *Tennessee's Radical Army,* 121–44.

3. Peter Maslowski, *Treason Must Be Made Odious: Military Occupation*

and Wartime Reconstruction in Nashville, 1862–1865 (Millwood, N.Y.: KTO, 1978), 148; Walter T. Durham, *Nashville, The Occupied City: The First Seventeen Months—February 16, 1862, to June 30, 1863* (Nashville: Tennessee Historical Society, 1985), 254–55; Stanley F. Rose, "Nashville and Its Leadership Elite" (master's thesis, University of Virginia, 1965), 30–31, 36–37, 67; Coulter, *Brownlow,* 341–42; Patton, *Unionism and Reconstruction,* 227–29; *Nashville Daily Press and Times,* September 29, 1866.

4. *Ninth Census,* vol. 1, *The Statistics of the Population of the United States* (Washington, D.C.: U.S. Government Printing Office, 1872), table III, p. 262, and table XXV, p. 654; Patton, *Unionism and Reconstruction,* 229; Robert M. McBride, "Northern, Military, Corrupt, and Transitory: Augustus E. Alden, Nashville's Carpetbagger Mayor," *Tennessee Historical Quarterly* 37 (1978): 63–65; William G. McBride, "Blacks and the Race Issue in Tennessee Politics, 1865–1876" (Ph.D. diss., University of Virginia, 1985), 262–64.

5. LeRoy P. Graf, Ralph W. Haskins, and Paul H. Bergeron, eds., *The Papers of Andrew Johnson,* 16 vols. (Knoxville: University of Tennessee Press, 1967–2000), 13:40–43; Patton, *Unionism and Reconstruction,* 229–31; Gary L. Kornell, "Reconstruction in Nashville, 1867–1869," *Tennessee Historical Quarterly* 30 (1971): 278; *Nashville Daily Press and Times,* October 2, 1867; Nashville Petition to Governor Brownlow, September 14, 1867, E. E. Patton Papers, Calvin M. McClung Historical Collection, East Tennessee History Center, Knoxville.

6. *Nashville Republican Banner,* September 17, 20, 1867; *New York Times,* September 23, 1867; McBride, "Blacks and the Race Issue," 264; Graf, Haskins, and Bergeron, eds., *Papers of Andrew Johnson,* 13:82; Rose, "Nashville and Its Leadership Elite," 68; Severance, *Tennessee's Radical Army,* 51–52; *Nashville Union and Dispatch,* September 17, 1867. Brownlow's legal position was supported by the Radical state supreme court, which, in its decision in *Ridley v. Sherbrook* (March 21, 1867), upheld the constitutionality of the franchise acts. See Patton, *Unionism and Reconstruction,* 120–23.

7. Governor Brownlow to General Cooper, September 22, 1867, GP 21, reel 1, box 1, folder 1, Papers of the Governors, Tennessee State Library and Archives, Nashville; Special Orders Nos. 133 (September 21, 1867), 136 (September 25, 1867), 139, 143 (September 26, 1867), Tennessee Adjutant General's Office (TAGO), Papers, reel 9, vol. 33, RG 21, Tennessee State Library and Archives; *Nashville Daily Press and Times,* September 25, October 1, 1867; *Knoxville Whig,* September 19, 1867.

8. See name index references for each listed militia officer in Severance, *Tennessee's Radical Army.*

9. State Guard Proclamation, September 23, 1867, GP 21, reel 1, box 1,

folder 1, Papers of the Governors; *Nashville Daily Press and Times,* September 25, 1867; *Nashville Republican Banner,* September 24, 26, 1867; *Nashville Union and Dispatch,* September 25, 27, 1867; Kornell, "Reconstruction in Nashville," 281. In rendering their opinions, some of the lawyers cited *Dartmouth College v. Woodward* (1819), the U.S. Supreme Court case that declared lawful charters inviolable unless all parties agreed to any modifications. *Nashville Republican Banner,* September 19, 1867.

10. Harvey W. Crew, *History of Nashville, Tenn.* (Nashville: Barbee & Smith, 1890), 150; Howard N. Rabinowitz, "The Conflict between Blacks and the Police in the Urban South, 1865–1900," *The Historian* 39 (1976): 68–69; Rose, "Nashville and Its Leadership Elite," 36; *Nashville Union and Dispatch,* September 21, 25, 27, 1867; *Nashville Daily Press and Times,* September 21, 23, 30, 1867. A longtime member of the municipal police, R. S. Patterson commanded a militia company of Nashville Confederates prior to the Union capture of the city. See *Nashville Daily Gazette,* December 1, 1861.

11. U.S. Congress, *House Executive Documents, Report of the Secretary of War,* 40th Cong., 2nd Sess., 1867, ser. no. 1324 (hereafter cited as *Report of the Secretary of War* [1867]), p. 186; *Nashville Union and Dispatch,* September 21, 1867; *Nashville Daily Press and Times,* September 25, 1867; Graf, Haskins, and Bergeron, eds., *Papers of Andrew Johnson,* 13:99–101.

12. *Report of the Secretary of War* (1867), 184–85, 187–88; *Nashville Daily Press and Times,* September 28, 1867; John Y. Simons, ed., *The Papers of Ulysses S. Grant,* 24 vols. to date (Carbondale: Southern Illinois Press, 1967–), 17:360–62. It should be noted that, because Tennessee was readmitted to the Union in July 1866 and, therefore, was not subject to the Reconstruction Acts, the U.S. Army did not possess the sweeping power it wielded in the other former Confederate states.

13. *Knoxville Whig,* September 25, 1867; *Nashville Union and Dispatch,* September 27, 29, 1867; *New York Times,* September 26, 1867; Governor Brownlow to General Cooper, September 25, 1867, GP 21, reel 1, box 1, folder 1, Papers of the Governors; Special Orders Nos. 139 and 144–46 (September 26, 1867), 147 and 149 (September 27, 1867), TAGO, reel 9, vol. 33; Governor's Proclamation, September 27, 1867, GP 21, reel 1, box 2, folder 11, Papers of the Governors; *Nashville Daily Press and Times,* September 28, 1867; *Nashville Republican Banner,* September 26, 1867.

14. *Report of the Secretary of War* (1867), 189–91; James E. Sefton, *The United States Army and Reconstruction, 1865–1877* (Baton Rouge: Louisiana State University Press, 1967), 229–30; John T. Morse Jr., ed., *Diary of Gideon Welles, Secretary of Navy under Lincoln and Johnson,* 3 vols. (Boston: Houghton Mifflin, 1911), 3:211–12.

15. *Report of the Secretary of War* (1867), 191–92, 460–61; *Nashville Republican Banner,* September 28, 1867; *Nashville Union and Dispatch,* September 28, 1867; *Nashville Daily Press and Times,* September 28, 1867; *New York Times,* September 28, 1867; Graf, Haskins, and Bergeron, eds., *Papers of Andrew Johnson,* 13:116. Johnson shared Brown's disgust with the actions of Grant and Thomas, but the president learned of the army's deployment too late to countermand its orders. Brooks D. Simpson, *Let Us Have Peace: Ulysses S. Grant and the Politics of War and Reconstruction, 1861–1868* (Chapel Hill: University of North Carolina Press, 1991), 201–2.

16. *Nashville Republican Banner,* September 27, October 2, 1867; *Nashville Union and Dispatch,* September 29, 1867.

17. *Report of the Secretary of War* (1867), 193–97; *Nashville Daily Press and Times,* September 28, 1867; Special Orders No. 152, September 28, 1867, TAGO, reel 9, vol. 33; Patton, *Unionism and Reconstruction,* 231; *Nashville Republican Banner,* September 29, 1867; *Nashville Union and Dispatch,* September 29, 1867. It is worth noting that Cooper served under General Thomas at the Battle of Nashville in December 1864; thus, the militia general was not averse to deferring to his former commander in matters of military protocol.

18. Kornell, "Reconstruction in Nashville," 280; Rose, "Nashville and Its Leadership Elite," 39; *New York Times,* September 29, 1867; McBride, "Blacks and the Race Issue," 265–66; *Nashville Union and Dispatch,* September 29, 1867; *Nashville Republican Banner,* September 28, 1867; Governor Brownlow to General Cooper, September 29, 1867, GP 21, reel 1, box 1, folder 1, Papers of the Governors; *Nashville Daily Press and Times,* September 28, 30, 1867; Simons, eds., *Papers of Ulysses S. Grant,* 17:362.

19. Patton, *Unionism and Reconstruction,* 231; *Nashville Union and Dispatch,* October 3, 1867; *Nashville Republican Banner,* October 2, 3, 1867; Certification Statement of B. J. Sheridan, October 1, 1867, MS 823, Samuel Arnell Papers, McClung Collection, Knoxville Tennessee, box 1, folder 12; Governor Brownlow to General Cooper, October 2, 1867, GP 21, reel 1, box 1, folder 1, Papers of the Governors; General Cooper to Captain Blackburn, October 2, 1867, TAGO, reel 9, vol. 33.

20. *Nashville Republican Banner,* October 3, 1867; *Nashville Union and Dispatch,* October 3, 1867; *Knoxville Whig,* October 9, 1867; Kornell, "Reconstruction in Nashville," 279–81.

21. *Nashville Republican Banner,* October 4, 1867; *Nashville Daily Press and Times,* October 4, 1867; Henry Stone to Governor Brownlow, October 31, 1867, GP 21, reel 1, box 2, folder 2, Papers of the Governors; Kornell, "Reconstruction in Nashville," 282–85; McBride, "Northern, Military, Corrupt, and Transitory," 65–66. The so-called Alden Ring included the black activists Randal Brown and

James Sumner, who won council seats the following year. Rose, "Nashville and Its Leadership Elite," 68.

22. *Nashville Republican Banner,* October 2, 1867; *Knoxville Whig,* October 2, 1867.

23. *Nashville Republican Banner,* September 29, October 4, 1867; Sefton, *United States Army and Reconstruction,* 229.

After the Horror

Kentucky in Reconstruction

B. Franklin Cooling

Thomas Parsons, a Kentucky Unionist farmer and wartime home guard member, recalled in 1901 how four decades earlier Confederate soldiers from southwest Virginia had gone to Mt. Sterling for parole. The intent, he said, "was to muster out the Rebel armies and get the country back as nearly to its normal condition as possible." While watching the surrender, which lasted for several days, he recognized many of the ex-Confederates as his former school chums. A little later, one approached him and queried: "Mr., what are they going to do with us fellows?" Presumably, the fear was imprisonment or worse. Parsons pointed out that it depended on how much the questioner respected his parole. The conversation then turned to a nearby contingent of U.S. Colored Troops. The former Rebel sneered with hate at what he called "Smoked Yankees." Parsons noted ironically that it was the man's kind who "made it necessary for the Government to call these people into the army to suppress that rebellion." Even yet, one can imagine the bedraggled prisoner scratching his head before rejoining that the Kentuckians were the "damnedest people out of hell." What Kentuckians? replied a quizzical Parsons. Why, the Southerners who in the beginning of the conflict "sent their sons out to fight for the South" and then before conflict's end "sent their Negroes out to kill their sons." Parsons must have smiled wryly, remembering: "I thought I had never heard the situation better expressed." In truth, what to do about returning Kentucky rebels, and what to do about the emancipated blacks, basically shaped Kentucky's transit from war to reconstruction.[1]

America's Solemn Mission

America periodically goes on a nation-building binge. It started, perhaps, in the 1780s when we built our own, and we have not stopped trying to do it for others ever since. Sometimes we are successful—everyone points to the post–World War II rebuilding of Germany and Japan and, by extension, much of Western Europe and Asia before and during the cold war era. More often than not, the results prove mixed—the Philippines, Caribbean and Latin American countries, Somalia, Bosnia. Current efforts in Afghanistan and Iraq await definitive result. As Cynthia Watson suggests, the United States has chosen this theme "as a major course of U.S. policy for the initial years of the twenty-first century," assuming that, by helping create "a world of democratic, free market states, the attacks resulting from the hatred of nineteen terrorists on September 11, 2001, will be prevented from recurring." She observes that the belief that the United States offers the rest of the world "a model of freedom, hope, ethics, and equality is not new" but has been "woven throughout our history." She could just as well observe, however, that actions have often conflicted with these lofty goals. Moreover, Americans might well look to blemishes as well as successes in our past, just as in other countries over the centuries. In what many scholars argue was our greatest failure—post–Civil War Reconstruction—we as a people have averted our gaze from that dreary postwar performance by government and people at all levels.[2]

The striking difference between then and now, of course, resides with today's powerful blending of national political crusade with a barrage of well-wishers and prescriptive manuals, an explosion of bureaucratic players, agendas, and goals, and a veritable food fight as to whether military or civilian instruments of national power should stand in the forefront. This rush of resources and enthusiasm cuts vertically through government and nongovernment entities as well as horizontally across the international picture. Nothing like that was possible in 1860s America because the philosophy and structure of governance and, frankly, the biases of hearts and minds hardened by four years of carnage mitigated against such a crusade. As James J. Carafano suggests about today's weaknesses in postconflict operations—lack of historical memory, unrealistic expectations, and longstanding flaws—so too, "among the traditions, experiences, preconceptions, and routine practices that determine how the military wages the fight for peace, the most powerful force shaping its thinking is a 'tradition of forgetting.'" He quotes the official army report on U.S. participation in the occupation of the Rhineland after World War I as noting that, "despite the precedents of military governments in Mexico, California, the Southern States, Cuba, Puerto Rico, Panama, China, the Philippines, and elsewhere, the lesson seemingly has not been learned." Explanation of this tradition lies beyond the purview of this essay. However, the theme helps reexplore Kentucky as a case study.[3]

Watson's "enduring questions in nation-building" can inform any discussion of post–Civil War Reconstruction. She defines *nation building* as "ending military conflict and rebuilding economic and political infrastructures," for which she means basic services, including the armed forces, police, government, banks, transportation networks, communications, health and medical care, and schools, among other basics of a functional society. Stopping violence, constructing a society based on rule of law and other norms so that it can function autonomously and to the benefit of the population, all sounds altruistic enough. And, of course, in a nineteenth-century variant, that is precisely what happened in each of the reconstructed Rebel and border states. Today, this might involve outside intervention—peacekeeping, preemption, humanitarian relief, institution building, conflict avoidance, liberation, or revenge—all good terms lending credence and form to activities of government as well as private-sector intentions and international activities. Whether in Afghanistan and Iraq, in Kentucky, or anywhere else in the South in the 1860s, such concepts can be examined in context.[4]

In addition to asking what is included in *nation building*, Watson wonders whether this phenomenon can "be brought to a people or does it need to be home grown?" Many observers, she contends, see the culture of entrepreneurship and suspicion of government in people's lives, together with optimism and blending of nationalities, as factors in U.S. success. The question can be asked of Kentucky in microcosm, adding, as she does, that the country as a whole "appears to have developed this commitment to democracy because it was a system developed from within." But, in a sense, for states of the post–Civil War South, the determinant of outside interposition stemmed from national government and nonindigenous contributors, and the results of self-redemption were anything but positive in many cases. In fact, Watson also observes another enduring question of nation building: whether outside intervention actually thwarts accomplishment. Closely related to this issue is that of whether nation building is a military operation or a civilian activity with the U.S. Army, itself a very controversial force in post–Civil War Reconstruction in Kentucky and elsewhere.[5]

Today, we think of a bounteously funded, technically efficient American military machine as exquisitely equipped for both war and nation building. Such was not the case after the Civil War, for a variety of reasons, although a disturbing similarity surfaces over numerical "boots on the ground" to stabilize and suppress continuing violent insurgency now and then as a stabilizing part of reconstruction. Today, politicians, policymakers, and uniformed professionals have complicated discussion when they ask, "How does nation building relate to peacekeeping operations, humanitarian operations, or so-called 'operations other than war'?" Frankly, throughout history, these terms flow together, and it remains to be seen whether today's lexicon gymnastics prove any more effective in result than, say, their application in Kentucky's postconflict reconstruction.[6]

Several of today's "eternal questions" obviously do not relate to postbellum Kentucky. Watson mentions the role of supranational organizations and the international community and how structured military civil affairs or so-called psychological operations fit into the picture (although, arguably, today's terms have historical counterparts even in the Kentucky experience). More fascinating for Kentucky analysis are Watson's citations of other modern considerations like:

- How do nongovernment organizations relate to U.S. government operations in nation building?
- How much of nation building relates to democratization and how much to the free market?
- Is nation building an exploration of lesser-developed states?
- At what point is belligerency over and nation building beginning?
- What are the metrics of success in nation building?
- How much resistance does a leader tolerate from his population in trying to accomplish the goals of nation building?

Kentucky and the Solemn Mission

In each case, extrapolation of such modern didactics to the Kentucky experience fits well with more traditional examination of the Bluegrass experience during war and Reconstruction. Watson concludes that nation building "is as complicated as any other public-policy question facing any state" with trade-offs, "best" or "worst" lying mostly in the eye of the beholder rather than in some empirical answer. Although history does not guarantee the future, nation building, she suggests, proves successful "only when done from within because the challenges facing outsiders in any culture or society are so vast." Yet was this really the case in Southern reconstruction and Kentucky reconstruction in particular? "Within" lay with native sons, both white and black and how they effected result; "outsiders" identified with the federal government and the victorious North and what they brought to bear in the Bluegrass. Edward L. Ayers saw the epoch as "the interlocking stories of three major groups," Southern whites, Southern blacks, and white Northerners all in conflict, all part of shifting alliances and alignments and patterns. Kentucky fits that paradigm.[7]

Whether in modern or historical nation building, the trajectory between cause, crisis, war, pacification/stabilization, reconstruction, and reconciliation forms a continuum. More simply put, there is wartime reconstruction and postwar reconstruction, illustrated nicely by Kentucky. In addition, a vertical dimension also stems from the idea that, not only national, but also local—even tribal—levels configure the subject matter. Massachusetts congressman Tip O'Neill once contended that all politics is local; so too is all history. Increasingly, the lessons of nation building suggest that tribalism remains the key element in broken or uncongealed states. While we as a nation and a people often forget our own preunification history or likewise fail to amalgamate and integrate our past holistically, the Civil War epoch provides opportunity for understanding, not merely a war of consolidation in which revolution nested, but also a time of transformation and reconstitution of structure at state and local as well as national levels. Revolutionary, transformational, remarkably complex is reconstruction, varying "sharply from one place to another in the South and from one year to the next," suggests Ayers. Yet this part of the experience has been overshadowed by the blood and gore, battles and leaders and glories of the fighting man in American popular mythology. Kentucky provides a case in point.

The Bluegrass State's own experience with the Reconstruction era should not be separated from the broader spectrum of antebellum to reconciliatory years. One need not belabor the details of prewar Kentucky politics, economics, or society (all intertwined with both region and section) or the state at war. The bright economic progress built on agriculture and expanding transportation infrastructure for commerce, nascent industry, and sociocultural development (at least for the white population) could be seen as marred by the continued existence of slavery as the labor base. However, Kentucky's politics and politicians spoke to compromise and balm as response to the severely fragmented nation on that issue. Some of this approach carried over to the war period itself as, according to Penny M. Miller, the Civil War and Reconstruction "affected Kentucky far more than would have been expected in a state that remained in the Union." In a sense, the very location as well as western rivers and the Louisville and Nashville Railroad that commercially and culturally linked Kentucky with sister states to the south sealed its fate rather quickly on the outbreak of hostilities.[8]

Despite the state's politicians' resolve to remain neutral while its national spokesmen spoke of compromise and consequent violation by both warring sections, Kentucky's fate was quickly sealed via the Union's relentless military advance to conquer the rebellious states, coupled with Confederate irresolution to stand and defend the upper heartland. A state whose people proved as divided in sentiment and allegiance as the Union itself at the time, Kentucky found that its geographic position conditioned events. Twin rebel defeats at Mill Springs and Forts Henry and Donelson at opposite ends of the Confederate general Albert Sidney Johnston's western defense line in the winter of 1862 effectively extinguished any dream of a Kentucky star in the Confederate national banner. True, there arose a provisional Confederate Kentucky regime under Governors George W. Johnson and Richard Hawes, and the dream of a Confederate western frontier on the Ohio River forever drove strategists in Richmond as well as Kentuckians in exile. But the dream died. Kentucky remained a divided border Union state (under secession-leaning Beriah Magoffin until pushed aside for conservative Unionist Thomas Bramlette), with national military occupation, stabilization, and repression of dissent conditioning the state as much as redemptive attempts by Braxton Bragg and Edmund Kirby Smith or the periodic heroics of beau ideal cavalryman John Hunt Morgan, much less John Bell Hood's stillborn goal that perished at Franklin and Nashville, Tennessee, in late 1864.[9]

Indeed, "the dark and bloody ground" escaped the worst of major battles, fire and sword, compared to that visited on the South in Tennessee, Georgia, and Mississippi. More like Maryland, but not quite like Missouri in terms of borderland strife, Kentucky slipped into the virulent destabilizing fever of localized partisan activity and eventual banditry, persecution of neighbors, prosecution and repression of dissidence, and edge-teetering allegiance to one side or the other. Miller speaks of the state's experience as "an internal battleground for its own soul—and politics." Never wholeheartedly trusted by either Union or Confederate authorities because of wavering positions from neutrality at the beginning to tepid response to Confederate raids as well as the unceasing presence of Federal troops, Kentucky experienced such explosive touchstones as the emancipation of slaves and the suppression of civil liberties. True, it retained civil governance (compared to Andrew Johnson's military governance of neighboring Tennessee) yet suffered as much disruption as if it had been an occupied area of the conquered rebellion. Older state sovereignty tradition vied with a unifying cathartic revolution of modernism evidenced by centralizing national government carried on the tides of wartime. In a confrontation as old as the Republic itself, Kentucky (the author of the famous Resolutions of 1798) rejected its presidential native son's policies and programs that would help push a reunited nation on the inevitable path to modernity. Ironically, then, it may have been Abraham Lincoln (until martyred) whose policies and administration tipped the Bluegrass into the notion that the loyal state in wartime could become disloyal on the return of peace. That perception long carried validity in Kentucky political folklore.[10]

Kentucky Wartime Reconstruction

In many ways, Kentucky's wartime experience (like that of the country as a whole) was more one of reconstitution than reconstruction. True, the two went hand in hand with both internal and external forces at play. Every cause and effect related to change, to transformation, with Kentuckians fighting against or embracing such to some ill-defined degree. Civil War statistics remain suspect, but official soldier count placed some 75,760 Kentuckians in Union blue; perhaps 30,000 went with the Confederacy. Of course, there is no accurate way to know how many "irregulars" participated on either side, while inclusion of partisan rangers and home guards might well raise totals appreciably for either cause. Yet every commentator points to a severely divided populace, and the Unionist apologist Thomas W. Speed wrote after the turn of the century that "every part of the State was Union in sentiment, except the extreme west end," and from all the other portions of the commonwealth, including the Bluegrass middle, were drawn the men in blue. Given such divisions, wartime Kentucky was destined to remain unsettled, the ultimate decision of the war notwithstanding. With its first families politically torn, their sons enlisting on both sides, the white working class similarly pulled in different directions. Only the African American slave proletariat might have seemed immune, just as everywhere across the Deeper South. In fact, slaves became something of a makeweight for Kentucky in both war and the return of peace. As they were elsewhere, they provided an important ingredient in the war effort, regardless of legal status, and provided the seed for Kentucky's divisive climate from antebellum, to bellum, to postbellum environment.[11]

Early threat of secession and ever-present force of arms via invasion, raid, and partisan activity evoked response from loyal state authority (government and politicians), harshly imposed national policies and instruments (military and civil), and second/third-tier effects unanticipated and clumsily handled. The General Assembly legislated restrictions on Confederate sympathizers early in the war (loyalty oaths, penalties against recruiters for Southern forces), and these eventually evolved into both state and national clamps on press freedoms and other expressions of sentiment, disenfranchisement of politically suspect citizens, imposition of martial law, and, by July 1864, suspension of the writ of habeas corpus as well as trade restrictions. When original national requests for state volunteers changed to registration and conscription of manpower (white and black), Kentuckians bridled and balked in dismay. When the Union military (many units and personalities homegrown Kentucky, and all serving under national authority) was not interfering with local, state, and even national elections, it harassed Kentucky citizens and oppressed the populace to the point of a perceived "reign of terror" by the summer of 1864. Gen. Eleazer A. Paine, the culprit in this case (in cahoots with Paducah's Union League of America), arbitrarily imposed fines and exile on locals in the Jackson Purchase section of the state who were suspected of aiding and abetting partisans. His extortion included taxing the mails, earning a full-scale investigation for crime and corruption. More unpardonable to Kentuckians, however, was that he apparently took it too far, summarily executing innocent combatants among outlawed guerrilla prisoners. Yet Paine only followed in the train of other paranoid authorities from Bramlette to zealous military officials charged with Kentucky affairs such as Jeremiah Boyle, Ambrose Burnside, and Stephen Burbridge.[12]

In turn, these authorities—even loyal Governor Thomas Bramlette—simply responded to frenetic raids by Kentuckians Morgan, Adam R. "Stovepipe" Johnson, and Hylan B. Lyon as well as outsiders Nathan Bedford Forrest, Roy S. Cluke, and, by the waning moments of hostilities, the infamous Missouri/Kansas war criminals William Clarke Quantrill and M. Jerome "Sue" Mundy, who sought sanctuary in Kentucky's continued destabilization. The fabled work of Confederate guerrilla Champ Ferguson and Unionist partisan Tinker Dave Beatty provided the stuff of legends in the Appalachian region of the state, capturing the essence of postwar feuds of even greater fame. Chicanery of a more venal variety enticed General Burbridge and Maj. Henry C. Symonds in the "Great Hog Swindle" whereby the Union commissariat bilked Kentucky hog farmers of at least $300,000 through favored pork speculators and illicit regulations. Lowell Harrison and James Klotter have concluded: "The animosity generated by such federal officials and policies turned most Kentuckians against the national administration."[13]

Here, Kentucky "became an early example of the hostility of an aggrieved, occupied population, depressed and injured by the suppression of a guerilla war," senses Miller. Indeed, one can also see in the destructive actions of raiders like Kentuckian Lyon another inherent thread that would transcend war and peace—state and national conflict. Sent on a late war raid through western Kentucky, Lyon struck a path of fire venting against Federal occupation authority—not merely military targets, but militarily fortified courthouse sites. Symbols of oppression due to occupancy by Federal troops, they might have been spared nonetheless as local government property in a loyal state. Yet those positions at the courthouse towns Hopkinsville, Cadiz, and Princeton, as well as five other places, contained black U.S. defenders. Lyon, termed by one subsequent Kentucky author as "the courthouse burnin'est general" in all the Confederate forces may, thus, have been reflecting another core peeve. One wartime, nationally imposed issue above all else inflamed the senses of Kentuckians (and all Southerners, for that matter), perhaps. That was emancipation, coupled with the enrollment and drafting of black troops.[14]

Not that Lincoln's Emancipation Proclamation directly affected Kentuckians per se. Exempt, like citizens of other loyal slaveholding states, they nonetheless saw the handwriting on the wall. Ersatz emancipation or liberation of slaves by transiting Union military followed with national confiscation acts as well as prohibition of slavery in the District of Columbia and then the territories. National recruitment of black soldiers and the tertiary problems of vagabondage, impact on labor productivity (numbers and attitude), and general refugee supplication all hardened racial prejudices as well as raising anti-Washington bile in the Bluegrass State. Washington's need for manpower to prosecute the war, however understandable, flew in the face of antebellum paranoia about arming black slaves. The Confiscation Acts of 1861 and 1862, plus Lincoln's proclamation, barely concealed the fact that slavery as an economic as well as a sociocultural institution would be dead come Union victory against the rebellion. Yet, observes Eric Foner, "resistance to change proved greatest in Kentucky."[15]

Moreover, Lincoln, according to Harrison, was "anxious to get emancipation in his native state." His efforts to secure acceptance among its political spokesmen for compensated emancipation form part of a convoluted story leading to the January 1, 1863, proclamation. Absence of any urban or other abolitionist (or antislavery) catalyst of consequence to lead the way, a loyal Union party "distinguished by its timidity" (in the opinion of Gen. John M. Palmer, the last Federal commander responsible for the state), and the obvious economic investment that conditioned Kentuckians' views above all else made ease of transition to a free labor postwar environment extremely problematic. Kentucky's reluctance to "anticipate the end of slavery and prepare for it" quietly, notes Harrison, would cause great strain and stress in postwar readjustment. At war's end, at least sixty-five thousand Kentucky blacks remained in legal bondage, and the state legislature made no effort to ratify the Thirteenth Amendment, which officially ended slavery in America.[16]

Kentucky and Peacetime Reconstruction

Indeed, along with the rights of returned Kentucky Confederates—"the Orphans" of wartime fame— the chief issue of the August 1865 congressional and state office elections was the Thirteenth Amendment. Appomattox, in fact, was but a milepost on the road still stretching from wartime stabilization and reconstruction efforts to postconflict restoration/reconstruction and eventual reconciliation. The overt hostilities ended, and Johnny (both blue and gray) came marching home. Many wanted simply to forget; others more grudgingly wished to remember and seek retribution. Factionalism, feuds, and unrequited urges for lawlessness and violence continued past war's end, with Appalachia and elsewhere witness to clan and community disarray. Whether or not the later famous Hatfield-McCoy feud traced to the violent 1860s, unabated violence all over the Bluegrass State did, "systematized" with murders and other criminality to the point that felons like Frank and Jesse James followed in the train of the Quantrill fugitives entering and exiting the state at will after the war. Such conduct came to symbolize a retarded culture in the minds of outsiders. And, for months, robberies, violence, and social upheaval continued no matter how Kentucky and the nation reacted to Lee's surrender or Lincoln's assassination. Such far-distant events affected the Bluegrass as the spring and summer of 1865 resumed the inevitable cycle of seasons. The war's survivors greeted the future with sorrow, hope, and anticipation as well as trepidation. A so-called Kentucky world at that point was filled "with bitter memories, wartime scars, and long-felt hurts." The outskirts of a city like Louisville stood abandoned on the sentinels, as one historian suggests, eleven forts that should not have been built, but appropriate monuments to a war that should not have been fought.[17]

After the fighting subsides, the issues of the demobilization and reconversion of the economy, society, and governance center, in part, on the reinsertion of the living back to some sense of normality. The mustering out of Union soldiers vied with the vast influx of blacks thinking themselves free after the rebellion's demise and plagued Louisville, bringing peace, but not calm, to that river city. The destitution of the vagabond slaves mixed with the drunken and disorderly demobilizing white volunteers as government authority had no idea of how to deal with the ills of either. If perhaps thirty thousand Kentuckians never returned from the conflict, countless others did—with empty sleeves and psychological damage mixed with the elixir of victory or the gall of defeat. For them, the challenge lay in recovering neglected farms, overgrown paths, and interrupted or defunct businesses while helping restore society's infra-structure—churches, schools, places of enterprise—as well as coping with the poisoned feelings engendered by the conflict. Congregations, classes, and newspaper readership as well as the commerce of Kentucky's major towns and cities—Louisville, Lexington, Paducah, Bowling Green, and Hopkinsville, for example—all required rebuilding to some extent.[18]

Here, then, was one part of Kentucky's reconstruction, along with replacing nearly 90,000 horses, 37,000 mules, 172,000 cattle, and miles of fence and creating a new labor pool. The state lost 4 million acres in cultivation during the war—as much a reflection of labor problems associ-ated with slavery's end as anything else. Land values naturally slumped from $225,000,000 to $174,000,000 by 1862 yet rebounded to nearly $200,000,000 three years later. The prewar hemp industry enjoyed mo-mentary revival along with the return of cotton production across the South, but, soon, newer methods (including the use of wood and metal binding) eclipsed that prosperous Kentucky crop. Prices for tobacco and cotton seemed stable, and, despite Miller's contention that federal aid dur-ing the war "was in the form of arms," one might also suggest that the presence of U.S. money for military-related provisions and services should be factored into such contention. Of course, Kentucky suffered nothing compared to heavier portions of the war zone to the south, in fact just across the border in Tennessee. In conventional American style, recovery in this case would demand the pioneer spirit of individualism and pluck that had built Kentucky in the first place. There would be no national programs for recovery on a scale associated with twentieth-century post-conflict situations. Yet the continuation of the Freedmen's Bureau, run by the War Department, suggested the beginnings of federal welfare for some of Kentucky's population.[19]

The major question of postwar readjustment in Kentucky was sim-ply who would guide or even dictate such adjustment—outsiders via the national government or Kentucky insiders at both the state and the local level. Rule of law, civil rights, payment of wartime debt—in short, the major issues of postwar federal-state relations—loomed large. Other is-sues—especially with economic and social implications—remained very much internal concerns. Traditional dislike or mistrust between pro-Union urban centers on the Ohio (notwithstanding Paducah's secessionist identity) and rural farm communities carried over to postwar issues like railroad, bank, and urban exploitation. Renewed and unregulated river and rail commercialism returned as the Treasury Department lifted wartime restrictions and steamboat ownership and operation returned to private enterprise from government contracts. The war-stressed Louisville and Nashville Railroad regained traction from important infrastructure and rolling stock losses and overuse in logistic support of the Union. The restored power of that line in the state legislature would stymie postwar construction of any competitive north-south lines through the state to tap into a new East Tennessee–Georgia trade axis, reflecting a predictable conflict between monopoly and competition, while blocking for a time more balanced postbellum state economic development and progress. How long such obstructionism might retard natural recovery and pent-up economic expansion for the state and region remained to be seen. Just how much the Civil War retarded the natural march of American commerce and industrialization anyway has long been a historical controversy. In any event, Kentucky played its own role in both the restoration of old, natural economic patterns and the adjustment to the new role, in some might say, a new nation.[20]

Discussion of Kentucky internal redevelopment in the postconflict phase forms the material of good local history or even specialized history dealing with transportation, education, and the role of minorities as well as government. Louisville's merchant princes, trying to maintain the same kind of economic and social hegemony when faced with rising industrialism after the war as they had encountered with professional groups before the conflict, are a story of their own. Yet, for this essay, fascination must lie rather with the national-state government contest for control of Kentucky's postwar direction. While different from the Reconstruction of the Confederate South, in terms of the imposition of a national government struggle for control between branches and agencies of government, the postconflict readjustment story in the Bluegrass State continued the abiding confrontation of states' rights versus federalism in the American System. A state's right to secede or leave the Union had been bloodily resolved in the war. A state's right to control its people, property, and economic and social activities within its own boundaries was decidedly not. As Miller advances: "Reconstruction also pitted many fiefdoms—'Little Kingdoms'—against the federal government when it attempted to encroach upon their control over local affairs." While Kentucky's economy and society remained in disarray, its politics stayed factionalized. And, because political historians long dominated the field of analysis, the central theme of federal-state conflict in Kentucky can be painted against a political canvas. The transition from war to peace scarcely stilled the drumbeat of rhetoric, fervor, and bile in the state's politics regarding national intrusion.[21]

While man, woman, and child in Kentucky transitioned along the road of war and reconstruction, the state's politicians evidenced little break from the power game pitting Frankfort against Washington. Antebellum irresolution of the constitutional issues morphed during the war as new party fault lines soon surfaced over local implementation of national policies and programs, rules, regulations, and restrictions. If Washington officials poorly understood the unique Kentucky predicament, so too Kentucky politicos seemingly looked for every occasion to offer obstruction and opposition without surcease. Perhaps this was a natural breakdown in the antebellum supremacy of the Whig Party, which then transformed into the wartime turbulence of secessionist, democratic conservatism and the new player, republicanism (itself too freely associated with abolition, military rule, and government centralism). Wartime animosity generated by Federal officials on the ground in the state (associated with the absentee domination of the Lincoln administration in Washington) and the vote for McClellan and the Democratic ticket in 1864 both encapsulated an environment soon transferred to a postconflict political maelstrom at every turn. While progress (or the lack thereof) in the restoration of individual and corporate enterprise might take place beyond this turbulence, history (or historians) has placed great, if even undue, attention on that phenomenon in explaining the state's place in the postwar Union.[22]

Harrison and Klotter may be correct when they assert that the fluid political situation was "uncertain, unstable and unsteady" in the environment of the late 1860s. They further assert that "three virtually new political parties" sprang up in the commonwealth. A wartime Union Party translated to a postwar Republican entity supporting the three civil rights amendments to the U.S. Constitution. More moderate at the Kentucky level than the national Radical Republican level, the membership included former Unionists and Whigs who sought a progressive, modernizing face for national as well as state consumption. Opponents, however, chose to identify this crowd as radicals, Jacobins, and militarists and pinned on them all the perceived ills of black suffrage and racial equality. Principal among these opponents was a Conservative or States' Rights Party—Democrats in any other guise, including ex-Confederates and some Unionists as well as old Bourbons who despised Washington on military, constitutional, and racial grounds. They fought all constitutional amendments, any extension of black rights, and sought actively to retain the free and unconquered states' right approach as the pure tradition of Washington's and Jefferson's precepts. Of course, standing apart from the two polarized parties was something termed the Conservative Union or Constitutional Union Democratic Party—a third party that disagreed with both the "radical" policies of the Republicans and the reactionary tide of the resurgent democracy. This third way captured the notion of the Union and that of the Constitution as they had been before the revolutionary tides of wartime change but with less stridency than the competitors, perhaps.[23]

In truth, this tripartite political split catered to national issues like Southern Reconstruction, racial prejudice, and constitutional interpretation—but with a Kentucky cast. Little wonder that, when a veritable propaganda war opened for the hearts and minds of postwar Kentuckians, voices were muted as Lexington newsman William C. P. Breckinridge, a sometime Confederate, called for a New South and a new postwar Kentucky in October 1866, one with extended railroads, reopened waterways, extracted mineral wealth, and new mills and manufactories so that the state might apply its zeal and energy to compete with other parts of the Union. Such modernism quickly drew rebuttal from agrarian-oriented Bourbons of the old school. It sounded too much like the Republican philosophy of progress—anathema to veterans of the vicissitudes of Kentucky politics during wartime occupation. The political testing in Frankfort came, not over reconstructive issues of valid economic sense, but, rather, over a continuing obsession about Washington intrusion and concern with the black man. The initial sparring as delineated by historians showed the rejection of the Thirteenth Amendment ending slavery, the repeal of the wartime expatriation act ensuring former Kentucky Confederates' pardons and redress from reprisals, and a decided renaissance of favor for those people who had actually brought on the war and the "time of troubles" in the first place. Indeed, little wonder then, despite the return of peace, that martial law continued in the state of Kentucky, that military intimidation continued to be felt at the polls and as a continued stabilizer against insurgency, crime, and disruption. This hypermilitary activity led President Andrew Johnson to order an end of martial law in the Bluegrass State on October 12, 1865. Still, the fact that Kentucky could not adjust easily to the new world of minority rights brought a threat of federal intervention by early 1866—one quite precedential for modern reconstructive efforts by a national government.[24]

Kentucky's continuing intransigence regarding slavery and freed people caused extension of the War Department's Freedmen's Bureau activity from Tennessee to its northern neighbor. Kentucky's steadfast stubbornness regarding the constitutional amendment, the nullification of the state's own slave code, and the provision for the destitute freed people as well as protection against terrorist actions by the white's postwar equivalent to wartime guerrillas—soon to be termed Ku Kluxers, Regulators—caused the assistant bureau commissioner, Brig. Gen. Clinton B. Fisk, to make the January 1866 move. By March, the state had been divided into three subdistricts by the chief, Gen. John Ely. Subdistrict headquarters were located in Louisville, Lexington, and Paducah, reflecting that immediate postwar tendency of the freed people to flock to urban sanctuaries while refugee camps had been opened at wartime Union training and freed-people rendezvous like Camps Nelson and Dick Robinson as well as other major towns and cities.[25]

Bureau responsibility went beyond merely caring for the needy and sick at those facilities, however, as education became a paramount concern for federal authorities as well as the freed people themselves, along with the appointment of citizen agents to assist the new freed labor in fair contract negotiations. At least, some Kentucky newspapers like the *Louisville Daily Journal* thought that Fisk meant to do right by his subjects as well as administering the bureau "in such a manner as to be the least offensive to the community." Six months later, however, the editor plumbed for legislative action to rectify the former slaves' plight, perhaps more under the guise of getting rid of the hated bureau's presence in the state than any humanitarian epiphany. On the other hand, outraged Kentuckians agreed with the Frankfort *Daily Kentucky Yeoman*'s stance that the state had been repaid for its wartime loyalty with treatment like a "conquered territory." Rhetoric appealed to the unapologetic, unrepentant, and decidedly racist masses as "the victors" lost the peace.[26]

Minor skirmishes before both off-year and state elections, even before the next presidential race in 1868, set the tone for postwar Kentucky politics—the introduction of heroes and villains in the guise of personae as politicians who had served loyally in either blue or gray uniforms. Political shuttlecocks continued to be the constitutional amendments and other national legislation on behalf of blacks, the federal presence in the guise of the Freedmen's Bureau, and bickering over perceived national government "robbery" of private property through uncompensated emancipation—in essence, the continuation of wartime federalism from Washington as translated to postwar congressional or Radical reconstruction. Eventually, as is typical in American politics, the third party (Conservative Union) effectively died by 1867, and divergent interest groups split apart the commonwealth's focus into western, central, northern, and eastern blocks with the agrarian conflict with commercial power reshaping populist insurgencies of the future. Crop niche sectionalism (old hemp-growing Bluegrass against tobacco-growing western Kentucky) might be identified. Even more prophetic, as state matters overtook nationally imposed ones in the late 1860s, the wisdom of William Breckinridge surfaced in earnest. Bourbon Democrats reflected the old and seemingly worshiped "at the dead shrine of the dead past," while New Departure Democrats sought a reborn Kentucky while putting the issues of the antebellum and wartime periods behind them. New Kentucky reflected New South regionalism—one enlightened on the role of blacks (to modest degree), industrialization, education, and internal improvements, in short, progress and change. Both factions of the Democratic Party stood in contradistinction to the Republicans. And Kentucky Republicans could not even get their war hero Ulysses S. Grant the state's electoral vote in the 1868 election.[27]

Outside help came for black enfranchisement in Kentucky and, ironically, not through national government intervention. While the state legislature overwhelmingly rejected the Fifteenth Amendment in January 1869, ratification by other states made it the law of the land. Despite the imposition of residence requirements or boundary changes at local levels to inhibit (and prohibit) black male voters, that sector of the population soon did vote in pivotal precincts while generally identifying with the party of Lincoln. Still, that party could not break identification with wartime oppression and postwar readjustment. Democratic control of the state was itself sharply divided, as shown by bitter maneuvering to overcome emergent sectionalism in opposition to the construction of the Cincinnati Southern Railroad to East Tennessee. Yet, by the mid-1870s, Reconstruction began to fade as an issue. Federal military or bureaucratic presence had ended in the state, and even party schisms abated. Black integration took place in places with Jim Crow, segregation, and local rules for vagrancy lying in the future. Unfortunately, Kentucky's reputation for violence, especially against freed people, never seemed to subside. The commonwealth's stubbornness on the race issue and Breckinridge's confidence that slavery would ultimately die without emancipation could be updated to suggest that racial barriers and prejudices would do likewise. But just when was anyone's guess in the decades after 1865.[28]

National or formal Reconstruction of the Confederate South ended with the Compromise of 1877 and the withdrawal of the last federal occupation troops the following year. Kentuckian Benjamin H. Bristow played a prominent role in engineering Republican Rutherford B. Hayes's ascendancy to the White House. Bristow was a progressive exponent of a South influenced by prosperity built on free institutions and untapped resources. Civil War–era issues had become historical anachronisms as he sought North-South reconciliation (reflected in the deal sending Hayes to Washington). Yet, in some measure, Kentucky in reconstruction had ended several years earlier. At least, some historians think so. The Democratic governor J. B. McCreary, himself an ex-Confederate colonel, declared in his 1875 inaugural address that he wished to see "the records of secession, coercion and reconstruction filed away forever," with the American people advocating peace and reconciliation "under the Constitution as the guarantee of our liberties and the safeguard of every citizen."[29]

Even then, the campaign leading to McCreary's election had underscored new focus. The former Unionist John Marshall Harlan (who eventually became one of the most widely acclaimed justices of the U.S. Supreme Court) honed in on state issues, while McCreary pounded those more closely national. Violence in the commonwealth would plague the victor's term, as it had for all the wartime and postwar reconstruction phases. Kentucky, even at epoch's end, still identified with unrepentant destabilization and wistful yearning to join the defunct Confederacy in spirit, masking the modernizing progress everywhere, perhaps, but in the hearts and actions of some leaders and followers. It took another two decades for the 1873 push for constitutional reform to revise the old 1849 basic charter that had condoned slavery so as to give all Kentuckians control of their government and ensure "the new order" springing forth in the breasts of more enlightened politicians and citizens the chance for fruition.[30]

Destruction and Reconstruction

Shortly after midnight on January 11, 1865, Louisville's famed hostelry the Galt House burned to the ground. The loss of life was small, but the structure could not saved. "The stately edifice, so long the pride and fame of our city, is now a huge, unshapely mass," wailed the *Louisville Democrat*. The building's destruction somehow symbolized the war years' cataclysm, the loss of institutions and lives for the American South, if not precisely for Kentucky. Nonetheless, no Kentuckian quite knew what impended in the new year, although rebuilding, if not the hotel, certainly the state and nation, had to occupy old patriarchs and nouveau characters alike. The Galt House had hosted numerous public figures, civilian and military alike, drawn to or through Kentucky by the conflict. The hotel had helped the river town transition to the commercial and technological revolution that wedded steam to boat and then to land rail car. As the Civil War wound toward its close, survivors had to return to harnessing that revolution. Now, while binding up wounds and mourning the dead, they needed to erect a new commonwealth on social as well as other revolutions. The question would be, could they do so, and in what form?[31]

Native sons and wartime visitors had driven both intrastate and nation-state difficulties. The antebellum Bourbonism of the Clays and Breckinridges as well as the upstart wartime disruptions of Bramlette, Boyle and Burbridge, Morgan, Basil Duke, and "Stovepipe" Johnson all provided a legacy that would drive postwar directions in Kentucky's world. Crisis and chaos in people's lives as well among institutions hampered the way toward progress and enlightened decisions. New Departure

Democracy may, ultimately, have been as predictable as the immediate simmering embers of bile and gall, and just how and when one would be superseded and the other emerge would remain shrouded in the wake of rebellion's defeat. The abiding questions of reconstruction, whether during war or peace, were principally the schisms that rent the commonwealth to begin with—states' rights versus federalism or nationalism and the human and economic dimensions whereby Africans found an adjusted place in Kentucky's society. If the state never quite fit Secretary of War Edwin Stanton's cryptic "pariah among the elect" in retrospect, those words evoke the bitterness of the age. Kentucky certainly supplied the supreme irony—a loyal border slave state oppressed for its allegiance, confronted with the process of national unification and modernization through artificially imposed nation building, yet saddled by the reactive, protective inclinations of local tribalism seeking to preserve the comfortable stability of the past, the known, and perhaps patriarchal rule. Overlying the scene was a social taboo of racism.

Each generation will reexamine the era of Civil War and Reconstruction, perhaps redefining its parameters and paradigms. Traditional negative definition via the William Dunning school has changed through the reinterpretations of John Hope Franklin and Eric Foner (to name two) and the new synthesis via the work of Richard Curry and Michael Fitzgerald. For a state like Kentucky—avowedly one of the stars missing from the Confederate Stars and Bars—whether or not it seemed to join the Lost Cause after the war remains a moot question today. The generation to which that mattered has long passed. The traditional interpretation of E. Merton Coulter notwithstanding, the more nuanced language of Lowell Harrison, James C. Klotter, Ross A. Webb, and Victor Howard suggests a freshness of new visitation of old evidence and broader scope. Throughout the South, familial curiosity concerning forebears' participation in Union blue as well as Confederate gray has reshaped the honor of the dead and the appreciation of the living. Perhaps today's generation will interpret the occupied American South with Kentucky included, in the lens of nation building in the Middle East and Southwest Asia. Cynthia Watson's concluding thought remains prophetic: "Nation-building appears one of the predominant challenges facing the world in this decade, if not this century." Americans and Kentuckians certainly thought so 150 years ago.

Perhaps their experience counsels the lesson of patience amid despair, the need to end outside (if well-intentioned) meddling to resolve inherent problems of internal tribalism, measured readjustment of men, institutions, policies, and programs and not to expect instant reconciliation following rancid rancor of political conflict based on high economic stakes and constitutionalism, familial division, and, above all, ethnic hatred.[32]

In addition to Watson's, analysis by another modern scholar, T. David Mason, on sustaining peace after civil war introduces the thought that "outsiders" (in this case, the international community) can reduce the chances of the resumption of armed conflict after civil strife by first "introducing peacekeeping forces," then "investing in economic development and reconstruction," and, finally, "establishing democratic political institutions tailored to the configuration or ethnic and religious cleavages in the society." Confederate general Richard Taylor, born at "Springfields" near Louisville, appropriately entitled his postwar memoirs *Destruction and Reconstruction*. However, replacing fences, butchered livestock, and disrupted patterns of living—the destruction of war—required less time than anticipated for Kentuckians, left alone to resolve that part of the destruction. By the end of the 1860s, the state and the region had a thirst for new directions—for commerce, enterprise, and self-control of their own destiny. Outside intervention from the national government, which had continued in the postcombat phase, still butted against that destiny, with the central cause for such intervention—matters of race—remaining contentious for decades thereafter. A revolution ending human bondage gravitated but slowly toward human equality. Slow to embrace the realities of emancipation and the protections of constitutional amendment, Kentucky mind-sets concerning lost human property meant that this part of America's nation building would take longer—perhaps a whole century at least, or even more. There would necessarily be new wine in old bottles to effect the solution of the problem of race and the problems of federalism as they affected the commonwealth. Even today, impatient Americans still cannot grasp the element of time required for democratizing the world, and leading by example is lost where perception speaks as loudly as words to a globalized information age. Kentucky's sons and daughters of the Tragic Era might teach us something about mind-sets and problems. They may even contradict today's conventional wisdom concerning civil war and reconstruction.[33]

Notes

1. Frank Furlong Mathias, ed., *Incidents and Experiences in the Life of Thomas W. Parsons from 1826 to 1900* (Lexington: University Press of Kentucky, 1975), 143–44.

2. Cynthia A. Watson, *Nation-Building: A Reference Handbook* (Santa Barbara, Calif.: ABC Clio, 2004), 3. See also Robert C. Orr, ed., *Winning the Peace: An American Strategy for Post-Conflict Reconstruction* (Washington, D.C.: CSIS, July 2004); U.S. Department of Defense, Directive 3000.05, Military Support for Stability, Security, Transition and Reconstruction (SSTR) Operations, Washington, D.C., November 28, 2005; James Dobbins et al., *America's Role in Nation-Building, from Germany to Iraq* (Santa Monica, Calif.: Rand, 2003).

3. James Jay Carafano, "Post-Conflict Operations from Europe to Iraq," *Heritage Lectures,* no. 844, June 21, 2004 (Washington, D.C.: Heritage Foundation, July 13, 2004).

4. Watson, *Nation-Building,* chap. 2, esp. pp. 10–11.

5. Ibid., 12–13.

6. Ibid., 12, 14.

7. Ibid., 13–19; Edward L. Ayers, *What Caused the Civil War? Reflections on the South and Southern History* (New York: Norton, 2005), 148–49.

8. Penny M. Miller, *Kentucky Politics and Government: Do We Stand United?* (Lincoln: University of Nebraska Press, 1994), 24–25; Lowell H. Harrison and James C. Klotter, *A New History of Kentucky* (Lexington: University Press of Kentucky, 1997), pts. 1 and 2, esp. chaps. 10–13; E. Merton Coulter, *The Civil War and Readjustment in Kentucky* (Chapel Hill: University of North Carolina Press, 1926), chaps. 1–5.

9. Harrison and Klotter, *New History,* chap. 14; Lowell H. Harrison, *The Civil War in Kentucky* (Lexington: University Press of Kentucky, 1975), chaps. 1–4. See also my *Forts Henry and Donelson: Key to the Confederate Heartland* (Knoxville: University of Tennessee Press, 1987), and *Fort Donelson's Legacy: War and Society in Kentucky and Tennessee, 1862–1863* (Knoxville: University of Tennessee Press, 1997).

10. Miller, *Kentucky Politics and Government,* 25 (quoting John Ed Pearce, *Divide and Dissent: Kentucky Politics, 1930–1963* [Lexington: University Press of Kentucky, 1987], 13); Coulter, *Civil War and Readjustment,* chaps. 6–10; Harrison and Klotter, *New History,* 195–207; Harrison, *Civil War in Kentucky,* chap. 5; Schott J. Lucas, "Indignities, Wrongs, and Outrages: Military and Guerrilla Incursions on Kentucky's Civil War Home Front," *Filson Club Quarterly* 73 (1999): 355–76.

11. See Victor B. Howard, *Black Liberation in Kentucky: Emancipation and Freedom, 1862-1864* (Lexington: University Press of Kentucky, 1983), chaps. 1-2; Thomas W. Speed, *The Union Cause in Kentucky, 1860-1865* (New York: Putnam's, 1907), 15-161; U.S. War Department, *The War of the Rebellion: A Compilation of the Official Records of the Union and Confederate Armies, 1861-1865,* 70 vols. in 128 pts. (Washington, D.C.: U.S. Government Printing Office, 1880-1901), ser. 3, vol. 4, p. 1269, and ser. 4, vol. 1, p. 962; Amy Murrell Taylor, *The Divided Family in Civil War America* (Chapel Hill: University of North Carolina Press, 2005), 3, 4, 15, 29-32, 42, 127; Mary Clay Berry, *Voices from the Century Before: The Odyssey of a Nineteenth Century Kentucky Family* (New York: Arcade, 1997); John David Smith and William Cooper Jr., eds., *A Union Woman in Civil War Kentucky: The Diary of Frances Peter* (Lexington: University Press of Kentucky, 2000); and Richard Troutman, ed., *The Heavens Are Weeping: The Diaries of George R. Browder, 1852-1886* (Grand Rapids, Mich.: Zondervan, 1987).

12. The details of Kentucky wartime reconstruction can be traced in Lewis Collins and Richard H. Collins, *History of Kentucky,* 2 vols. (Covington, Ky.: Collins, 1882), 1:85-150 ("Annals of Kentucky"); James Louis Head, *Atonement of John Brooks: The Story of the True Johnny "Reb" Who Did Not Come Marching Home* (Geneva, Fla.: Heritage, 2001); and Sean Michael O'Brien, *Mountain Partisans: Guerrilla Warfare in the Southern Appalachians, 1861-1865* (Westport, Conn.: Praeger, 1999), chap. 6.

13. Harrison and Klotter, *New History,* 205-6; Michael A. Flannery, "Kentucky History Revisited: The Role of the Civil War in Shaping Kentucky's Collective Consciousness," *Filson Club Quarterly* 71 (1997): 27-51; Palmer H. Boeger, "The Great Kentucky Hog Swindle of 1864," *Journal of Southern History* 28 (February 1962): 50-70; William J. Davis, ed., *The Partisan Rangers of the Confederate States Army: Memoirs of General Adam R. Johnson* (Austin, Tex.: State House, 1995); John Sickles, *The Legends of Sue Mundy and One Armed Berry: Confederate Guerrillas* (Merrillville, Ind.: Heritage, 1999); Thomas Shelby Watson, *Confederate Guerrilla Sue Mundy: A Biography of Confederate Soldier Jerome Clarke* (Jefferson, N.C.: McFarland, 2008); and Marion B. Lucas, "Camp Nelson, Kentucky during the Civil War: Cradle of Liberty or Refugee Death Camp?" *Filson Club Quarterly* 63 (October 1989): 439-52.

14. On Lyon, see B. L. Roberson, "The Courthouse Burnin'est General," *Tennessee Historical Quarterly* 23 (December 1964): 372-78 (citing Hall Allen, *Center of Conflict* [Paducah, n.d.], 146; and Edward M. Coffman, ed., "Memoirs of Hylan B. Lyon, Brigadier General, C.S.A.," *Tennessee Historical Quarterly* 18 [March 1959]: 35-53).

15. Eric Foner, *Reconstruction: America's Unfinished Revolution, 1863-1877*

(New York: Harper & Row, 1988), 37–38; see also Silvana R. Siddali, *From Property to Person: Slavery and the Confiscation Acts, 1861–1862* (Baton Rouge: Louisiana State University Press, 2005).

16. Coulter, *Civil War and Readjustment*, 258–61; Harrison, *Civil War in Kentucky*, 88–94; Miller, *Kentucky Politics and Government*, 25; Foner, *Reconstruction*, 38.

17. The details of postwar Kentucky reconstruction can be traced in Collins and Collins, *History of Kentucky*, 1:151–246; Robert Emmett McDowell, *City of Conflict: Louisville in the Civil War, 1861–1865* (Louisville, Ky.: Louisville Civil War Round Table, 1962), chaps. 13–14; O. S. Barton, *Quantrill: A True Story Told by His Scout John McCorkle* (Norman: University of Oklahoma Press, 1992), chap. 13; Gary Robert Matthews, *Basil Wilson Duke, CSA: The Right Man in the Right Place* (Lexington: University Press of Kentucky, 2005), chap. 14; Altina L. Waller, *Feud: Hatfields, McCoys, and Social Change in Appalachia, 1860–1900* (Chapel Hill: University of North Carolina Press, 1988); and T. J. Stiles, *Jesse James: Last Rebel of the Civil War* (New York: Knopf, 2002), 196–98, 201, 216, 218–20.

18. McDowell, *City of Conflict*, chap. 14; Harrison, *Civil War in Kentucky*, 101–2.

19. Harrison, *Civil War in Kentucky*, 101–2; Harrison and Klotter, *New History*, chaps. 15–16; Miller, *Kentucky Politics and Government*, 37; Coulter, *Civil War and Readjustment*, chaps. 12, 15, 17–18; Ross A. Webb, "Kentucky: 'Pariah among the Elect,'" in *Radicalism, Racism, and Party Realignment: The Border States during Reconstruction*, ed. Richard O. Curry (Baltimore: Johns Hopkins University Press, 1969), chap. 4; James F. Hopkins, *A History of the Hemp Industry in Kentucky* (Lexington: University of Kentucky Press, 1951), chap. 6.

20. Leonard P. Curry, *Rail Routes South: Louisville's Fight for the Southern Market, 1865–1872* (Lexington: University of Kentucky Press, 1969), chaps. 2–4; George H. Yater, *Two Hundred Years at the Falls of the Ohio: A History of Louisville and Jefferson County* (Louisville, Ky.: Filson Club, 1987), chap. 9.

21. Miller, *Kentucky Politics and Government*, 25–27.

22. Coulter, *Civil War and Readjustment*, chaps. 9–10.

23. Harrison and Klotter, *New History*, 239–40; Coulter, *Civil War and Readjustment*, chap. 13; Hambleton Tapp and James C. Klotter, *Kentucky: Decades of Discord, 1865–1900* (Frankfort: Kentucky Historical Society, 1977), chaps. 1–2.

24. Webb, "'Pariah among the Elect,'" 118–19.

25. Ross A. Webb, "'The Past Is Never Dead, It's Not Even Past': Benjamin P. Runkle and the Freedmen's Bureau in Kentucky, 1866–1870," *Register of the Kentucky Historical Society* 84 (1986): 344–57; Richard E. Sears, *Camp Nelson*,

Kentucky: A Civil War History (Lexington: University Press of Kentucky, 2002), li–lxiv, chaps. 4–8.

26. Harrison and Klotter, *New History*, 240; Webb, "'The Past Is Never Dead,'" 344–46 (citing *Daily Kentucky Yeoman* [Frankfort], January 17, 24, 1866; and *Louisville Daily Journal*, January 4, February 8, June 11, 1866).

27. Coulter, *Civil War and Readjustment*, 416–17; Harrison and Klotter, *New History*, 243; Webb, "'Pariah among the Elect,'" 124–25.

28. See Howard, *Black Liberation in Kentucky*, chaps. 9–11; Harrison and Klotter, *New History*, 234–39, 247–48.

29. Harrison and Klotter, *New History*, 239–46; Webb, "'Pariah among the Elect,'" 134–40.

30. Harrison and Klotter, *New History*, 249–58; Tapp and Klotter, *Decades of Discord*, chap. 12.

31. Yater, *Two Hundred Years at the Falls*, 95; McDowell, *City of Conflict*, 185–86.

32. Watson, *Nation-Building*, 19; Richard Taylor, *Destruction and Reconstruction: Personal Experiences of the Late War* (New York: D. Appleton, 1879).

33. T. David Mason, *Sustaining the Peace after Civil War* (Carlisle, Pa.: U.S. Army War College, Strategic Studies Institute, 2007), iii, 70–78.

Afterword

John V. Cimprich

Over twenty years ago, Benjamin Franklin Cooling argued that events in Kentucky and Tennessee determined the outcome of the Civil War. Certainly, major campaigns there led to an extensive Federal occupation as well as important Confederate invasions, cavalry raids, and guerrilla activity. In any case, developments in the two states illustrate much about the nature of the war in all the Upper South. This collection offers insights into a wide range of topics beyond the well-known battles.[1]

From the essays of Gary R. Matthews, Thomas C. Mackey, Derek W. Frisby, Robert Tracy McKenzie, and John D. Fowler, one can conclude that the secession movement faced similar obstacles and opportunities in both states. Neither state experienced the full force of Southern sectionalism's anxieties, and many voters had imbibed the strong nationalism cultivated in the region during Henry Clay's long political career. Kentucky and Tennessee yeoman tended to conceive of their economic interests as being like those of Northern farmers. A high volume of trade tied the region to the Midwest. Still, the two states had more slaves and slaveholders than several of the original Confederate states. Those realities fostered Southern identities in some. So deep division of opinion existed, sometimes within the same mind.[2]

William G. Brownlow, like Clay, greatly influenced political attitudes, although the middle-aged Tennessean did so on a much less idealistic level than the deceased Kentuckian. The strength of Unionism made secessionist leaders feel hard-pressed. In Tennessee, disunionists frustrated in one referendum turned in a second vote to fraud and force, methods that they did not invent but that had appeared periodically in the nation's prewar mass participation politics.[3] President Abraham Lincoln tipped the balance for some citizens (such as Sidney Smith Stanton, according to W. Calvin Dickinson) through his decision to go to war against the seceded states. Yet, by showing more respect than the Confederate army did for Kentucky's official position of neutrality, Lincoln kept that state on his side.

Recruits from both states, as described by Dickinson, Kenneth W. Noe, and Kent T. Dollar, fit well-known patterns. Not surprisingly, those who joined the Union army generally were nationalists from Unionist communities. Wartime experiences eventually turned a few—fewer than in the Union army as a whole—against slavery. Confederate enlistees motivated themselves by upholding Southern independence, personal liberties, and their families' security. In both armies, good officers, a sense of brotherhood with comrades, hatred of the enemy, and deepening religious convictions could help troops endure deprivations.[4]

Ugly, irregular forms of warfare commonly appeared behind Federal lines. Brian D. McKnight points to the roles of paranoia, terrorism, and a dehumanizing hate for enemies in causing preemptive killing by guerrillas such as Champ Ferguson. To be successful, guerrillas needed prudence, caution, and intelligence. Michael R. Bradley demonstrates how both partisan warfare and abuses of civilians easily escalated brutality into a cycle of revenge. Angry men in the ranks most often initiated abuse of the easy targets, those who could not resist. Officers like the notorious Gen. Eleazer A. Paine made matters worse by ordering or encouraging atrocities. Significantly, not everyone succumbed to these temptations. The majority of soldiers in all ranks in both armies probably objected or refused to participate. The Confederate general John Breckinridge ordered Champ Ferguson's arrest for killing captured Federal soldiers, and the Union general James Garfield condemned depredations against civilians.[5] Wartime atrocities are a difficult and sensitive subject. As these essays demonstrate, historians need to document alleged injustices thoroughly with firsthand, contemporary evidence that has been cross-checked whenever possible. Other kinds of evidence can too easily convey rumors or truths embroidered for greater impact.

Two major groups, victimized or empowered in different circumstances during the war, were slaves and white women. The war's impact on slavery in occupied states is well-known,[6] but Marion B. Lucas and Richard D. Sears offer insights into the special situation of Kentucky, the loyal state with the largest number of slaves. Slavery there remained perfectly legal yet floundered amid the disruptive forces of the war. At first, masters received much open aid from Federal authorities in preserving the institution. The 1864 wintertime expulsion of slave women and children from Camp Nelson after their men had enlisted became notorious because many died from exposure or starvation. It was a turning point and resulted in much more use of the Union army's might against the state's government and proslavery masters. Enlistment would give more slave men and their families a Federal freedom in Kentucky than elsewhere.

Defined as dependent, weak, and less important, women were especially vulnerable before heavy-handed armies. The idealized position of the "lady" in Victorian culture has long received careful study.[7] Kristen L. Streater shows how "the divisive nature of the war in Kentucky [and the South generally] had made women's actions significant." Their familial duties to support and help provide for men led to a partisanship benefited by the culture's high respect for "ladies" and their responsibilities. Many soldiers were reluctant to be harsh with them and sometimes had to be ordered to act so.

While Kentucky had an existing civilian government to deal with wartime issues, Tennessee fell under Federal military rule after the Union troops' advances caused the collapse of the Confederate state structure. Handicapped by an unconstructive prewar political record, and challenged by the state's complexly divided society, the military governor, Andrew Johnson, according to Jonathan M. Atkins, could not avoid controversy. He had to use delays and disfranchisement to get prowar, Unionist electoral victories. He had to accept emancipation, although not racial equality, to keep Lincoln's confidence. In attaining his goal of restoring civilian state rule, he did the best job possible.[8]

In the postwar South, charitable aid to transition the needy back to work was inadequate or nonexistent. Sears adds that the Freedmen's Bureau was in an excessive hurry to end federal support for black and white refugees (the latter group had often been ignored during the war as well). When many Southerners grew hostile toward economic development because the Republican-controlled central government favored it, harmful consequences followed, given the continued decline of agricultural economies. Rebuilding requires an end to violence, but the postwar occupation lacked enough troops to assure order, and not all officers had the prudence exemplified in the case of the 1867 Nashville election. Unionist state governments did not build sufficient popular support for their reconstruction efforts. Fowler and Ben H. Severance emphasize that Tennessee Unionists especially failed at this through suppressing and alienating ex-Confederates. Kentucky's government represented popular opinion by refusing to enforce emancipation. But that only led to more hostility toward the federal government, when, through the Freedmen's Bureau, it imposed an end to slavery and rights for freedmen. By refusing to accept the Union victory and viewing all reconstruction as invalid and oppressive, the more recalcitrant ex-Confederates proceeded to turn the majority of Southern whites in a reactionary direction.[9]

Tennessee and Kentucky are just pieces in the Civil War story. Comparative analysis is very useful here. B. Franklin Cooling does so in a world context, which has general benefits for dissecting the big processes of civil war and reconstruction. Several of the authors consider other Southern states for comparisons, such as Cooling's observation that guerrilla war in Kentucky (I would add Tennessee) falls between the less intense level in Maryland and the much worse case of Missouri. Such an approach can offer more numerous and specific insights. It is to be hoped that future studies will continue to use comparative analysis to aid understanding of the Civil War's local, regional, and national impact.

Notes

1. Benjamin Franklin Cooling, *Forts Henry and Donelson: The Key to the Confederate Heartland* (Knoxville: University of Tennessee Press, 1987), esp. 276–78. For synopses of major campaigns in the region, also see Stephen D. Engle, *The Struggle for the Heartland: The Campaigns from Fort Henry to Corinth* (Lincoln: University of Nebraska Press, 2001); Earl J. Hess, *Banners to the Breeze: The Kentucky Campaign, Corinth, and Stones River* (Lincoln: University of Nebraska Press, 2000); Steven E. Woodworth, *Six Armies in Tennessee: The Chickamauga and Chattanooga Campaigns* (Lincoln: University of Nebraska Press, 1998); and Anne J. Bailey, *The Chessboard of War: Sherman and Hood in the Autumn Campaigns of 1864* (Lincoln: University of Nebraska Press, 2000).

2. See also Daniel W. Crofts, *Reluctant Confederates: Upper South Unionists in the Secession Crisis* (Chapel Hill: University of North Carolina Press, 1989).

3. Glenn C. Altschuler and Stuart H. Blumin, *Rude Republic: Americans and Their Politics in the Nineteenth Century* (Princeton, N.J.: Princeton University Press, 2000), 73–84; Daniel W. Crofts, ed., "Re-Electing Lincoln: The Struggle in Newark," *Civil War History* 30 (1984): 54–79.

4. James M. McPherson, *What They Fought For, 1861–1865* (Baton Rouge: Louisiana State University, 1994).

5. See also Daniel E. Sutherland, ed., *Guerrillas, Unionists, and Violence on the Confederate Home Front* (Fayetteville: University of Arkansas Press, 1999); and James Ramage, "Recent Historiography of Guerrilla Warfare in the Civil War: A Review Essay," *Register of the Kentucky Historical Society* 103 (2005): 517–41. George S. Burkhardt (*Confederate Rage, Yankee Wrath: No Quarter in the Civil War* [Carbondale: Southern Illinois University Press, 2007]) argues that retribution became unwritten military policy, while Mark E. Neely (*The Civil War and the Limits of Destruction* [Cambridge, Mass.: Harvard University Press, 2007]) rejects that thesis.

6. Leon F. Litwack, *Been in the Storm So Long: The Aftermath of Slavery* (New York: Knopf, 1979); Ira Berlin et al., eds., *The Destruction of Slavery*, vol. 1, ser. 1, of *Freedom: A Documentary History of Emancipation, 1861–1867, Selected from the Holdings of the National Archives of the United States* (New York: Cambridge University Press, 1985); John Cimprich, *Slavery's End in Tennessee, 1861–1865* (Tuscaloosa: University of Alabama Press, 1985).

7. George C. Rable, *Civil Wars: Women and the Crisis of Southern Nationalism* (Urbana: University of Illinois Press, 1989), 154–79; Drew Gilpin Faust, *Mothers of Invention: Women of the Slaveholding South in the American Civil War* (Chapel Hill: University of North Carolina Press, 2004), 196–219.

8. See also William C. Harris, *With Charity for All: Lincoln and the Restoration of the Union* (Lexington: University Press of Kentucky, 1997).

9. See also Eric Foner, *Reconstruction: America's Unfinished Revolution, 1863–1877* (New York: Harper & Row, 1988); Dan T. Carter, *When the War Was Over: The Failure of Self-Reconstruction in the South* (Baton Rouge: Louisiana State University Press, 1985), 34, 48, 58; and James E. Sefton, *The United States Army and Reconstruction, 1865–1877* (Baton Rouge: Louisiana State University Press, 1967).

Contributors

Jonathan M. Atkins is professor of history at Berry College in Georgia and specializes in nineteenth-century politics. His most well-known works are *Politics, Parties, and the Sectional Conflict in Tennessee, 1832-1861* (1997) and several articles published in the *Journal of Southern History* and the *Tennessee Historical Quarterly*.

Michael R. Bradley taught history at Motlow State Community College in Tullahoma, Tennessee, and has written extensively on the Civil War. Among his books are *Nathan Bedford Forrest's Escort and Staff* (2006), *With Blood and Fire: Life behind Union Lines in Middle Tennessee, 1863-65* (2003), and *Tullahoma: The 1863 Campaign for the Control of Middle Tennessee* (1999).

A professor of history at Thomas More College in Crestview Hills, Kentucky, John V. Cimprich has authored several works on the Civil War, including *Fort Pillow, a Civil War Massacre, and Public Memory* (2005) and *Slavery's End in Tennessee, 1861-1865* (1985). His project in progress centers on runaway slaves during the Civil War.

B. Franklin Cooling is professor of national security studies at the Industrial College of the Armed Forces in Washington, D.C. His many publications include *Forts Henry and Donelson: The Key to the Confederate Heartland* (2003), *Fort Donelson's Legacy: War and Society in Kentucky and Tennessee, 1862-1863* (1997), *Jubal Early's Raid on Washington: 1864* (1995), and *Symbol, Sword, and Shield: Defending Washington during the Civil War* (1991).

W. Calvin Dickinson is professor emeritus of history at Tennessee Technological University. He has published dozens of articles and books, the most recent of which are *Tennessee: State of the Nation* (2006), coedited with Larry H. Whiteaker; *Rural Life and Culture in the Upper Cumberland* (2004), coedited with Michael E. Birdwell; *Tennessee Tales That Textbooks Don't Tell* (2002), coauthored with Eloise Hitchcock; and *A Bibliography of Tennessee History, 1973-1996* (1998), coedited with Jennie Ivey.

Kent T. Dollar is assistant professor of history at Tennessee Technological University in Cookeville. He is the author of *Soldiers of the Cross: Confederate Soldier-Christians and the Impact of War on Their Faith* (2005). His current project examines the activities of Christian soldiers, both Union and Confederate, in the early months of the Civil War.

An associate professor of history at Kennesaw State University in Georgia, **John D. Fowler** is the author of *Mountaineers in Gray: The Story of the Nineteenth Tennessee Volunteer Infantry Regiment, C.S.A.* (2004) and *The Confederate Experience Reader* (2008). He is also the director of the Center for the Study of the Civil War Era.

Derek W. Frisby is a history professor at Middle Tennessee State University in Murfreesboro and has authored several articles on the Civil War. He has a work in progress on guerrilla warfare in West Tennessee.

Marion B. Lucas is professor emeritus of history at Western Kentucky University in Bowling Green. His publications include *A History of Blacks in Kentucky: From Slavery to Segregation, 1760–1891* (2003) and *Sherman and the Burning of Columbia* (1976).

A professor of history at the University of Louisville, **Thomas C. Mackey** has authored several books, the most recent of which is *Pursuing Johns: Criminal Law Reform, Defending Character, and New York City's Committee of Fourteen, 1920–1930* (2005). He is a constitutional scholar who specializes in the Civil War and Reconstruction era.

Gary R. Matthews is a freelance writer who lives in Lexington, Kentucky. He is the author of *Basil Wilson Duke, CSA: The Right Man in the Right Place* (2005).

Professor and Donald A. Logan Chair of American history at the University of Washington, **Robert Tracy McKenzie** has authored over a dozen articles and books relating to the antebellum South and the Civil War, including *One South or Many? Plantation Belt and Upcountry in Civil War–Era Tennessee* (1994). His most recent publication is on Knoxville and is titled *Lincolnites and Rebels: A Divided Town in the American Civil War* (2006).

Brian D. McKnight is assistant professor of history at Angelo State University in San Angelo, Texas. He has written several articles on the Civil War and two books on the war in Appalachia: *Contested Borderland: The Civil War in Appalachian Kentucky and Virginia* (2006) and *To Perish by the Sword: Champ Ferguson's Bloody Civil War* (forthcoming).

The Draughon Professor of Southern History at Auburn University, **Kenneth W. Noe** has authored numerous books on the Civil War. His major publications include *Perryville: This Grand Havoc of Battle* (2002), *The Civil War in Appalachia: Collected Essays* (1997), coedited with Shannon H. Wilson, *A Southern Boy in Blue: The Memoir of Marcus Woodcock, 9th Kentucky Infantry (U.S.A.)* (1996), and *Southwest Virginia's Railroad: Modernization and the Sectional Crisis* (1994).

The Tripp Professor of the Humanities at Berea College in Berea, Kentucky, **Richard D. Sears** has published several books on American history, including *A Utopian Experiment in Kentucky* (1996), *Camp Nelson, Kentucky: A Civil War History* (2002), and *The Day of Small Things: Abolitionism in the Midst of Slavery* (3rd ed., 2008). He was a contributor to the *Kentucky Encyclopedia* and is currently writing entries for the forthcoming *Kentucky African American Encyclopedia*. He recently published eight volumes of a genealogical study called *Founders and Presidents of Berea College*.

An assistant professor of history at Auburn University, Montgomery, **Ben H. Severance** is the author of *Tennessee's Radical Army: The State Guard and Its Role in Reconstruction, 1867–1869* (2005). Currently, he is working on two projects: the Alabama edition of the Civil War series *Portraits of Conflict* (published by the University of Arkansas Press) and a political biography of the Tennessee congressman Horace Maynard, who served eight terms in the U.S. House during the Civil War era.

Kristen L. Streater is associate professor of history at Colin County Community College in Texas. She has a forthcoming article in *Occupied Women: Gender, Military Occupation, and the American Civil War*, edited by LeeAnn Whites and Alecia Long.

Larry H. Whiteaker is professor emeritus of history at Tennessee Technological University. He has written extensively on the Civil War as well as on nineteenth-century America. Among his books are *Tennessee: State of the Nation* (2006), coedited with W. Calvin Dickinson, *Seduction, Prostitution, and Moral Reform in New York, 1830–1860* (1997), and *The Individual and Society in America* (1979).

Index

Thomas, Lorenzo, 194, 199, 201, 229
Thompson, Newcomb, 174
Tolley, Burton, 175
Tolley, John, 175
Tompkinsville (Ky.), 127–28, 290
Topp, Robertson, 53, 59
Travelstead, Harvey, 180–81
Trenton (Tenn.), 173
Troy Press, 62
True American, 19
Tullahoma (Tenn.), 178, 275, 277, 308
Tupelo (Miss.), 292
Tuttle, John W., 141

Underground Railroad, 80
Union and Dispatch, 325
Union League of America, 321, 323–24, 345
Union Party, 289, 310
United States: nation building and, 339–42, 357–58; September 11, 2001, and, 339
U.S. Colored Troops. *See* black regiments

Van Buren, Martin, 4
Van Dorn, Earl, 173
Vaughn, Emily, 252
Veteran Volunteer Act, 134
Vetters, John, 232
Vicksburg Campaign, 173

Wakefield, Samuel J., 174
Walker, Leroy P., 39
Walker, Thomas, 2
Wallace, Ellen, 250
Wallace, Lew, 192
Wallace, Mrs. R. W., 176
Warfield, William A., 236
War Hawks, 4
War of 1812, 4, 127
Warren County (Ky.), 254
Warren County (Tenn.), 292

Wartrace (Tenn.), 170
Washington, D.C., 26
Washington Peace Conference, 70n25
Watson, Cynthia, 339–42, 357–58
Watson, Samuel J., 284n12
Weatherred, John, 152
Webb, Ross A., 357
Weekly Anglo-African, 236
Weigley, Russell, 27, 33–34
West, Thomas R., 174
West, Benjamin, 174
Western Europe, 339
West Point Military Academy, 177, 179
West Tennessee: 1863 election in, 304; election of 1865 in, 314; February 1861 referendum and, 53–54, 288; June 1861 referendum and, 64–65; prosecession sentiment in, 315; secessionists' actions in, 65; slavery in, 56; the secession crisis and, 49, 51, 65, 97; Unionism in, 306; Unionists' actions in, 51, 53; Union occupation of, 272, 303; voting patterns of, 66n5
West Tennessee Whig, 57, 63
Wheeler, Joseph, 149, 156, 160
Whig Party, 4, 5, 13–14, 29, 75, 287, 300
White, Hugh Lawson, 4
White, William, 174
Whiteaker, W. C., 174
White County (Tenn.), 144, 152–54, 289, 293
Whitier, Newton, 175
Whitier, Philander, 175
Whitthorn, Selica, 176
Wild Cat Creek, Battle of, 152–53
Wilderness Trail, 10, 16
Wiley, Bell I., 124, 132
Williams, Alpheus, 175
Williams, John S., 159
Wilmot Proviso, 5
Wilson County (Tenn.), 293
Wolford, Frank L., 148, 194

225938LV00003B/112/P

9 780813 125411